ACTS

ACTS

The Gospel of the Spirit

Justo L. González

ORBIS BOOKS

Maryknoll, New York 10545

This book is a translation, revision, and updating of *Hechos* by Justo L. González, part of the Comentario Bíblico Hispanoamericano, published in 1992 by Editorial Caribe, 9200 South Dadeland Boulevard, Suite 209, Miami, Florida 33156.

Library of Congress Cataloging-in-Publication Data

González, Justo L.
  Acts : the gospel of the spirit / Justo L. González.
    p. cm.
  Includes bibliographical references and index.
  ISBN 1-57075-398-9
    1. Bible. N. T. Acts—Commentaries. I. Title.

BS2625.53 .G66 2001
226.6'07—dc21
                                      2001036537

Contents

Preface

This commentary was originally written in Spanish, as part of a projected Comentario Bíblico Hispanoamericano. It was addressed primarily at Spanish-speaking readers—mostly, but not exclusively, Protestant—both in Latin America and in the United States. The intent was to provide a commentary that, while taking into account contemporary scholarship, stressed the relevance of Acts for the current struggles of Christians in Latin America and in the Latino churches in the United States. Two different typefaces were used in order to make that purpose clear: one typeface for what the Editorial Board called "the text in its context," and another for "the text in our context."

In the process of preparing an English edition, I debated whether to produce a translation or an adaptation. Eventually I decided for the former, inviting English readers to "look over the shoulders" of Hispanics as we seek to read Scripture in our own context, and to decide for themselves how much of this is relevant to their own situations. Thus, the adaptations I have made are minor, and mostly limited to clarifying points that might not be entirely clear to those who are not acquainted with the context in which the book was originally envisioned. I have also made minor adaptations at points in which English translations—particularly the NRSV—pose different problems or questions than the Spanish translations to which the original referred.

As in the case of the Spanish edition, this commentary is printed in two typefaces, one for what we originally called "the text in its context," and another for "the text in our context." Clearly, that is a distinction that should not be exaggerated. We always read a text from our own context, and there is no such thing as an "objective" reading of a text. The text and our context are in a constant dialogue, so that the movement between them is circular rather than linear. Still, one must make an effort to respect the "otherness" of the text, for otherwise there would be no reason to read it. That is what the distinction between the two typefaces seeks to show.

Finally, a word of gratitude. I am particularly grateful to Dr. Sharon Ringe, of Wesley Theological Seminary, and to Dr. William Burrows, of Orbis Books, for their encouragement to translate the commentary into English. And I thank Ms. Jane Gleim for her care and patience in transcribing my first, rather garbled, translation!

J.L.G.

Abbreviations

BIBLE TRANSLATIONS

CEV	Contemporary English Version
JB	Jerusalem Bible
KJV	King James Version
NASB	New American Standard Bible
NEB	New English Bible
NIV	New International Version
NRSV	New Revised Standard Version
RSV	Revised Standard Version

OTHER ABBREVIATIONS

AndUnivSem	*St. Andrews University Seminary Studies* (Berrien Springs, MI)
ANF	*The Ante-Nicene Fathers* (American Edition)
AngThRev	*Anglican Theological Review* (Evanston, IL)
Ant	*Antonianum* (Roma)
AusBibRev	*Australian Biblical Review* (Melbourne)
BangThF	*Bangalore Theological Forum* (Bangalore)
Bib	*Biblica* (Roma)
BibArch	*Biblical Archaelogist* (Durham, NC)
BibLitur	*Bibel und Liturgie* (Klosterneuburg)
BibOr	*Bibliotheca Orientalis* (Leiden)
BibTo	*The Bible Today* (Collegeville, MI)
BibTrans	*Bible Translator* (London)
BibZeit	*Biblische Zeitschrift* (Paderborn)
Bsäch	*Berichte über die Verhandlungen der königlich sächsischen Gesellshaft der Wissenschaften* (Leipzig)
BZ	*Biblische Zeitschrift* (Freiburg i.B.; Paderborn)
BZntW	*Beihefte zur Zeitschrift für die neutestamentlich Wissenshaft* (Giessen; Berlin)

CBQ	*Catholic Biblical Quarterly* (Washington)
Christus	*Christus: Revista mensual* (México)
CollTheol	*Collectanea Theologica* (Warsaw)
Comm	*Communio* (Sevilla)
Conc	*Concilium* (New York)
ConcThM	*Concordia Theological Monthly* (St. Louis)
Dia	*Dialog* (St. Paul)
EphThLov	*Ephemerides Theologicae Lovanienses* (Leuven)
EstBib	*Estudios Bíblicos* (Madrid)
EstEcl	*Estudios Eclesiásticos* (Madrid)
EtThRel	*Etudes Théologiques et Religieuses* (Montpellier)
EvTh	*Evangelische Theologie* (München)
Exp	*The Expositor* (London)
ExpTim	*The Expository Times* (London)
FilolNt	*Filología neotestamentaria* (Córdoba, Esp.)
GuL	*Geist und Leben* (München)
HTR	*Harvard Theological Review* (Cambridge, MA)
IDB	*The Interpreter's Dictionary of the Bible* (4 vols. + suppl., Abingdon, Nashville, 1962)
Int	*Interpretation: A Journal of Bible and Theology* (Richmond)
IntRevMiss	*International Review of Missions* (Geneva)
JBL	*Journal of Biblical Literature* (New Haven, Boston, etc.)
JEH	*Journal of Ecclesiastical History* (London)
JfdT	*Jahrbücher für deutsche Theologie* (Göttingen)
JJewSt	*Journal of Jewish Studies* (Oxford)
JnRyl	*Journal of the John Rylands Library* (Manchester)
JQR	*The Jewish Quarterly Review* (Merion Station, PA)
JR	*The Journal of Religion* (Chicago)
JRomSt	*The Journal of Roman Studies* (London)
JStNT	*Journal for the Study of the New Testament* (Sheffield)
JTS	*The Journal of Theological Studies* (Oxford)

LMD	*La Maison Dieu* (Paris)
MiscB	*Miscelanea Biblica* (Roma)
Neot	*Neotestamentica* (Stellenbosch, South Africa)
NkZ	*Neue kirchliche Zeitschrift* (Leipzig)
NRT	*Nouvelle Revue Théologuique* (Tournai)
NT	*Novum Testamentum* (Leuven)
NTSt	*New Testament Studies: An International Journal* (Cambridge, Eng.)
PalExQ	*Palestine Exploration Quarterly* (London)
Prot	*Protestantesimo* (Roma)
RCatalT	*Revista Catalana de Teología* (Barcelona)
RechScR	*Recherches de Science Religieuse* (Paris)
RelStudRev	*Religious Studies Review* (Macon, GA)
RestorQ	*Restoration Quarterly* (Abilene, TX)
RevBib	*Revue Biblique* (Jérusalem)
RevisBib	*Revista Bíblica con Sección Litúrgica* (Madrid)
RevScPhTh	*Revue des Sciences Philosophiques et Théologiques* (Paris)
RevThLouv	*Revue Théologique de Louvain* (Louvain)
RevThom	*Revue Thomiste* (Toulouse)
RHE	*Revue d'Histoire Ecclésiastique* (Louvain)
RHPR	*Revue d'Histoire et de Philosophie Religieuses* (Strasbourg)
RHR	*Revue de l'Histoire des Religions* (Paris)
RicRel	*Ricerche Religiose* (Roma)
RivBib	*Rivista Biblica* (Brescia)
RScR	*Revue des Sciences Religieuses* (Strasbourg)
RTP	*Revue de Théologie et de Philosophie* (Genève; Lausanne)
Salm	*Salmanticensis* (Salamanca)
ScEccl	*Sciences Ecclésiastiques* (Paris)
SecCent	*Second Century* (Macon, GA)
ST	*Studia Theologica* (Lund)
StNTUmv	*Studien zum Neuen Testament und seiner Umvelt* (Linz)
StRelScRel	*Studies in Religion / Sciences Religieuses* (Waterloo, Ontario)

Th	*Theology: A Journal of Historical Christianity* (London)
ThQ	*Theologische Quartalschrift* (Tübingen)
ThRund	*Theologische Rundschau* (Tübingen)
ThSt	*Theological Studies* (New York)
ThuGl	*Theologie und Glaube* (Paderborn)
ThWzNT	*Theologisches Wörterbuch zum Neuen Testament* (10 vols., ed. G. Kittel, W. Kohlhammer, Stuttgart, 1933–79)
TynBull	*Tyndale Bulletin* (Cambridge, Eng.)
TZ	*Theologische Zeitschrift* (Basel)
VyP	*Vida y Pensamiento* (San José)
WaW	*Word and World* (St. Paul)
ZKgesch	*Zeitschrift für Kirchengeschichte* (Stuttgart)
ZkT	*Zeitschrift für katholische Theologie* (Innsbruck)
ZntW	*Zeitschrift für die neutestamentlich Wissenshaft* (Giessen; Berlin)

General Introduction

There is no better way to study a book of the Bible than reading that book itself. Therefore, many of the matters that commentaries often include in their introductions will here be left for appropriate places in the commentary itself. At this point, as a general introduction to Acts, a few brief words will suffice on such subjects as the nature of the book, its author, date, purpose, context, historical value, and text.

A. THE NATURE OF THE BOOK

Acts is a unique book in the entire canon of the New Testament. The books before it, the Gospels, are a literary genre to themselves, perhaps created by the author of Mark. The books after it, the Epistles, follow the accepted structures of the epistolary genre as it was practiced then, abandoning them only when the circumstances and content so require. The Book of Revelation is an example—certainly the most influential—of the apocalyptic literature circulating at the time among Jews as well as among Christians. Acts, however, does not fit any of these categories. It is not a gospel, nor an epistle, nor an apocalypse.

It is markedly different from all these other books in that it is a sequel to one of the four Gospels. It does not seem to have occurred to the other three evangelists to follow the narrative of the life and teachings of Jesus with a second book. Because, in the present order of the New Testament, the Gospel of John appears between Luke and Acts, the connection between the two tends to be lost, when in fact Luke and Acts are really the two volumes of a single work. This connection is shown in the dedication of both books to "Theophilus," and in the reference to the "first book" in Acts 1:1.[1] However, the Gospel of Luke already gives us a hint of its interest in carrying the story of Jesus beyond his resurrection. The other three evangelists do not carry their story beyond the resurrection of Jesus, or at best beyond some final words on the actions and teachings of the Risen Lord. Only the Gospel of Luke tells us of the ascen-

---

1. On who "Theophilus" might have been, and how many "books" Luke wrote or intended to write, see the commentary on Acts 1:1–3. (Particularly, on Theophilus, notes 3–5; on the possibility of a third book, note 2.)

sion of Jesus (Luke 24:50–52a), and gives us a hint of what happened next: "they . . . returned to Jerusalem with great joy; and they were continually in the temple blessing God" (Luke 24:52b–53). These final verses of Luke's Gospel show that its author is interested in the continuation of the narrative—and may be even hinting at his sequel or "second book."

B. THE AUTHOR

Who wrote this unique book in the New Testament? When was it written, and with what purpose? The traditional view has been that both books were written by "Luke, the beloved physician" who sends greetings to the Colossians in one of Paul's letters (Col. 4:14), and who later appears also in the salutations in Philemon 24 and II Timothy 4:11. This opinion is first expressed in the Muratorian Canon, a document from the second half of the second century, and in its contemporary Irenaeus.[2] One should also point out that already by the middle of the second century Marcion (eventually condemned as a heretic for other reasons) included it in his canon of the New Testament, besides the Epistles of Paul, the Gospel of Luke, whose authority Marcion grounded on Luke's having been Paul's companion. Later, beginning in the fourth century, some have suggested that Luke is the same as the "Lucius of Cyrene" mentioned in Acts 13:1.

At this point one must distinguish two different questions. The first is whether the author of the Third Gospel, no matter what his name, is also the author of Acts. The second is whether this author is the "Luke" to whom the Epistles refer.

On the first question, there is a general consensus that the two books are indeed the work of a single author. This is based, not just on the initial words of both books, but also on the stylistic continuity between the two, which points to a single authorship. This continuity is such that some have even suggested that the two were originally a single book, which was then divided so that the first section would be parallel to the other three Gospels.[3] This theory has not gained widespread acceptance.

What is still in question is whether the author of these two books is in fact "Luke, the beloved physician." The two books themselves give no indication one way or the other. The title "Gospel according to Luke," like the other titles for books in the New Testament, was added in the second century, and therefore is no proof that the author of these books was indeed named Luke. Some have defended Lukan authorship on the basis of the interest of Luke/Acts in medical matters.[4] Others respond that such an interest does not really go beyond what could be expected in any moderately educated person in the Helle-

---

2. Irenaeus, *Adv. haer.* iii, 1:1, 10:1, 12:1–15, 14:1.

3. See the commentary on 1:9–11.

4. The texts most often cited in this regard are Luke 4:38, 5:18, 22:44; and Acts 3:7, 9:18, 28:8.

nistic world, and that in the two books there is not a single proof that their author had any specialized knowledge of medicine. The matter cannot be easily resolved, which in itself shows that the evidence for "Luke, the beloved physician" is feeble.

The main argument of those who hold that Luke, Paul's companion, could not have written these two books (and particularly Acts) is a series of apparent contradictions or discrepancies between Acts and the Pauline Epistles. These will be discussed more fully as we come to the pertinent places in the commentary itself. It may be well, however, to summarize some of the most important:

First, there are some apparently factual matters in which it is difficult to harmonize what Acts tells us with what Paul says in his Epistles. One such case is the matter of Paul's visits to Jerusalem. How many times, and to what ends, did Paul visit Jerusalem after his conversion? In 9:26, Acts tells us that Paul went to Jerusalem, apparently shortly after his conversion. In Galatians 1:15–21, Paul declares that after his conversion, without going to Jerusalem, he went to Arabia, and that three years later he returned to Damascus, and then to Jerusalem. However, as will be seen in the commentary on 9:20–31, it is possible to explain this discrepancy. The same is true of the differences between Acts and the Epistles in the manner they present and interpret the apostolic gathering at Jerusalem usually called the "Apostolic council."

Second, there are differences between Paul's personality and theology as seen in his own Epistles and as presented in Acts. For the author of Luke/Acts, the "apostles" are usually the Twelve, and Paul is not one of them (although in 14:4,14 both Paul and Barnabas are given that title). In contrast, in his Epistles, Paul argues forcefully for his right to be considered an apostle, and seems to equate his position in this regard with that of the Twelve. It must be pointed out, however, that this apparent contrast is based on a reading of Acts as supporting the authority of the "Twelve" in a way that this commentary questions.[5]

Another case deals with the matter of what was to be expected from converted Gentiles. According to 15:29, there were four requirements placed on them. According to Galatians 2:9, the "pillars" of Jerusalem—James, Peter, and John—gave Barnabas and Paul "the right hand of fellowship," and placed no further demands on the Gentiles. However, when posing these objections, many interpreters are still reading the story of early Christianity through the lenses of the famous but now questioned school of Tübingen. That school, whose main exponent was F. C. Bauer, held that in the early Church there was a serious conflict between the "Judaizing" tendencies of James and the openness of Paul toward the Gentiles. From this perspective, the "later" books of the New Testament, such as Acts, reflect the compromise that was eventually

---

5. See, for instance, the commentary on the election of Matthias (1:12–26), and on the election of the "seven" (6:1–7).

reached. Even though many of the premises of the school of Tübingen are no longer held, it is still customary to think in terms of a great conflict and tension between Paul and the Christian authorities in Jerusalem.[6]

A further problem is posed by the existence within the Book of Acts of several sections (16:10–17, 20:5–15, 21:1–18, 27:1–28:16) where the narrative appears in the first person plural ("we" sections). These portions of the text have caused much debate. The main difficulty is that, if the "we" is taken literally, it is not always easy to see where or when the narrator joins Paul and his companions, or leaves them. This has led to several hypotheses. The most common are: (1) that the author of Acts made use of a "travelogue" of one of Paul's companions or some other traveler, and that the "we" appears in the sections taken from that document; (2) that the "we" is a theological or stylistic clue with which the author seeks to signal something.[7] Neither of these hypotheses is fully convincing. If the author was indeed employing a travelogue, it would have been quite simple to change a narrative from the first person to the third, so as to make it agree with the rest of the work. The author of Luke/Acts is careful with style, and a discrepancy in the use of grammatical persons would not have been left unnoticed. Likewise, in all its diverse versions the second hypothesis implies that the Book of Acts is written in code, and that this code was not really broken until modern interpreters suggesting a particular hypothesis came along. The most simple and probable notion is to accept that the "we" refers, as the text would lead us to think, to one of Paul's companions, who is also the author of the book. Because, as will be abundantly shown, the book does not claim to be a detailed narrative of everything that took place, it does not tell us when or why this particular person joined or left the group. Not only the "we" narrator, but also an entire series of other characters, including Peter, appear and disappear in the narrative, without a word being said as to where they went or what they were doing during their absence. Furthermore, at the end of the book the same happens with reference to Paul, for the final outcome of his story is not told.

Could this companion be the same person whom Paul calls "Luke, the beloved physician"? It is impossible to know for certain. The book itself—like the Third Gospel—does not tell us who wrote it. Nor does the rest of the New Testament shed any light on this matter. As has already been pointed out, the hints of possible medical knowledge on the part of the author are insufficient to reach a conclusion. However, a very ancient tradition, at least as old as the

---

6. There is no doubt that Paul did have serious encounters with "Judaizers," as may be seen in Galatians. However, this does not mean that those Judaizers had the support of the Christian leadership in Jerusalem. See J. Munck, *Paul and the Salvation of Mankind* (London: SCM, 1959).

7. See the bibliographical references, and the summaries of various positions, in the commentary to 16:10.

second century, unanimously affirms that the name of the author of Acts was Luke, and that he was indeed Paul's medical companion.[8]

For all these reasons, in this commentary the author of Acts and of the Third Gospel will simply be called "Luke." However, the use of this name does not mean that there is any certainty that the author of these books is the person by that name in the Epistles of Paul.

C. DATE OF COMPOSITION

When was Acts written? The book itself provides no dates. It has been suggested that the reason the book ends without telling us of the final outcome of Paul's imprisonment in Rome is that it was written when Paul was still awaiting trial.[9] This hypothesis, however, raises many objections. The most important has to do with the date of composition of the Gospel of Luke. Most scholars agree that the earliest of the four Gospels was Mark, written late in the decade of the sixties. Luke must have been written some time later. Because Acts is its sequel, it must have been written still later. The dedication in Acts implies that Theophilus, its addressee, would already have had time to receive and read Luke's Gospel. Furthermore, the fact that Luke speaks of the church in Jerusalem at the beginning of his book and then leaves it aside seems to indicate that by the time when Acts was being written that church no longer existed. Because this came about around the year 70, when Jerusalem was taken by the Romans and the Christians there fled to Pella, it is most likely that Acts was written after that date.

On the other hand, Acts does not even mention the Epistles of Paul, and this leads to the supposition that it was written before those Epistles were compiled and began enjoying the great prestige they soon achieved. Furthermore, there is the possibility that the publication of Acts itself may have been one of the catalytic events leading to the compilation of Paul's Epistles. Also, many ancient Christian writers, some as early as Clement of Rome toward the end of the first century, seem to know of Acts. Certainly, by the middle of the second century, it was granted great authority throughout the Church. Therefore, it would seem that the book was written around the year 80.

As to where it was written, it is impossible to know. Traditionally it has been thought that both the Gospel of Luke and Acts were written at Antioch, mostly on the basis of the place that the church of Antioch plays in the Book of Acts. However, there simply are not sufficient indications to determine where the book was written.

---

8. See a summary of the arguments for this theory in I. Howard Marshall, *The Acts of the Apostles* (Leicester: Inter-Varsity Press, 1980), pp. 44–46.

9. For another explanation of this abrupt end, see the commentary on 28:30–31.

D. THE PURPOSE OF THE BOOK

The first impression we receive when we begin reading Acts is that Luke is telling us the history of early Christianity. This is supported both by the present title of the book and by the first verses. Given that assumption, we read through the entire book taking for granted that it is a history of the Church in its first generation. But, when after such a reading we review the content of the book, it is obvious that this is a strange sort of history. Certainly, historians must always select among the materials that they have, for it is patently impossible to tell everything that happened. Still, Luke's selection is strange. At first, his attention focuses on the church of Jerusalem, which he then abandons in order not to return to it except much later when Paul returns to Jerusalem (21:17–25). Very little is said about the life and actions of the Twelve Apostles. Although their names are listed in 1:13, most of them are ignored from there on, and the only ones who appear in the rest of the narrative are Peter, John, and James (who dies in 12:2, and is to be distinguished from the other James, brother of the Lord, who does appear later in the narrative). In chapter 8, Philip, who is not one of the Twelve but one of the Seven, takes center stage; but then he disappears, and is only mentioned again in passing in 21:8–9. Paul's companions enter and leave the stage, most often without our being told when they left or when they joined the group.

Therefore, although Acts is certainly a narrative, it is a selective narrative. Luke tells of some incidents and omits others. This leads to the crucial question for the interpretation of the entire book: on what basis does Luke make such selections? The entire interpretation of the book depends on the manner in which we respond to that question.

In modern times those who first posed the question of the purpose of the book and sought to respond to it were the scholars of the school of Tübingen. That school, deeply influenced by Hegel's philosophy, read history as a series of theses that were opposed by various antitheses, until each conflict was resolved in a synthesis. In the history of the primitive Church, a series of conflicts appeared between the more traditional or Judaizing elements, whose leader and prototype was James, and those of Hellenistic tendencies, represented by Paul. According to the Tübingen school, that conflict appears in the foreground in Paul's Epistles, especially in Galatians. Eventually a synthesis or compromise was reached, which reconciled both positions, excluding their extreme expressions. That is what we find in Acts, whose purpose is to present the history of early Christianity so as to make it appear that there was always unity and agreement between Peter and Paul, and especially between James and Paul.[10]

For many reasons, that theory is no longer generally accepted among most scholars. Even though there certainly existed in the early Church a multi-

---

10. The main exponent of these theories was F. C. Bauer, especially in his book *Paulus, der Apostel Jesu Christi*, published in 1845.

plicity of perspectives and interpretations, the contrasts and the generalizations of the Tübingen school were too clearly determined by its Hegelian philosophical presuppositions. Therefore, soon many scholars began pointing out the weaknesses in this hypothesis, and how it failed to account for much in the text of Acts as well as in the rest of the New Testament.

Another theory that gained a measure of acceptance, and which has many supporters, sees in Acts an apologetic work, written in order to show that Christianity is not really opposed to the Roman Empire. This theory takes different shapes. Some suggest, for instance, that Theophilus was a Roman officer, and that Luke addressed his double work to him in order to show him that the empire had no reason to persecute the Church. Others believe that Acts was written in preparation for Paul's defense in Rome, and that it was addressed to an officer who would be involved in the trial.[11] This theory also has its weak points. One of them is that even though, toward the end of the book, there are a number of episodes that could be interpreted as having an apologetic purpose, the theory itself does not explain the purpose of the book as a whole. Furthermore, as we shall see repeatedly in the commentary itself, Luke does not always present Roman authorities in the best light, but rather points to their weakness, corruption, and injustice.[12]

What then is the purpose of Acts? If we place ourselves where the author would have been, let us say around the year 80, it would not be very difficult to respond to this question. The Church, which had begun with a vision of the power of God and with great hope that the advance of its mission would lead to the fulfillment of God's promises, now found itself in a serious conflict both with the Roman Empire and with the surrounding culture and civilization. There were political conflicts, whose extreme expression would lead to persecution, and there were conflicts of culture and values. The style of life that Christians proposed and followed was not that of society at large. It was not even that of the best elements in that society. Christians, who had begun their mission as heralds of a new age, were now in danger of severe discouragement as they clashed with the powers of the old age.

In that situation, what was necessary was a guide to lead Christians in their behavior and in their faith during those difficult times. In the midst of conflict with Rome, with Judaism, and with civilization itself, what are we to do? What is to be our attitude? Why take courage? Luke responds to these questions with a double work. The first part is a Gospel in which it is clear that

---

11. These theories and many others are well summarized in E. Haenchen, *The Acts of the Apostles* (Philadelphia: Westminster, 1971), pp. 14–50. A good example of the interpretation of Acts as an apology is B. S. Easton, *Early Christianity* (Greenwich, Conn.: Seabury Press, 1955), pp. 33–118.

12. There is an excellent criticism of the interpretation of Acts as an apology in R. J. Cassidy, *Society and Politics in the Acts of the Apostles* (Maryknoll, N.Y.: Orbis, 1968), pp. 145–57.

Jesus, although not a revolutionary after the manner of the Zealots, clashed with those in authority both among his own Jewish people and among the Romans. The second part shows that the same was true with reference to the early disciples. That is why Luke takes time to tell us about the confrontations between the first disciples and the Sanhedrin, the martyrdom of Stephen, the repeated appearances of Paul before Jewish and Roman authorities, the episode in the Areopagus in Athens, and the manner in which the wise of his time mocked Paul in spite of his cultured erudition. Christians in Luke's time were having similar experiences, and the Book of Acts has the purpose of strengthening and directing them through such conflicts.[13]

The consequence of this purpose is that the main character in the Book of Acts is not the apostles, nor even Paul, but the Holy Spirit. As will be seen later on, Luke states very clearly at the beginning of the book that he intends to speak of the manner in which Jesus continued working in the Church through the Spirit.

This in turn means that our reading of Acts must be very different from traditional readings. Traditionally, we have read this book as a sort of first book of discipline of the early Church, where the apostles and others set the procedures and practices to be followed throughout the ages. Thus, for instance, the election of the Seven in chapter 6 has become the paradigm and the biblical basis for the election and role of deacons at later times. If, on the other hand, the main character of the book is the Holy Spirit, we should be free to see cases in which the Spirit seems to correct, and perhaps even slightly to mock, what the apostles and other leaders of the Church do and decide. Many such cases will appear in the course of this commentary. When read in this manner, the Book of Acts becomes a call to Christians to be open to the action of the Spirit, not only leading them to confront values and practices in society that may need to be subverted, but perhaps even leading them to subvert or question practices and values within the Church itself.

Such action of the Spirit, however, always take place within a concrete context. Therefore, it is necessary, however briefly, to describe that context.

E. CONTEXT

The entire narrative of Acts evolves within the Roman Empire. This was a variegated empire, whose provinces and cities were governed in various ways according to their particular history and circumstances. Thus, for instance, beginning in the year 27 B.C.E., there were "imperial" and "senatorial" provinces, and each of these had its own form of government. The imperial provinces were under the direct government of the emperor, who named a "procurator" as his representative. Provinces and cities added to the empire kept many of their traditional laws. Some cities and their citizens received special legal con-

---

13. Such is the thesis, well supported by argument, of Cassidy, *Society and Politics*, pp. 158–70.

sideration. Thus there were, for instance, "colonies," free cities, etc. It is remarkable that Luke always refers to the officers of each city or province with their correct titles, as will be seen in the commentary itself.

The political situation in Judea changed during the period encompassed in Acts. Beginning in the year 6 B.C.E, most of the region had been under the rule of Roman procurators, even though the successors of Herod the Great had jurisdiction over some of the outlying territories. At the beginning of the narrative in Acts, Herod Philip was "tetrarch" of an area near Judea toward the northeast of Galilee. In the year 37 C.E., Caligula granted these territories as well as others to Herod Agrippa I. Thanks to his loyal collaboration with Roman power, his territories and authority were repeatedly extended, until he became king of Judea and Samaria in the year 41 C.E., which gave him lands as extensive as those of Herod the Great. When he died three years later, his son Herod Agrippa II was quite young, and the Romans did not grant him his father's throne.[14] Therefore, throughout the rest of the narrative in Acts—for instance, upon Paul's last visit to Jerusalem—Herod Agrippa II, although still retaining the title of king, did not rule over Judea. He did have certain special prerogatives, such as appointing the high priest and being the guardian of the temple treasure. But his authority was quite limited.

What has just been said about the appointment of the high priest is an indication of the manner in which politics affected the religious life of Judea. The Romans respected the various religions of their subjects, but took great care to keep them under their control, in order to prevent their being employed to incite rebellion. In consequence, the religious leaders of Israel had to be constantly concerned about their relations with the Romans, and to avoid any religious act that could be construed as subversive or inciting to riot. In the early chapters of Acts, this situation impacts the manner in which the Sanhedrin and in general the leaders of Judaism react against Christianity. On the other hand, the very fact that the religious leaders appeared to the people to be serving a foreign power lessened their prestige and forced them to even harsher action in order to keep their control over the people and thus avoid riots or actions against their authority.

From the point of view of Rome, the first duty of every government official was to keep order. Any disorder or riot was severely punished. At various points in the course of this commentary it will be clear that the authorities are afraid that there may be a riot (*stasis*) for which they might be blamed. Therefore, it was almost inevitable that the Christians would soon clash with the authorities, because their preaching led to debates and disturbances. This appears already in the conflicts with the Sanhedrin in the early chapters of the book, and will continue to be the case as Paul and his companions make their way into other parts of the Roman Empire. When Luke wrote Acts, the same situation still existed.

---

14. See the commentary on 25:13.

The date in which Christianity begins to make its way into the world coincides with the time of greatest glory of the Roman Empire. As every empire must do, the Roman Empire justified its existence on the basis of an ideology. In its case, this was the ideology of Rome as a civilizing agent. The very word "civilization" comes from the same root as "city"; and the manner in which the Romans understood their civilizing task was precisely the "cityfication" of the world. For them, the greatest human creation was precisely the city, and their purpose in history was to promote city life throughout their empire. Therefore, during its years of greatest glory the Roman Empire embellished cities with beautiful buildings, constructed roads joining one city to another, and even founded cities where until then there was nothing but fallow land or even unhealthy marshes. Construction became the main occupation of the Mediterranean world. The rich built luxurious mansions with marble and other stones of various colors: yellow from the quarries of Simitu in Africa, green from Greece, red from Egypt, and purple from the Felsberg. Those who really wished to show their wealth and liberality had public buildings, temples, and other architectural jewels built at their own expense in order to embellish the cities and proclaim the glory of the donor. Never before had the Mediterranean world seen such civilization or cityfication.

On the other hand, such prosperity, as is usually the case, also had its negative side. Cities require the product of agriculture in order to survive, and their ever-growing markets helped the development of *latifundia*, large agricultural estates dependent on the labor of slaves or near-slaves. This was made even worse because the rich and powerful paid little or no taxes, while the fiscal burden fell mostly on peasants and laborers. Therefore, while the first centuries of the Christian era witnessed the progressive disappearance of the small farms that had been the very foundation of the ancient Roman Republic, the senatorial families and other members of the aristocracy amassed ever-increasing extensions of land. Many who had previously been small landholders either remained to work under new masters or joined the growing mass of the partially disemployed that congregated in the cities. Thus, the very cities in which the most beautiful buildings were rising also had a growing number of persons living in slumlike conditions.

Such were the cities that Paul visited in his travels. When we see him in Athens, "deeply distressed to see that the city was full of idols" (17:16), we must imagine him amidst the architectural jewels of the Acropolis and all that in more recent times the Romans had built around that ancient site; likewise when we read about the riot in Ephesus, and about the theater in that city (19:29). At the same time, that very riot reminds us of the other reality, the impoverished and unemployed masses that were also part of the scene and a consequence of the economic "progress" of the empire. (See the commentary on 17:5.)

In the midst of this situation, there appear first in Jerusalem, and then in other cities of the empire, some people who go about speaking of a reign of God, and of a "Lord" Jesus Christ. That reign and that Lord, by their mere existence, bring into question the justice and order of Caesar, and deny his absolute authority.[15] What Luke then tells us is the story of the mission of those early Christians, impelled and strengthened by the Spirit, and how that mission led them to ever-increasing conflicts with the surrounding society. As Cassidy correctly states, "as Luke gradually unfolds his narrative, the image of Paul as a great missionary is replaced with the image of Paul as a Roman prisoner and the image of Paul as a witness before Roman officials."[16]

This particular commentary is written from the perspective of one who has witnessed many similar situations both in his own native Latin America and in the United States, where he now lives. Seeking to be obedient in their context, Christians to this day find themselves forced to question and challenge the values of a society that insists on ignoring the gospel. As a consequence, there have been and will be many conflicts similar to those of which we read in Acts. The result is that, although it is true that Luke wrote for Christians in his time, who were beginning to face the great challenge of the conflict with Rome, he also wrote for us, who do not yet know the challenges before us.

F. TEXT

When comparing the various extant manuscripts of Acts, it is clear that the book has come to our time in two distinct versions or traditions. That found in the majority of the more ancient manuscripts and which seems to be original, is usually the "Egyptian," "common," or "neutral" text. The other is commonly called the "Western" text.[17] Other books of the New Testament also exist in these two versions, but none shows as frequent or extensive differences between the two as does the Book of Acts. From as early as the second century there are authors and translations that use each of the two versions—indicating that both versions are quite old. It has even been suggested that both come from the author, who revised his own work a few years after writing it. A few scholars hold that the original text is the Western, and that the Egyptian version is a later revision.[18] However, most biblical scholars agree that the Egyptian text is the original, and that the Western text is a later revision, even though in a few isolated cases the Western text may be closer to the original.

In general, the NRSV and other English translations follow the Egyptian text, although there have been some translators who have argued for the Western text. In this commentary, the Western text will also be taken into account where what it says seems to be relevant or to clarify a point.

---

15. In 25:26 there is the first case in the surviving ancient literature in which the emperor is called "Lord." That title, which the Christians gave to Jesus, would be the cause of many of their conflicts with the state and its authorities.

16. Cassidy, *Society and Politics*, p. 162.

17. It is possible to speak also of a "Byzantine text" and of a "Caesarean text." But these are only variants of the main traditions mentioned above.

18. See Haenchen, *Acts*, p. 51, for the pertinent bibliography.

It seems clear that the Western text reflects some of the biases of its own author. Thus, for instance, this Western text has a clear anti-feminine prejudice and seems to reflect the general anti-feminine reaction that took place in the Church toward the end of the first century and early in the second.[19] In any case, the purpose of a commentary such as this is to study the text itself. Let us therefore turn to it.

---

19. For instance, while the Egyptian text, except in one case where the grammar requires it, speaks of "Priscilla and Aquila," the Western text invariably calls them "Aquila and Priscilla." In 17:12 the Western text changes the words, so that the qualifier "of high standing" does not apply specifically to the women, as it does in the Egyptian text. In 17:34, it completely omits Damaris.

1

Introduction
(1:1–26)

A. DEDICATION AND PROLOGUE (1:1–3)

The very first words of Acts indicate that this book is the continuation of another.[1] As was seen in the General Introduction, that previous book is the Gospel of Luke, whose sequel Acts is.[2] It is impossible to tell who was the "Theophilus" to whom the two books are addressed.[3] The name itself means "lover of God," and therefore many have suggested that this did not really refer to a particular person, but is rather a symbolic name that Luke gives to all his readers. On the other hand, there are reasons to think otherwise. In the first place, the name itself of Theophilus was relatively common in the first century, not only among Gentiles (because the name is itself is Greek), but also even among Jews. Second, in Luke 1:3 Luke calls this Theophilus "most excellent." This was a formal honorific address normally reserved for Romans of the equestrian class—that is, the rank immediately below the senatorial ar-

---

1. On some of the literary and structural issues relating to the prologue of Acts, see: Prosper Alfaric, "Les prologues de Luc," *RHR*, 115 (1937), 37–52; Emanuel Hirsch, *Frügeschichte des Evangeliums* (Tübingen: J. C. B. Mohr, 1951), pp. xxx–xxxix; Eduardo Iglesias, "El libro de los Hechos: El prólogo," *Christus*, 1 (1935–36), 429–436.

2. The Greek form employed here in describing the "first book" (*prôtos* instead of *prôteros*) would technically imply that there was to be a third book. T. Zahn, "Das dritte Buch des Lukas," *NkZ*, 28 (1917), 373–95. The truth is that the Hellenistic Greek of Luke's time no longer distinguished clearly between *prôtos* and *prôteros*. Therefore, it is not necessary to suppose, as some have done, that Luke wrote or planned to write a third book. E. Haenchen, *The Acts of the Apostles: A Commentary* (Philadelphia: Westminster, 1975), p. 137, n. 1.

3. Edgar J. Goodspeed, "Was Theophilus Luke's Publisher?", *JBL*, 73 (1954), 84; H. Mulder, "Theophilus, de 'Godvrezende'," in N. J. Holmes et al., eds., *Arcana Revelata* (Kampen: J. H. Kok, 1951), pp. 77–88. Without attempting to solve the question of the identity of

istocracy. Even though one could argue that Luke did not employ this address in its strict technical sense,[4] it is certainly an indication that the two books were addressed to a person of a certain social standing. Third, it was quite customary in those times to dedicate a book to an illustrious and powerful person, who then promoted its circulation. For all these reasons it seems possible that Luke did indeed address his book to a distinguished Christian whose name was Theophilus, and that he did this, not only so that Theophilus would read it, but also so that it would circulate among others.[5]

At any rate, the very fact that a book such as the Gospel of Luke carries a preface that in many ways follows the conventional structures of the best literature of the time,[6] and that the book is addressed to a Christian with certain social standing such as Theophilus, implies that, by the time Luke writes, the Christian Church is beginning to make headway at least among some members of the middle and higher ranks of society. The ensuing problems are part of the background for Luke's writing.

The word that the NRSV translates as "book" is *logos*. It is the same word that appears in the prologue of the Fourth Gospel, and which is there translated as "word."

What the NRSV translates as "all that Jesus did and taught from the beginning" could also be translated as does the NIV: "all that Jesus began to do

---

Theophilus, Paul S. Minear offers an excellent study of the challenges facing the readers of Luke, and therefore of the purpose of Acts, in "Dear Theo: The Kerygmatic Intention and Claim of the Book of Acts," *Int*, 27 (1973), 131–50. There is a good summary of the various positions regarding the identity of Theophilus in F. F. Bruce, *Commentary on the Book of Acts*, 2nd ed. (Grand Rapids: Eerdmans, 1954), pp. 30–32.

4. Although against such a position stands the fact that Luke does use this address in its proper sense in Acts 24:3 and 26:25.

5. That Theophilus was a Christian would seem to be implied by Luke 1:4, where the book is addressed to him "so that you may know the truth concerning the things about which you have been instructed." It is true that such words could also have been addressed to a judge or another officer who had authority to judge the Christians, and in that case they could be understood as referring to the reports that Theophilus had received. Such an interpretation has not found great support among scholars. Also, at various times in the history of the interpretation of Acts various candidates have been suggested as persons to whom Luke referred under the pseudonym of "Theophilus." The one most frequently mentioned is Flavius Clemens, the Roman aristocrat who died in the time of Domitian, late in the first century, apparently as a Christian martyr. There have also been attempts to identify him with other persons of the same name: one who appears in Seneca's Seventh Epistle (which is not by Seneca, but is actually a Christian writing under a pseudonym), and another who appears in Pseudo-Clementine literature (*Recog.* 10.1). But such attempts are only hypotheses or theories that are impossible to test or prove.

6. Victoriano Larrañaga, "El proemio-transición de Act 1:1-3 en los métodos literarios de la historiografía griega," *MiscB*, 2 (1934), 311–74; D. W. Palmer, "The literary background of Acts 1:1-14," *NTSt*, 33 (1987), 427–38; P. W. ven der Host, "Hellenistic parallels to the Acts of the Apostles: 1:1–26," *ZntW*, 74 (1983), 17–26.

and to teach." The implication is that the first book dealt with the things that Jesus began to do "until the day when he was taken up to heaven," and the second book will deal with what Jesus continued to do and to teach after his ascension, now through the Holy Spirit.[7] The assertion that Jesus gave instructions "through the Holy Spirit" (1:2) helps to entwine the two books. In the first, when Jesus was physically present, the Holy Spirit acted through him. In this second book, after the ascension, Jesus would continue acting through the Holy Spirit.[8]

The "convincing truths" of verse 3 (NRSV and NIV) or "demonstrations" (JB) probably refer, not only to the manifestations of Jesus to his disciples, but also to his insistence on his physical resurrection. In Luke 24:37–43, when the disciples were "terrified and thought they were seeing a ghost," Jesus showed them his hands and his feet and invited them to touch him. Finally, as a final proof of his physical resurrection he received from them a piece of broiled fish, "and he took it and ate it in their presence."

The "forty days" in this verse are not to be taken literally, for it is a phrase frequently employed in the sense of "many days." Luke himself uses it thus in Luke 4:2 (see also, for instance, Genesis 7:4, 14, 17; Exodus 24:11; Ezekiel 4:6; in Acts: 7:30, 36, 42). The Church soon noted the parallelism between these "forty days" and what is said about the time that Moses spent on Mount Sinai receiving the law (Exodus 24:18). Just as Moses during those forty days received instructions about the future conduct of Israel, so did Jesus during these other forty days instruct the apostles for their future tasks.[9]

Finally, Luke summarizes what Jesus taught during those "forty days" as "the kingdom of God."[10] As will be seen in the next section, the subject of the reign or kingdom of God is closely related to the expectations of the disciples.

---

7. It is also possible to understand the "began" as a Greek idiom that simply adds strength to the main verbs, and therefore to translate the passage simply as "what Jesus did and taught."

8. Greek grammar would allow for two other translations. One would make the phrase "by the Holy Spirit" refer not only to the instructions, but also to the choosing of the apostles. The other would refer the action of the Spirit only to the choosing, and not to the teachings of Jesus. The NRSV translation is the most natural. See Lorenzo Turrado, *Hechos de los Apóstoles y Epístola a los Romanos* (Madrid: Biblioteca de Autores Cristianos, 1975), pp. 27–28.

9. See Jürgen Roloff, *Hechos de los Apóstoles* (Madrid: Cristiandad, 1984), pp. 46–47; William H. Roscher, "Die Tessarakontaden and Tessarakontadenlehren der Griechen und anderer Völker," *Bsäch*, 61 (1909), 17–206. Roloff also stresses the purpose of the "forty days" as a way of setting a term for the manifestations of the Risen Lord. After those days and the ascension, there may be visions of Jesus, but no more physical manifestations.

10. On the direct verbal teachings of Jesus as they appear in Acts, see A. Wikenhauser, "Las instrucciones que Cristo Resucitado dio según los Hechos de los Apóstoles 1:3," *Revis-Bib*, 17 (1955), 117–22.

THE ACTS OF THE SPIRIT

The very first words of Acts are "in the first book." This lets us know that this book is not to be read by itself. It is a continuation of the Gospel of Luke, the "the first book" addressed to the same Theophilus to whom this one speaks. What we have here is a two-part history. The first deals with the acts of Jesus, and the second with the acts of the Spirit after the ascension of Jesus. But Luke does not want us to imagine that these are two completely separate matters. That is why he refers to the subject of his first book as those things that Jesus began to do and to teach. In saying "began," he suggests that this second book, even though it speaks about what took place after the ascension of Jesus, still deals with his ministry, which did not end with the ascension, but rather continues in the work of the Spirit and therefore also in the life of the Church. This second book tells the sequel of what was already told in the first. The acts of the Spirit are a continuation and part of the Gospel.

At the beginning of this second book, Luke feels the need to summarize what he said in the first. He obviously cannot repeat all of it, but rather must find a way to bring it all together under one phrase that will somehow encompass the acts and teachings of Jesus. For Luke, there is no better way to do this than by referring to the message of the reign of God. This is why he tells Theophilus (and now also tells us) that, during the time Jesus spent with his disciples between the resurrection and the ascension, he taught them "about the kingdom of God." Even a rapid reading of the Gospel of Luke will show that the central theme of the teachings of Jesus is the reign of God. Most of the parables refer to it. The good news that merits the message the title of "evangel" is precisely that the reign of God has approached in the person and acts of Jesus (see, for instance, Luke 10:9, 11). This subject will be discussed again in the next section (the commentary on 1:4–8). However, at this point it is important to underscore the significance of the continuity between Luke's two books.

Part of what Luke is telling us is that it is impossible to know Jesus without the intervention of the Holy Spirit. Paul says the same thing in other words: "no one can say 'Jesus is Lord' except by the Holy Spirit" (I Cor. 12:3). Luke indicates this at the beginning of his Gospel by affirming that Mary conceived by action of the Holy Spirit (Luke 1:35), giving several examples of people who recognize Jesus by the Spirit (Luke 1:41, 2:25–27), and affirming that the Spirit descended on Jesus at his baptism, at the moment when he was ready to begin his ministry (Luke 3:22).

In order to be a Christian, it is not enough to have grown up among Christians or to belong to a supposedly "Christian" culture. Jesus becomes known to us as Lord and Savior, not merely by human action or inference, but by the work of the Holy Spirit, who employs those human experiences to reveal the true character and power of Jesus. Without the Holy Spirit, it is impossible to be a Christian.

The other significant point here is that the function of the Spirit is to lead people to Jesus. Whatever the Spirit does today, Jesus is doing through the Spirit. That is why Luke declares that his first treatise deals with the things that Jesus *began* to do and to teach. By the Spirit, Jesus continues acting and teaching. That is precisely the subject of the "second book." What the Spirit will teach is not a revelation beyond that which Jesus brought; it is the same as Jesus taught.

Understanding this relationship between Jesus and the Holy Spirit is very important for the Church today. There is among us a common opinion that the revelation of God takes place in three successive stages, each higher than the previous one, so that each excels the other. According to that opinion, first came the revelation of the Father in the Old Testament; then that of the Son in the Gospel; and finally that of the Spirit, in the Church after the ascension of Jesus, and particularly with the contemporary outpouring of charismatic gifts. Such a notion is not new, for similar ideas were held in the second century by the Montanists, and in the Middle Ages by the followers of Joachim of Foire.

The attraction of such opinions for many generations as well as ours is in that it fits well with a certain understanding of "spirituality." For many, "spirituality" consists in leaving behind all that is physical or material. Because Jesus is a physical person, with material flesh and bones, it would seem that "the religion of the Spirit" would be superior to that of Jesus. Such notions, which still challenge the Church today, already were a challenge in New Testament times. That is why in I John 4:2–3, where it is a matter of testing the spirits, the test is precisely in the relationship between such spirits and the flesh of Jesus: "By this you know the spirit of God: every spirit that confesses that Jesus is come in the flesh is from God, and every spirit that does not confess Jesus is not from God." The purpose of the entire Book of Acts is to describe the action of the Spirit leading us to the same Jesus who has come in flesh and who, by means of the Spirit, is still active in the Church.

This has practical consequences. If the "religion of the spirit" is higher, it would seem that the best way to serve God is to deal only with "spiritual" things and to forget the material. In a hemisphere burdened by poverty, hunger, malnutrition, and all sorts of physical evil, the Church would not then have to be concerned with such things, and its sole task would be to preach the "gospel." Naturally, such a "gospel," as Luke abundantly shows in his two books, is not the Gospel of Jesus Christ, and therefore it is also not the result of the work of the Holy Spirit.

B. THE PROMISE OF THE SPIRIT (1:4–8)

This section and the one following (1:9–11) take up what was already discussed at the end of the "first book."[11] They serve as a bridge between the two books. The instruction to remain in Jerusalem and the promise of the Holy Spirit, which are the subjects of this section, are also summarized in Luke 24:49. The ascension of the Lord, which will appear in the next section in Acts, is also mentioned much more briefly in Luke 24. However, what appears in the

---

11. See José Ramos García, "La restauración de Israel," *EstBib*, 8 (1949), 75–133.

Gospel as conclusion serves here as an introduction; what there completed the narrative, here sets the tone for all that will follow.

Luke, as well as Paul in Galatians, uses two Greek words that are both translated as "Jerusalem": *Ierousalēm* (Jerusalem) and *Hierosolyma* (Jerosolyma). The first comes from the Hebrew, whereas the latter is Hellenistic. Normally, Luke uses the first when his references are religious or relate to the Temple; whereas the second is simply the geographical name of the city.[12]

In verse 4,[13] what the NRSV translates as "staying with them" literally means "sharing salt," and therefore translations such as that in JB and NIV are closer to the original. This reminds us that one of the "convincing proofs" that the Lord gave of his resurrection according to Luke was eating with his disciples, and that Luke as well as John refer to meals which the Risen Lord shared with his followers.

In the same verse, "the promise of the Father" (which appears in the parallel passage in Luke 24:29) is the Holy Spirit, as verse 5 makes clear: "for John baptized with water, but you will be baptized with the Holy Spirit not many days from now."[14] This contrast between the baptism of John and that of Jesus appears in all the Gospels, usually uttered by John the Baptist (Matthew 3:11, Mark 1:8, Luke 3:16, John 1:33). The words, which in the Gospels John pronounces at the beginning of the ministry of Jesus, appear here once again at the end of that ministry, but now in the mouth of Jesus himself.

In verses 6 to 8, "those who are gathered" ask Jesus about the restoration of the kingdom of Israel, and it is in response to that question that Jesus clarifies the promise of the Holy Spirit.[15] There are some points in this passage that merit special attention. The first is that it is not clear that those who asked the question were the apostles. In this particular case, it does not appear that Luke is trying to underscore the mental obfuscation of the apostles, who after "forty days" of special instruction after the resurrection of the Lord still do not comprehend the nature of the message of Jesus. Later on (1:15) we shall see that those gathered in Jerusalem were some 120 persons. Therefore, it is possible to interpret the text simply in the sense that the question was asked by some of

---

12. There is a good study of these two words and their theological significance: G. Morales Gómez, "Jerusalén-Jerosólima en el vocabulario y la geografía de Lucas," *RCatalT*, 7 (1982), 131–86. See also I. De la Potterie, "Les deux noms de Jérusalem dans les Actes des Apôtres," *Bib*, 63 (1982), 153–87.

13. William H. P. Hatch, "The Meaning of Acts 1:4," *JBL*, 30 (1911), 123–28.

14. Ernest Best, "Spirit-baptism," *NT*, 4 (1960–61), 236–43. The grammatical construction of this phrase allows also for a translation in the sense that John baptized "in" water, and the disciples will be baptized "in" the Holy Spirit.

15. On the manner in which Luke understands the Church as the "restoration of Israel," see J. Schmitt, "L'église de Jérusalem ou la 'restauration' d'Israël d'après les cinq premiers chapîtres des Actes," *RScR*, 27, (1953) 209–18; D. L. Tiede, "The exaltation of Jesus and the restoration of Israel in Acts 1," *HTR*, 79 (1986), 278–86.

those gathered. However, the fact that Luke does not identify the speakers, but seems to tell us that they were the ones who had received the teachings of Jesus since the resurrection, would seem to point to a theme that will appear repeatedly in this book: the disciples of Jesus are not always clear as to their Lord's will, and often the Holy Spirit will amend their actions and decisions.

At any rate, it is necessary to clarify Jesus' response. Sometimes we are told that this passage shows that the disciples were still thinking in materialistic terms, and in the restoration of a political kingdom, and that Jesus corrects them because that was not really the nature of his message. The text does not say that. Jesus certainly does correct his disciples, but not because their interests are too materialistic or political. Actually, the very word "kingdom," which is central to the message of Jesus, necessarily has political connotations.[16] Jesus corrects them rather for two other reasons: first, because they wish "to know the times or periods that the Father has set by his own authority"; and second (and this more by implication than directly), because the reign of God is not to be restored only to Israel, but also will include the Samaritans[17] and all other peoples, "to the ends of the earth."[18]

Luke has just told us that Jesus spent the forty days after his resurrection telling his disciples about the reign of God. The reign of God is the center of the message of Jesus in the Gospel, and would also be at the heart of the message of the apostles and others in Acts. That reign, in the biblical view, is not a purely spiritual place where the souls of the dead go. It is the consummation of the will of God for all of creation, physical as well as spiritual. It is about this that Jesus has spoken to them for forty days, and it is about this that they now pose a question. In his answer, Jesus does not tell them that such a reign will not come, but simply warns them against being concerned about the time when this would come about. The coming of God's reign will take place in the time and period that "the Father has set by his own authority." What is rejected here is not the idea itself of the reign, or even of a restoration; what is rejected is interest in finding out when it is to come.

---

16. D. L. Tiede, "Acts 1:6–8 and the theo-political claims of Christian witness," *WaW*, 1 (1981), 41–51, shows that Luke was quite aware of the political and religious nature of Jesus' message regarding the inauguration of the reign of God, and that his disciples were sent as his "agents." The message of the reign or kingdom of God is a radical critique of all the political claims of the kings of the Gentiles, including the Roman Empire.

17. See Morton S. Enslin, "Luke and the Samaritans," *HTR*, 36 (1943), 277–97.

18. There is an unusual interpretation in D. R. Schwartz, "The end of the *Ge* (Acts 1:8)," *JBL*, 105 (1986), 669–76. According to Schwartz, the quote "ends of the earth" are not the boundaries of the inhabited earth, but rather the boundaries of the land promised to Israel. In that case, it would seem that Jesus is giving his disciples a rather limited view of their mission, and that it is only later, as events develop in the Book of Acts, that there will be talk of a wider vision. See also the note regarding Ethiopia in 8:27.

On the other hand, these verses do deny the limitation of the reign of God to Israel alone.[19] The disciples inquire about the restoration of the kingdom "to Israel"; the Lord responds by speaking to them of the need to be witnesses "to the ends of the earth." The contrast is not clarified any further at this point. The rest of the book will be the narrative of the manner in which, thanks to the leading of the Spirit, the disciples will discover that the reign is not only for Israel.

It has often been pointed out that the last part of verse 8 may be read as an outline for the entire book: "in Jerusalem, in all Judea, in Samaria, and to the ends of the earth." What has not been sufficiently understood is that in this entire process Christians themselves are discovering, by means of the Spirit, that the reign of God is much wider than they themselves thought or expected.

The function of the disciples is to be "witnesses."[20] The text itself says no more. However, according to Lukan theology, God has given the Lordship to Jesus. Therefore, the message of God's reign is also the message that with the advent of Jesus that reign has been initiated. That is why being witnesses for Jesus is also being witnesses to the kingdom of God. The reign itself, as an idea and a hope, had no need of "witnesses" among Jews. It was part of the expectation of all faithful Jews. That to which the disciples are to testify is not simply the idea or the promise of a coming reign of God, but the fact that in Jesus that kingdom has dawned. It is important to underscore that historical nature of the "witness" of the disciples. One cannot "witness" to an idea or a doctrine. One is a "witness" of a fact, an event, the actions and words of a person. The witness for which the disciples are empowered is the concrete announcement of what God has done in the life, death, and resurrection of Jesus.

THE REIGN OF GOD AND OUR REALITY

The message of Jesus in the Gospel according to Luke is the reign of God, and now Luke begins the second book summarizing that message once again in terms of the reign. It is important to remember this, for throughout this second book the subject of God's reign will appear repeatedly, although most often implicitly rather than explicitly. In order to understand the acts of the Spirit as this book does we have to see them as the acts of the Spirit within the reign and toward the reign. In the first book, Luke clarified the significance of this reign, which stands at the very heart of the teachings of Jesus. In Luke 4:43, Jesus declares, "I must proclaim the good news of the kingdom of God, for I was sent for

---

19. Walter J. Galus, *The Universality of the Kingdom of God in the Gospels and the Acts of the Apostles*, doctoral dissertation, Catholic University of America, Washington, D.C., 1945.

20. Edouard Burnier, *La Notion de Témoignage dans le Nouveau Testament. Notes de Théologie Biblique* (Lausanne: F. Roth, 1939); Eduardo Iglesias, "El Libro de Hechos: ¡Seréis mis testigos!," *Christus*, 2 (1936), 637–42; Vittorio Subilia, "Nota sulla nozione di testimonianza nel Nuovo Testamento," *Prot*, 4 (1949), 1–22.

this purpose." His miracles are signs of the kingdom. His parables are promises and descriptions of life in the reign of God. His own life is the inauguration of that reign.

It is, however, a rather strange kingdom, which can be compared to a mustard seed (Luke 13:18–19) or a bit of leaven (Luke 13:20–21). It is a reign different from all the present kingdoms, because "the greatest among you must become like the youngest, and the leader like the one who serves" (Luke 22:26). Furthermore, even though we might not like it, it is a kingdom in which the poor, the hungry, those who mourn, and those who are hated are blessed; whereas the opposite is the case with those who live well and are well thought of: "Woe to you who are rich, for you have received your consolation. Woe to you who are full now, for you will be hungry. Woe to you who are laughing now, for you will mourn and weep. Woe to you when all speak well of you, for that is what their ancestors did to the false prophets" (Luke 6:24–26).

Acts too is about this strange kingdom. The story here is about the acts of a Spirit who makes it possible for believers to live, even amidst the kingdoms of this world, as citizens of that other kingdom. Much of the Book of Acts tells how that strange order of God's reign becomes a reality in the life of the Church when it is obedient to the dictates of the Spirit.

Meanwhile, the events of the old order continue. Still the rich enjoy. Still those who eat more than is necessary rejoice in their feasting. Still newspapers are more interested in the powerful than in those who suffer. But those of us who have heard "the gospel of the kingdom of God" know that this new reign is an unavoidable reality and seek to organize our lives and our actions, even while living in the old order, in such a way that they will witness to the new order for which we are preparing and which we already in a way enjoy.

That is clearly the situation of the Latin American Church. Our lands and our people have an abundance of human and natural resources, which in themselves are signs of God's reign. However, even amidst such abundance millions live in abject poverty. The condition of the poor in Latin America, rather than improving, grows worse as time passes. The same is true of Hispanics in the United States, among whom according to the latest census almost two out of every five children live below the level of poverty.

Sometimes it seems difficult to see where there is true fear of the Lord. The powerful exploit the weak as if there were no God to see and judge their actions. In the Church itself there are "leaders" who become rich by preaching the gospel while the people starve. Certainly, even though the reign of God has dawned, we are still living under the old regime, in which the powerful take advantage of the rest, and the privileged flaunt their privilege.

The first few verses of Acts warn us about two temptations. The second will become clear as we discuss the ascension of the Lord (1:9–11), but the first is similar to that of the disciples who asked the Lord if he was about to restore the kingdom to Israel (1:6). Israel had been oppressed for centuries, and throughout all that time had been awaiting its liberation. There were many political parties among the Jews in Jesus' time. Most of them, each in its own way, spoke of the day in which the kingdom would be restored to Israel. The exception were those who had so profited from the "prosperity" and the "peace" brought about by the Roman Empire that they had become practically foreigners among their own people. Therefore, the question that the disciples asked is not surprising. What is surprising is Jesus' response by widening their understanding of God's reign. They ask him about restoration of the kingdom *to Israel*; he responds by speaking to them of a mission "to the ends of the earth." Fortunately, most of the Latin American Church has not lost its expectation of God's reign. However, for many of us the greatest temptation is in narrowing the borders of that reign, very much as the disciples did. Those of us who are Protestant in Latin America, and who sometimes feel oppressed or marginalized for religious reasons, and all of us Hispanics in the United States, where we often feel marginalized for ethnic and economic reasons, ardently hope for the coming of God's reign among us. Our hope is that the reign will end our own suffering and, therefore, instead of asking how we are to witness in ever-wider spheres, we simply ask when the reign will be ours.

This is understandable, as we can also understand the attitude of those suffering Jewish disciples who ask the Lord whether the kingdom would then be restored to Israel. The text in Acts warns us that we are not to seek to know the time events will take place, but that our task consists rather in receiving the power of the Holy Spirit and then being witnesses "to the ends of the earth." This means that our witness must reach as far as reaches the creative work of God.[21]

There are some who seem to think that the Holy Spirit will tell them when the end is to come. In our day, in some Protestant circles, some look to the new state of Israel, and on the basis of this supposed "restoration of Israel" and of what they say has been revealed to them by the Spirit, claim this to be a sign that the end is near. Such people need to hear again what the text says, that the Holy Spirit is not given to us in order to foretell the future, but in order to empower us as witnesses. It is by the power of the Spirit that we have faith; it is by the power of the Spirit that we can live in hope even in the worst of circumstances; it is by the power of the Spirit that we know that we are loved children of God even while the world tramples us. But that power has been given to us, not just so that we may enjoy it in our own lives, but above all so that we may be witnesses to Jesus and to God's reign.

On the other hand, it is necessary to clarify the meaning of the word "witness," which is what the disciples are to be by the power of the Spirit. There are various sorts of truths, and each of them must be communicated in its own way. For instance, it is true that two and two are four; but we do not claim that someone is a "witness" to the fact that two and two are four. That sort of truth is normally communicated, not by witnesses but by teachers. But when it is necessary

---

21. Perhaps at this point we ought to learn from those early Christians who prayed "for the delay of the end," in order to be able to proclaim the gospel further. Tertullian, *Apol.* 32.

to establish facts before a court, what is called for is not teachers but witnesses. The teacher says, "Such and such is always thus, by its own nature"; the witness says, "Such and such an event has happened thusly." Therefore, the first characteristic of witnessing is that it refers, not to invariable truths such as those in mathematics, but to historical fact. It is important to understand this, because the message of the gospel is not a series of doctrines but a series of events. What we proclaim is not our knowledge of theories or doctrines, no matter how true these may be. What we proclaim are events, the actions and the promises—for the latter are simply future events—of God in Jesus Christ. Unfortunately, sometimes Christians have confused these two, and then we act as if the gospel were a series of doctrines, and as if our task were to make everybody accept these particular four, ten, or two hundred points of doctrine. But that is not the case. The gospel is the good news of what God has done, is doing and will do in Jesus Christ. The gospel is neither a philosophy nor a style of life. It is news! And, as all news, those who communicate it are witnesses to it.

There certainly is a relationship between eternal reality and the events that are the subject of witness, just as there is a relationship between the mathematical principle that two and two are four and the experience of someone who sees that two stones and two stones make four stones. But what makes a witness truly such is knowing, not just primarily an eternal truth, but what one has seen in life and history.

This means that that to which we witness is the concrete and historical event of Jesus in the flesh, and the events, also concrete and historical, that result from it. That is why Christian witness always takes into account the context. It is not a series of words that we repeat in all times and circumstances, but the manner in which Christians of each time and in each circumstance give witness to that which took place in the first century in the life of Jesus, and to that which takes place in our own century in our own lives and in our own history. The history of our people, then, is not something that we can ignore as we are witnesses. The history of our people—our own history—is the proper field for witnessing. A witness that is not incarnate in its own history neither is a true witness nor does it truly refer to the Lord who has been made flesh in our human history. Therefore, when throughout this commentary we seek to relate what we read in Acts with our own life and history, what we are doing is not optional, something that we do because we choose to do so, but rather something absolutely necessary as we seek to be the sort of witnesses that we are called to be.

C. THE ASCENSION (1:9–11)

This text is parallel to Luke 24:50–52.[22] Some point to the differences between the two texts, for here we hear of an ascension that took place after "forty days," and in Luke the impression is that it took place the same day as the resurrection. On the basis of this discrepancy, some have argued that the

---

22. On the relationship between the two texts, see Philippe H. Menoud, "Remarques sur les textes de l'ascension dans Luc-Actes," *BZntW*, 21 (1954), 148–56; Heinrich Schlier,

two books were originally a single one, and that, in separating them, some careless redactor produced this disagreement.[23] The truth is that the Gospel of Luke does not actually say that the ascension took place immediately after the resurrection, and that therefore the discrepancy is not as large as it seems. The same may be said regarding the location of the ascension. In Luke, it is in Bethany; here, it is on the Mount of Olives (1:12). In fact, Bethany is on the slope of the Mount of Olives, some three kilometers from Jerusalem. Therefore, the only difference would be that in Luke the ascension seems to take place some three kilometers away from Jerusalem, whereas in Acts it is "a Sabbath day's journey away," which is closer to a kilometer.

There is, however, a clear difference in the emphasis in each of the two texts. In Luke, in spite of the brevity of the story, we are told that Jesus was blessing his disciples when he left them, and that they then "returned to Jerusalem with great joy." In Acts, the stress falls on what happens immediately after the ascension. While those present are still looking to the sky, "two men in white robes" come before them and ask them, "Men of Galilee, why do you stand looking up toward heaven? This Jesus who has been taken up from you into heaven, will come in the same way as you saw him go into heaven." These two messengers remind us of the "two men in dazzling clothes" who first announced the resurrection of Jesus (Luke 24:4–5). In both cases, what they do is to point the attention of the disciples in a different direction. In the first, they tell the women no longer to look in the empty tomb. In the second, they tell the disciples to cease looking at the sky, but rather simply to trust that Jesus will return.

A SIGHT SET ON HEAVEN

In commenting on the previous passage, we saw that one of the temptations constantly before Christians is that of narrowing the borders of God's reign. Now we note that the second temptation is religious escapism: to remain standing looking to heaven, where Jesus is. Jesus had told his disciples that after his ascension they should go to Jerusalem, where they would receive the power of the Holy Spirit. But after the ascension the disciples remained immobilized, with their sight set on heaven, and it was necessary for the "two men in white robes" to remind them that this was not what they were supposed to do. Jesus will return from heaven, certainly, they are told; but meanwhile there are other things to be done. It is about those other things that Acts speaks.

"Jesu Himmelfahrt nach den lukanischen Schriften," *GuL*, 34 (1961), 91–99; P. A. Stempvoort, "The interpretation of the ascension in Luke and Acts," *NTSt*, 5 (1958–59), 30–42. Even though somewhat dated, probably the most thorough study is still that of Victoriano Larrañaga, *La Ascensión del Señor en el Nuevo Testamento*, 2 vols. (Madrid: Instituto Francisco Suárez, 1943).

23. Etienne Trocmé, *Le "Livre des Actes" et l'Histoire* (Paris: Presses Universitaires de France, Paris, 1957), pp. 30–41.

What the two men promised the disciples is not that they too will go to heaven, but rather that Jesus will return to earth. If the former were the case, they could forget about Jerusalem, and about all the rest of the places mentioned in Acts. But the promise is that Jesus will return to earth, and that meanwhile it is on this earth that disciples must be obedient, in the midst of very earthly circumstances and challenges.

Too often, we Christians remain with our sights set on heaven, and forget that we have been placed on earth in order to fulfill a mission. Speaking as a Protestant of Latin American background, I can say that this is a common temptation in the community in which I was formed and to which I belong. Due to a series of historical, political, and social circumstances, we have heard the preaching of a "gospel" that has little to do with the total reign of God over all of creation, and often is reduced to the promise that the soul will continue living eternally in heaven. From the point of view of today's kingdoms, such a "gospel" is innocuous; it does not challenge them in any way. If the "kingdom" has to do with the "beyond," those who preach it will have no conflict with the "here and now." That is why such a truncation of the gospel is attractive, not only to those who conduct affairs in the present reign, but also to many Christians who thereby seek to avoid problems and conflicts with the present order.

We pay a high price for such tranquility. Our preaching, so concerned about the beyond, frequently runs the risk of having little to say to those who must still live amidst the injustice and suffering of the present. (Much like that ancient philosopher, who was so enthralled by the study of the stars that he fell into a well.) At least for the time being, and as long as that is the divine will, we are not called to heaven, but first of all to Jerusalem, to prepare to be obedient, and then we are called to the world, "to the ends of the earth."

There is, however, another way of looking at heaven that does have a positive value. The reason for this is not that heaven is "spiritual," but the ascension itself.[24] The victory of Jesus has already taken place in heaven.[25] This is a warranty, not only of the victory of Jesus, but also of ours. As John Calvin states in his *Institutes of the Christian Religion*,

> from this our faith receives many benefits. First it understands that the Lord by his ascent to heaven opened the way into the heavenly kingdom, which had been closed through Adam. Since he entered heaven in our flesh, as if in our name, it follows, as the apostle says, that in a

---

24. On the history of the interpretation of the ascension and the place it has had in the history of Christian thought, see J. G. Davies, *He Ascended into Heaven: A Study in the History of Doctrine* (London: Lutterworth Press, 1958).

25. This may seem very strange to those of us who believe that heaven, in contrast with earth, is and has always been a place of calm and purity. In the New Testament, it appears that part of the victory of Jesus consists precisely in expelling evil from heaven. See Luke 10:18 and Revelation 12:12–13.

sense we already "sit with God in the heavenly places in him," so that we do not await heaven with a bare hope, but in our Head already possess it.[26]

The Epistle to the Hebrews interprets the ascension likewise, when commenting on Psalm 8:6, where it is stated that everything has been subjected to the human. Hebrews asserts that we do not actually see that such has taken place, for we certainly do not rule over all creation; however, "we do see Jesus, who for a little while was made lower than the angels, now crowned with glory and honor" (Hebrews 2:9).

This is of the utmost importance for us today. We constantly see human beings trampled and oppressed by forces they cannot control. Hunger, poverty, and oppression are a common experience among the Latin American and Hispanic peoples. If we were to consider only what we see, we would have to confess that we are miserable beings without future or hope. From that, it is only one step to acquiescing to misery and oppression. But that is not the case. Although we do not yet see ourselves in glory, we do see our Head, Jesus Christ, in glory. It is there that he is currently in our stead. As Paul says, "your life is hidden with Christ in God. When Christ who is your life is revealed, then you also will be revealed with Him in glory" (Col. 3:3–4).

In contrast to this, there is a style of preaching and a sort of theology, unfortunately widespread in our day, that seem to believe that the best way to exalt God is to denigrate the human creature. Thus we are taught to declare, "I am but a lowly worm." The Bible, on the other hand, speaks very differently. One of us is already sitting at the right hand of the Father. All of us will reign with him in glory. We are not worms. We are kings and priests (Rev. 1:6, 5:10), "a chosen race, a royal priesthood, holy nation, God's own people" (I Pet. 2:9). Let no one dare denigrate or oppress us!

If the one who sits at the right hand of God is "one of us," that is, a human being, every human being is worthy of the highest respect. Sometimes Christians have employed their claim to be "kings and priests" in order to impose their will on those who do not believe as they do. This is not what is meant here. Not only we Christians, but every human being, is like the one who already sits at the right hand of God. Therefore, if as Christians we are to resist any oppression that might seek to subject us, also as Christians we must resist the temptation to oppress others. When a Christian, for whatever reason, is tempted to exploit, humiliate, or marginalize another human being, that Christian must see, seated at the right hand of God, another who is like that other human being.

In Latin America for too long we have suffered from a vision of Jesus that sees him mostly as the crucified, but not as the risen one who sits at the right hand of God. That vision was employed at the time of the Conquest in order to seek to convince the original inhabitants of these lands that they were to accept

---

26. *Inst.* 2.16, Trans. Ford Lewis Battles (Philadelphia: Westminster, 1960), p. 524.

the sufferings imposed on them by the Conquistadores. It was employed in colonial times in order to support the privilege of the power elites. And it is still employed in that fashion today. This is not the perogative of any particular branch of the Christian faith.

D. THE ELECTION OF MATTHIAS (1:12–26)

The last section in this introductory chapter deals with the election of Matthias.[27] After the ascension of Jesus, the disciples return to Jerusalem (see also Luke 24:52), and there they gather in the "upper room." This seems to have been the same place where Jesus had his last supper with the disciples before the crucifixion (Luke 22:12, Mark 14:15).[28] Here we are further told that the Twelve lodged in this upper room. Luke repeats the list of their names, which he gave us earlier in the Gospel (Luke 6:14–16).[29] To the Twelve were joined others who devoted themselves to prayer. Among them, "certain women, including Mary the mother of Jesus, as well as his brothers." About these "brothers" there has been much discussion, not because the text itself raises any issues, but because their possible existence obviously involves the perpetual virginity of Mary. Apart from that question, there is no way to know whether they are in fact the brothers of Jesus or other relatives.

The subject of the "women" must engage our attention. Apparently they are the same women, several of them affluent, who accompanied Jesus and took care of at least some of his expenses, as is affirmed in Luke 8:2–3. A manuscript from about the year 500, the "Codex Bezae," says "the wives and children," thus implying that these women were dependents of the male disciples. This particular manuscript, like the rest of the Western text that it reflects, shows a certain anti-feminine prejudice, and therefore it would seem that the purpose of this different reading is to lessen the importance of these women who accompanied Jesus in his ministry, covered his expenses, and apparently also participated in the events of Pentecost.

---

27. Paul Gaechter, "Die Wahl des Matthias," *ZkT*, 71 (1949), 318–46; Eduardo Iglesias, "Los Hechos de los Apóstoles: Muéstranos al que has elegido," *Christus*, 2 (1936), 902–8; Charles Massan, "La reconstitution du collège des douze, d'après Actes 1:15–26," *RTP*, série 2, 5 (1955), 193–201; Philippe Menoud, "Les additions au groupe des douze apôtres, d'après le livre des Actes," *RHPR*, 37 (1957), 71–80; K. H. Rengstorf, "Die Zuwaahl des Matthias," *ST* 15, (1961), 35–67; J. Rius-Camps, "L'elecció de Maties: Restauració pòstuma del Nou Israel," *RCatalT*, 12 (1987), 1–27; L. S. Thornton, "The choice of Matthias," *JTS*, 46 (1945), 51–59; J. DuPont, "Le douxième apôtre (Actes 1:15–26) à propos d'une explication récente," *BibOr*, 24 (1982), 193–98.

28. Even though the Greek word that Luke employs here (*hyperiòn*) is different from the one he uses in the Gospel (*anagaion*).

29. The New Testament lists of the Twelve do not always agree. See the study of Wilhelm Weber, "Die neutestamentlichen Apostellisten," *ZkT*, 54 (1912), 8–31.

What complicates the matter is that in verse 16 Peter addresses a group that seems to be exclusively masculine. Some seek to solve the contradiction by supposing that the scene has changed between verses 14 and 15, so that the 120 gathered when Peter speaks are a group different from the one described in verses 13 and 14. There is no doubt that at some point along this passage the scene has changed, for it is inconceivable that in the upper room there would be space for the 120 people in verse 15. However, the most likely place for such a change is between verse 13, where we are told that the Twelve dwelled in the upper room, and verse 14 where the women and others are added. In that case, what Luke is telling us is that after returning to Jerusalem and the upper room, the apostles gathered with others in some unnamed place, and the number of those congregated was of some 120 persons. If that is the case, beginning with verse 15 Luke is describing a scene such as could take place in any synagogue or other assembly in which women were present but did not share in the process of decision making. In some such cases, the men gathered in the center of the room and the women at the edges. In this case, apparently within a mixed assembly, Peter addresses the men, asking them to appoint another to take the place that Jesus has left vacant among the apostles. (This phenomenon of a change of scene without letting the reader know happens repeatedly in Acts—for instance, in the event of Pentecost itself.)

There follows Peter's speech, urging the "brothers" to elect a successor to take Judas's place. Although the speech is put in the mouth of Peter, it is in truth Luke's.[30] This becomes clear in verse 19, where Peter explains that *hakeldama* means field of blood "in their language." Speaking Aramaic, among people who spoke the same language, Peter would have had no need to explain the meaning of such a word.[31] Likewise, the quotations from Psalms 109:8 and 69:25, which appear in verse 20, are not taken from the Hebrew text but from the Greek version of the Hebrew Scriptures known as the Septuagint.[32] Therefore, Luke is describing the scene in general terms, adapting it for

---

30. Approximately thirty percent of Acts consists of speeches that Luke places in the mouths of various actors. There has been much discussion on the authenticity of such speeches, and especially those that proclaim the gospel. This will be discussed more fully in the study of the speeches of Peter in chapters 2 and 3.

31. On *hakeldama* and its background, see Max Wilcox, *The Semitisms of Acts* (Oxford: Clarendon, 1965), pp. 87–89.

32. Although it is customary to speak of the "Septuagint" as if there had been an official Greek translation, the fact is that, apart from the Pentateuch, what existed in the time of the New Testament was a series of diverse translations circulating independently. It was not until the third century, or perhaps even the fourth, that they were gathered as a whole. Having made that clarification, however, one may speak of the "Septuagint," meaning by that the totality of these independent translations, and the consensus among them. See Sidney Jellicoe, *The Septuagint and Modern Study* (Oxford: Clarendon, 1968).

his readers, who speak Greek and could therefore use the Septuagint and need to have Hebrew and Aramaic words explained.

Peter's speech revolves around two necessities: in verse 16, the betrayal by Judas is couched in the need to fulfill Scripture, and later on we are told that someone "must" become a witness of the resurrection in place of Judas. The Greek word in both cases is the same. In any case, Peter is not really dealing with the much-debated matter of the relationship between divine predestination and human responsibility. He is simply asserting that, in fulfillment of Scripture, Judas betrayed the Lord. The second necessity refers to the present responsibility: in light of what has happened, it is necessary to name another to take the place of Judas.[33] As to what happened to Judas after his betrayal, the New Testament reflects two different traditions. According to one of them, which appears in Matthew 27:3–8, Judas cast away the coins in the Temple and then hanged himself. The priests then used that money to buy the "field of blood." According to the other tradition, which is reflected here in Acts, it was Judas himself who bought the field, and in it he fell and died.[34] From an early time it became customary to join these two traditions declaring that Judas hanged himself, but that either the rope or the branch to which he tied it broke, so that he fell on his head and burst open.

What Peter proposed is that someone else should take "his position." The Greek text from the Psalms that Luke quotes refers to that position as an *episkope*. This word, later understood as "episcopacy," in ancient times did refer to a position, function, or supervisory capacity. However, as years went by it became more and more limited to the Christian episcopacy, and the notion developed that the bishops—those who occupied the episcopacy—were the successors of the apostles. This text played an important role in that process, because in it the office of an apostle is called an "episcopacy." Peter suggests that from among the "men"—which is literally what verse 21 says—who have

---

33. I. H. Marshall, *The Acts of the Apostles* (Leicester, England: Inter-Varsity Press, 1980), pp. 65–66, indicates that the reason someone must be elected to take the place of Judas is not in order to fulfill the prophecies of old, but rather to complete the number of the witnesses to the resurrection of Jesus.

34. There was also in the ancient Church a third tradition, claiming that Judas swelled up. It appears in a fragment of Papias: "Judas walked about in this world a sad example of impiety; for his body having swollen to such an extent that he could not pass where a chariot could pass easily, he was crushed by the chariot, so that his bowels gushed out" (*ANF*, 1:153). Perhaps this tradition is connected with the one reflected in Acts, that "he burst open in the middle." The two traditions are briefly compared by Rubén Darío García, *La Iglesia, el pueblo del Espíritu* (Barcelona: Ediciones Don Bosco, 1983), pp. 63–64. García also offers a number of references to intertestamentary literature that illustrate the use of similar images and traditions. See also: Pierre Benoit, "La mort de Judas," in *Synoptische Studien: Alfred Wikenhauser zum siebzigsten Geburstag* (München: Karl Zink, 1953), pp. 1–19; H. G. Hoelemann, *Letzte Bibelstudien* (Leipzig: Gustav Wolf, 1985), pp. 104–60; W. Wrede, *Vorträge und Studien* (Tübingen: J. C. B. Mohr, 1907), pp. 127–46.

been with Jesus from the very beginning of his ministry someone be chosen to take the place of Judas. That requirement is both strange and interesting, because not all twelve had "accompanied us during all the time that the Lord Jesus went in and out among us, beginning from the baptism of John on to the day he was taken up from us." In John 1:40–41 we are told that Peter and Andrew did fulfill that requirement, but there is no indication that the same was true of the others. In any case, those gathered[35] suggest two names: Joseph Barsabbas[36] "the just" and Matthias. Nothing is known about either beyond what this text tells us. In Acts 15:22 there is reference to a Judas Barsabbas, who may well have been a brother of Joseph. About Matthias, who finally was chosen, the New Testament remains silent. According to a later tradition, he preached in Judea and died as a martyr, stoned to death.[37]

As to the manner in which the lots were cast, the text offers no further clarification. The most common procedure was to write the names of candidates in small stones, putting them in a container, and shaking it until one came out.

MISSION AND STRUCTURE

What are we to say about the election of Matthias and its application to our day? This depends on how we interpret the message and purpose of the entire book of Acts. It has often been thought that Acts was written in order to uphold the role and authority of the apostles. In such a case, the purpose of this passage would be to show that Matthias, the twelfth of the apostles, was elected by the Lord just as the others were. On the other hand, the fact remains that Matthias is never again mentioned, either in Acts or in the rest of the New Testament. Therefore, it seems more appropriate to see in this episode a step in a transition that will be clear throughout the early chapters of Acts. In those chapters, at the same time that the mission of the Church advances, new leadership emerges. The apostles and the early disciples, grounded in their biblical tradition, saw a special significance in the number twelve, which is clearly related to the twelve tribes of Israel. From that perspective, they do what makes sense: they name another to complete that number. But the Spirit is ready to do new things, opening the Church to a wider world, which requires other leaders. The task of being witnesses, not only in Jerusalem and in Judea, but also in Samaria and to the ends of the earth, required people who could participate in that mission. For that reason, it has become commonplace to say that the disciples chose Mat-

---

35. Codex Bezae says that it was Peter who proposed the two names. All that is required for this different meaning is a minor change in the verb, turning it into a singular instead of the plural. Most likely, Codex Bezae is seeking to underscore Peter's authority as the one who proposes the names of the candidates.

36. Some manuscripts say "Barrabas," but that is clearly an error.

37. Clement, *Strom.*, ii.163, vii.318; Eusebius, *Hist. Ecl.* i.12.2, iii.25.6; Epiphanius, *Pan.* i.20.

thias, but the Spirit chose Paul. Although such a statement is not to be taken literally, it certainly points to one of the themes in Acts, which is the manner in which the Spirit calls new leaders and new structures for new circumstances.[38]

Later chapters in Acts will make this clearer. At any rate, the issues posed by this passage should be familiar to Christians who seek to be faithful to what God is doing in their world today. As the mission is transformed, so is it necessary to seek new structures and new leadership that are adequate to new dimensions in mission. Too often in Christian circles a question about the structure of the Church and how it is to be governed is answered by seeking in the New Testament—or in some other period of the Church—a fixed pattern, a model to be copied. However, what the entire book of Acts abundantly shows is that the heart of the matter is not the *structure* of the Church, but its *mission*. The eleven seek to keep the structure by naming one to take the place of Judas. That may be alright. But soon the Spirit will call the Church to a new dimension in mission that will require a sort of leadership different from even the apostles themselves.

There are other ways in which the text resonates with the experiences of many Latino Christians. The "old guard," that is the eleven, seems to believe that the structure of the Church must forever be the same that they knew, and they even seek leaders whose experiences and perspectives are the same as theirs. The "Twelve," now reduced to eleven, think that the election of another like themselves is absolutely essential. They even set up requirements in the election—requirements that some of them themselves did not meet. Whoever has not had the same experiences as they have had has no place in the leadership of the Church. Does that not remind us of many of the elections that take place in our churches? Rather than asking ourselves who can make a better contribution to the mission in an ever-changing world, we seek someone who can continue what has been done previously, someone who fits well in the patterns established by earlier generations, someone who will not challenge nor widen the view of those who are currently in charge. When this happens, we are in fact raising structure above mission, and giving clear signals that what seems most important to us is not the mission in the world, but to safeguard the structures which have served so far—or, perhaps more precisely, that have served us. As will be seen in the chapters that follow, the Holy Spirit does not tolerate such practices, and constantly forces the Church to be reformed in faithfulness to its mission. The very fact that Matthias is never again mentioned should serve as a warning: do not try to force the Spirit to act according to our own purposes!

---

38. On the difference between the election of the Twelve by Jesus and this election of Matthias, the following words are worth quoting: "Luke has taken care to make clear in the prologue to Acts that Jesus chose the twelve moved by the Holy Spirit. The reason for this clarification, which does not appear in Luke 6:13, is now clear: Luke wishes to contrast the choosing of the twelve, made by Jesus, with the restoration of that number by the 120 gathered, when Jesus is no longer with them, and before the coming of the Spirit." Josep Rius-Camps, *El Camino de Pablo a la Misión a los Paganos* (Madrid: Cristiandad, 1984), p. 24.

2

Pentecost
(2:1–41)[1]

A. THE OUTPOURING OF THE HOLY SPIRIT (2:1–13)

The events to which Acts now turns take place on the day of Pentecost. The word "Pentecost" originally means "fiftieth." It was the name that Greek-speaking Jews gave to the "festival of weeks."[2] It was celebrated at the end of the seventh week after Passover (that is, after a "week of weeks"). It was originally an agricultural celebration, having to do with the completion of the harvest, in which a symbolic sacrifice was presented to God consisting of two loaves of bread made with the recently harvested grain, as well as certain animals the law established (Lev. 23:15–21). After the destruction of the first Temple, the feast of Pentecost slowly evolved to become a celebration of the delivery of the law to Moses on Sinai.

Some interpreters[3] see a relationship between the Jewish celebration of the granting of the law at Pentecost and the granting of the Spirit on the date of that celebration. In that case, one could conclude that Luke intends to tell us that, just as God delivered the ancient law on Mount Sinai on Pentecost, so

---

1. How one divides and outlines the text of Acts is a matter of opinion. For instance, G. Krodel, "The Holy Spirit, the Holy Catholic Church: Interpretation of Acts 2:1–42," *Dia*, 23 (1984), 97–103, argues that the passage about Pentecost continues to verse 42, which I take to be the outline or summary of what follows after Pentecost.

2. Ex. 34:22, Deut. 16:10, Num. 28:26, II Cor. 8:13.

3. For instance, W. L. Knox, *The Acts of the Apostles* (Cambridge, U.K.: Cambridge University Press, 1948), p. 75.

did God deliver the new law of the Spirit on Pentecost.[4] Although such a hypothesis is attractive, it remains no more than a possibility.[5]

At any rate, it is clear that Luke places these events on the day of Pentecost because that feast brought a large number of Jewish pilgrims from all parts of the world, who came to worship in Jerusalem. It is precisely the presence of these people of various backgrounds that provides the opportunity for the miracle of tongues.[6]

Verse 1 tells us that "they were all together in one place." This "all," which appears again in verse 4, is to be understood in the sense that not only the Twelve are present, but also the women and the other disciples who are mentioned in 1:13–15. It was over all of these, and not only the Twelve, that the Spirit descended.[7]

Verses 2 and 3 describe two extraordinary phenomena whose overwhelming power is often hid from us because we already know that verse 4 will tell us that all of this was a manifestation of the Holy Spirit. If one reads the text in order, as one who does not know what comes next, the dramatic nature of the narrative becomes clearer. The disciples are gathered in prayer, as apparently they have been for several days since the ascension of the Lord (see 1:14). They are sitting in a house. This scene, although one of expectation, is tranquil. *Suddenly*, with no previous announcement, unexpectedly, a sound comes from heaven "like the rush of a violent wind." This fills the entire house where they are gathered. The text does not say that there was indeed a mighty wind, but only that there was a noise that the author compares with the sound of such wind and that this noise filled the house. Immediately, to what is heard is joined what is seen: "Divided tongues, as of fire, appeared among them, and a tongue rested on each of them." What has been described to this point is a frightening scene.

It is in verse 4 that Luke finally tells us why these things are happening: "All of them were filled with the Holy Spirit." In consequence, they, "began to speak in other languages." (Note the play on words between the tongues of fire and the tongues that the believers spoke. In Greek, as in English, the word is

---

4. This conjecture is further strengthened by the existence of a Jewish tradition that when God gave the law on Mount Sinai God's Word was made manifest in the seventy languages of all the nations. On the rabbinic traditions about Pentecost, see H. L. Strack and P. Billerbeck, *Kommentar zum Neuen Testament aus Talmud und Midrash*, 6 vols. (München: C. H. Beck, 1922–61), 2:597–602.

5. Interestingly, Paul relates the gift of the Spirit with the first fruits rather than with the revelation of the law on Sinai (Rom. 8:23).

6. A. Causse, "Le pélerinage à Jérusalem et la première Pentecôte," *RHPR*, 20 (1940), 120–41.

7. Antonio Salas Farragut, "Estaban 'todos' reunidos (Hch. 2.1); Precisiones críticas sobre los 'testigos' de Pentecostés," *Salm*, 28 (1981), 299–314, interprets this point as meaning that the full communication of the Spirit requires and leads to the participation both of the hierarchy and of the grassroots.

the same.)[8] The Greek verb that the NRSV translates as "to speak" is *apophtheggomai*, a verb that appears in the New Testament only in Acts (1:4, 14; 26:25). It means to speak solemnly, although not necessarily ecstatically.[9]

Luke then makes a parenthesis in his narrative (1:5) to let us know that there were Jews "from every nation under heaven" in Jerusalem. This parenthesis is necessary if we are to understand what follows. Luke, as a good narrator, tells us what we need to know and no more, in order not to interrupt his story. Most commentators think that these Jews would be mostly pilgrims who had come to Jerusalem for the religious festivities[10]—as many as a hundred thousand.[11] At any rate, although there certainly were many pilgrims on such occasions, it is also true that there were many pious Jews from the Diaspora (that is, those who lived in other parts of the world) who went to Jerusalem in order to finish their lives there (see below, the commentary on 6:1).

Luke then retakes the narrative telling us that "at this sound the crowd gathered." Somehow the scene has changed, for before we were in a "house" and now we seem to be in a wider space, perhaps a square in front of the house.[12] The mental picture that most of us have is that the noise that attracts the attention of the multitude is the result of the disciples speaking in various tongues. However, it most likely refers to the sound from heaven in 2:2.[13] Whatever the case may be, those who came because of the noise were "bewildered." This is interesting, because it is customary to speak of Pentecost as the reversal of the story of the Tower of Babel, claiming that whereas in Babel humanity was divided by different tongues, in Pentecost that division was overcome. The fact is that according to the text the first reaction of the crowd is bewilderment, "because each one heard them speaking in the native language of each." It should also be noted that this is not exactly the same as the glossolalia that appears in Paul's Epistles, for there the tongues spoken cannot be understood by those who hear but require an interpreter; whereas here in the event of Pentecost the very act of speaking in tongues has the purpose of communicating the message, and therefore translators are not needed.

---

8. Cf. J. Rius-Camps, "Pentecostés versus Babel: Estudio crítico de Hch. 2," *FilolNt*, 1 (1988), 35–61.

9. Gerhard Kittel, *ThWzNT*, 1:448.

10. For the contrary position, that is, that they were Diaspora Jews who now lived permanently in Jerusalem, see E. Haenchen, *The Acts of the Apostles* (Philadelphia: Westminster, 1971), p. 168.

11. Joachim Jeremias, *Jerusalén en tiempos de Jesús: Estudio económico y social del mundo del Nuevo Testamento* (Madrid: Cristiandad, 1985), pp. 95–102.

12. This has led some interpreters to suggest that the "house" was the Temple, and that the action has now moved to the courtyard. However, Luke does not normally speak of the Temple as a "house."

13. Although the Greek words for both sounds are different.

Those who listen are surprised because all those who are speaking, and can be understood by the rest, are "Galileans." That word can be understood in different ways. In some cases it was used as a pejorative name for the followers of Jesus. If that is the meaning here, the question being asked is, "Are not all those who speak Christians?" However, such a question would make little sense in this context, where those who listen have no reason to know that the speakers are followers of Jesus, nor would that question have anything to do with the variety of tongues. Another possibility is that those who hear recognize the Galilean accent of the speakers (as in Matt. 26:73). This also would seem strange, because the point of the story is that those who comment hear each in their own tongue. All that can be said then is that, for whatever reason, those who listen recognize the speakers as Galileans, people despised by the more sophisticated Jews of Jerusalem, and that therefore the meaning of the question is more something like, "Are not all these people ignorant and backward Galileans? How is it then that we hear them speak each in our own tongue?"

Scholars have long debated the nature and the origin of the list of the nations from which those who listen come. What is under discussion is mostly the relationship between this list and others.[14] What Luke wants to stress is that they come from all the known world, even from Parthia, far beyond the limits of the Roman Empire. The "Romans" mentioned in the list are also Jews coming from Rome, and not Gentile Romans. The text makes it clear that all those who are present are Jews, if not by birth, at least by conversion ("proselytes" in 2:10).

The theme of which the believers speak is "God's deeds of power" (1:11). That is all that Luke tells us. Given the context, and the speech by Peter that follows, one is led to suppose that they were not speaking only of the death and resurrection of Jesus, but of all that God had done throughout history.

---

14. The most discussed of these lists is that of Paul of Alexandria, who in the year 378 B.C.E. wrote a treatise on astrology in which he related the signs of the zodiac with the nations existing under each of them. The list of nations that he employs is much older than his treatise, and is similar to that in Acts, although not exactly the same. Obviously, Luke does not include Greeks and Jews because he needs to mention nationalities with which it would be difficult for Jews to communicate. The "Medes" and the "Elamites" were no longer called that at the time, and it is possible that Luke has decided to use these names in imitation of the Septuagint, where they do appear as existing people. On this entire question, see Haenchen, *Acts*, pp. 169–70, n. 5; Stefan Weinstock, "The geographical catalogue in Acts 2:9–11," *JRomSt*, 38 (1948), 43–46; J. Brinkman, "The literary background of the 'catalogue of nations' (Acts 2:9–11)," *CBQ*, 25 (1963), 418–27. In the list as it appears in Acts, also the word "Judea" has caused some debate, for there are a number of reasons leading to think that the original text read otherwise. On this point, see F. F. Bruce, *Commentary on the Book of Acts*, 2nd ed. (Grand Rapids: Eerdmans, 1954), p. 58, n. 13.

It is also interesting to note that those who hear, although coming from different areas and speaking different languages, can somehow communicate among themselves, even apart from the Pentecostal miracle, asking each other what is the meaning of what they are witnessing (2:12).

There are, however, others who mock (2:13). Once again, in reading the text we read into it the traditional mental image according to which they are mocking the Christians who are speaking in tongues, and that it is those believers who are accused of being drunk. However, the text can also be interpreted in a different way that probably makes more sense. Those who sneer are "others," that is to say, they are not the ones who hear the believers speaking in their own tongues. For some reason that the text does not tell us, these "others" do not perceive the miracle. They are present with the multitude, but the miracle is hidden from them. The text does not say why. One possibility would be that they are Jews from the area, who expect to understand what is being said, and for whom therefore the fact that they can hear in their own tongue is no cause for wonder. On not perceiving the miracle, they sneer. Whom are they mocking? Only the speakers? Or are they also sneering at the listeners who are acting as if something great had happened? Possibly both. Because they cannot see the miracle, they decide that all involved, the speakers as well as the listeners, are "filled with new wine."

The Disadvantage of the Advantaged

There is an interesting detail in the narrative that has just been studied: not all perceive what seems to be an obvious miracle. It is one of the most surprising miracles in the New Testament. A large crowd of people speaking different tongues can understand what the followers of Jesus are saying after they have received the Holy Spirit. Still, there are some who do not see the miracle, but simply claim that those who speak (or perhaps those who act as if they are amazed) "are filled with wine."

How can this be? How is it that some, instead of perceiving a miracle, see only something to mock? Probably, because those who sneer speak the language of the country. Because they expect to understand whatever is said, the very fact that they now understand is no cause for wonder. If I expect my language to be spoken, how could I be surprised when I understand what is being said? And if I am not surprised, wouldn't I come to the conclusion that those who act surprised are either drunk or out of their minds?

If this is what is happening, those who sneer are precisely the ones who in another way would be advantaged. They are at home. When someone speaks, they expect to understand. Therefore, Pentecost is no miracle for them.

If that is the case, what is happening here is an example of what Jesus said so many times in his parables, namely, that the first will be last, and that those who think that the reign of God belongs to them are at risk of losing it. The Spirit is manifested with power, and those who would otherwise seem to be advantaged, because they are at home, are now at a disadvantage, precisely because they cannot see the extraordinary events that are taking place. In the next section we shall encounter Peter describing the "leveling" power of the Holy Spirit. However, Peter's words are not necessary for us to see that power, which is manifest in many other places in Scripture. Here, in the very event of Pentecost and in the various reactions to it, we see that leveling power.

There is much that could be said about this passage that is pertinent to our situation today. In many of our churches, there is great emphasis on the presence and the power of the Holy Spirit. Many Protestant Christians in Latin America are not surprised when those who look at them from outside claim that they are "filled with new wine." Our enthusiastic response to the gospel, and frequently our emotional reaction to it, confuse onlookers. Why such joy and such noise? And then we are accused of being irrational, emotive, and ignorant.

In such cases, it is possible that what is taking place is something similar to what we have just seen. Those who look at us and think that we are "filled with new wine" are precisely those who are accustomed to being advantaged in the social order. They seem to think that what they have and what they are they have and they are because they have earned it. They are like those Judeans who, precisely because they were at home, expected to understand, and who were therefore not surprised by the miracle of Pentecost. Because they expected to understand, they could not understand! Likewise, many of the sophisticated today find it difficult to be surprised by the miracle of God's grace. Because they cannot be surprised, they sneer at those who are. That is why it is possible to speak of the "disadvantage of the advantaged."

On the other hand, it is dangerous to rely on our own advantage. Christians, precisely because we are Christians, are always tempted to trust in our own advantage, in our own religious experience, and not in the surprising power of the Spirit. Thus, there is in many of our Latino churches, besides the phenomenon just described, another one that seems to be its opposite, but which in truth is simply the other side of the same coin: we claim the Holy Spirit as our own possession. We demand that the Spirit be always manifested in a particular way that we have determined. For some it is speaking in tongues. For others it is worship done "decently and in order." If we demand that the Spirit always be manifested by speaking tongues, when someone does not share that experience we claim that that person does not have the Spirit. If we think that the Spirit always acts according to the order our rituals prescribe, we refuse to acknowledge the presence of the Spirit when someone does speak in tongues. Both are denials of the freedom of the Spirit, who like the wind blows from where it wishes, and whose variety is always surprising (I Cor. 12:8–11— note in particular the end of verse 11, "the same Spirit, who allots to each individually just as the Spirit chooses").

The trap in each case is in claiming an advantage. Whoever believes to be advantaged, loses any advantage. Whoever claims to know how the Holy Spirit will act, may not be able to see that action when it takes place. If there is something that the Book of Acts tells us quite clearly, it is precisely that the activity of the Holy Spirit is always surprising and overpowering.

EACH IN OUR OWN TONGUE

It has become commonplace to establish a contrast between Babel and Pentecost, saying that whereas the first results in confusion through the multiplicity of tongues, the latter leads to unity. That is true to an extent, but there is also a grave error in it—an error that can be used to seek within the Church a uniformity the Spirit does not demand.

In the story of Babel, humans used their linguistic unity to unleash their pride, attempting to build a tower so high that it would reach heaven. In response, God produces a multiplicity of tongues, from which confusion results.

However, the contrast with Pentecost is not absolute. In Pentecost too God produces a multiplicity of tongues. For that reason, it has been claimed that Pentecost is not quite the opposite of Babel, but rather "a second Babel."[15]

In order to have the multitude understand what the disciples of Jesus were saying, the Holy Spirit had two options: one was to make all understand the Aramaic the disciples spoke; the other was to make each understand in their own tongue. Significantly, the Spirit chooses the latter route. This has important consequences for the way we understand the place of culture and language in the Church. Had the Spirit made all the listeners understand the language of the apostles, we would be justified in a centripetal understanding of mission, one in which all who come in are expected to be like those who invite them. However, because what the Spirit did was exactly the opposite, this leads us to a centrifugal understanding of mission, one in which as the gospel moves toward new languages and new cultures, it is ready to take forms that are understandable within those languages and cultures. In other words, had there been an "Aramaic only" movement in first-century Palestine, Pentecost was a resounding no! to that movement. And it is still a resounding no! to any movement within the Church that seeks to make all Christians think alike, speak alike, and behave alike. The first translator of the gospel is the Holy Spirit, and a church that claims to have the Holy Spirit must be willing to follow that lead. That is why it has correctly been stated that whereas Babel was a monument to human pride, the Church is called to be a monument to the humiliation of any who seek to make their language or culture dominant.[16]

B. EXPLANATION AND RESPONSE (2:14–41)

1. Peter's Speech (2:14–36)

It is as a response to the accusation of being drunk that Peter explains what is happening. There has been much discussion among scholars about the speeches in Acts, and especially the "kerygmatic" ones—that is, those proclaiming the gospel. Much of that discussion has revolved around the thesis of

---

15. I. G. Malcolm, "The Christian teacher in the multicultural classroom," *Journal of Christian Education*, 74 (1982), p. 53.

16. Ibid.

C. H. Dodd that these speeches allow us to reconstruct an outline of the contents of apostolic preaching, as there are certain constant elements in that outline.[17] Over time the consensus has developed that Luke has his own theology, and that his speeches are a way of presenting it.[18] This does not necessarily mean, however, that Luke has invented such pieces out of whole cloth, but rather that he has employed ancient materials that somehow have become part of the tradition of the Church, and from them he has composed his own speeches. At the same time, there are indications that there is in Luke at least a certain degree of consciousness of the fact that Christian thought has evolved from the origins to his own day, and that he must take that into account. Therefore, in the Acts speeches there is a combination of ancient materials, Luke's own theology, and his attempt to depict a theological development.

The manner and measure in which those various elements are combined varies from speech to speech. This may be seen by contrasting the speech by Peter in Acts 2 with the one that appears in the following chapter. The speech at Pentecost has every sign of having been composed by Luke, summarizing the essential points of his own theology, while including some elements that may be Petrine in origin. The speech in the next chapter has an undeniable archaic flavor, and possibly is much closer to the early preaching of the Church.[19]

What seems to determine the nature of Peter's speech is, first of all, the quote from Joel that serves as its starting point, and also the role that this speech plays in the entire book, which is similar to the role in Luke's Gospel of the quotation from Isaiah and the sermon by Jesus in chapter 4. In both cases, Luke presents a biblical text that summarizes or announces what is to follow. Therefore, the sermon in Acts 2 has the clear stamp of Luke the theologian, whereas in the speech in Acts 3, Luke the historian offers us more ancient materials.

Turning then to the speech in chapter 2, the word that the NRSV translates as "standing" was usually employed for the action of an orator who stood up in order to make a formal speech. The verb for what Peter does in speaking is the same that appears in 2:4, and usually refers to a solemn or formal speech. Peter's opening words also reflect the beginning of such a speech.

---

17. C. H. Dodd, *The Apostolic Preaching and Its Development* (New York: Harper, 1936). The same thesis appears in F. F. Bruce, *The Speeches in Acts* (London: Tyndale, 1942) and in Etienne Trocmé, *Le "Livre des Actes" et l'Histoire* (Paris: Presses Universitaires de France, 1957), p. 208.

18. Ulrich Wilckens, *Die Missionsreden der Apostelgeschichte* (Neukirchen-Vluyn: Neukirchener Verlag, 1963). Cf. J. DuPont, "Les discours missionaires des Actes des Apôtres," *RevBib*, 69 (1962), 37–60.

19. This has been demonstrated in abundant detail by Richard F. Zehnle, *Peter's Pentecost Discourse: Tradition and Lukan Reinterpretation in Peter's Speeches of Acts 2 and 3* (Nashville: Abingdon, 1971).

Therefore, in spite of the mental image that we have of Peter's fiery character, Luke is presenting him here as making a formal oration.

The speech itself is divided into three parts, each of which begins with a call to the audience: "men of Judea" (2:14); "you who are Israelites" (2:22); "fellow Israelites" (2:29). Each of these three parts of the speech revolves around biblical quotes, the first from Joel and the others from the Psalms.

In the first section, Peter simply responds to the comment of those who claim that those witnessing and participating in the miracle are drunk. His answer is quite simple: it is only nine o'clock in the morning (literally, "the third hour of the day"). There have been attempts to relate this with the Jewish hours of prayer or other similar practices. However, most likely Peter is simply taking the commentary on drunkenness as a starting point and simply responding that it is just too early to be drunk.[20]

Then follows Peter's understanding of what is taking place. As in all sorts of speeches, what Luke offers us here is both a summary of what he says that Peter told those who were listening and what Luke wishes "Theophilus" and his other readers to understand. This leads to a number of anachronisms, of which the most significant is that the biblical text that Luke puts on the lips of Peter are taken, not from the Hebrew text nor from an Aramaic translation, but from the Septuagint (the Greek version that has already been mentioned). Quoting that version,[21] Peter explains that what is taking place is the fulfillment of Joel's prophecy ("*this is* what is spoken through the prophet Joel").

The prophecy is said to refer to "the last days," that is the coming of God's reign. This is of crucial importance in order to understand not only Peter's speech, but the entire Book of Acts. What is happening there is that the reign of God is moving forward. We are "in the last days," no matter how long these last days may be (as Jesus said, "It is not for you to know the times or periods," 1:7). The fact is that with the death and resurrection of Jesus, and with the gift of the Spirit, the reign of God has been inaugurated. What is now lacking is the final fulfillment, when the "last days" finally end.

---

20. David John Williams, *Acts* (New York: Harper & Row, 1985), pp. 39–40.

21. Actually, there has been much scholarly discussion on this particular quote, for the texts of the Septuagint that have been preserved do not completely agree with what Peter quotes. The main difference is that none of those texts includes the phrase "in the last days." What is then debated is whether Luke took this from a text that has been lost, or rather adapted the quotation for his own use. Cf. Zehnle, *Peter's Discourse*, pp. 28–30. On this discussion, it may seem best to follow the opinion of Edesio Sánchez Cetina: "When we compare the Hebrew text, the Greek text of the Septuagint and the Greek text of Acts, we realize that Luke has adapted the quotation so that it corresponds more graphically to the event he is describing. . . . This deliberate alteration of the text is due to the manner in which the author is using it. He does not move from Scripture to the event, but rather in the opposite direction. He begins from the event and goes to Scripture to show the connection between that event and the prophecy: Behold, today has been fulfilled what the prophets promised!", "Pentecostés en Joel 2:18–32, en Hechos 2, y en nuestros días," *VyP*, 4:1–2 (1984), p. 53.

The work of the Spirit in these "last days," as described in the text that Peter quotes, could be described both as leveling (2:17–18) and as catastrophic (2:19–20). It is leveling, because the Spirit will be poured out upon "all flesh" (that is to say, it will not be the exclusive prerogative of prophets or priests). This includes sons and daughters, young and old, slaves, both male and female.[22] It is catastrophic in that it includes "portents in the heaven above and signs in the earth below." The outcome of all of this will be "the coming of the Lord's great and glorious day." That day, as throughout the rest of the prophetic tradition, produces both danger and fear, and therefore leads to the final word of hope and invitation: "then everyone who calls on the name of the Lord shall be saved."

It is necessary to insist that this quotation of Joel is central for the entire Book of Acts, where it plays a role similar to that which the quote from Isaiah in Luke 4 plays in the entire Gospel. There, that quote summarizes the nature of the ministry of Jesus. Here, the quote from Joel summarizes the nature of the work of the Spirit. In a way, all that follows in the rest of the book is the unfolding of what was already implicit in the quote from Joel.[23]

In 2:22, by saying "as you yourselves know," Peter seems to indicate that his listeners, although perhaps pilgrims in Jerusalem, are aware of what has happened in the last few months. The other quotations Peter uses are taken from the Psalms. It was already common in the first century for Jewish exegetes to interpret the Psalms that originally referred to the kings of Israel in Messianic terms. Now Peter does likewise. It seems that the early Church also did this quite commonly, as may be seen in the repeated use of a text such as Psalm 110:1 (in the New Testament, it appears not only here in 2:34–35, but also in Matt. 22:43–45, Mark 12:36-37, Luke 20:42–44, I Cor. 15:25, Heb. 1:13 and 10:13, and many other possible allusions).[24]

Finally, note that in 2:32, when Peter says "and of that all of us are witnesses," this seems to indicate that this is the beginning of the fulfillment of the promise that Jesus made when he told his followers that, by the power of the Holy Spirit, they would be witnesses. Now, at the very moment when they have just received that power, they are already witnessing.

---

22. Acts says "*my* slaves." The possessive adjective does not appear in the Hebrew text nor in the Septuagint. Does this mean that Acts "spiritualizes" the condition of servant or of slave, just as today we speak as someone as a "servant of the Lord," or does it mean rather that God raises the category of slaves by making them God's? The text does not say.

23. See, for instance, C. H. Talbert, ed., *Perspectives on Luke-Acts* (Edinburgh: T. & T. Clark, 1978), p. 195.

24. It was probably in reaction to such Christian exegesis that later Jewish exegetes refused to interpret this or any other Psalm in Messianic terms, as had been quite common before their controversy with Christians.

2. The Response of the Crowd (2:37–41)

Luke continues telling us that those who heard[25] "were cut to the heart." The NRSV translates the Greek quite literally here, for what is meant is a very profound pain. The manner in which they now address the apostles, calling them "brothers"—no longer simply "Galileans"—is a sign of their favorable attitude. Peter's response includes both an invitation and a promise. The invitation is to repentance and baptism. Although the NRSV does not make it completely clear, the phrase "everyone of you" refers both to repentance and to baptism. The promise also has two elements: the forgiveness of sins and the gift of the Spirit.

Verse 39 helps to eliminate something of the anti-Jewish impression that Peter's speech may have given. Peter accuses his listeners of being accomplices in the death of the Lord; but immediately he reminds them that they are the particular heirs of the promise. The phrase "for all who are far away" is not to be understood, as in the case of a similar phrase in Ephesians, as referring to the Gentiles. On the contrary, throughout the narrative of Acts Luke clearly shows that there is progress in the understanding that the apostles have regarding the scope and reach of the promise. The point of conversion for Peter in this sense will be in chapter 10. Therefore, here Peter is referring rather to the Jews of the entire world, including those from the Diaspora, whose representatives are most of his audience. Luke has introduced verse 40 in order to let us know that what he has quoted from Peter is just a summary of all that the apostle said and thought.

Finally, verse 41 tells us the outcome of Peter's speech and invitation: some three thousand people are baptized. According to what Peter promised them in 2:38, one should expect that they also received the gift of the Holy Spirit, although we are not told that this was accompanied by extraordinary signs such as speaking in tongues. Normally, in the Book of Acts baptism and the gift of the Spirit go together, although there are also some exceptions (8:16, 10:44, 19:2–6).

THE COMMUNITY OF THE SPIRIT

The passage about Pentecost frames the whole book, giving us a glimpse as to the manner in which the Spirit works and how the Church, the community of the Spirit, is to live. Therefore, the study of this passage and of its implications for today is crucial if we are to see what Acts tells us within our context. Along these lines, there are several elements in these passages worthy of attention.

1. The Last Days

The first of these is that, as Peter says, "the last days" have begun with the resurrection of Jesus and the gift of the Spirit. While it is important for us to look at

---

25. Codex Bezae, apparently in order to avoid the impression that they were all converted, says, "Some of those who heard."

our social, cultural, political, and economic context, we must also look at that context within the order of God's times. The two are not mutually exclusive, for in fact the understanding of each of these two dimensions of our context illumines the other.

Within the order of God's time, we are already living "in the last days." Such days could well last only a few seconds more, or twenty thousand centuries; but in either case we are still living in "the last days." What this means is not that there are so many days until the final consummation of history. What it means is that such consummation has already begun, that God's reign is not only in the future but also among us, no matter how difficult it may be for us to see this in daily life. Whether the world lasts millenia more or not even a second, right now we are living "between the times" (between the beginning of the end and the final end), and therefore we live in two reigns, the reign of God that has been inaugurated and the ancient reign that still remains.

It is important to clarify this, for an erroneous understanding of the relationship between these two "reigns" leads to an erroneous understanding of the Christian message and of our responsibility in the present order. This could be explained by saying (1) that the biblical contrast between the two reigns is temporal rather than spatial, and (2) that it has to do with relationships among creatures rather than with the nature itself of those creatures.

Temporal rather than spatial. To think of the two "reigns" in a spatial sense would lead us to think in terms of a reign that is the world in which we live and another to be found elsewhere, in the "beyond." But the reign we seek as God's children is not a matter of a "beyond," but rather of a "day of the Lord," of a future that comes from God. The difference between what we have and what we hope for is not best expressed in terms of a "beyond," but rather in a "not yet." From this perspective, the gift of the Spirit is a "now" or a "finally." This is what Peter tells his listeners. The power of the Spirit promised in 1:8 is precisely the power to be witnesses of Jesus and of his reign while living in the present reign as those who have the first fruits of the order to come.

The contrast between these two reigns has to do with relations among creatures, rather than with the nature itself of those creatures. When one speaks of "two reigns" or of "two kingdoms," very often we think that there are things that belong to one of them and other things that belong to the other. At various points in the history of the Church there has been talk of a reign of the souls and a reign of the bodies, and it has even been claimed that the gospel is to rule over the one, whereas civil law should rule over the other.[26] This, however, is not what is meant by the contrast between the present reign and the coming one. The contrast is not based on the nature of things or the stuff of which they are made, nor on whether they are physical or spiritual. The contrast has to do

---

26. This is the manner in which Luther has often been interpreted and employed when he speaks of "two kingdoms." In the thirteenth century, Pope Innocent III said: "Just as God the Creator of the universe established two great lights in the firmament, the greater to preside over day and the lesser to preside over night, so also did God establish two great

rather with the order in each of those two reigns. In one of them the powerful rule, all seek their own, and those who have no one to defend them are oppressed. In the other, God reigns, and therefore the standard is the law of love, which leads to true justice. Therefore, to live in the present reign as citizens of God's reign in no way means ignoring physical reality, but rather placing all things, physical as well as spiritual, under the rule of God's will, which is a will of peace, justice, and equity.

Returning then to the passage in Acts and to the text from Joel which Peter quotes, we see that what Peter is proclaiming is precisely that we are living in "the last days," and that a sign of this is the leveling action of the Spirit, who is poured on all flesh, male and female, young and elderly, and upon servants, both male and female. As will become clear throughout this commentary, an important part of the message of Acts is how Christians are to live as subjects of the reign to come even while in the midst of a present reign that does not acknowledge that new order.

2. Dual Citizenship

To complicate matters further, it is important to point out that all of this does not mean simply that the new order is to be found in the Church, among those who have and acknowledge the power of the Spirit, and the old order in all the rest. In the case itself of Pentecost, the new order is manifest in the communication that becomes possible by the power of the Spirit. Listeners from various parts of the world can understand in their own tongues what is being said. This, however, should not exclude the fact that there is already a measure of communication among these people, even apart from the extraordinary manifestation of the Spirit. As is clear from the text, those who hear can communicate among themselves. They can communicate because they are part of a vast empire that facilitates such communication. Later on in our story, Christians will make use of Roman roads, of the means of communication that have resulted from Roman imperialism, in order to communicate among themselves and also to spread the gospel. Therefore, even apart from the unity that is the result of the Pentecostal gift, there is a unity that is the result of Roman imperialism. The problem is then how to affirm that unity without affirming the imperialism that produced it. On the other hand, nor can one say that the life of the Church is always a sign of God's reign, or that living in the Church always means that we live according to that new order. Later on Luke will make it plain that the old order still exists in the Church, and that part of the constant work of the Spirit consists in unveiling, challenging, and destroying it.

How then were Christians to live in the Roman Empire as citizens of God's reign? This is one of the central themes of the entire book. That is part of the difficult situation in which Christians in Acts find themselves. Sometimes in the

---

authorities in the firmament of the universal church. . . . The greater to preside over the souls as days, and the lesser to preside over bodies as nights. These two are the pontifical authority and royal power." *Reges.* 1.401.

book, this situation comes to the surface and leads to great difficulties and hard decisions.

That is precisely one of the most burning issues for Christianity today. The existing order is in many ways opposed to the order of God's reign. We live under a series of powers that oppress the poor and exploit the weak. This is true both in the social order within nations and at the international level, in which poor countries, already burdened by debts that they cannot possibly pay, are forced to participate in economic systems that continue impoverishing them, while economic resources flow toward the more powerful nations. At the same time, it is important to recognize that the existing order has also produced positive elements: roads, schools, means of communication, medical advances, and so on. All of these latter elements may be seen as signs of the abundant life that God wills for all, just as the same could have been said of many aspects of life under the Roman Empire. Given such circumstances, the problem is how to evaluate the order in which we live, how far to participate in it, how to try to change it, and so forth. These questions are to be posed both about the general order of society and about the order and structure of the Church.

The problem is not new. The early Christians already had to face it, finding themselves subjects of the most advanced and powerful empire the Mediterranean had ever known, but of an empire that in many ways represented the old order and its opposition to the new order that had been inaugurated in the "last days" of the resurrection and Pentecost.

Because the problem is not new, the Christians of whom Acts speaks had to face it. For the same reason, throughout this study it will be important for us to seek to discern the signs of the reign of God while we live "between the times," in these "last days" which began with the resurrection of Jesus and the gift of the Spirit.

3. A Leveling Spirit

For the time being, the story of Pentecost and Peter's speech already give us an important direction: this Holy Spirit who is the first fruit of the new order is manifested as a leveling power that destroys privilege. As the text from Joel says, the Spirit is poured upon "all flesh," sons and daughters, young and old, male and female servants.

The story of Pentecost itself witnesses to this. This may be seen at least in two points. The first is the possibility that those who did not perceive the miracle—those who claimed that the others were drunk—did not perceive it because they did not think there was anything extraordinary in being able to understand what was being said. They were people from the area. In that situation, they were privileged. They expected their own language to be spoken. And precisely because they were privileged and expected to understand, they were able to understand what was being said, but they could not see the miracle. The privileged, by the very fact of being such, turn out to be disadvantaged. For Christians today living in regions of the world in which another culture is dominant, this is particularly important. Such is the case of Hispanics in the United

States, or native peoples in various countries of Latin America. Over against the prejudice of culture and language that so often remains in the Church, someone has correctly declared that the miracle of Pentecost "made it very clear that within the Christian community no language should ever be more important than the others."[27]

The same is true of all the other means society employs to measure the value or the prestige of a person. The leveling spirit works in such a way that its power is much more difficult to appreciate for the powerful, the rich, and the wise than for the weak, the poor, and the unlearned. This does not mean that we should seek to be ignorant, hungry, or oppressed in order to be able to perceive the work of the Spirit; but it certainly does mean that we are mistaken if we think that our erudition will make us more able to see that work. This fact is well known throughout the churches in Latin America as well as Latino churches in the United States, where one constantly sees how the Spirit is freely made manifest among the poor and the oppressed.

All of this has to do also with relationships within the Church and the order that reigns within it. The Church has always been tempted to accept within itself the order of the world. There were times when it was customary for bishops to belong to rich and powerful families. Even though much of this has changed, much still remains. The same happens in many Protestant churches in Latino contexts. Because we have been a small and marginal group for a long time, when we find that there are among ourselves some persons of power, prestige, or wealth, we immediately think that they should occupy special places within the Church. At other times, we almost demand that the Spirit act through the systems and channels we have created and the persons whom we have appointed to wield power. That, however, does not work. The Holy Spirit is a leveling power, destroyer of privilege.

Latin America offers many examples of this. In the Roman Catholic Church, the resistance of much of the hierarchy to Basic Christian Communities (*Comunidades de Base*) and to lay leadership is to a great extent a fear that these may threaten the traditional control of the Church by the hierarchy. Also in many Protestant churches, the unexpected work of the Spirit has often clashed with the ecclesiastical authorities that seek to control the Church. The result has been that quite often those structures have not been able to respond to the challenges of the time. In some of the more traditional Protestant churches the "disorder" of those who claim to have received the Spirit is criticized, supposedly for theological reasons but in fact because there is fear that the structures of control will lose their authority, or that the rest of society will look down on the church as a group of ignorant and emotional people. In some Pentecostal congregations and denominations, there are leaders who try to use the "power" of the Holy Spirit

27. Charles Yrigoyen, *Hechos para nuestro tiempo: Un estudio de los Hechos de los Apóstoles* (New York: Junta General de Ministerios Globales de la Iglesia Metodista Unida, 1986), p. 18.

in order to establish their rule and dominance over others. The same fear seems to be present in the many attempts, in Protestantism as well as within Catholicism, to limit the role of women. But the fact remains that all of this opposes the leveling power of the Spirit as manifest in Acts, where the Spirit is poured upon "all flesh" and upon "sons and daughters."

The second point worthy of special mention is the manner in which those who listen refer to those who speak. At the beginning, in spite of the miracle, they see in them some "Galileans," that is, people who are not quite as important or as valuable or as faithful as the true Judeans.[28] After verse 37, they refer to these "Galileans" as "brothers." And finally, in verse 42, the same people now accept those "Galileans"—as leaders in whose teaching they persevere.

At the beginning of his Gospel, Luke places on the lips of Mary a song in which she says, among other things, that God "has scattered the proud in the thoughts of their hearts. He has brought down the powerful from their thrones, and lifted up the lowly. He has filled the hungry with good things, and sent the rich away empty" (Luke 1:51–53). Now, at the beginning of Acts, he tells a story that corroborates Mary's song.

For the Spanish-speaking Church, both in Latin America and in the United States, mostly composed of people who have been marginalized, who frequently suffer pressure and even persecution because of their opposition to many elements in the existing order, these words are both a comfort and a challenge.

---

28. The subject of Galilee as a sign of ethnic and cultural mixing as well as of marginality has been crucial in the development of Hispanic theology in the United States. See Virgilio Elizondo, *Galilean Journey: The Mexican-American Journey* (Maryknoll, N.Y.: Orbis, 1983); Orlando Costas, "Evangelism from the periphery: A Galilean model," *Apuntes*, 2 (1982), pp. 51–59; Orlando Costas, "Evangelism from the periphery: The universality of Galilee," *Apuntes*, 2 (1982), pp. 75–84.

3

The Church in Jerusalem
(2:42–8:3)

As the story in Acts unfolds, we now come to the manner in which, by the power of the Holy Spirit, the disciples become witnesses in Jerusalem. Here we shall find descriptions of the life of the early Church, as well as some selected incidents in that life. After this section, very little will be said about the church in Jerusalem. Were Acts in fact a history of the Church, or a history of the apostles, we would have reason to complain that Luke leaves us hanging, without telling us about the later history of that church or the life of its various leaders. But, because the purpose of this book is not to give an account of the early history of the Church, but rather to show how the Holy Spirit allows the Church to discover and rediscover its mission, as soon as the edge of that mission moves from Jerusalem, the church in that city will recede in the author's interest.

A. A SUMMARY (2:42–47)

Throughout the Book of Acts, there are several "summaries" that have provoked discussion among scholars (besides this particular one, the most extensive ones are 4:32–35 and 5:12–16; but there are many briefer ones: 6:7, 9:31, 19:20, 28:31, etc.).[1] Much of these discussions revolves around the sources Luke may have employed for such summaries, and therefore has little to do with the interpretation of the text for our situation. As to the function of the summaries, it should be clear: Luke seeks a balance between simply telling

---

1. See the bibliography in E. Haenchen, *The Acts of the Apostles* (Philadelphia: Westminster, 1971), p. 190. To this should be added: J. Lach, "Katechese über die Kirche von Jerusalem in der Apostelgeschichte 2, 42–47; 4, 32–35; 5, 12–16," *CollTheol*, 52, supplement (1982), 141–53; H. Zimmermann, "Die Sammelberichte der Apostelgeschichte," *BZ*, 5 (1961), 71–82.

particular instances and a more generalized overview of what is in fact taking place.[2]

The first of these summaries describes the daily life of early Christians. The theme that is emphasized here is perseverance, which is a strong connotation of the verb that the NRSV translates as "they devoted themselves." This was a very important subject in Luke's time, for by then it was becoming increasingly clear that Christians would have serious clashes with the rest of society. In verse 42, we are told that Christians "devoted themselves" to four things: (1) the apostles' teaching, (2) fellowship, (3) the breaking of bread, (4) prayers. In a way, these four things are a summary of the rest of the summary.[3]

Persevering in the "teaching" of the apostles does not only mean that they did not deviate from the doctrines of the apostles or that they remained orthodox. It means also that they persevered in the practice of learning from the apostles—that they were eager students or disciples under them. This apostolic "teaching" was not limited to verbal instruction, for in verse 43 we are told that the apostles continued doing "many wonders and signs." In order to understand fully this matter of the "teaching of the apostles," it is important to remember that "apostle" means "envoy," and that therefore the "apostolic" doctrine is by definition missionary doctrine, an open and flexible doctrine oriented toward mission. However, it is also clear that an important part of the teaching of the apostles consisted in the narration and repetition of the facts and sayings of Jesus, whom the new converts had not personally met.

The "fellowship" requires special attention. The word thus translated in the NRSV is *koinōnia*.[4] Few Greek words are as common among Christians today as is *koinōnia*. In some circles, all claim to know the meaning of *koinōnia*, which is "fellowship." However, such a translation reflects only one of the many shades of meaning of this word, and perhaps not even the most important. In its common use in the daily life of the first century, *koinōnia* did not refer only to a good feeling or fellowship among friends. It also meant "corporation," "common enterprise," or "company," similar to the way today we might say that Peter and John own a "company," that they are "partners," or

---

2. As a historian myself, I have written a number of books on the history of the Church and of its theology. In that process, I have repeatedly found myself in the same situation that led Luke to include these summaries: on the one hand, the narrative at some point has to deal with specific individuals and incidents; on the other, occasionally it is necessary to include generalizations that help the reader to see the total picture.

3. The relationship between perseverance and these four elements is such that P. H. Menoud organizes his study of this text around four themes: perseverance in the teaching of the apostles, perseverance in fellowship, perseverance in the breaking of bread, and perseverance in prayers. His conclusion: "the entire life of the faithful is nothing but a constant perseverance." *La Vie de l'Eglise naissante* (Neuchatel: Delachaux & Niestlé, 1952).

4. On this word and others with similar roots, see *ThWzNT*, 3:789–810. See also Arthur Carr, "The fellowship of Acts 2:42 and cognate words," *Exp*, series 8, 5 (1913), 458–64.

that they have a "corporation."[5] There is no doubt that *koinōnia* is fellowship, but it is also solidarity and the sharing of feelings, goods, and actions.

Verses 44 and 45 are then an explanation of this *koinōnia*. This consisted precisely in that they "had all things in common"—the word translated as "common" comes from the same root as "communion" or *koinōnia*.[6] This does not mean, as it is often thought, that they simply sold all their resources and put them in a common fund, so that no one any longer had anything. The verbs in this verse are in the imperfect, which means that they used to sell and used to distribute resources. This implies a continued action, done "as any had need." This will be discussed again when dealing with the summary in 4:32–35, and also with the story of Ananias and Sapphira (4:36–5:11).

The "breaking of the bread" does not mean only that they ate together. It refers to the celebration of communion, which from the beginning and for many centuries has been the center of Christian worship.[7] That is why in verse 46, where Luke returns to the same subject, it is joined to attendance at the Temple. According to this verse, Christians persevered both in their attendance at the Temple (their worship as Jews, which they all were) and in breaking bread (the new form of Christian worship that was developing).[8] In the same verse we are told that this was done "with glad and generous hearts." Originally, the Eucharist was a celebration, for what was remembered was not only the death of Jesus, but also and particularly his resurrection and his future coming in glory. It was later, through a process that took centuries, that the emphasis was laid on the crucifixion, and that the Eucharist took the solemn and in some cases even funereal overtones that in many circles it still has.

We are not told much about the "prayers," partly because later we shall see a picture of the Church and prayer. For the moment, all that we are told in

---

5. In Luke 5:10, where the NRSV tells us that James and John were "partners" with Simon, what the Greek text says is that they were *koinōnoi*—that is to say, they jointly owned the boat. Likewise, whenever in the New Testament there is mention of *koinōnia* of the Spirit, or of the *koinōnia* of Jesus, this is to be understood, not only in the sense that there is love and fellowship among Christians by reason of the Spirit or of the presence of Jesus, but also in the sense that Christians are jointly owners, heirs, participants, in Jesus or in the Spirit. In *Amherst Papyri*, eds. B. P. Grenfell and A. S. Hunt, 100, 4, there is a case in which a fisherman named Hermes makes another his *koinōnos* or partner.

6. See Franz Meffert, *Der kommunistische und proletarische Charakter des Urchristentums* (Recklinghausen: Bitter, 1946).

7. Allen Cabanis, "Liturgy-making factors in primitive Christianity," *JR*, 23 (1943), 43–58; R. Orlett, "The breaking of bread in Acts," *BibTo*, 1 (1962), 108–13. A good summary of what is known about communion in the New Testament is to be found in C. P. M. Jones et al., eds., *The Study of Liturgy* (New York: Oxford University Press, 1973), pp. 148–69.

8. F. Montagnini, "La comunità primitiva come luogo cultuale. Nota da At. 2, 42–46," *RivBib*, 35 (1987), 477–84, interprets the entire passage in such a way that it culminates in the cultic life of the community.

verse 47 is that they were "praising God." It is also in this verse that we are told that they had "the goodwill of all the people."[9] As the story unfolds, through the early chapters of Acts the "people" either support the preaching of the disciples or at least do not oppose it. The opposition comes from the leaders, who often moderate their stance for fear of the "people."

THE CHURCH BETWEEN FEAR AND JOY

After the brief outline of verse 42, this summary of the life of the Church opens with overwhelming words: "awe came upon everyone." This could also be translated in the sense that "fear came over everyone." Then toward the end of the summary, we are told that they ate their food "with glad and generous hearts." Between the fear and awe of the beginning of the passage and the gladness and the generosity at the end stands the reality of a life in community and obedience. The text also tells us, with such brevity that it almost sounds like shorthand, that such life in community and obedience consists in persevering on four fronts.

The first of these is the teaching of the apostles. As we have seen, this is not mere orthodoxy. It is not simply believing whatever it was that the apostles believed. What the text points to is a perseverance in learning, in study, in deepening of faith and understanding. It is not a matter of the first Christians being converted and then remaining as immovable rocks. It is rather that they were converted and from there on they persevered in learning, while the apostles themselves also persevered in teaching them more and more of what they had learned from Jesus.

Perseverance in study and learning must become one of the marks of the Church if it is to be truly faithful, and to be able to move from fear into joy. In some of our Latino churches we have been taught that "it is enough to have faith"—which in a certain context is true. But we have not been taught that this one in whom we believe is a Lord who has abundant riches to offer at each step, if we would only ask.

The "teaching of the apostles" is not the mere repetition of what the apostles taught. It is above all the teaching and the studying that allow us to carry forth our own apostolate, our mission today. The Church lives in an ever-changing world. Because the mission is a bridge between the message of what has taken place in Jesus Christ and the reality in which the addressees live, missionary or apostolic study must always take into account the world in which the Church lives. That is why it is not enough to repeat what has always been said, in the same way in which it has been said before. It is necessary to study both the Word and the world to which it is to be communicated. Perseverance in

---

9. The Greek text could also be translated in other ways: "having the grace [of God] before all the people," or "giving thanks [to God] before all the people" (David John Williams, *Acts* [New York: Harper & Row, 1985], p. 46). However, the manner in which the NRSV translates the text is probably the intended meaning.

such a study is today's equivalent of the early Church's perseverance in the teaching of the apostles.

There are circles in some of our churches where people fear that study (except perhaps for Bible study) leads to unbelief, when in fact study motivated by faith leads us to a deeper and more mature faith, and any belief that is threatened by study is not true faith. We live at a time that poses urgent and complicated problems. If we are to respond to those problems with faithfulness and joy, without being led by fear, we must be equipped for it by persevering in study, by entering ever more deeply in Scripture, by analyzing the problems that contemporary society poses with the best instruments at hand.

On the other hand, if Christians are to persevere in learning, their teachers must persevere both in teaching and in their own learning. There are too many sermons in which the same is said over and over again. There are too many Sunday School classes where there is no serious commitment to the careful study of the biblical text.

The second aspect of this perseverance that leads from fear to joy is "fellowship," or even better, sharing and solidarity. Luke describes a community in which love takes concrete shape. Shortly after Luke—or perhaps even at about the same time—an anonymous Christian wrote, "if we share in the immortal things, should we not share in those that are mortal?"[10] If we call each other "brother" and "sister," should we not behave as such? In a world of social injustice such as the one in which we live, there is always a temptation to allow such injustice to enter into the Church, and even to determine its life and structure. However, love must take concrete form, and the same is true about the announcement of God's reign. If we proclaim justice, if we speak of the need for justice in our society, we must make a special effort so that the life itself of the Church may be an image, however imperfect, of the order that we proclaim. (What this might mean in our present society will be discussed further when studying 4:32–5:11.)

The gift of the Spirit, Peter told us in an earlier passage, is a sign that we are living in the "last days"; that the reign of God is at hand; that already in a way, precisely because we have the Spirit, we have the first fruits of the kingdom. This is a message of joy. The practice of *koinōnia* in the Church is one of the ways in which we can live now, even while still in the midst of the old reign, as those who are already tasting the future one.

The third aspect of the perseverance of those early Christians was in worship. This meant both worship at the Temple, which they still continued practicing as good Jews, and the eucharistic celebration, a remembrance of the unparalleled event of the resurrection of Jesus, and an announcement of the equally great event of his return at the fulfillment of the promise. This is perhaps one of the strongest features in many of our Latino churches. We are a worshipping

---

10. *Didajé*, 4.8. What the Greek text literally says is that we are *koinōnoi* in immortal things, and therefore we ought to be also in those that are mortal.

church. In other circles, worship is sometimes eclipsed by indifference or by an activism that soon loses its thrust. To this day, the vast majority of the Spanish-speaking Church has not allowed itself to be swept by such currents, and that is the reason there often is in our churches a joy that is not seen elsewhere. Also, if we are to be faithful and persevere in seeking justice, we must have in worship the source of our strength.

This worship takes place in community. This is true both of the services in the Temple and of the Eucharist. It is important for us not to forget that Christianity is a communal faith. It certainly has its profoundly personal dimension. But a purely private faith, no matter how apparently orthodox, is not Christian!

Here too does the Latin Church have something to contribute. Most of the Bible was originally written to be read in public amidst the community of faith. This is true of both the Old Testament and of most of the New. Perhaps the main exception is the Epistle to Philemon. In Spanish, this is constantly apparent in the use of the second person plural: *vosotros* or *ustedes*. The language of many who brought the Protestant faith to us, English, does not make that distinction. *Tú* is "you," and *ustedes* is also "you."[11] Therefore, the error of reading the Bible in purely individualistic terms is much easier for those who read the Bible in English than for those read it in Spanish. However, because many who taught us to read the Bible read it in English, sometimes they brought to us, jointly with the biblical message, an individualism that is not part of it.

Thanks to the importance of public worship among us, we are slowly leaving behind much of that unfortunate individualistic inheritance. It is therefore, important for us to cultivate public worship, in the hope that this may help us make a significant contribution to those who originally brought the Bible to us.

The fourth element of the perseverance that Luke describes is prayer (2:42) or praise (2:47). In describing such prayer in terms of praise, we are being told that the Church attributed all that it was and all that it had to God. Such is the nature of praise: "Thank you, God for. . . ." If fear is to give way to joy, it is necessary to persevere in praise. If that which we are and that which we have is a result of God's grace, we have no need to be constantly anxious for fear of losing it. This is true of the three other elements of our perseverance already discussed. Study must be made in praise. Justice and equity are to be sought and practiced in praise. Worship is to center in praise. In all things, glory to God. If we truly believe and live this, what fear can overshadow our joy?

Luke ends his summary by declaring that "day by day the Lord added to their number[12] those who were being saved." In many of our churches there is much talk of "evangelism," even to the point of an obsession: "We have to be most evangelistic"; "we need to win more souls for Christ"; "we need to dis-

---

11. The plural *ye*, which appears in earlier versions such as the KJV, has such an archaic flavor that its plural form does not come across with full clarity.

12. Some manuscripts say "to the church." Although that is probably what is meant, the common text simply says "the Lord added each day those who were being saved."

cover new methods of evangelism." In the midst of that obsession, we are at risk of losing the "glad and generous hearts" of which the text speaks.

Luke presents matters in a different way. It is the Lord who adds to the Church. The Church must certainly give witness, and the various aspects of its perseverance that we have just studied are part of its witness. But in the end it is the Lord who adds to the Church.

Many of our churches have experienced this. While in other parts of the world, and particularly in the traditionally Christian North Atlantic, there is concern over diminishing church membership, the Latino Church, both in Latin America and in English-speaking North America, continues growing rapidly. Why? Because it is a Church where people experience some of the gladness and generosity of heart of which Luke speaks.

The church that Luke describes kept on growing because, thanks to the Holy Spirit, it had "the good will of all the people." This does not mean that it was constantly preoccupied with its public relations, or with seeking to win the favor of the people, or that it was not a "controversial" community. In order to understand what this means we must move to the next portion in Luke's book.

B. A MIRACLE AND ITS CONSEQUENCES (3:1–4:31)

After the summary just studied, Luke tells us a particular story that illustrates the summary and then tells us something of its consequences. This is a device he employs repeatedly. For instance, in the section immediately following this one (4:32–5:11), he offers first a summary of the life of Christians and how they employ their goods, in order then to tell us specifically of the incidents whose protagonists are Barnabas, Ananias, and Sapphira. In the case we now study we have an amplification and clarification of the meaning of the phrase in the summary, "having the good will of all the people" (2:47).

1. The Miracle (3:1–10)

The narrative is clear,[13] and it suffices to read the story in order to understand it. Therefore, this section of our commentary will only clarify some details. What the NRSV translates as "three o'clock in the afternoon" is the same as the "ninth hour" of some other translations; the latter is more literal but does not convey the meaning as well. As will be seen later on (4:3), it is precisely because of the lateness of the time that the Council is called for the next day.

The gate called "the beautiful gate" poses some difficulties, for as far as we know there was no gate with such a name. Some think it was Nicanor's gate, which Luke calls "beautiful" because it was of burnished bronze. Others sug-

---

13. R. Filippini, "Atti 3, 1–10: Proposta di analisis del racconto," *RivBib*, 28 (1980), 307–17.

gest various alternatives.[14] In any case, what interests Luke is not the geography of the Temple, but the miracle and its consequences.

The "look at us" of 3:4 contrasts with 3:12, where Peter asks the people "why do you stare at us?" When the lame man looks at them, Peter utters the best-known words in the entire episode: "I have no silver or gold, but what I have I give you; in the name of Jesus Christ of Nazareth, stand up and walk."[15]

The "name" of Jesus Christ is worthy of special attention, for it appears repeatedly in this section. On its meaning see the commentary on 4:12. Finally, the lame man's jumping (3:8) is reminiscent of the prophecy of Isaiah 35:6: "then the lame shall leap like a deer."

2. Peter's Explanation (3:11–26)

Immediately, Luke takes us to where Peter gives a speech in which he explains what has happened. Peter and John have now moved to "the portico called Solomon's portico."[16] The lame man has not let them go, and by the time they reach this portico, there is a crowd gathered (in a hyperbole, the text says that "all the people ran together to them").

In this verse and a half, which serve as an introduction to Peter's speech (3:11–12a), the word "people"—*laos*[17]—appears twice. This is important, for when we come to 4:1–2a we shall note that Luke is establishing a contrast between the "people" and its leadership. (Remember also that in the last verse of the previous section, 2:47, we are told that Christians had "the goodwill of all the people.")

Peter's speech seeks to make it clear that the credit for what has taken place is due to Jesus, and not to Peter or John. Peter says to those who are listening that they should not stare at them as if it was they who have healed the lame man. The verb he employs here is the same verb used in 3:4, where Peter

---

14. S. Corbett, "Some observations on the gateways to the Herodian Temple in Jerusalem," *PalExQ*, 84 (1952), 7–15; Ethelbert Stauffer, "Das Tor des Nikanor," *ZntW*, 44 (1952–53), 44–66; E. Wisenberg, "The Nicanor Gate," *JJewSt*, 3 (1952), 14–29.

15. E. Iglesias, "No tengo plata ni oro . . . ," *Christus*, 4 (1937), 661–65, 745–50; Paul Jaggi, *Was ich aber habe, das gebe ich dir: Eine Deutung der Heilung des Lahmen ver der schönen Tempelpforte nach Apostelgeschichte 3 and 4* (Bern: Christliches Verlagshaus, 1953).

16. Because we do not know exactly which was the "beautiful gate," it is also impossible to trace the apostles' steps in the Temple.

17. Luke employs two words that may be translated as "people": *laos* and *ochlos*. Both may refer to the "common people," but the second has more of the connotation of "crowd," "multitude," whereas *laos* also refers to the people as a nation—as for instance in the phrase "people of God." In these first chapters of Acts, Luke will only use the term *laos*, and he will reserve the other for chapter 14, when he is talking about a disorganized multitude in Lystra, and for 17:8, where he is speaking about a riot in Thessalonica. See below, 4:1–6.

"looked intently" at the man. Peter tells his hearers not to do with him what he did with the lame man. The difference is in that Peter stared at the needy man in order to see his need and to respond to it; whereas these people stare at Peter, not in order to see his need, but as a sign of admiration or almost of worship.

Twice in 3:16 Peter declares that the lame man has been healed "by faith"; but he does not tell us whether this is the lame man's faith (although apparently he had not heard of Jesus before), or the faith of Peter and John. In any case, what Peter says is that the God of the people to whom he is speaking, the God of Abraham, Isaac, and the rest, is the same one who has glorified Jesus.[18] This is the same Jesus whom they have denied. The tragedy of this situation comes to a climax in the contrast in 3:15: "You killed the Author of life."

However, that is not the end of the story. God raised Jesus from the dead (3:15b), therefore now the *name* of Jesus is powerful—to which we shall return on dealing with 4:7-12—and it is by faith in that *name* that the lame man has been healed. The story does not have a tragic ending because God is powerful to overcome the evil perpetrated by human beings. Furthermore, even for those who did kill the Author of life there is still the open door of repentance and conversion (3:17-26). Peter tells them that they did this out of ignorance, their own and that of their rulers (3:17),[19] and also that it was necessary for the Christ to suffer (3:18). Therefore, he invites them to repent and convert, accepting Jesus Christ, who was announced by "all the prophets" (3:24).

The literary character and the style of this speech differ greatly from Peter's other speech at Pentecost, as has been amply shown by Richard Zehnle.[20] This may be seen in the titles that Peter gives to God ("God of Abraham, God of Isaac, and the God of Jacob, the God of our ancestors" [3:13]), those he gives to Jesus ("Author of life" [3:15], "Child" of God [3:13, 26],[21] the "Holy" and "Just" [3:14]), and those he gives to his listeners ("descendants of the prophets and of the covenant" [3:25]). Zehnle also points out that there are here several other words that are not typical of Luke's vocabulary. This would seem to indicate that in writing this speech Luke was using earlier materials, perhaps from the primitive Church. Zehnle, however, would go as far as to affirm that they come from Peter himself.

---

18. This may be understood as referring to the glorification of Jesus in his resurrection and ascension, or as referring to the miracle itself, which also glorifies Jesus.

19. See however C. Escudero Freire, "Kata agnoian (Hch. 3.13): ¿Disculpa o acusación?", *Comm*, 9 (1976), 221-31.

20. Richard F. Zehnle, *Peter's Pentecost Discourse: Tradition and Lukan Reinterpretation in Peter's Speeches of Acts 2 and 3* (Nashville: Abingdon, 1971), pp. 44-60.

21. The NRSV translates the word here as "servant." The word that appears in the Greek is *pais*. This means "child" and is not the same as *huios*, which is the term that Luke usually employs to refer to the Son of God.

3. The Reaction of the Powerful (4:1–22)

a. The Intervention (4:1–6)

The entire speech is addressed by Peter to the people, who are astonished at the miracle that they have seen. Now, however, the authorities break into the scene, and react quite negatively. Their motivation is made apparent in 4:1–2. Peter and John[22] are still speaking to the *people* when "the priest, the captain of the Temple, and the Sadducees came to them, much annoyed because they were teaching the *people* and proclaiming that in Jesus there is the resurrection of the dead."

The theme of the "people" (*laos*) is very important for Luke, both in the Gospel and in Acts. In the Gospel, that word appears twenty-nine times, and in only two of them is there a parallel use in the other Gospels. In Acts, it is employed forty-eight times. In most of these cases it has positive connotations (the main exceptions are 6:12 and 12:1).[23] In studying the manner in which Luke uses this word, it becomes apparent that it has two dimensions: on the one hand, it points to the importance of the community for the life of faith; on the other, when it is used in contrast with the "rulers" or other important people, it points to the "popular" character of the Christian message and to the opposition of those whose power is threatened by that message.

Luke makes it apparent that in the action undertaken against Peter and John there are two motivations. One is theological in nature: the Sadducees did not believe in the resurrection of the dead, and the preaching of Peter and John clearly opposed their doctrines. But the text also shows that that was not the real cause for the intervention by the authorities. The real cause is that they were "annoyed because they were teaching the people"—in other words, that they were usurping and subverting the authority of the priests and other leaders. The "captain of the Temple"—literally, the "general of the Temple"—was the captain of the guard, which was entirely composed of Levites. The Sadducees, although a religious party more than an authorized structure of authority, were mostly representatives of the higher echelons of Jewish society. Therefore, Luke acknowledges here that there are official structures of power such as the captain of the guard of the Temple, and others that even though unofficial are equally powerful, such as the Sadducees; and he also acknowledges that these come together when their control over the people is in danger. That such is the case here, Luke makes clear when he says that "many of those who heard the word believed; and they numbered about five thousand" (4:4).

---

22. Although in the previous chapter there is only mention of Peter's speech, now we are told that John is also speaking. Once again, Luke is not attempting to give us a word-for-word account of all that was said, or of all who spoke, but simply to underscore the most important points.

23. See Zehnle, *Peter's Discourse*, pp. 63–66, which underlines the community dimension of *laos* rather than its contrast with the leaders and the powerful.

It is the powerful, fearing for their power and prestige, who imprison Peter and John until the next day, because it is too late in the day to bring them to trial (see 3:1).[24]

Verse 14 sounds strange, almost an interruption in the middle of the narrative. The apostles have just been imprisoned, and rather than continuing with the events of their imprisonment and trial, Luke tells us that "many of those who heard the word believed; and they numbered about five thousand." The Greek actually says that the *men* numbered that many. The fact of counting only the men is a sign of the patriarchal character of that culture, and it is implied that the rest of their families came with them, just as today we speak of a church having "fifty families." But what is most surprising in the text is that, precisely at a moment of great threat and even impending defeat, Luke tells us of all these thousands of conversions. John Chrysostom, one of the greatest preachers of all ages, underlines the surprise that Luke springs here:

> How can this be? Did they see them honored? Did they not rather see them in chains? How then would they believe? Doesn't this manifest the power of God? It was to be expected that even those who had believed earlier would waver in their faith on seeing the apostles imprisoned. But what happens is all the opposite, because Peter's sermon had sown the seed so deeply in them and it had so well entered their minds. For that reason the enemies become even more resentful, because they are afraid of them.[25]

Chrysostom is arguing that Luke places this verse precisely at this point in the narrative in order to point out that faith is to be such not only during the good times, and that prestige and power are not necessary so that people will believe. On the contrary, it is precisely at the point where the powerful show their disapproval, and do so by taking strong action against the preaching of the gospel, that the number of believers explodes.

On the next day, those who gather to judge the apostles are members of the same echelons of society that imprisoned them: "their rulers, elders, and scribes assembled in Jerusalem, with Annas the high priest, Caiaphas, John, and Alexander, and all who were of the high priestly family" (4:5–6).[26] Annas

---

24. It was not common at that time to use imprisonment as punishment. Rather it was used to hold the accused until they could be brought to trial. Most punishment was corporal—death, lashing, forced labor—as well as fines and removal from positions of authority and responsibility. Also, according to the Mishnah (*Sanh.* 4.1) trials on capital matters should be completed the same day in which they were begun.

25. *Hom. x in Act.*

26. Paul Gaechter, "The hatred of the House of Annas," *ThSt*, 8 (1947), 3–34; Robert Eisler, *The Enigma of the Fourth Gospel, Its Author and Its Writer* (London: Methuen, 1938), pp. 39–45.

was no longer the high priest; but it was customary to keep using that title for any who had borne it before—just as we do today with senators and governors. Caiaphas, the high priest at the moment, was the son-in-law of Annas. No more than what is said in this text is known about John and Alexander— unless the Western text is correct in calling him "Jonathan" rather than John, for Jonathan succeeded his brother-in-law Caiaphas in the year 36.

b. Peter's Speech (4:7–12)

The trial takes place before the Council or Sanhedrin.[27] This was composed mostly of the Jewish aristocracy and the main scribes. Because most of the aristocrats were Sadducees, and the scribes tended to be Pharisees, there frequently were strong debates within the Council itself. Apparently, the body had been dominated by the Sadducees until the beginning of the Christian era, when the Pharisees began attempting to take some of their power. By the time of the Jewish wars and the destruction of Jerusalem in the year 70, the Pharisees controlled the Sanhedrin.[28]

At the beginning of the trial, Peter and John are not asked what they have done, but on what authority they have done it (4:7). What is actually at stake is power and control.

Peter's answer, inspired by the Holy Spirit ("filled with the Holy Spirit"), addresses the chiefs of the people ("rulers of the people and elders"), but reminds them that his answer is also for all the people ("let it be known to all of you, and to all the people of Israel" [4:10]).

The manner in which Peter expresses the miracle that has taken place is significant, for the Greek word that the NRSV translates as "sick"[29] actually means "lacking in power," or "weak," and the verb translated as "healing" also means "saving" or "liberating."[30] Therefore, what Peter is saying is both that a sick man has been healed and that a weak person, oppressed by an illness, has been healed, saved, liberated, strengthened.

The leaders have asked him in what name, or on what authority, he and John have performed this miracle; and Peter answers quite clearly that this has been done "by the name of Jesus Christ of Nazareth." Quoting Psalm 118:22,

---

27. Sidney Benjamin Hoenig, *The Great Sanhedrin* (Philadelphia: Dropsie College for Hebrew and Cognate Learning, 1953); Hugo Mantel, *Studies in the History of the Sanhedrin* (Cambridge, Mass.: Harvard University Press, 1961).

28. On the background of this situation see William Wagner Buehler, *The Pre-Herodian Civil War and Social Debate: Jewish Society in the Period 74–40 B.C., and the Social Factors Contributing to the Rise of the Pharisees and the Sadducees* (Basel: Friedrich Reinhardt, 1964); Louis Finkelstein, *The Pharisees: The Sociological Background of Their Faith* (Philadelphia: Jewish Publication Society of America, 1940); M. Simon, *Las sectas judías en el tiempo de Jesús* (Buenos Aires: EUDEBA, 1962).

29. *ThWzNT*, 1:488–92.

30. *ThWzNT*, 7:966–1024.

he declares that Jesus is "the stone that was rejected by you, the builders" (4:11); that is to say, you the leaders who were supposed to be the builders of Israel.

The repetition of the "name" throughout this passage is important.[31] Here the name means much more than the mere sound of the two syllables, "Jesus." The name is the essence itself of a thing or a person. That is why Yahweh's name is sacred; because Yahweh is sacred. The "name" is the authority and power with which an action is performed. The leaders of Israel ask Peter and John in what "name," with what authority, they have performed this miracle. Peter tells them that they have done this "by the name of Jesus of Nazareth." The "name" of Jesus is none other than Jesus himself.

It is at this point that Peter comes to his much-quoted conclusion: "For there is no other name under heaven given among mortals by which we must be saved" (4:12). It is important to remember that the verb employed here may refer to eternal salvation as well as to the salvation of the body—that is, health. In the New Testament there is not the distance between saving and healing that there is in most of our minds. Therefore, what Peter declares could also be translated as "there is no other name under heaven given among mortals by which we must be healed."[32] What Peter is saying here is not only that all "salvation" comes from Jesus, but also, and much more directly in the particular context of this narrative, that all health is given by the same name. Far from limiting the scope of Peter's claim for Jesus' power, this widens that scope. By affirming that all health and all salvation (physical and spiritual health, social salvation, etc.) come from Jesus, Peter is affirming the universal lordship of that Jesus in whose name the lame man has been healed/saved/liberated/strengthened. This has enormous consequences, for the affirmation of the universal power of that "name" is also a claim that the supposed authority of the powerful who are sitting in judgment before Peter and John is limited.

c. The Verdict (4:13–22)

The judges marvel at the "boldness" of Peter and John. Once again, although Luke only offers a summary of Peter's speech, he implies that both spoke. It is important to remember once again that Luke is not attempting to give us a literal and tachygraphic version of all that each person says, but rather a narrative of the most important points, always seeking to show the manner in which the Holy Spirit works. The "boldness" (NRSV), "courage" (NIV) or "assurance" with which the apostles speak is the same for which the church later prays (4:29) and will receive (4:31). The words that the NRSV translates as "uneducated and ordinary" (agrammatos and idiôtês) literally mean unlettered and common or untrained.

---

31. ThWzNT, 5:242–83.

32. On this point, and the inconsistency in translations, see Irene W. Foulkes, "Two semantic problems in the translation of Acts 4:5–20," BibTrans, 29 (1978), 121–28.

Perhaps the most surprising affirmation in 4:13 is that the leaders "recognized them as companions of Jesus." Obviously, this cannot mean that it is only at this moment that they recognize that Peter and John are disciples of Jesus. They probably knew it well already. What they now acknowledge is that, although they thought they had finally dealt with Jesus by crucifying him, they are still not rid of the problem, for now they have to deal with others who from their perspective seem to be as stubborn as Jesus. What makes matters worse is that they cannot deny the miracle, for the man who used to be lame is now there "standing beside them." Furthermore, these who now dare argue with them are "uneducated and ordinary men," that is to say, people who will normally not dare speak before such a distinguished assembly as the Council.

The account has a particularly realistic touch. The powerful are puzzled as to what to do. What has happened is absolutely clear, and therefore they say "we can not deny it" (4:16). The obvious implication is that if they could they would indeed deny it, even though they know it to be true. The only solution they can find, because they cannot deny the truth, is to hide it: "to keep it from spreading further among the people." Once again, what is at stake is control over the people, in this particular case by means of the control of information.

In order to control information, one has to control its sources, and therefore, what the council decides is to threaten the apostles, so that they will not continue speaking or teaching in the name of Jesus. The response of the apostles, "uneducated and ordinary men," reveals the pusillanimity of the Council, for they are told that because they are judges, supposedly teachers of the law of God, they are to judge on their own verdict. The inevitable conclusion is that the judges are judged by the very law that they will not obey.

The judges find no way of punishing the apostles, and simply threaten them again and let them go. They let them go, not for the sake of justice, but "because of the people." Therefore, as has been seen throughout this entire episode, what is taking place must be seen as a struggle over control and authority.

4. The Response of the Faithful (4:23–31)

Peter and John then go and tell "their friends" (literally, "their own"; does this mean the entire congregation, or their closest friends?) what has taken place. Apparently they especially tell them of the threats that have been made against them, because the response of the believers is to utter a prayer that deals precisely with the subject of threats.

The prayer itself is interesting.[33] The first part (4:24–27) poses the old and difficult problem of how a sovereign God, maker of all that exists, allows the group to be persecuted and oppressed. The conspiracy against Jesus and his followers is powerful: Herod, Pontius Pilate, the Gentiles, and the people of Is-

---

33. Didier Rimaud, "La première prière dans le livre des Actes 4:23–31 (Ps. 2 et 145)," *LMD*, 51 (1957), 99–115.

rael. (Note that here the people are included on the negative side. The people allowed themselves to be led by their leaders, but that does not free them from responsibility.) How is it that God allows such things? That question, often asked in anguish, has no answer from the human perspective, and therefore often can be paralyzing. But these believers, even while expressing and acknowledging the difficulty, at the end admit that the final answer is in God's own designs (4:28). Then they go on to ask for "boldness" in order to speak the word, and that there be "signs and wonders" performed by the name of Jesus. What is significant about this is that the disciples are asking for what they already have. Signs and wonders had taken place, and it was precisely for that reason that Peter and John were taken before the Council. There before that Council, they showed the same "boldness" for which they now pray to God.

In verse 31 their prayer is answered. That is the meaning of the shaking of the earth where they were gathered. Having received power from the Holy Spirit, they again speak the word "with boldness."

TODAY'S CONFLICTS

The story that Luke tells sounds particularly contemporary to us. The first thing we notice is the marked difference between the "people" and their supposed "leaders." The people are ready to believe. They recognize the lame man, and they rejoice that he has been healed. The leaders are more interested in their power and their own ideology than in the well-being of the lame man; and they are only concerned over the people in order to make certain that they continue accepting the authority of their supposed leaders. It is clear that the same happens today. There are countries in Latin America where power is concentrated on "twelve families" or "thirty families," which own almost all the land, practically own the entire nation, and whose representatives take turns in government. There are cities in the United States where it is also possible to speak of the "thirty" who control finance, trade, industry, and much of government. Within the Council, there were differences of opinion, for the Pharisees and the Sadducees disagreed in matters of doctrine and they generally represented different social classes; but in the end both are more interested in their own power and prestige than in the well-being of the lame man or of the people. The same thing happens in many of our countries, when a congress elected in a more or less democratic fashion, and where there are certainly differences between members and parties, all or almost all agree in using the people as a stepping stone towards greater power.

In the text, it is a matter both of official and of extra-official structures of power. The Council, the high priest, and the captain of the guard of the Temple are officially constituted authorities. The Sadducees, on the other hand, are a relatively amorphous group of people who are generally affluent, and who are also conservative in their theology as well as in their politics. Because they are conservative in their theology, they reject the notion of the resurrection of the dead, which according to them is recent teaching lacking foundation in Israel's ancient faith. Because they are conservative in their politics, they tend to collaborate with the Roman Empire, and to receive economic and other benefits in return.

It would be difficult to find a more accurate description of what happens in many of our Latin American countries. There are official structures: presidents, provincial or state governors, senators and representatives. There are also semi-official structures, that sometimes even claim not to exist, but which in fact have much more power than they legally should. Such is the case, for instance of many of our armies, whose legal purpose is to defend the country against supposed threats or invasions, but whose real power is often much more extensive. Sometimes that power includes naming and removing presidents; and sometimes they also become judges and executioners, as has happened so often in nations where "death squadrons" have been organized, or where the army itself has "disappeared" those who stood in its way or threatened its power. Another of those semi-official structures is the political party, for in some of our nations there are parties that are so powerful that their inner circles actually determine the results of supposedly democratic elections. In the United States itself, the "two-party system," which includes only two very similar parties, is such that outside of that structure there is very little possibility of political success.

Then there are extra-official structures of power: rich families that intermarry and retain all the land and much of the power; the newly enriched who have accumulated capital on the basis of trade or industry, and now make certain that any possible competition is destroyed before it becomes too strong, and thereby smother the economic development of our nations; those who control the mass media, through which they also manipulate information and public opinion.

The text speaks of some "builders" who did not build well (4:12) and of some judges who did not judge well (4:19). The scribes themselves sometimes were called "builders." Those who have been placed in order to edify and build up the people have rejected the cornerstone of the building. Those who have been placed to be guardians of truth and to seek the well-being of the people have uttered false judgment, ordering Peter and John to hide the truth. Unfortunately, that also is often the practice of many of our rulers. There are some whose function was to defend and to develop the economy of the nation, but instead mortgaged it to such a point that the external debt has become an "eternal debt." There are those who were set to watch over the economic and social well-being of the citizenship, but who employed their authority to open the way for the powerful, accepting bribes and participating in enterprises that enriched them, but not the people. There are those who had been set to stand for law and justice, but who instead issued laws protecting their own interests, named judges who would rule falsely, and punished any who in any way questioned or threatened their power.

The text also speaks of the Sadducees as part of the opposition that the apostles encountered. The Sadducees opposed the apostles for two reasons: the matter of authority and the issue of resurrection. In 4:2 we are told that the apostles were subjected to repression both because they taught the people and because they proclaimed the resurrection of the dead. Thus, perhaps the starting point of the conflict is that the doctrine of the resurrection of the dead is rejected by the Sadducees, who therefore believe the apostles to be teaching heresy. However, very soon the doctrinal issue is forgotten, and the trial seems to deal only with the matter of the authority on which the apostles dared heal the lame man and then teach the people. What we have here is a typical case in which theological disagreement becomes an excuse hiding the true motivations, which have to do with power and control.

The same thing happens often in many of our own circles. Someone is accused of teaching false doctrines; but what is really meant is that the accused is somehow subverting the established order, or questioning those who currently hold power. This is nothing new, for it has happened again and again throughout the history of the Church. Certainly, there are cases in which doctrines that threaten the very heart of the faith must be rejected. In the early Church, that was the case with Gnosticism, which the Church rejected categorically. The same is true in our days, when it is necessary to reject and critique doctrines such as the various new forms of Gnosticism, the "Moonies," the so-called Christian Science, Jehovah's Witnesses, Scientology, and many others. However, this should not hide from us another reality: that very often, both in the past and today, Christians who have power so cling to it that in defense of their own interests they have claimed to see grave heresy where in fact there was little more than resistance to their own authority.

Many cases could be cited. One coming out of the history of Latin America is the case of Dominican friar Gil González de San Nicolás, who worked in Chile at the time of the conquest, and who declared that to make war on the natives in order to take their lands was a mortal sin, and that therefore those who did not repent—which necessarily involved returning the stolen lands—would be excommunicated. Following his guidance, many other Dominicans, Franciscans, and others refused to hear the confessions of those who held lands taken illegally from the natives. Many in the laity refused to participate in the ongoing wars of conquest. The cause of the Conquistadores was threatened. Because González based his claims in generally accepted principles of theology and Christian ethics, it was difficult to refute him. In the end, the subterfuge was used of accusing González of heresy because he had declared that the actual sins of the parents were inherited by the children.[34]

It would be easy to imagine that such a thing happened only in the time of the Conquest, and only in the Church of that century. However, in our own day, and in many ecclesiastical circles in Latin America, similar events take place repeatedly. As in the case of the Sadducees, political conservatism is often confused with supposedly theological conservatism, and one of these is used as an excuse and as support for the other.

---

34. Antonio de Egaña, *Historia de la Iglesia en la América española: Hemisferio sur* (Madrid: Biblioteca de Autores Cristianos, 1966), p. 209.

The realistic and contemporary note of this passage goes further. The Council wishes to control and manipulate information. Its preference would have been to suppress the news about the healing of the lame man. But because the miracle is well known and undeniable, they seek ways to make certain that the people know only what their leaders determine, and that unwanted information is not spread too widely. The purpose of their action is not to punish the apostles for a crime they might have committed, nor even protecting orthodoxy. Their purpose is "to keep it from spreading further among the people," and that if the news about the healing of the lame man spreads, it would not be connected with the name of Jesus.

This too could have been written in very recent times. Some years ago I was visiting a country where people "disappeared" daily. Because very often their family, friends, and neighbors knew that they had disappeared, and had made a claim before the authorities, the newspapers would include a small notice declaring that "it is not known what has become of. . . ." A few days later there would appear another notice: "The body of . . . has been found, apparently the result of foul play," or "in such and such a lake the body of such and such a person has been found, apparently the victim of a drowning." Such news, when it appeared, would only be found in a small corner of the newspaper, where it was hoped that it would draw little attention. In such cases, because what has happened cannot be hidden, an effort is made to make it appear less important, and to make it difficult for readers to relate what is said on page four about someone who has disappeared to what is said on page fifteen about a body that has been found. In a village in the same country there was a massacre. When I was visiting, there was an official campaign seeking to blame various groups, but never mentioning the army, which was the obvious perpetrator.

In other places similar things happen, although less dramatically. But there too there is a tendency to subvert or to manipulate truth in order to bolster various interests.[35] Sometimes what is said is true, but the manner in which it is said serves purposes that are not explicitly stated. We even have a newly coined word for such practices: "spin." A case having to do with the Latino population in the United States should be obvious. According to various projections from the U.S. Bureau of the Census, by the year 2080 there will be 150 million Latinos in the United States. That bit of statistics, which may well be true, is then employed in articles that seem to rejoice in the "Hispanic future" of the nation, but whose true purpose is to sow fear and distrust toward Hispanics among African Americans and other minorities. What is being said may be true. But it is

---

35. On the manner in which this takes place in the United States see for instance E. S. Herman and N. Chomsky, *Manufacturing Consent: The Political Economy of the Mass Media* (New York: Pantheon Books, 1988) and H. I. Schiller, *Culture, Inc.: The Corporate Takeover of Public Expression* (New York: Oxford Press, 1989). These two books offer concrete examples. A more theoretical work is that of A. and M. Mattelart, *Pensar sobre los medios: Comunicación y crítica social* (San José: DEI, 1988).

said in a way that foments division among the various minorities in the country. It is not necessary to add that this serves the interests of those who are currently benefiting from the inferior status of African Americans, Latinos, and other minorities.

The Council was seeking ways to subvert truth in order to avoid the possible subversion that the apostles would bring about. The same has been done throughout the ages. When Luke wrote about this episode, he already knew about another sad chapter in the history of the Church. In the year 64, there was a great fire in Rome. The houses where much of the lower echelons of society lived burned. Soon people began saying that it was Emperor Nero himself who had ordered the fire. Most probably there was no truth to such rumors. In any case, Nero, rather than responding to such rumors by seeking to discover the truth, circulated other rumors that were at least as false as the previous ones: it was the Christians who had set fire to the city. The result was the first persecution of Christians by Roman authorities.

All of this should serve as a calling for Christians to understand how information is handled and manipulated in our own circles and societies. It has often been said that Christians should read the Bible in one hand and the newspaper in the other. On that saying, deceased Puerto Rican theologian Orlando Costas commented that "it all depends on which newspaper." Newspapers certainly manipulate information, and one has to be aware of their particular bias in order to interpret what they say. In some Latin American countries, at various times, the government has openly controlled information, establishing more or less official systems of censorship. In other places, each newspaper belongs to the representatives of a certain ideology, and the news is manipulated in such a way as to support that ideology. In many more, newspapers are privately held by powerful economic sectors whose representatives control not only the media, but also banking and commerce, industry, and political power. It should come as no surprise that the press then tends to favor and to defend the interests of that sector of society. Finally, one must add the fact that the media often live by the sale of publicity. Newspapers are supported mostly by advertisers. If they publish something that is not to the liking of their sponsors, the latter will withdraw their support, and the newspaper will find itself in difficult straits. The same is true of magazines, television, radio, and the various other media of information. That is why, when Christians adopt attitudes that do not agree with the desires of those who control the means of information, they are called communist, extremist, reactionary, subversive, or anything else that may undercut their credibility.

Sadly, similar things sometimes happen in ecclesiastical circles, where there are pastors who do not tell the laity what they know, with the excuse that "they will be scandalized," when in truth this is their means of retaining their power and supposed authority. These so-called "builders" refuse to build the household of God if it is not done under their control and direction.

How does the church in the text we are studying respond to such maneuverings and threats? The first thing it does is to acknowledge its own perplexity before what is taking place. There is a note of holy protest in verses 24 to 26, where the believers cry to God demanding, if God is so powerful and made the heaven and earth, why is it that "the Gentiles rage and the peoples imagine vain things"? It is important to acknowledge that attitude of holy protest, which is part of the biblical faith, and which we often repress both in ourselves and in our churches. It should suffice to read the Psalms (from which comes part of this particular church's prayer) in order to see that the God of Israel is not offended because believers express their doubts, their frustrations, and even their rebellion: "How long, O Lord? Will you forget me forever? How long will you hide your face from me?" (Ps. 13:1). "My God, my God, why have you forsaken me? Why are you so far from helping me, from the words of my groaning? O my God, I cry by day, but you do not answer: and by night, but find no rest" (Ps. 22:1–2). "O God, why do you cast us out forever? Why does your anger smoke against the sheep of your pasture?" (Ps. 74:1).[36]

In many of our churches there is the impression that to ask such questions is a sign of lack of faith. But the truth is exactly the opposite. Faith implies such a relationship with God that we are able to deal with God frankly and openly. To hide our perplexities, our anguish, and our doubt is not a sign of faith, but rather of its lack. The church described in Acts begins by freely expressing its perplexity, in order finally to acknowledge that somehow what is taking place must be seen within the context of the mysterious designs of God (4:28)—which however does not diminish the responsibility of the guilty parties nor the evil of what is taking place. Those Christians strongly assert that what is taking place is evil. They also affirm that all is in the hands of God, who does not wish evil. Finally, they affirm that in some mysterious way that they do not claim to understand both of these are true. And in the midst of that, they continue believing in a God who is ready to listen to their complaints, their perplexities and doubts.

But there is more. That church moves from expressing its anguish to asking God for power to respond to the situation. It is here that we have much to learn from the text. Those early Christians could have asked God to take away the threats, to free them from further difficulties, to help them avoid conflict with the powerful within their nation. But instead they ask the opposite. They ask that there may be "signs and wonders" performed "through the name of your Holy Servant, Jesus" (4:30). They also ask for power to continue speaking with "boldness." They had just been threatened by the authorities precisely because of a wonder that has been performed in the name of Jesus. They have been ordered to be silent and not to continue healing and teaching in the name of Jesus. What they now ask for is more wonders like the one that brought about the threats from the powerful, and that they be given the power to disobey the order of the Council and to continue preaching in the name of Jesus with boldness.

---

36. Ingrid González, "Salmos de lamentación: Protesta ante el sufrimiento," *VyP*, 4 (1984), 69–88.

We have much to learn from those ancient sisters and brothers in the faith. In many of our churches, the most common way of making certain that something is not said or done is to call it "controversial." In many of our churches when we are about to make a decision about any particular program, one of the first things we ask is how will it impact the manner in which we are seen in society. We live in a continent full of people in need—of people, so to speak, who are weak and lame. We live in a continent that has need of the proclamation of the name of Jesus Christ as the Lord who saves us, not only from eternal death, but also from acquiescence before the many deaths—full and partial deaths— that the social order perpetrates daily. In the midst of such a continent and such a situation, too often we are tempted to say, "Lord, help us to avoid difficulties." When we see the cases of manipulation of information that have already been discussed, we are tempted to say, "Lord, help us to be silent." When someone in the Church begins to respond to the needs of the oppressed, and the oppressors begin pressuring the Church, we are tempted to say, "Lord, do not allow those extremists to create difficulties."

However, what this text invites us to say and to do is exactly the opposite. Instead of saying, "Lord, help us to avoid problems," the text invites us to say, "Lord, give us more signs of your power, which is what has created the problem in the first place." Instead of saying, "Lord, help us to be silent," the text invites us to say, "Lord, grant to your servants to speak your word with all boldness." Instead of saying, "Lord, do not allow those extremists to create difficulties," the text invites us to say, "Lord, give us more extremists."

Sometimes we are told that if we do not look after the prestige of the Church, our evangelizing mission will be in danger. To that also the text provides an answer, which may be found in verse 4. At the very moment when Peter and John have been imprisoned as controversial extremists, the Lord adds to the church five thousand families. It is in the most difficult moments, precisely when the Church risks its own prestige and well-being in favor of truth and of the well-being of the weak and the oppressed, that God gives growth. We have already been told in an earlier passage (2:47) that the disciples of Jesus had "the goodwill of all of the people," and that "the Lord added to their number those who were being saved." Having the goodwill of the people does not mean simply pleasing everybody, but rather taking a stand in favor of the people in the face of those who oppress it, and of those who seek to control it by falsifying or spinning information.

To speak the word of God with "boldness" is a gift of the Holy Spirit (4:31). To speak it thus is to speak it with integrity, even though this may cause controversy and even bring about threats from those who wish to control everything. This is an urgent need in Latin America. The Church must earn the goodwill of the people by taking its side, by placing the Church's spiritual, material and human resources at the service of the people. When the Church remains at the margin of the needs and struggles of the people, or when it seeks to profit by identifying itself with a particular group that holds or seeks power, its life and its witness are very different from what Luke describes in these verses in Acts.

C. THE USE OF GOODS (4:32–5:11)

1. Another Summary (4:32–35)

We come now to another of those summaries that Luke includes in his narrative in order to offer generalizations and commentaries, which are later illustrated or discussed in particular instances. This summary deals with the economic life of the early Church. Because in our churches economic matters are not discussed as often as they should be, a careful study of this text is important.

In reading this summary (as well as the briefer one in 2:44–45), the first question often asked is whether this actually happened. Is it true that the early Christians practiced the sort of communal property described here, or is it rather a fiction of Luke's imagination, who projects on the life of the Church in the past a romantic or idealized vision? We have to pose this question, because some scholars have done so, arguing that what is described here is in fact the ideal community as it was conceived among some Greek and Hellenistic philosophers—especially the Pythagoreans—and that therefore this is only an attempt to depict the early Christian community as an ideal one. Such is, for instance, the interpretation that sees this passage as an attempt to symbolize the authority of the apostles.[37] To support this thesis, an entire list of Greek and Hellenistic sources is given for Luke's ideas: Plato, a proverb quoted by Aristotle, the lives of Pythagoras written by Diogenes Laertius, Porphyry, and Iamblichus.[38] In other words, the argument is that, when Luke seeks to describe the early Christian community, he draws on Hellenistic sources regarding the value of unity and friendship, and in particular on the manner in which such unity and friendship are revealed in the community of goods.

Such an interpretation does not take into sufficient account the significant differences between the Pythagorean ideal and what is described in this text. That ideal is an elitist association of philosophers who share goods because this helps them be devoted to the "philosophical life"; what we have in Acts is an open community that rejoices as its numbers increase, and whose ability to share is the result of the gift of the Spirit and of its own eschatological expectation.

At any rate, it is possible to put an end to this discussion if one shows that not only at the time Acts was written, but also for some time thereafter, the sort of community of goods described here was still practiced in the Church. That is certainly the case, as will be shown in a moment.

---

37. L. T. Johnson, *The Literary Function of Possessions in Luke-Acts* (Missoula, Mont.: Scholars Press, 1977), pp. 189–98. The same ideas appear also in D. L. Mealand, "Community of goods and utopian allusions in Acts II–IV," *JTS*, 28 (1977), 96–99; J. Downey, "The early Jerusalem Christians," *BibTo*, 91 (1977), 1295–1303.

38. L. T. Johnson, *Sharing Possessions: Mandate and Symbol of Faith* (Philadelphia: Fortress Press, 1981), p. 119.

However, before moving to that historical account, there is another common interpretation of this passage and of its importance that must be discussed and rejected. According to that interpretation, the early Church did indeed hold the community of goods described here, but that practice was soon abandoned. Frequently this explanation is joined to the notion—totally lacking in foundation in the text itself—that the poverty that existed sometime later in the church in Jerusalem was due, at least in part, to that practice of sharing goods, and that this was why Paul had to work at collecting an offering for the poor in Jerusalem. This opinion is expressed in its most characteristic form in the following quotation, taken from one of the commentaries most frequently employed in the United States until recent date:

> Whatever may have been the extent of this "communistic" experiment in Jerusalem, it appears very soon to have broken down, first, perhaps on account of the dissention between "Hellenists" and "Hebrews" (6:1), and second because the administrators who had been appointed as a result of the dispute had been driven from the city by the Jews. Probably also the eager expectation of the Parousia led to improvidence for the future so that the Jerusalem community was always poor.[39]

This notion that the poverty of Christians in Jerusalem was the result of their earlier practice of the community of goods is relatively common. However, there is no basis for such an interpretation, be it in Acts itself, or in other ancient documents. On the contrary, Acts does speak of a great famine and implies that this was the reason the church in Jerusalem was in need of help from others (11:27–30). Josephus also refers to a great famine that took place in Judea, which reached its high point around the year 46.[40] And Roman historians Tacitus and Suetonius mention in their writings several periods of famine during the reign of Claudius (which is also the date at which Acts places the famine that made necessary the collection for the poor in Jerusalem).[41]

In order to respond to both the interpretation that turns the text into an idyllic view of the past and the other interpretation that claims that the commonality of goods was an economic disaster, the first point must be to clarify the nature of the commonality of goods that Acts describes. In commenting

---

39. H. C. Macgregor, in *The Interpreter's Bible*, 9:73; R. J. Sider, *Rich Christians in an Age of Hunger* (Downers Grove, Ill.: Intervarsity Press, 1977), p. 101, quotes a similar opinion of another modern author, J. A. Ziesler, *Christian Asceticism* (Grand Rapids, Mich.: Eerdmans, 1973), p. 110: "The trouble in Jerusalem was that they turned their capital into income and had no cushion for hard times, and the Gentile Christians had to come to their rescue."

40. *Ant.* 20.5.

41. Tacitus, *Ann.* 12.43; Suetonius, *Claud.* 18.

on Acts 2:42, 44–45, the meaning of the word *koinōnia* has already been clarified, as well as the fact that in both that passage and this one the verbs are in the imperfect tense. In summary, what was said there is that these verbs in imperfect tense imply that it was not a matter of people going and selling whatever they had, as in later monastic communities, but rather that, as the need arose, people would sell what they had in order to respond to the various needs of the community.

The present text adds two other elements to the similar summary in chapter 2:[42] first, that "there was not a needy person among them"; second, that "the proceeds of what was sold" was "laid at the apostles' feet."

The first is a reference to Deuteronomy 15:4–11, where Israel is encouraged to obey the law of God in such a way that there "be no one in need among you" and that if there is, people will share with such a needy person. Perhaps this helps to explain an interesting phenomenon when one compares the two books of Luke/Acts: it has been pointed out that, whereas in the Gospel of Luke the poor are a constant theme, in Acts the word "poor" does not even appear.[43] This is the only place where the subject of the needy is mentioned, and even here a different word is employed, which does not convey the radical poverty that appears repeatedly in Luke. How is this to be explained? A possible explanation is that Luke is telling us that, by virtue of the gift of the Spirit, the promise of Deuteronomy is being fulfilled in the early Church.

The second detail that this text adds to what has been said in chapter 2 is that the result of the sales was placed "at the apostles' feet." Perhaps this is to be understood literally, as if the apostles were presiding at the assembly and believers would place the money at their feet. More likely it simply means that it was put at the disposal of the apostles. In any case, what is added here is that there was a method for the distribution of resources, and that this method consisted simply in trusting the apostles to distribute what was available according to each one's need.

In conclusion, what this summary describes is not a regime in which all go at once and sell what they have, put it in a common coffer, and then live off it. Rather it describes a community in which mutual love is such that if someone has need others go and sell their real estate in order to respond to those needs. Also, in this second summary, apparently the community has grown enough that it has become more difficult to offer direct assistance to the needy, and therefore a system has developed whereby those who sell properties bring

---

42. It also clarifies what it was that Christians would sell. In 2:45, the words "possessions" and "goods" are relatively imprecise. According to 4:34, what they would sell were "lands" or "houses," that is, real estate.

43. J. A. Bergquist, "'Good News to the Poor': Why does this Lucan motif appear to run dry in the Book of Acts?", *BangThF*, 18 (1986), argues that this means that the theme of the poor is not as crucial for Luke as we have often imagined. According to him, what is important is the message of salvation, which God brings in Jesus Christ.

the proceeds to the apostles, who in turn are responsible for the distribution of resources.

Having clarified this point, it is now possible to return to the question that was left pending, namely, whether there are other indications of similar practices in the early Church besides these passages in Acts. The first response that comes to mind is the collection for the poor in Jerusalem, which occupies such a prominent place in Paul's Epistles. When one examines what Paul says about that collection, it is clear that what we have there is a continuation of the *koinōnia* described in Acts, although now widened to include the Church in various cities.[44] Acts was written after Paul's letters, in a circle where Paul's influence was strong. That is why a major part of the book deals with Paul's ministry. Therefore, instead of suggesting that the community of goods described in Acts is the result of Hellenistic influences or of the idealization of the primitive community, one could argue that—even though a few phrases in Acts 2 and 4 may parallel similar phrases in earlier Greek literature—what Luke is describing is the sense of *koinōnia* that existed at the very heart of Paul's ministry. If that is the case, what Acts describes here is not an ephemeral moment in the life of the Church nor an idyllic dream of how things ought to have been in the early days of the life of the Church, but a fundamental aspect of the life of the Church both in its origins and in Luke's own time.

Furthermore, the commonality of goods, far from being an ephemeral element in the life of the early Church, continued for a long time. In the *Didache*, a document that could well date from the end of the first century or early in the second, we are told that "you are not to overlook the needy but rather are to share [*synkoinōnein*, that is, being *koinōnoi* jointly] all things with your brother, and are not to say that they are your own. Because if we are partners [*koinōnoi*] in the eternal, how are we not to be partners even more in that which perishes?"[45] The same ideas appear, perhaps some fifty years later, in the so-called *Epistle of Barnabas*.[46] At about the same time, that is, toward the middle of the second century, the *Address to Diognetus* claims that Christians "share a single table, but not a bed."[47] This is probably a brief way of distinguishing the commonality of goods that Christians practice from that which had been proposed by Plato and others, which also included sexual promiscuity. In any case, what is important is that the commonality of goods described in Acts continued at the time of that other writing. Furthermore, similar asser-

---

44. In *Faith and Wealth: The Origins, Significance, and Use of Money in the Early Church* (San Francisco: Harper & Row, 1990), I have included a study of the Pauline correspondence along these lines, showing precisely that the collection for the poor is an extension of the earlier *koinōnia*.

45. *Did.* 4.7–8.

46. *Barn.* 19.8.

47. *Diog.* 5.7.

tions appear in the writings of Justin Martyr, also from the middle of the second century,[48] and after that in Tertulian, toward the end of that century.[49]

Therefore, interpretations that seek to set aside this text claiming that it was a failed and ephemeral experiment in the early Church are clearly contradicted by the historical record.

2.   Concrete Cases (4:36–5:11)

Luke interweaves his summaries with concrete examples. Here he offers two such cases, the one positive (4:36–37) and the other negative (5:1–11). (In the next chapter, he will offer another example, and the manner in which the church dealt with it.)

The first case is that of a man whose true name was Joseph, but whom the apostles had named "Barnabas."[50] We are told that he was a Levite, "a native of Cyprus," and that he sold a field. The text does not clarify whether the property itself was near Jerusalem or in Cyprus. Luke tells us that "Barnabas" means "son of encouragement," but it is difficult to connect such an etymology with Hebrew or Aramaic.

The fact that what Barnabas did is mentioned specifically does not mean that it was an extraordinary case, which would contradict what Luke has just told us.[51] This is simply one more case in which Luke, after a general summary, offers a concrete example. He also uses the opportunity to introduce a person who will be important for the rest of his story.

Then follows the case of Ananias and Sapphira.[52] Although the text does not say so, the sequence in the narrative and the loving name that the apostles had given to Barnabas strongly suggest that Ananias and Sapphira were moved by jealousy, or by the desire to be admired as much as Barnabas. Whatever the case, the narrative itself is clear. First Ananias and then Sapphira lie regarding the prize for which they sold the property, giving the impression that they are

---

48. *I Apol.* 14.2, 15.10, 67.1, 6.

49. *Apol.* 39.

50. The words that the NRSV translates in this manner could also be understood as "Barnabas of the apostles," in which case they would mean that Barnabas was one of the apostles. There would be no difficulty in this, for in the early church the title of apostle was not reserved for the Twelve (see, for instance, 14:4, 14). However, such a translation would require interpreting the text as an unusual grammatical construction. C. V. Burch, "The Name Barnabas and the Paraclete," *ExpTim*, 27 (1951–56), 524.

51. It is thus that Haenchen interprets the passage, *Acts*, 233. However, Haenchen seems to have decided to discount all that Luke says on economic matters.

52. P. H. Menoud, "La mort d'Ananias et de Saphira," in *Aux sources de la tradition chrétienne: Mélanges offerts à M. Maurice Goguel à l'occasion de son soixante-dixième anniversaire (Neuchâtel: Delachaux & Niestlé,* 1950), pp. 146–54; J. S. Ruef, *Ananias and Sapphira: A Study of the Community Disciplinary Practices Underlying Acts 5:1–11,* doctoral dissertation, Harvard, 1960; R. Schmacher, "Ananias und Sapphira," *ThuGl,* 5 (1913), 824–30.

turning all of it over to the community, and as a consequence of their lie they are struck dead. The use of an unusual Greek verb, translated in the NRSV as to "keep back," relates this episode with another in which the same verb appears, that of Achan in Joshua 7 (in the Septuagint, which is the translation that Luke employs). However, whereas Achan took what was not his, Ananias simply kept a part of what was his, and claimed to have contributed the whole to the community.

The narrative itself presents some problems regarding the sequence of events. Ananias dies, and the young men of the congregation take him out to be buried, apparently without even telling his widow. Sapphira, three hours later, has no idea what has happened. There is no explanation regarding the haste in burying Ananias. The reader's impression is that Peter did this precisely in order to catch Sapphira as an accomplice to her husband's lie. Some point out that there were laws ordering that dead bodies were to be taken out of the city before a certain time of day. According to the story, the young men who took Ananias's body took three hours in burying him and returning. Therefore, one could imagine that, having to hurry in burying the body, there was no time to tell Sapphira. However, all of these are mere conjectures, for the text simply leaves us puzzled.

The "young men" who bury Ananias are not necessarily a specific group—in contrast, for instance, to the "elders," who indeed represented an office. It is simply that in order to perform this duty, which requires some physical labor, the young men were a natural choice. As to the burial place itself, according to custom, it probably was not a hole in the ground, but rather a cave or a hole in the rock, which was then covered with stones. This also would require the strength of youth.

Beside such details that can only be conjectures, this story itself reaffirms that the community of goods to which the summary refers was voluntary and ongoing. It was not a matter of everyone going out and selling whatever they had, but rather of a continuing process of selling property as this became necessary in order to fill the needs of the less fortunate. Although in 4:32 we are told that "all" who had properties used to sell them, this seems a hyperbole, for here Peter tells Ananias that he had no obligation to sell what he had, and that even after selling it he was free to bring or not to bring the proceeds.[53] Their sin is not in keeping some of what was theirs in any case, but rather in lying to the Spirit.

---

53. On this point, see, besides the dissertion by Ruef quoted in the previous footnote, F. Scheidweiler, "Zu Act. 5:4," *ZntW*, 49 (1958), 136–37; B. J. Capper, "The interpretation of Acts 5.4," *JStNT*, 19 (1983), 117–31. The latter argues that what we have here is the existence of varying degrees of initiation or perfection in the primitive Church. Ananias and Sapphira did not have to sell their property, nor to bring all the proceeds of the sale, because they were not full members of the community. The argument has not convinced many scholars.

The terrible punishment that befalls Ananias and Sapphira seems to be completely out of proportion with their crime until we realize that, as Peter sees the matter, what they have done is to lie, not just to the church, but to God. Peter sees the situation as a great conflict between Satan and God. What has happened to Ananias is that Satan has filled his heart, and therefore he has lied to the Holy Spirit (5:3) or, what is the same, to God (5:4). Sapphira hears a similar judgment from Peter: she has "put the Spirit of the Lord to the test" (5:9).[54]

Luke summarizes the results of all this in 5:11. In this particular case it is not clear who are "the whole church" and who are "all who heard." The text may be understood as meaning that those who were gathered learned of the event immediately, and others heard about it later. It may also mean that people outside the church were seized by the same fear as believers. A third possibility is that what we have here is the typical Semitic parallel construction where the same thing is said twice with different words. In any case, what Luke wishes to emphasize is the general fear that resulted from these events.

THE NATURE OF THE CHURCH AND ITS INNER LIFE

1. Interpretation and Ideology

The passages we have just studied are frequently misinterpreted or twisted. Catholic as well as Protestant interpreters seem to make every possible effort to take the bite out of what is being said. They do this in various ways: (1) arguing that what we have here is an ideal image of the early Church as depicted by Luke, but one which never existed; (2) claiming that what is described here was a failed attempt, which at most lasted for a few weeks or months; (3) exaggerating what the text says, ignoring the verbal tenses in imperfect, and therefore implying that the economic difficulties that the church in Jerusalem had to face later were the result of their having "burnt their assets." However, as has already been said, neither the text nor other documents of the time support any such interpretation. Furthermore, what was said above regarding the meaning of the word *koinōnia* (see 2:42) indicates that what is described here may be found wherever in the New Testament or in ancient Christian documents there is reference to *koinōnia*.

What has clearly happened in this case is that interpreters, including those who most insist on the authority of Scripture, have allowed themselves to be carried by their own ideologies, and therefore have not taken the text itself very seriously.

---

54. A. Mettayer, "Ambiguité et terrorisme du sacré: Analyse d'un texte des Actes des Apôtres (4:31–5:11)," *StRelScRel*, 7 (1978), 415–24, underlines the parallelism between the terror in this passage and that at Pentecost, as well as between the function of the Spirit in both passages. There is a good discussion of the various reactions to this text in F. F. Bruce, *Commentary on the Book of Acts*, 2nd ed. (Grand Rapids: Eerdmans, 1954), pp. 110–12.

This should serve as a warning to us. It does not suffice to declare or even to believe that the final authority resides in Scripture. It is necessary to deal with the text with the seriousness and reverence that such an assertion requires. Much of what is often called "biblical" is little more than a tendentious interpretation, which itself lacks respect and obedience to the text. The text says what it says, no matter whether we like it or not. The function of the interpreter is not to take the sting out of the text, but to clarify it and bring it to bear on our situation.

In 4:2, the Sadducees disguised their interest in controlling the situation under the cloak of a theological discussion on the resurrection of the dead. Later on, when discussing 19:23–40, we shall see a case in which it is pagans who hide their true economic motives behind supposedly religious matters. It is significant that Luke seems to be aware of such a manipulation of religious discourse—an awareness that we often think is a modern discovery. More remarkable still is the fact that, in spite of the clarity with which Acts describes such manipulations, we still practice them. A typical case is the manner in which interpreters and Christians in general twist the passages we are studying. Therefore, our first reaction to this study must be to become aware of the danger of tendentious interpretations resulting from our economic interests or our ideological convictions.

2. Mission and the Use of Resources

The obvious theme of the entire passage, 4:32—5:11, is money; but behind that theme and all that is said about it here there is a particular understanding of the Church and its mission.

The story about the commonality of goods is not, as so many interpreters claim, an attempt to apply to the life of the early Church Hellenistic notions about what should be an ideal society. It is rather the result of what Peter declared in his Pentecost speech: "it shall be in the last days. . . ." In other words, what is taking place with the resurrection of Jesus and the gift of the Spirit is that the last days have begun. Christians live in two kingdoms: the present one of sin and the coming reign of God. From this perspective, the Church is seen as a sign of the reign to which it belongs. That is why the outpouring of the Spirit on "all flesh," and the fact that the daughters and the sons prophesy, was seen as a sign of those last days.

However, the reign of God is characterized above all by love, peace, abundance, and justice. The images of that reign that appear throughout the Old Testament emphasize one or another of these various elements of the *shalom* of God. Therefore, when Luke tells us about the Church as a community in which love reigned ("the whole group of those who believed were of one heart and soul") and in which this was so real that "no one claimed private ownership of any possessions," with the result that "there was not a needy person among them," he is describing, not the life of an ideal community, but rather the life of a community that is indeed a sign and a foretaste of the coming order. As Peter would say, this is a community living "in the last days." When we read the story in this manner, it does not call us to look to the past, as if it were a matter of attempting to reconstruct the ideal Church of Acts (which never existed, for Luke speaks of a very real Church in which people like Ananias and Sapphira still participate), but rather looking toward the future, as those who seek to point toward the coming community of God's reign.

Commonality of goods is not an end in itself. The mission of the Church is not to practice such commonality, but to practice love. That is how it happens that, even in the midst of a church that practiced the commonality of goods, Ananias could have retained his property, without selling it or giving any of the proceeds to the apostles. This is not a legislated communalism, but rather it is the sort of communalism that is an expression of the love and the new life in the Spirit.

Therefore, even apart from whatever we might say today about the commonality of goods, this text tells us much about the nature of the Church. Rather, it illustrates what has already been said: that the Church is that community which, by virtue of the gift of the Spirit, lives in the last days even in the midst of this world, which still lives in the old order.

It is within this context that the enormity of the sin of Ananias and Sapphira becomes apparent. Even a cursory glance at the various commentaries on this passage will reveal how difficult it is for modern interpreters to come to terms with what Luke says here. The problem is not so much the miraculous nature of the death of Ananias and Sapphira, but rather the apparently disproportionate punishment. Ananias did not have to sell his property, as Peter tells him. Even having sold it, he did not have to turn over the proceeds to the apostles. Therefore, it would seem that Ananias and Sapphira pay with their lives for not having done something they did not have to do.

But that is not the manner in which the text presents the situation. The sin is not in selling or not selling, in giving or not giving. The sin is in the lie. And that lie is not only before the church, but also before God (5:3, 4).

This is closely related to the matter of the nature of the Church. Because by virtue of the Holy Spirit the Church is the community of the last days, to lie to it is to lie to God. Apparently, it is then impossible to lie only to the human members of the Church. In the Church the Holy Spirit is also present, supporting it. To lie to the Church is to lie to God. This is not to be taken lightly. It is as Peter says, a satanic action.

If everyone who lies in church today were to drop dead, our membership would be diminished drastically! Very few dare to be totally candid with the Church. Furthermore, one could even argue that the Church is one of the places in which it is most difficult to be absolutely sincere. Apparently we have lost the custom of speaking the truth in Church. For instance, if we have doubts about a point of doctrine, rarely do we dare express them in the midst of a Sunday School class, or to ask others for help. If some sin or temptation eats away at our lives, seldom do we dare confess it before the congregation and, even though in Latino communities it is customary to speak of personal problems more frankly than in other cultures, as we become more adapted to modern urban life or move up in the social scale it becomes increasingly difficult for us to speak of problems we might have at home or at work.

The main reason it is so difficult to speak the truth is that others do not speak it either. Because others do not speak of their doubts, mine seem exceptional. Because no one speaks of their sins, mine seem enormous. Because no one speaks of their problems, I must have caused mine. In other words, we lie to the Church because within it lies and appearances have taken the place of love and truth.

What is tragic about this situation, as the text indicates, is not only that we lose the comfort that we might draw from others. The tragedy is rather that our hypocrisy and prevarication open the way to Satan, so that we end up lying to God and denying the very nature of the Church. If the Church itself lies, one can question whether it is truly the Church of the Holy Spirit.

In many of our Latino churches there is much talk of the presence and the gifts of the Spirit. This is good and correct. But too often we forget that the Spirit is to lead us to all truth (John 16:13), and that the highest of all the gifts of the Spirit is love (I Cor. 12:31–13:13). Too often, while we claim to have the Spirit of God, we lie to each other claiming to be holier than we really are, to have more faith than we really have, or to make greater sacrifices than we really make. Or we lie to each other with half truths, or we manipulate the truth about others with whom we disagree, so that they may not be able to oppose our opinions or positions. According to the biblical text, when we do these things we lie to the very Spirit of God. And the worst consequence of all this is that the lie grows, and because of our own lying others do not dare tell the truth.

3. The Price of Grace

Dietrich Bonhoeffer affirms that a common problem among Christians is that we are constantly seeking the ideal Church, and that in so doing we leave aside the real ones. The fact is that there is no such thing as the ideal Church. Luke describes a Church with a beautiful spiritual and communal life; but it is still not ideal.[55] What may be very difficult, although necessary, for us to understand is that this conglomerate of weak and sinful human beings that we are can in truth be the Church of Christ, where the Holy Spirit dwells. At the very root of the sin of Ananias and Sapphira lies this difficulty. As Luke makes clear, they were not the only ones having problems and conflicts in the church in Jerusalem (see for instance 6:1). Their sin was not in being less perfect than the rest. It was rather in not being able to discern, in that community of people just like them, the presence of the Holy Spirit.

Because the text deals specifically with money and property, it is important to relate it to those issues today, for it is precisely in matters of money and finances that Christians are quite often tempted to lie, and the Church is tempted to be untrue to its mission. The commonality of goods described in Acts is an es-

---

55. D. Bonhoeffer, *El precio de la gracia* (Salamanca: Sígueme, 1968), pp. 334*ff.*

chatological sign; that is to say it is a sign pointing toward the final day when there will no longer be any one in need, and when there will be perfect peace and justice. Because the Church is a community of the Spirit or, what is the same, a community of "the last days," part of its mission is to witness to the future that God has promised. That testimony must be given, not only in words, nor merely through the individual lives of Christians, but also through the communal life of the Church. In order to be true to its mission, the Church must seek, to the highest measure possible, to be a sign of the coming reign of God.

This may be clarified by means of an illustration. Suppose that a friend tells you that Japan is the best country in the world, that there is no culture like Japanese culture, and that as soon as possible he will move to Japan, where he hopes to spend the rest of his days. Suppose then that you ask your friend what he is doing while he awaits the day he can move to Japan. And suppose finally that he tells you that, while he waits to move to Japan, he is studying Italian! You would laugh in his face. His present actions are a radical denial of what he claims to be his future plan. If he truly expects to live in Japan he would begin right now to practice for life in that country, and therefore would be studying Japanese. Christians can spend hours and days speaking about the coming reign of God, and eloquently preaching about it; but if we do not give signs that our hope is genuine, people will not believe us. We may spend a lifetime proclaiming a coming order of justice and of peace; but if we do not deliver as those who truly believe in that future, we will not be taken seriously.

That is one of the reasons the inner order of the Church is so important. In the first of the summaries in which Luke mentions the commonality of goods, he adds that "day by day the Lord added to their number those who were being saved" (2:47). The commonality of goods and the love among the members of the church were means of witnessing. The opposite is also true: a church that simply accepts the social and economic distinctions of the wider society, and in which everyone claims that what they have is their own to use as they see fit (in contrast with 4:32), cannot be a faithful witness to Jesus and to the coming reign.

It is true that modern life is very complicated, and that a simple commonality of goods such as is described in Acts presents enormous difficulties. But this does not free us from the need to seek ways in which our community may be a sign pointing toward the coming reign of God, toward the day in which the prophet says, "they shall all sit under their own vines and under their own fig trees" (Mic. 4:4). Such ways can be found, if we only look for them. Thus, for instance, in some of the poorest communities in Latin America, churches participate actively in "common pots" in which the residents, sometimes with the help of ecclesiastical and para-ecclesiatical organizations, join what they have, prepare it together, and thereby seek to meet the needs of all. When such things take place, quite often the words of Acts 2:47 become a reality, and the church finds itself once again "having the goodwill of all the people." I know the case of a poor community in Buenos Aires in which a Protestant church prepares and organizes a common pot. A baker went to the church and offered bread and sweets so that the poor people in the community could celebrate Christmas.

"But," he said, "please come and pick up the baked goods on Friday, because I am Jewish and do not work on Saturday." Because it is concerned with the needs of his community, because it not only announces the reign of God, but really lives as those who expect it, because it truly lives out the presence of the Holy Spirit, that church enjoys the "goodwill of all the people."

Ananias and Sapphira lied to the Holy Spirit, and they paid with their lives. Some will feel uncomfortable reading this passage, for it will seem to them that it speaks of an excessively severe God. But the fact is that the God of the Bible must be taken seriously. God is not to be trifled with. And because God is a serious matter, God's Church must also be a serious matter. One can not "play church" like children who "play doctor." To lie to the Church is to lie to God. To say that all we have is God's and then to deny it to our sisters and brothers in need is to mock God. The price in the case of Ananias and Sapphira was physical death. The price in our case may be even greater: spiritual death.

D. PERSECUTION INCREASES (5:12–42)

This section is a cycle similar to that in 4:1–31: miracles lead to jealously, which in turn lead to a trial, at the end of which the message continues moving forward.

1.   The Gospel Gains Popularity (5:12–16)

The cycle begins with another of the summaries, which we have found repeatedly in the early chapters of Acts. In this case, that summary deals almost exclusively with the miracles that were taking place, and the growing popularity of Christians. Once again, the center of activity seems to be the porch of Solomon, although now those who seek miracles follow Peter, placing the diseased where he has to pass by, in the hope that his mere shadow will heal them.[56]

As before, here again the contrast appears between the "people" and the powerful. Through the apostles, many miracles were done "among the people" (5:12), and therefore "the people held them in high esteem" (5:13). However, in this very verse we also hear about "the rest," of whom none dared "to join them." Who these others might have been, the text does not say, but the entire context would seem to support the opinion of Martin Dibelius, who suggests that the "rulers" or "chiefs" of the people are the ones who would not join.[57] In that case, what the text implies is that the social and religious elite so pressured

---

56. On the healing power of shadows in ancient religiosity, and the importance of this matter in this context, see Werner Bieder, "Der Petrusschatten, Apg. 5:15," *TZ*, 16 (1960), 407–9; P. W. van der Horst, "Peter's shadow: The religio-historical background of Acts v. 15," *NTSt*, 23 (1977), 204–12.

57. *Studies in the Acts of the Apostles* (New York: Scribner's, 1956), p. 91.

its members that even those would like to join the disciples did not dare to do so (which reminds us of the case of Nicodemus, who came to Jesus at night).

Miracles continue and multiply and, in spite of the wish of the Council (4:17: "to keep it from spreading further among the people"), there are ever more people who believe and who come in quest of health.

2.   Another Attempt to Silence Peter and John (5:17–42)[58]

Verse 17 explicitly states that those who sought to silence the apostles were moved by jealousy. Throughout the entire passage, those who seek to silence Peter and John are the high priest (5:17, 21, 24, 27), the chief priests (5:24), and the captain of the guard of the Temple (5:24, 26), whereas the apostles teach the *people* (5:20, 25), and the Temple police fear to be stoned by the *people* (5:26).

A miraculous intervention to free the disciples from prison appears, not only in this passage, but also in 12:6–11 (where Peter is freed) and in 16:26–27 (where it is Paul and Silas who benefit from the miracle). In reading here the word "angel," we must not necessarily think of a shiny being, with white robes and wings. In the Bible, an "angel" is simply a messenger, and frequently such messengers give no indication that they are different from any human being, to the point that it is even possible to offer them hospitality without knowing it (see Heb. 13:2).

The morning after the arrest of the apostles, the Temple police find the jail empty, and they report to their superiors. Suddenly the powerful are perplexed (verse 24); but as soon as they learn that Peter and John are once again teaching in the Temple, they have them arrested again, although without violence, for fear of the *people*.

It is interesting to note that in the trial that follows the matter of having escaped from jail is not even mentioned. This may be due in part to the fact that imprisonment, as noted earlier, was usually not a punishment, but only a means of making certain that the accused were present at their trial, or were held for punishment. Because Peter and John have left their imprisonment but have not attempted to flee, there is no reason to insist on the matter, and the trial goes on as if nothing had happened.

This second trial is almost the continuation of the first, for the high priest begins by reminding the accused of what they had been ordered before,[59] and they in turn respond as they had before: "We must obey God rather than any human authority" (5:29; see 4:19). Also, the manner in which Luke here sum-

---

58. E. Iglesias, "El libro de los Hechos: Las primeras persecuciones," *Christus*, 5 (1938), 55–63.

59. The law required that before flogging a person, there must be clear warnings regarding that person's conduct, and that this be done in the presence of two witnesses. Therefore, it is possible that by reminding the accused of the previous order the high priest is actually affirming that the law has been obeyed, for the apostles were clearly warned in the previous trial.

marizes the teaching of the apostles (5:30–32) is similar to what appears in 4:10–12.

The response of the council is now more extreme, for they want to kill the accused (5:33). It is at this point that Gamaliel intervenes with his famous advice.[60] His historical references to Theudas and Judas the Galilean raise some difficulties.[61] The only rebel called Theudas of whom there is historical notice arose around the year 45, several years after the incident that Luke is narrating. There are also difficulties with the exact date of the rebellion of Judas the Galilean (around the year 4). In any case, what Luke places on the lips of Gamaliel is wise advice, although based on a dubious argument: that Peter and John should not be killed, because "if this plan or this undertaking is of human origin, it will fail; but if it is of God, you would not be able to overthrow them" (5:38–39).[62] The advice is wise because the people are at the edge of rioting, and if the apostles are killed the Council will lose much of the little prestige it still has. The other members of the Council accept Gamaliel's advice, probably because that will allow them to practice the apparent mercy of condemning the accused to a flogging, instead of a more severe penalty, and also to ignore the fact that they have not been found guilty of any crime.

Although the Council accepted Gamaliel's general advice, it did not accept his argument, for before letting the apostles go they had them flogged and they ordered them once again to remain silent. The number of lashes in such cases was usually thirty-nine, a high enough number that sometimes the accused died as a result of the flogging. Therefore, although they were not killed, Peter and John were severely punished.

In spite of all of this, Peter and John go out rejoicing, for they "were considered worthy to suffer this honor for the sake of the name" (5:41). Such an attitude of joy and even of gratitude in the face of suffering became characteristic of Christian martyrs throughout the early centuries of persecution.

Finally, the passage ends with a summary that closes the incident.

---

60. Gamaliel is also known from other writings of the time. Apparently he was indeed a Pharisee, and a leader in that party. Herman L. Strack and Paul Billerbeck, *Kommentar zum Neuen Testament aus Talmud und Midrash* (Munich: Beck, 1922–61), vol. 2, pp. 636–39.

61. J. Spencer Kennard Jr., "Judas of Galilee and his clan," *JQR*, 36 (1945–46); Lucien Campeau, "Theudas le faux prophète et Judas le Galiléen," *ScEccl*, 5 (1953), 235–45; William R. Farmer, *Maccabees, Zealots and Josephus: An Inquiry into Jewish Nationalism in the Graeco-Roman Period* (New York: Columbia University Press, 1956); P. Winter, "Miszellen zur Apostelgeschichte. I: Acta 5:36," *EvTh*, 17 (1957), 398–99. On this subject, see the excellent book by R. A. Horsely and J. S. Hanson, *Bandits, Prophets, and Messiahs: Popular Movements at the Time of Jesus* (San Francisco: Harper & Row, 1985).

62. W. C. Bishop, "Was Gamaliel's counsel to the Sanhedrin based on sound reasoning?", *ConcThM*, 10 (1939), 676–83. The argument is dubious, because it would lead to an absolute quietism. In the face of any difficult situation, it will be possible to avoid responsibility by placing it on God: whatever God wills will happen anyway.

THE MATTER OF MIRACLES

The Book of Acts is full of stories of miracles, to such a point that it is impossible to read it without taking miracles into account. Because this section speaks of the "many signs and wonders" done through the prophets, this is an appropriate place to consider the matter of miracles.

The frequency of stories of miracles in the Book of Acts has led many to deny its historicity. It is difficult for many to even entertain the notion of miracles because the modern worldview is that of a closed universe, a system of causes and effects that may be explained by mechanicist principles. In our day, if a given event is not completely explainable by such principles, the reason for this is our own ignorance of causes and relationships, and not the order of the universe itself. The universe so conceived is closed to any divine intervention, and functions on the basis of inalterable laws that can never be changed nor subjected to other powers. This view of the universe as a closed, mechanistic system is a fundamental aspect of modernity. As Rudolf Bultmann says, "it is impossible to use electric light and the wireless and avail ourselves of modern medical and surgical discoveries, and at the same time to believe in the New Testament world of spirits and miracles."[63]

The truth is, however, that what Bultmann declares to be impossible is not just possible, but even frequent. Throughout the world, including much of the Spanish-speaking community of faith, people not only use electricity and radio, but also computers and the Internet in order to tell of the great wonders that God has performed in their lives.

The fact is that between the world vision of Bultmann and those who hold his position and that of these believers who speak of the wonders God has done, there is an ideological dissonance. Those who do not admit the possibility of miracles base their disbelief on "reason." Indeed, but, which reason? "Reason" is not a universal and constant principle, but is itself conditioned by our own perspective on life. Ever since the writings of Emmanuel Kant, we have been aware of the possibility that the human mind does not really adapt to the world in order to know and describe it, but rather imposes its own order and limits on the world in order then to conceive it. Later, with the work of Marx, Freud, and their successors, we have also learned that "reason" does not exist in a vacuum, but is conditioned by historical, psychological, economic, and social factors. We have also learned that "reason" functions in such a way that it is able to hide those factors from itself. Therefore, when we are told that "reason" demands that we believe in a closed universe, our first question must be: which reason?

The answer should be obvious. The definition of reason in mechanicist terms, so that any possible disruption or divine intervention is excluded, serves the interests of the status quo, and part of its purpose is to discourage those whose only hope is in a radical and practically unexplainable change in the

---

63. *Kerygma and Myth* (New York: Harper & Row, 1961), p. 5.

present order. If all that is to be will only be the result of what already is, there is no reason to hope for a new order; and without that hope, the struggle and resistance against the present order lose their momentum. The understanding of reason promoted by such interests is very similar to the attitude of the Sadducees and the "builders" in the Council, who wish to know "by what name" the apostles have dared disrupt the existing order. However, for those who have no other hope than a radical change, a truly new thing, an intervention from on high, the mechanicist and closed view of the universe is only one more burden added to the weight of their oppression.

This is why so often in Latino churches (or at least in Latino churches that have not succumbed to the pressure of the mechanicist worldview in the surrounding society), there has always been the belief in an active God and in a world that is open to God's action. As the creed says, God is "maker of heaven and earth." The world as it now exists, "earth" with its physical law principles is indeed God's creation. But that "earth" is not all that God has created and rules. God is also creator and ruler of "heaven," of that which we do not see, of the mystery that intervenes in this "earth" of established orders and predictable results. The miracles in Acts, far from turning it into a distant and incomprehensible book, bring us closer to it, for we are a Church and a community that live by faith and trust in a God who does intervene in our lives and our history.

BEWARE OF GAMALIEL!

Belief in an "open universe" also has its dangers. The main danger lies in thinking that, because God intervenes in history, we are not to take our responsibility within that history too seriously. That is how Gamaliel is sometimes used in our churches. If a controversial issue arises, rather than analyzing the situation and acting responsibly, we say like Gamaliel that if it is a matter of God, we cannot really oppose it, and if it is a human matter, it will fail anyhow. With such an excuse we avoid problems and decisions. With that excuse, we allow injustice to continue rampant in our society.

However, when we use Gamaliel's advice in this fashion we forget that this is not all that he said. Part of his advice is that one ought to avoid "fighting against God." Even though it is true that God's will shall be done, it is also true that we humans can either serve that will or oppose it. God intervenes indeed; but God also intervenes through human action. What in the previous section we called "heaven" is still active, and the will of God will be fulfilled because of that activity; but "earth," the field of human activity, the sphere where natural laws do reign, is also God's creation, and it is our duty to be faithful within it.

When we only listen to the first part of Gamaliel's advice, what we are doing is surrendering to a fatalistic view of the world and of history. Such a view is not biblical, yet it has often led our churches to ignore the world around them—after all, if what is taking place is not God's will, it will be undone. However, the second part of Gamaliel's advice reminds us that God has placed us in this world with a task and a purpose, and it is not enough to believe in miracles and to wait for them. In a way, we ourselves, the Church, are to be the first and most evident of God's miracles leading the world toward the future that God proposes.

THOSE WHO TURN JUSTICE TO WORMWOOD

Much of what was said about the earlier trial before the Council (4:7–22) could be repeated about this other trial. What is at stake is the power of the leaders over the people. If the apostles continue their preaching, the blood of Jesus will come upon these leaders (5:28), who also are jealous for their power, which the apostles seem to subvert (5:17: note that in 5:13 we have been told about the apostles that "the people held them in high esteem"). As in that other case, much of what takes place in the trial and around it reflects situations and responses very similar to those which exist today in the Americas.

What this second trial adds is an example of how the most scrupulous observance of the laws can be used in order to uphold the power of those who are already dominant. The trial is quite formal. The Council neither mentions nor discusses the manner in which Peter and John have been freed from prison, for that is not the issue at hand. Most carefully, the high priest reminds the accused of the previous warning, which opens the way to physical punishment. On the basis of Gamaliel's advice, they decide not to kill the accused, which also convinces them that they are being merciful. However, in the end they have Peter and John flogged, without ever having come to the matter of whether they are guilty or not.

None of this should surprise Latino Christians, as we have lived in places where the very law that was supposed to protect equity and freedom has been used to benefit the powerful. Examples abound. In a certain Central American nation, thanks to the new means of transportation and refrigeration, cattle raising and the large-scale production of fruits, vegetables, and flowers become important and productive businesses. Soon the powerful in the nation, with the support of legal teams, begin claiming the ownership of lands that have been held by peasants for generations. If the peasants try to protect their lands, they are accused of being communist subversives. If they still insist, they are evicted by force. If they appeal to the courts, they find that the best legal teams, the courts, and even the power to legislate, are in the hands of those who covet their lands. The result is a form of legal theft very similar to the legal abuse to which Peter and John were subjected. Popular wisdom acknowledges this situation in traditional sayings such as "*el que hizo la ley hizo la trampa*"—whoever made the law also made the loophole—and "*el que tiene padrino se bautiza*"— whoever has a sponsor gets baptized.

There is another dimension in the trial of Peter and John that also merits attention. The powerful within the Council, those who judge the apostles, are themselves under another power, that of the Roman Empire. At that time, it was up to Roman authorities to determine who among possible candidates would be the high priest of Israel, and therefore, who would occupy the most important positions in the Temple and in the entire Jewish religious structure. The same was true of the economic structures of Judea. If the well-to-do Sadducees collaborated with Rome, this was partly because Rome had the power to enrich or ruin them. Therefore, those who seem to be powerful within the limited context of Judea are not really all that powerful within the wider context of the empire. For that reason their policies must take into account not only the people whom they try to control, but also the Roman authorities that control them. Quite often their interest in controlling the people is related to their fear of the consequences that the actions of the people might bring about, even to the point of provoking an imperial intervention. The manner in which this takes place in Judea may be seen in John 11:48, where the leaders among the Jews (including Caiaphas, who also appears in Acts) declare, "if we let him go on like this, everyone will believe in him, and the Romans will come and destroy both our holy place and our nation." The same concern may be seen in the case of the pagan authorities of Ephesus in 19:40.

The parallelism between this and the conditions in Latin America and throughout the Third World is obvious. We are part of a global system, and the powerful within our own nations can only retain their power if they behave according to the rules of that global system. Rich capitalists exploit their laborers partly to make more money, but also partly to compete with other rich investors who exploit other laborers in other parts of the world. There are also dictators who remain in power because they have the support of foreign powers or of economic interests that benefit from their policies. The situation described in Acts is very similar to our own situation.

Christians should not be surprised by this. The Christian Church has a long and glorious history of martyrs who died precisely because the law was twisted and justice was turned into wormwood. Unfortunately, that history even includes many incidents in which some Christians persecuted others because they did not accept their doctrines, because they subverted their systems, or because in any other way they awakened in the powerful jealousy similar to that which the apostles awakened in the Sadducees and the high priests.

In Latin America, for a long time Protestants were persecuted with supposedly legal subterfuges. In Colombia, vast territories were declared "mission lands," which made it illegal for anyone to preach a faith that was not the one officially recognized by the government. At that time and in those circumstances, many suffered the weight of an unjust law and of a justice turned into wormwood. In many of our countries there existed for a long time laws that limited the civil rights of Protestants: laws having to do with the civil registry, with marriage, with teaching and education, with cemeteries, and so on.

For all these reasons, Christians better than anyone else should be more acutely aware that it is a custom of the human race, sinful as it is, to use supposedly legal systems to silence those who, like Peter and John, say things that the powerful do not like. This should help us resist the fallacy that confuses the will of the powerful with the will of God.

Peter and John were preaching the gospel. They did not preach it in order to provoke jealousy, but simply to be faithful to what the Lord had told them to do.

If this provoked jealousy it was not their fault, but rather the fault of the powerful who were not ready to have their authority questioned. In our day, there are many Peters and many Johns—and many Marys and many Janes—who in a thousand different ways give witness to the gospel. Some preach from the pulpit, others teach in school, others help peasants reclaim their lands, others tend to the sick, others teach how to read. Given the sinful world in which we live—and as we still live in the midst of the passing reign of the present order—these signs of the coming reign of God frequently provoke jealousy and opposition in those who still serve the present reign. The first thing that this text tells us is what the history of the Church in its most glorious moments also tells us: do not be surprised that these things happen. The struggles between the Spirit and Satan to which Peter referred when dealing with Ananias continue to this day. What really should surprise us is lack of opposition, having everyone say that our message is marvelous. When that happens, we better beware, for there is a high probability that we have abandoned the message of the apostles!

But there is more. The apostles "as they left the Council, they rejoiced that they were considered worthy to suffer dishonor for the sake of the name." The normal and natural reaction is that a punishment such as they had suffered should destroy their joy. But this strange community, which is the Church, this community of the Spirit, has the power precisely by the Spirit to rejoice in the midst of tribulation. According to the Gospel of Matthew (16:21–25), it was this that Peter could not understand when Jesus began to speak of his coming sufferings and his death. The way of the cross is absolutely incomprehensible from the purely human natural perspective. But it was precisely that way of the cross that Peter and John were now able to understand thanks to the power of the Holy Spirit. It was that way of the cross that the members of the Council could not understand, for they believed that with threats and floggings they could put an end to the preaching of the apostles, which they considered subversive. It was this that could not be understood by those Roman authorities who later condemned martyrs to the lions. It is this that will never be understood by those who imagine that the preaching of the gospel and the commitment to live its fullness is a movement like any other, and that laws, punishments and threats will suffice to stop it. Gamaliel was right after all: this work is of God, and no one will be able to overthrow it!

E. HELLENISTS AND HEBREWS (6:1–7)

We come now to the moment in which conflicts arise within the early Church regarding the distribution of support for the widows, and in response to that situation seven men are elected to supervise that distribution. Luke does not tell us exactly when this happened, but says simply "during those days" (6:1). The fact that there already existed a "daily distribution of food" may be an indication that this was already sometime after Pentecost, for support to the needy had now evolved to the point that it had become a daily practice.[64] Some suggest that at least six years have taken place between Pentecost and the events that this text narrates.[65] Such a chronology fits with the rest of the book and with what we know about Paul's chronology.

Given the structures and the practices of society at that time, many of the needy would be widows. In a society in which women depended on men for their support, widows found themselves in difficult economic conditions.[66] It is for this reason that the Old Testament constantly reaffirms the obligation to look after widows (Deut. 14:29, 24:19, 26:12; Isa. 1:17; etc.). In the Christian community, as the breach between those who believed in Jesus and the other Jews became wider, Christian widows would find themselves increasingly in need to appeal to the church for their support (see James 1:27).[67] Naturally, this was not true in every case, but only in the case of those widows who did not have sons or other relatives who supported them.

The conflict arises because there are in the Christian community two groups: the "Hellenists" and the "Hebrews." Here the word "Hellenist" does not refer to people with any particular contact with Greece, but rather to Jews who grew up in the Diaspora, away from Palestine, and who therefore find themselves more at ease with Greek, which was the lingua franca of the eastern Mediterranean basin, than with Aramaic.[68] In contrast the "Hebrews" are Jews from Palestine, whose language is Aramaic—even though at that point this

---

64. There is an interesting interpretation of this passage, but one that has not been generally accepted, in N. Walter, "Apostelgeschichte 6.1 und die Anfänge der Urgemeinde in Jerusalem," *NTSt*, 29 (1983), 370–93. According to Walter, the dispute did not take place within the church, but in the community at large, and the response of the church in support of the Hellenistic widows helped the church make inroads into the Hellenistic community.

65. Rubén Darío García, *La Iglesia, el pueblo del Espíritu* (Barcelona: Ediciones Don Bosco, 1983), pp. 21–22, 29.

66. In Jerusalem, as a way of applying the laws of the Old Testament regarding the care of widows, the custom had been established that a widow could remain living in the house of her dead husband, and using his goods, for as long as she remained a widow.

67. As time went by, such widows who were dependent on the Church were given specific functions, to the point that they became a special category among functionaries in the Church (I Tim. 5:3–16; Ignatius, *Ad Smyr.*, 13.1; Polycarp, 4.3; etc.). In these various texts the widows are still women who have lost their husbands. Later the very title of "widow" seems to have become connected with a function of a woman in the Church, who may simply have been unmarried. On the manner in which the orders of deacons and widows intertwine, see Joseph Viteau, "L'institution des diacres et des veuves Actes 6:1–10; 8:4–40; 21:8," *RHE*, 22 (1926), 513–37.

68. Henry J. Cadbury, "Note 7. The Hellenists," in F. J. F. Jackson and K. Lake, eds., *The Beginnings of Christianity*, vol. 5 (London: Macmillan, 1933), pp. 599–74; E. C. Blackman, "The Hellenists of Acts 6:1," *ExpTim*, 48 (1936–37), 524–25; Walter Grundman, "Das Problem des Hellenistischen Christentums innerhalb der Jerusalemer Urgemeinde," *ZntW*, 38 (1939), 445–73; C. F. D. Moule, "Once more, who were the Hellenists?", *ExpTim*, 70 (1958–59), 100–2.

language was usually called "Hebrew." Whether members of one or the other group knew Hebrew or not depended on the religious instruction they had received. At any rate, in Palestine itself the "Hebrews" believed themselves to be better Jews, and they viewed the "Hellenists" with suspicion, for they seemed to have accepted customs and traditions that were alien to Israel.

In spite of the prejudices of the "Hebrews" the truth was that many of the "Hellenists" were Jews of profound religious conviction. This was even more so as many of them were elderly people who went to Jerusalem in order to spend their final days and to be interred in the Holy Land. For the same reason, there were in Jerusalem many Hellenistic widows, and the same was probably true of the young Church.

The conflict does not break out into open division, but is limited to complaints. This is enough for "the Twelve"[69] to take the matter seriously and call a meeting of the entire congregation. Because it was at the feet of the Twelve that the offerings were placed for their distribution (4:35), it is to be expected that the complaints were in fact against their management. It is now they who ask for help, requesting that seven others be charged with that function. The phrase "wait on tables," which is employed to describe the function of these seven (6:2), may well mean what it does today, namely to serve or distribute food, perhaps in a communal meal; but it may also mean the distribution of money, for "the tables" were also the place in which economic transactions took place, and therefore very often the management of money was called serving at the tables.

The Twelve, even though they were Galileans and therefore were considered second-class Jews by those from Jerusalem, were "Hebrews," for they had grown up in Palestine and their language was Aramaic. Therefore, it is not surprising that the needs of the Hellenists were not properly understood or met. On hearing the complaints, the Twelve asked the congregation to elect seven men. The only necessary qualification for these seven is that they be "full of the Spirit and of wisdom." Their function would be to manage the distribution, whereas the function of the Twelve would continue being "prayer" and "serving the word."

It is interesting to note that the seven elected all have Greek names. About Procorus, Nicanor, Timon, and Parmenas all that we know is their names. Nicolaus, according to the text, was "a proselyte of Antioch."[70] This means that he was not even a Jew by birth, but by conversion. On the other hand, Stephen becomes the main character in the rest of this chapter and the next, and about Philip and his ministry we learn in chapter 8 and much later in 21:8–9.

The fact that the "seven" seem to be Hellenists has led some scholars to suggest that what actually happened was that there was a separate governing

---

69. This is the only case in which Acts refers to the apostles as "the Twelve."

70. On the possible later history of Nicanor see, Adolf von Harnack, "The sect of the Nicolaitans and Nicolaus, the deacon in Jerusalem," *JR*, 3 (1923), 505–38; Bruce, *Acts*, pp. 129–30.

body organized to manage the affairs of the growing Hellenistic membership, while "the Twelve" would continue directing the affairs of the Aramaic-speaking community.[71]

The seven receive their office by the laying on of hands.[72] Although the practice of laying hands on a person appears sometimes in the Old Testament (see Num. 27:18), this is the first time that it is mentioned in the New Testament as a sign of conferring office.

Traditionally the seven have been called "deacons," and it has been thought that what we have here is the beginning of the diaconate.[73] It is true that here they are said to be responsible for the daily *diakonia* (6:1), and that the verb the NRSV translates as "waiting [on tables]" (6:2) is *diakonein*. But it is also true that the function the Twelve reserved for themselves is described as the *diakonia* of the word (6:4). Also, nowhere else in the New Testament is any of these seven called a "deacon." Therefore, it is doubtful that this text really refers to the founding of the diaconate.[74]

The passage ends with a brief summary (6:7). What this adds to the previous narrative is the conversion of "many of the priests." Up to this point, Luke has spoken of the "chief priests," who have opposed the preaching of the apostles. However, it has been estimated that by this time there were more than seven thousand priests in Jerusalem, most of whom lived in extreme poverty,[75] and therefore very distant in the social hierarchy from those who tried Peter and John in the Council. Perhaps Luke adds this note about the many priests in order to indicate that, now that the apostles are exclusively dedicated

---

71. Thus, for instance, Josep Rius-Camps, *El camino de Pablo a la Misión a los paganos* (Madrid: Cristiandad, 1984), p. 27, suggests that what was created was "a double administration. The twelve will for the time being be in charge of Hebrew community; the seven will be in charge of the administration of the communities from the Diaspora." The same is suggested by P. Gächter, *Petrus and seine Zeit* (Innsbruck: Tyrolia-Verlag, 1958), pp. 105–54, adding that later another seven "Hebrews" were elected and that these are the "elders" mentioned in 11:30.

72. The Greek text does not make it clear whether it was the apostles or the entire congregation who laid their hands on the seven. A grammatically literal translation would seem to imply that it was the entire congregation, whereas the thrust of the passage and the flow of the narrative would lead to the manner in which the NRSV translates the sentence, saying that it was the apostles who laid their hands on the seven.

73. This is affirmed in ancient times by Irenaeus (*Adv. haer.* 1.26, 3.12, 4.15), Cyprian (*Ep.* 3.3), and Eusebius (*Hist. Eccl.* 6.43).

74. Stephanus Bihel, "De septem diaconis (Act 6:1-7)," *Ant*, 3 (1928), 129–50; Hans Laurer, "Die 'Diakonie' im Neuen Testament," *NkZ*, 42 (1931), 325–26; Iglesias, "El libro . . . ," 748–51, 934–37; Karl L. Schmidt, "Amt und Aemter im Neuen Testament," *TZ*, 1 (1945), 309–11; P. Gaechter, "Die Sieben (Apg. 6:1-6)," *ZkT*, 74 (1952), 129–66.

75. According to Josephus, *Ant.* 20.181, some even died of starvation due to their exploitation and oppression by the chief priests.

to the "service of the word," they are able to have a greater impact among other "Hebrews."

PLURALISM IN THE CHURCH

This passage leads us to one of the main problems and perhaps the greatest opportunity facing the Spanish-speaking church, both in the United States and in Latin America. These are the issues posed by pluralism within the Church.

In the United States many Latino Christians belong to denominations in which their own culture is a minority, and which reflect customs, structures, worship practices, and so on, that are alien to much of Latino culture. In such cases, such Latinos are like the Hellenists of our text, for they belong to a church that has traditionally existed within another culture and is still dominated by those representing that culture—the "Hebrews," so to speak.

In Latin America the issues are often posed in a different way. There are some churches where those who lead and rule are mostly Spanish-speaking people, members of the dominant culture, whereas those who belong to the original cultures of the hemisphere are marginalized, and their own culture finds little expression in the worship and life of the church. In such cases, those of us who speak Spanish are the Hebrews, and the Hellenists are the others. It is no wonder that many such churches have attained limited growth—as would have happened if "the Twelve" had refused to listen to the complaints of the Hellenists, and to share authority with them.

Frequently, both in the United States and in Latin America, such situations lead to quarrels and divisions. Perhaps the first thing to learn from the passage we are studying is that the leaders of the church listen to the complaints of those who suffer injustice. They do not claim that these are unimportant matters, or the feelings of a small group of malcontents, or the manipulations of a particular clique in order to grab power. There is an injustice, the Twelve learn of it, and they seek a remedy, even though this requires acknowledging that the manner in which they have distributed resources is not perfect, and even though it may lead to a sharing of power.

As a result, seven men are elected in order to manage the daily distribution, that is, to manage the resources of the church. Significantly, all the ones elected have Hellenistic names. In our churches today, we often try to deal with similar problems of injustice by placing in a position of relative authority one or two token members of whatever group has been marginalized in the hope that this will satisfy those who complain. In other words, there is an attempt to solve the "problem" by means of a symbolic presence. What the church in Acts does is very different. Because the members of the group that suffers injustice are those who best know how such injustice functions, it is they who receive the authority to manage the resources of the church!

The vision behind all this follows directly from the events of Pentecost. In view of what we were taught in chapter 2, it is clear that the "problem" of pluralism in the Church is not the work of the Hellenists, but of the Holy Spirit of

God. The Church is a community of people representing different cultures, traditions and customs, not because some Johnny-come-latelies have joined it, but because inclusivity is the work and the purpose of God. Therefore, the English-speaking church in the United States, if it really believes in the Spirit poured out in Pentecost, cannot think that the Hispanic presence is a "problem." Nor can the Spanish-speaking church in Latin America think that the *quichés,* the *aymaras,* the *quechuas,* the *mapuches,* the *tobos,* or others are a "problem." The "problem," if there is one, is the result of the subversive inclusivity of the Holy Spirit.

The proper response to such a "problem" should be obvious: it is necessary to give those who would otherwise not be heard a decisive voice in all matters pertaining to the life of the Church. This is what the church in Acts does. This is what the Church must do today if it is to be open to what the Holy Spirit has done among us.

The same may be said with reference to missionary leadership in the Latin American churches. There are situations in which a church has found it very difficult to free itself from the control of foreign missionaries who deserve all the respect due to founders, but who have not known how to follow the example of "the Twelve," giving a place of authority and responsibility to their Latin American colleagues. Furthermore, sometimes the control over economic resources from abroad is employed to perpetuate authority systems established in the early days of the mission work. In such cases, the "problem" is not the nationals who complain that the structures of the Church no longer fit the present-day situation. The problem is rather in those structures themselves and in their inflexibility. In such a case, as in the case of the widows in Jerusalem, the only way to move toward a solution is to give more authority precisely to those who have been left aside.

There is no doubt this is a dangerous "solution." In Palestine there was much prejudice against the Hellenists. Many of them had recently arrived, and they were regarded with the supercilious contempt that is so often directed at recent arrivals, much as happens in the United States with immigrants from Latin America. Furthermore, it was generally thought that the Hellenists were not as good Jews as the "Hebrews." This raised the suspicion of the supposedly more orthodox. Because it is clearly attested in Scripture that the welfare of the land depends on the faithfulness of the people, the more nationalistic elements feared that the Hellenists were the ultimate cause of the difficult political circumstances in which the country found itself.

But there is much more. As we continue reading the Book of Acts, we discover that the decision with regard to the widows, apparently taken for a simple reason of justice, was of great importance for the mission of the Church. Up to that point, the Church had been led by the "Hebrews," especially by those who had come with Jesus from Galilee. Had the Church never broken out of that framework, it would have remained one of the many messianic sects that first-century Judaism produced. But in the very act of opening itself to the Hellenists, the Church opened itself to a portion of the community that would serve as a bridge for the mission to the Gentiles. Note that although the Twelve think that the "service of the word" will be reserved for them, immediately after this story it is Stephen (one of the "seven") who proclaims the word, and gives the highest witness to it with his own life. Indeed, Stephen, who is not supposed to be preaching at all, preaches the longest sermon in the entire Book of Acts! As a consequence of the death of Stephen, the followers of Jesus—especially the Hellenists—scatter, and that leads to a further expansion of the mission. Immediately after Stephen, it is Philip, another of the "seven," who takes center stage in leading the gospel first to Samaria and then to the Ethiopian eunuch. All of this prepares the mission to the Gentiles, which will be the subject of much of the rest of the book.

This points to the very close connection between justice and mission. A church cannot be truly missionary if it does not do justice to those who come to it as a result of that mission. Being a community of the Spirit, which implies being an inclusive community, is an indispensable requirement for being a missionary community. Even though the apostles did not know it, the future of the Church was in those Hellenists whom the Church had been slighting. Likewise, it is possible and even probable that the future of the Church is in the hands of those who until now have been left aside, and are now calling for their rights within the Church. (And all that has been said with reference to those who are marginalized by reason of their culture or language must also be said about those who are marginalized by reason of their social class, their education, their age, their sex, or their physical limitations.)

Finally, it is important to note that this text points to the manner in which we are to read the entire Book of Acts. The apostles seek to keep for themselves "the service of the word"; but the Spirit has other plans, and soon it is Stephen and Philip who are performing that ministry. What was done in 6:1–7 amplified the mission of the Church and therefore it was a wise decision; but not all that was done did receive the imprint of the Holy Spirit. The story in Acts is that of a Spirit who is constantly calling the Church to a new obedience in such a way that, although we can learn from the obedience of times past, we cannot limit ourselves to it. What would have happened to the Church if Stephen and Philip had said, "No, our ministry has to do with tables, and not with preaching?"

An example of how this may be relevant today is the entire matter of the role of women in the Church. The apostles asked that seven men be named. Even supposing that this was the founding of the diaconate, does this mean that only men can be deacons? Certainly not, for already in the New Testament there is the case of women holding that function (see Rom. 16:1). Or, if today we are trying to respond and to solve issues having to do with the oppression of women, does the story in Acts mean that today we should name a committee of men, with no women, in order to represent them? Certainly not, for the same Spirit who corrected that aspect of the apostles' decision that precluded Stephen and Philip from preaching may today be correcting the decision to have only men elected.

F. STEPHEN (6:8–8:3)

1. His Arrest (6:8–12)[76]

Without any indication of how much time has passed after the election of Stephen to serve at the tables, the first thing that Luke tells us is that Stephen "did great wondrous and signs among the people" and that he debated with some of the other Jews. Note that it was not Stephen who began the dispute. This may perhaps indicate that Stephen did not decide to preach on his own, against what had been decided by the Twelve, but that it was his opponents who forced him to it. Verse 9, where those opponents are named, is ambiguous, for it is not clear whether there is only one synagogue called "of the Freedmen," which included Cyrenians, Alexandrians, and others—which is how the NRSV translates the passage—or whether there were more than one synagogue involved—perhaps even as many as five.[77]

In any case, what is significant is that those who oppose the leadership of Stephen are not "Hebrews," but people whom the locals would have called "Hellenists." Now opposition no longer comes from the Temple and from the powerful scribes and Sadducees, but rather from other Hellenistic Jews. That opposition then works on the basis of lies and bribes that "stirred up the people as well as the elders and the scribes." This is almost the first time in Acts that "the people" oppose Christians and take the side of the religious leaders. (The one earlier example is 4:27, where the subject is the death of Jesus.) It is these rioting people who take Stephen before the Council, which apparently is already gathered for some other reason. The charges against Stephen are essentially two, for he is accused of blaspheming against the Temple and the Law. In 6:11 the witnesses say, "We have heard him speak blasphemous words against Moses and God"; in 6:13, they add that Stephen "never stops saying things against this holy place and the law"; and in 6:14 they insist that they "have heard him say that this Jesus of Nazareth will destroy this place and will change the customs that Moses handed on to us." It is interesting to note that the words about the destruction of the Temple, which the other Gospel writers include in their narrative about the passion of Jesus (Matt. 26:61, 27:40; Mark 14:58, 15:29; see John 2:19), Luke does not include in his Gospel, but rather

---

76. Iglesias, "El libro . . . ," *Christus,* 5 (1938), 1115–25, *Christus,* 7 (1939), 175–77; Marcel Simon, *St. Stephen and the Hellenists in the Primitive Church* (New York: Longmans, Green & Co., 1958); W. Foerster, "Stephanus und die Urgemeinde," in K. Jansen, *Dienst unter dem Wort* (Götersloh: Bertelsmann, 1953), pp. 9–30.

77. An additional problem is that four of the groups mentioned have to do with places, and that therefore the "Freedmen" do not seem to fit. Some have suggested that the original actually said "Libyans," and that the word that took its place was a copyist's error. The only basis for such a conjecture is the ancient Armenian version, which does say "Libyans." A possible solution is that the "Freedmen" may have been Jews from Rome, who had been taken there as captives when the Romans conquered the area, and who had now returned from Rome after being freed.

reserves them for the charges against Stephen. In any case, it has been shown that the opposition to the Temple in Jerusalem during the first century was not an exclusive theme of Christians, but something that existed much more widely within the Jewish community of the time.[78]

It is also interesting to note that in the arrest of Stephen there is a combination of legal formalities with other elements that have more the characteristics of a riot. Stephen's enemies bribe false witnesses, who are then the ones who appear and accuse him before the Council. But they also stir up the people, the elders, and the scribes (that is, both the common people and their more respected leaders), and it is these who take Stephen before the Council. The significance of this is that, now that the people are predisposed against Stephen, the Council has no need to act with the caution that it employed earlier with Peter and John, who did enjoy the favor of the people.

2. The Trial (6:13–7:56)

Verses 13 and 14 summarize the formal charges against Stephen. As already stated, these charges are twofold: blasphemy against the Temple claiming that Jesus will destroy it, and blasphemy against the Law, claiming that Jesus will change "the customs that Moses handed on to us."

When those who were part of the Council looked upon Stephen, they "saw that his face was like the face of an angel" (6:15). Possibly by including this assertion Luke is establishing a parallelism between Stephen and Moses, whose face shone when he descended from Sinai (Ex. 34:29–30). Jewish historian Flavius Josephus, writing roughly at the same time, says that the face of Joseph shone as a sign of the presence of the Spirit in him.[79] Stephen speaks with authority because, like Moses and Joseph, he has been with God.

To the question of the high priest, Stephen responds with a long speech on the history of Israel.[80] This is the longest speech in the entire Book of Acts, occupying roughly five percent of the book. It is not necessary to stop to consider each of the events in the history of Israel to which Stephen refers, but it is important to notice the manner in which Stephen himself interprets that history.

---

78. Oscar Cullmann, "L'opposition contre le temple de Jérusalem, motif commun de la théologie johannique et du monde ambiant," *NTSt*, 5 (1958–59), 157–73.

79. *Ant.* 14.8–9.

80. There has been much discussion regarding the structure of this speech as well as its sources. See, as basic bibliography: J. F. J. Foakes, "Stephen's speech in Acts," *JBL*, 49 (1930), 283–86; C. M. Menchini, *Il Discorso de S. Stefano Protomartire Nella Letteratura e Predicazione Cristiana Primitiva* (Rome: Servi di Maria, 1951); A. F. J. Kiln, "Stephen's speech—Acts 7:2–53," *NTSt*, 4 (1957–58), 25–31; M. H. Scharlemann, "Acts 7:2–53. Stephen's speech: A Lucan creation?", *Conc*, 4 (1978), 52–57; J. Dupont, "La structure oratoire de discours d'Etienne (Actes 7)," *Bib*, 66 (1985), 153–67. On the purpose of the speech and the relationship between that purpose and its structure see Bruce, *Acts*, p. 161; I. Howard Marshall, *The Acts of the Apostles* (Leicester: Inter-Varsity Press, 1980), pp. 131–32.

Verses 2–8 tell the story of Abraham. About that story, Luke has little to say that is new.[81] Abraham is the prototype that establishes the character of the chosen people as a pilgrim people, which will be a central theme throughout the speech. This is the significance of the words "he did not give him any of it as heritage, not even a foot's length" (7:5).[82]

After the rapid summary of the story of the patriarchs in verse 8, verses 9–16 deal with the story of Joseph. The main point that Stephen underscores here appears in verse 9, where we are told that the patriarchs, out of jealousy, sold Joseph, but that God was with him. Jointly with the theme of the pilgrim people, this other theme of being rejected by humans but approved by God is central throughout this speech. (About the burial of Joseph's brothers in Shechem, the Old Testament does not say a word. According to Josephus[83] they were buried in the cave of Machpelah.) Verses 13–43 are the heart of the speech, where Stephen tells the story of Moses. What he wishes to emphasize is the parallelism between Moses and Jesus, for Stephen is accusing his own ancestors of having done with Moses what more recently the leaders of the people have done with Jesus.[84] The story of Moses shows how the people of Israel have repeatedly rejected those who were sent to them. Thus rejected, Moses had to flee to Midian when he slew the Egyptian. However, as Stephen sees matters, "it was this Moses whom they rejected . . . whom God now sent as both ruler and liberator" (7:35). After this veiled allusion to the case of Jesus, Stephen continues his narrative, pointing out that the people of Israel have always lived between faith and apostasy. What is more, the very people who had been liberated by Moses continued rejecting him, for "in their hearts they turned back to Egypt" (7:39) when they asked Aaron to make gods whom they could adore. (The quotation from Amos 5:25–27 that appears in 7:42–43 is taken from the Septuagint, and for that reason does not exactly match what appears in the present translations of the Old Testament.)

It is in verse 44 that the speech takes a new turn, which will lead to Stephen's martyrdom. There he begins attacking the Temple and its religion.[85]

---

81. There is a small difference between what Stephen says and what may be read in Genesis. According to Stephen, God called Abraham "when he was in Mesopotamia, before he lived in Haran." In Genesis 12:1, the call takes place in Haran. This change in the story, however, does not seem to have originated with Stephen, Luke, or the early Christian community, for it can also be found in Philo of Alexandria, *De mig.* 62.66 and in Josephus, *Ant.* 1.154.

82. This not exactly true, for in Genesis 23 we are told that Abraham bought the cave of Machpelah in order to bury Sarah.

83. *Ant.* 2.198–99.

84. L. de Lorenzi, *Mosè e il Cristo Salvatore nel discorso di Stefano* (Rome: Pont. Univ. Lateranensis, 1959).

85. A. Pindherle, "Stefano el il templo 'manufatto,'" *RicRel*, 2 (1926), 326–36; M. Simon, "Saint Stephen and the Jerusalem Temple," *JEH*, 2 (1951), 127–42. Cp. M. Simon,

All that Israel had in the desert was the tent of testimony, built according to the instructions that God had given Moses. What David set out to build (7:46) was still not a temple, but a "dwelling place" or tabernacle.[86] Then comes the moment in which, according to Stephen, Israel lost its way: "but it was Solomon who built a house for him" (7:47). According to Stephen, the God of Israel is a pilgrim God always marching before the people, who cannot be circumscribed to a single place. Above everything else, Stephen is convinced that God "does not dwell in houses made with human hands." The religion of the Temple claims exactly the opposite: it seeks to confine God to a temple made by human hands.

All of this provides the basis for the harsh words in 7:1–53 with which the speech ends. God gave Abraham circumcision as a sign of the covenant; but these children of Abraham are "uncircumcised in heart and ears." Like their ancestors, they resist the Holy Spirit and they persecute the prophets.[87] It is here in verse 52 that we have the only explicitly christological reference in the entire speech: the prophets killed "those who foretold the coming of the Righteous One, and now you have become his betrayers and murderers." However, even though this is the only explicit reference to Jesus, it is clear that the entire speech has been constructed in order to show a double parallelism: (a) Joseph / Moses / prophets = Jesus; (b) Joseph's brothers / Israel in Egypt / those who killed the prophets = Stephen's audience.

At the end of this speech one might ask whether Stephen has really responded to the charges against him. That question, to which some exegetes respond in the negative, has led to a long discussion about the origin of the speech. Some suggest that Luke took it from some source that originally had nothing to do with the trial of Stephen. Others suggest that the speech itself does have to do with the trial, but that Luke incorporated materials from other sources.[88] All of this, however, is not germane. According to Luke, Stephen has been accused of attacking the Temple and criticizing Moses. His speech accepts the first charge and rejects the second. The Temple "made by hands" has led Israel to abandon the God of the "tent of testimony" in the desert, the pil-

---

"Retour du Christ et reconstruction du Temple dans la pensée chrétienne primitive," in *Mélanges Goguel*, pp. 247–57.

86. This verse involves a difficult textual problem. Most manuscripts (and the best among them) say that David was to provide a dwelling place for "the house" of Jacob. Other manuscripts, fewer in number and of lesser quality, say that the dwelling place was for "the God" of Jacob. The NRSV follows the majority of the manuscript tradition. The NIV and others say "the God of Jacob." At any rate, the point that Stephen wishes to make is that what David wanted to build was not, strictly speaking, a temple, but still a tabernacle or temporary dwelling place.

87. On the subject of the persecution of the prophets, see H. J. Schoeps, *Die jüdischen Prophetenmorde* (Tübingen: J. C. B. Mohr, 1950).

88. Haenchen, *Acts*, pp. 286–89, offers a good summary and discussion of the various theories proposed.

grim God who leads the people. That is not surprising, for already in the times of Moses (and even before, in the case of Joseph, and later in persecuting the prophets), the children of Israel have acted in similar fashion. Those who really reject Moses are not Stephen and those who hold to his beliefs, but rather those who accuse him. Moses, rejected by his own people but raised by God to become ruler and liberator, announced and in his very life prefigured Jesus, "the Righteous One, and now you have become his betrayers and murderers."

The initial reaction of those who hear is dramatically described in verse 54, as a sort of mute rage: "they became enraged and ground their teeth." But Stephen does not seem to be paying any attention to them, for he has a vision of the glory of God, with Jesus at God's right hand, and simply continues speaking and telling what he sees. In declaring, "I see the heavens opened and the Son of Man standing at the right hand of God," Stephen is affirming what the rest of his speech has already implied: that, just like Moses, Jesus has been raised by God in order to be made "ruler and liberator."

3. Stephen's Death: Beginning of Persecution (7:57–8:3)

This is just too much. Those who hear Stephen cover their ears and shout him down. This may seem strange to us today, for covering one's ears when someone speaks is a sign of a spoiled child. However, at that time it was the prescribed reaction when someone heard blasphemy, for by covering one's ears one prevented such blasphemies from entering into one's mind. What this means is that, without further discussion, it has been decided that Stephen is indeed guilty of blasphemy.

The text says that they "all rushed together against him." There is no formal verdict in this trial. There were precise and clear laws about how the Council was supposed to issue verdicts. This was particularly true in capital cases. What is more, at that time the Council did not have the authority to decree the death penalty. Therefore, what Luke describes is not a trial culminating in a verdict, but a trial that begins with a riot, includes a rather antagonistic speech by the accused, and ends with another riot. Although Stephen is stoned to death as was prescribed in ancient times, and although there are "witnesses" (7:58), what is taking place is not an execution, but a lynching.[89]

Whatever the case may be, Stephen's death is exemplary, for he imitates the manner in which Jesus dies according to Luke himself, commending his spirit to God (Luke 23:46) and praying for those who kill him (Luke 23:34).

---

89. Even beyond the bare fact that the Council could not impose a death penalty, there are many details to indicate that what took place was not the application of that penalty as Jewish law understood it. What Luke describes here is a scene in which Stephen, apparently standing, is stoned by various people until he falls on his knees and finally dies. The manner in which the death penalty was prescribed was very different, for the accused was thrown from a cliff, and then a heavy stone was thrown or laid on his chest, so that if he had not died from the fall, he would suffocate. See Haenchen, Acts, p. 296.

At the scene of Stephen's martyrdom, as in passing (7:58), we hear for the first time of a "young man named Saul," who will become an important character in the rest of the narrative. The word "young" does not mean that he was almost a child, for it was employed for any man who had not reached full maturity. Therefore, Saul (Paul) might even have been as old as thirty. Although this Saul does not appear to be more than a spectator at Stephen's death (7:58 and 8:1), he becomes a dominant figure in the ensuing persecution. It may be significant to note that among those who plotted against Stephen were the people from Cilicia (6:9). The capital of Cilicia was Tarsus, whence Saul hailed. Therefore, it is quite possible that his participation in the entire process went further than is usually assumed.

In 8:1–3, the order of the narrative is somewhat confusing, for first we are told that persecution broke out and Christians scattered, then (8:2) that there was great lamentation over Stephen's death, and finally that Saul persecuted the church. Were we to be telling the same story today, the order would be different, mentioning first the lamentation over Stephen's death, and then matters having to do with persecution. In ancient times stories were often told as Luke does here, introducing a subject before finishing the other one, so as to keep the reader's attention. At any rate, there are here several elements worthy of mention. In the first place, that "all except the apostles were scattered" is a hyperbole, for Luke himself declares (8:3) that Saul was going from house to house imprisoning those who had not left; and later on (9:26–27) he tells about a continuing Christian community in Jerusalem. Apparently, persecution broke out mainly against Hellenistic Christians, and not against the "Hebrews," and therefore the apostles as well as Barnabas and others were able to remain in Jerusalem. Second, verse 2 confirms that Stephen's death was not a formal execution, but a lynching, for it was forbidden to bury or to mourn over anyone who had been stoned to death,[90] but Stephen is both buried and mourned. Finally, one should note that what Saul did was not to kill the Christians, but to take them to prison—as a way of ensuring their presence at trial.

WHEN THE ENEMY CALLS US TO OBEDIENCE

The previous section told us how the congregation elected seven (apparently) Hellenists among its members, with the clear indication that their function was not to preach, but rather to manage. The present passage shows that, even though the decision to elect these seven was wise, the Holy Spirit had designs different than those of the Twelve, for immediately after the story of the election of the seven we are told that one of them is witnessing and eventually preaching.

There is much to be learned from this passage. The first is that the Church is a historical reality. Being a historical reality means that it evolves with history, so

---

90. Mishnah, *Sanh.* 6.5-6.

that what was wise and correct at the time is to serve, not as a chain tying the Church to the past, but rather as a springboard toward the future. If anything has limited the mission of the Church throughout its history it has been precisely in the failure to understand this. When good traditions become an excuse for not being obedient today, they cease being good. This was one of the central themes of the Protestant Reformation, and most recently it has become important in the Catholic reformation since the Second Vatican Council, and therefore it should not seem necessary to say much about it. However, in practice it is necessary to insist on this point, for in many of our Protestant Latino churches a tradition has been developing—sometimes the very recent tradition of what happened in the last fifty years, or what was taught to us by those who preached the gospel to us—that sometimes makes it difficult for us to respond to the challenges of the day. When a controversial matter comes up, we say, "That is not the mission of the Church," and with that we think we have solved the problem. Had Stephen been in our shoes, perhaps he would have said, "I was not elected to preach, but to manage. I have nothing to do with such matters."

In the case of Stephen something very interesting takes place. It is not his fellow believers, but his opponents disputing against him, who impel him to witness and to preach. According to the Church his function was purely administrative; but the challenge from outside forces him to widen that function. Stephen's vocation, his calling, comes to him from the Church only up to a point; his final vocation comes to him from those outside.

Furthermore, those from "outside" have some things in common with him. Stephen was elected as a leader in order to respond to the inner crisis of the Church because of the presence of Hellenists who were not sufficiently understood by the "Hebrews." He was elected to do justice and give representation to the Hellenists. His election, and that of the other six, is a sign that the Church is becoming more open to the Hellenists. But now those who dispute with Stephen and come to the point of bribing others who will bring false witness against him are Hellenists—that is, they are Jews from the Diaspora, from Cyrene, Alexandria, and elsewhere. It is possible to understand this when we remember that in Jerusalem the Hellenists were eyed with suspicion, and that therefore non-Christian Hellenists would be particularly interested in proving that they would not allow themselves to be "contaminated." The more the Church opens itself to the Hellenists, the more will other Hellenists who have not become Christians seek to show their Jewish orthodoxy, mostly by opposing Christianity. This is what stands at the root of the disputes and accusations against Stephen.

On the other hand, even unwittingly and unwillingly, these opponents are used as an instrument of the Holy Spirit in order to call Stephen to his vocation. The Twelve as well as the rest of the Church seem to have believed that all that the Spirit wanted from Stephen was that he be a good manager, serving at the tables. The Spirit, however, had other plans, and through these opponents called Stephen to the glorious distinction of being the first Christian martyr—the first to proclaim the gospel, not only by word, but also by shedding his own blood.

Is it possible that today the Holy Spirit may be acting in similar ways? We all know the challenges that are being posed to Christians and to the Church by the contemporary world. Sometimes the challenges and calls come to us from people or groups that look upon the Church with sympathy and support our work. Sometimes they come from people and groups that wish to hinder our tasks. In both cases, the question we must ask is not what might be the motivation of those who challenge us to undertake new forms of mission, but rather what might be the will of God. Who knows if, as in the case of Stephen, God could be using even enemies in order to lead us to our vocation!

Let us see a few examples. In a large city in the United States, three or four drug addicts begin visiting a small Latino church. The pastor and the members of the church welcome them, for that is what the gospel has taught them to do, but they do not worry about trying to find out who they are or where they come from. The neighbors, however, are upset. Some among them who have always opposed the church begin saying that the church is now being used for drug traffic. The police intervene. There are investigations. The pastor is taken to the police station and questioned. Throughout that entire process, both the pastor and several of the members of the church begin inquiring about drug trafficking in the barrio, and especially about the life of those three or four whose presence caused the initial suspicion. Slowly they become more interested and more involved in the issue. At the end, as a result of a very painful conflict, they have in the church a center for the rehabilitation of drug addicts, and they buy a neighboring house where they provide shelter for some of their clients. Through that ministry that little church receives new life, and becomes a center of renewal and hope in its community. Still many of those who presented the initial accusation are hostile to the church; but even unwittingly, they were used by the Holy Spirit in order to help that church discover God's will.

Another example: In a certain Latin American country, an evangelist with little schooling, but great devotion, begins visiting a small village every week, traveling through the woods on horseback. His only purpose is to organize a church in that community. Slowly that purpose is being achieved. But in the country itself there is much social and political conflict. The peasants are being organized in order to reclaim their lands; and in response death squadrons kill them and their leaders. In this particular village, some peasants fear that the visits of the pastor, and the small church that is beginning to gather every week, will be seen as subversive, and that the blame will fall on the entire village. They visit the authorities who in turn visit the church to make sure that they "stay in line." During that visit, in harsh and even abusive terms, some of the government officials inquire about the pastor's preaching, "Do you preach about what you revolutionaries call 'social justice'? What do you tell them about Amos and the prophets? What do you tell them about life here on earth?" In the very process of interrogation, the pastor becomes convinced that the Holy Spirit is calling him to widen his ministry and his message. He decides to move to the village, to live with the peasants, and to organize an agricultural cooperative.

Quite possibly, his story might end like Stephen's; but it is clear that those who sought to silence him actually called him to widen his message and his program of service.

An interesting element in both of these examples, as well as in the story of Stephen, is that in an odd way those who become enemies are the ones who should be closer to those whom they accuse. In the case of Stephen, they are members of the Hellenistic synagogues. In the case of the city in the United States, they are all Latinos from the same barrio. In the case of the village in Latin America, they are peasants from the same village. There is a saying in Spanish, "There is no worse wedge than one taken from the same wood." What often happens, as it did with the Hellenistic Jews who persecuted Stephen, with the neighbors who accused the pastor in the barrio, and with the peasants who called the attention of the authorities to the pastor, is that these people are also oppressed by others. Behind the Jewish elite—even the most powerful among them—was the Roman Empire. Likewise, many who oppress others are in turn oppressed themselves. Therefore, it is no wonder that the opposition often comes from those who should be allies. And still, in a wondrous way God employs that opposition to lead us to our vocation.

Finally, let us not forget that Stephen saw the heavens open and Jesus at the right hand of God, nor that Stephen prayed for those who killed him. The first means that, even amidst all of these conflicts and many others that might arise, we know that the final victory is ours. Jesus, to whom we witness and by whom we do whatever we do, is already at the right hand of God. He is almighty Lord of Lords and King of Kings. No one who might oppose us has greater power than He does. That is precisely why Stephen can forgive his enemies. He has seen Jesus at the right hand of God, and therefore he feels compassion toward those who stone him, who will face the judgment of that Jesus: "Lord do not hold this sin against them." Forgiving enemies—including those whom God may be using to call us to obedience—is not only a commandment of Jesus; it is also the outcome of the profound conviction that the Jesus who died on the cross, and who from the cross prayed for those who crucified him, is at the right hand of God, and that therefore our enemies are already defeated.

4

New Horizons
(8:4–12:24)

Now the narrative takes a new direction. As a result of the persecution unleashed in Jerusalem after Stephen's death, the witness of the believers reaches other parts of Judea and Samaria. The outline of 1:8 is generally being followed—"in Jerusalem, in all Judea and Samaria"—but that order is not strictly followed, for Luke will tell us first about Samaria and even Ethiopia, in order then to come to the conversion of Saul, and toward the end of this session to the witness of the believers in Judea.

In a way this entire section is a bridge between the foregoing and the rest of the book. Up to this point attention has been focused on Jerusalem. In the election of the seven we have encountered new leadership, which is now mostly Hellenistic Jews. Now we shall be told how that growing Hellenistic church took the message beyond the limits of Jerusalem and even of Palestine. In the next section, the center of the narrative will move to Antioch, and to the mission from it, which will occupy the rest of the book.

A. PHILIP (8:4–40)

The Twelve asked the congregation to elect seven men to serve at the tables, while they kept for themselves the ministry of preaching. Already in the case of Stephen the Holy Spirit contradicted the desire on the part of the Twelve to keep that ministry for themselves. Now, in chapter 8, it will be Philip who will proclaim the gospel—which once again raises the point that the Twelve (whose authority is not denied, but rather affirmed) erred in thinking that it would be only up to them to preach the word.

1. In Samaria (8:4–25)[1]

The passage begins with one of those summaries that we have encountered repeatedly in Acts. In this particular case it is very brief, for it is limited to verse 4; but it is important because, like the other summaries, it tells us that what follows is only a particular example of more general trends and principles.

Luke does not claim that Philip was the only one who went around preaching. Philip, on the contrary, is a concrete example of the general fact affirmed in this verse, and Samaria is a particular case of what was taking place "from place to place." As Joseph Kurzinger commented:

> We would very much like to know the details of this first Christian mission, which extended to Phoenicia, Cyprus and Antioch (11:19). We would like to know the names of the exiles who introduced that very important phase in the history of the church. We can think first of all of the group of which Stephen was part whose names are given in 6:5. Soon we will become acquainted with one of them: Philip. However, at the same time there must have been many others who became spokespersons for the gospel. What was the nature of the message they preached? At that point there still was no written gospel. The word and actions of the Lord were shared by oral tradition and expounded and applied as we have already seen in the earlier speeches in Acts. What these "servants of the word" (Luke 1, 2) told about Jesus, what they pondered and described with a theological sense of salvation, would later find the path that through a greater understanding of the message led to the Gospel writers, who from those spoken words drew the material for writing the Gospels.[2]

Luke does not claim that he is telling us the entire story of the expansion of the gospel, but is simply trying to connect that story with "Theophilus" and with the rest of his readers. Therefore, what he tells us is like a series of successive stages through which the message has reached his audience. This is something similar to what has so often been done in the study of what we call "universal" history: very little is said about the Far East, and we center our attention on Mesopotamia and the Mediterranean basin. After that we become interested in Western civilization and study little about the Byzantine or

---

1. F. García Bazán, "En torno a Hechos 8, 4–24: Milagro y magia entre los gnósticos," *RevisBib*, 40 (1978), 27–38; R. J. Coggins, "The Samaritans and Acts," *NTSt*, 28 (1982), 423–34.

2. Joseph Kurzinger, *Los Hechos de los Apóstoles* (Barcelona: Herder, 2 volumes, 1979), 1:209.

the Islamic civilizations. After that we are particularly interested in Great Britain, Spain, France, Italy, and Germany, and say very little about Poland, Scandinavia, and so on. We are aware that all those nations and civilizations have their history; but because that history does not lead directly to ours, we pay little attention to it. Likewise, Luke offers us glimpses of that entire different history in Galilee, Phoenecia, and elsewhere, but only deals in detail with some episodes that for some reason are of particular interest for his narrative and its purposes.

The "city of Samaria" where Philip goes (8:5) may well be Samaria itself (which was then called Sebaste) or Shechem,[3] which was also in Samaria.[4]

Sebaste was mostly a Gentile city, whereas Shechem was mostly Samaritan. For that reason many scholars suggest that the story refers to Shechem. What Philip does there is to preach and to do "signs" or miracles. People hear and see (8:6). Apparently in this verse "hearing" refers to the loud cries that were given by the unclean spirits as they left those who were possessed; and the "seeing" refers to the lame and others who were cured (8:7). However, the emphasis in the passage is not so much on such signs as it is on preaching. Philip's main function is not performing wonders but preaching. The "great joy" in verse 8 apparently refers both to those who were healed and to the message itself, the good news that Philip preached. As to the content of that message, Luke tells us that he "proclaimed the Messiah" (8:5); that is to say, the anointed one. This may be significant, for there was a strong Messianic expectation among the Samaritans, who also called the anointed one *Taeb*, "the one who restores." It is possible that all of this is also related with the miracles that took place, which are signs of restoration. We also know that the Samaritans opposed worship at the Temple in Jerusalem (see John 4:20–21). This is interesting, for we have already seen that in Stephen's speech he strongly critiqued the Temple made by human hands. Now Philip, another of the seven and therefore probably a member of the same circle as Stephen, will be working among the Samaritans, who also reject worship in the Temple.[5]

---

3. Sometimes Shechem, which appears repeatedly in the Old Testament, has been identified with the village of Sychar in John 4:5.

4. Some manuscripts do not say "the city of Samaria," but "a city of Samaria." In Old Testament times, the capital of the kingdom of Israel was Samaria, but when Herod rebuilt it he named it "Sebaste," which is the Greek equivalent of the Latin "Augusta," in honor of Augustus Caesar. Samaria was a very Hellenized city, with large numbers of pagans. The very name of "Sebaste" was seen as blasphemous by many Jews and Samaritans. Therefore, it would not be surprising for Luke to prefer the ancient name of "Samaria."

5. O. Cullmann, *Des sources de l'Evangile à la formation de la théologie chrétienne* (Neuchatel: Delachaux et Niestlé, 1969), p. 18.

In verse 9 we meet Simon,[6] known in later history as Simon Magus,[7] and Luke tells us about his prestige and authority, which were such that the Samaritans said, "This man is the power of God that is called great" (8:10).[8] This Simon is among the many persons converted by Philip's preaching. He is baptized and he follows Philip around. Although traditionally it has been said that Simon was a hypocrite, the text does not give any such indication. Therefore, it seems that Roloff departs from the text in claiming that "Simon has agreed to join the community in the hope of discovering the secret of Philip's wonder-working power; that is why he will not leave him alone, in order to observe him closely while he carries on his activities."[9]

Then the Twelve intervene (8:14) by sending Peter and John to Samaria. Upon arriving, the two discover that the believers there have not yet received the Holy Spirit, for "they had only been baptized in the name of the Lord Jesus" (8:15–16). The apostles lay their hands on them, and they receive the Holy Spirit (8:17). This particular passage has been used in various times in the history of the Church in very different ways, for there are several aspects of it that are not altogether clear. Sometimes it is used by those who claim that originally baptism was only in the name of Jesus, and that it should still be so. The same text is used by those who insist on the trinitarian formula at baptism, claiming that this text shows that baptism only in the name of Jesus is deficient. Then, others use this text to insist on the existence of two baptisms: one with water and another that takes place later, with the Holy Spirit. Finally,

---

6. There is extensive scholarly literature on Simon. There are two summaries of that literature: W. A. Meeks, "Simon Magus in recent research," *RelStudRev*, 4 (1977), 137–42; and K. Rudolph, "Simon—Magus oder Gnosticus? Zur Stand der Debatte," *ThRund*, 42 (1977), 279–359. Two later studies should be added: R. Bergmeier, "Die Gesttalt des Simon Magus in Act 8 in der simonischen Gnosis-Aporien einer Gesssamtdeutung," *ZntW*, 77 (1986), 267–75 and G. Ludemann, "The Acts of the Apostles and the beginnings of Simonian Gnosis," *NTSt*, 33 (1987), 420–26. The latter argues that the Gnosis that later took the name of Simon is indeed connected with him, and that Luke refers to it ironically when speaking of the *epinoia* of Simon in 8:22.

7. In patristic literature Simon is often accused of being the father of Gnosticism. This is certainly an exaggeration, but there are reasons to think that there is indeed a connection between Simon and early Gnosticism.

8. In the second century, Justin Martyr, who came from the same area, tells us about Simon that "almost all Samaritans, even though very few among other nations, adore him as the first God; and a certain Helen who at that time accompanied him in his wanderings and who before that had been a prostitute, they call the first mind [*ennoian*; hence the reference by Ludemann to the the *epínoia* mentioned in note 6] born from him" (*Apol.* I, 26.3). And elsewhere Justin himself says: "about the Samaritans, I have told the emperor that they are deceived by following the magician Simon, from among their own people, whom they claim to be god above every principle, power [*dynamis*, the same word that appears in Acts 8:10: 'the great power of God'] and potency" (*Dial.* 120.6).

9. Jürgen Roloff, *Hechos de los Apóstoles* (Madrid: Cristiandad, 1984), p. 186.

it is also on the basis of this text that some claim that, although baptism may be administered by any Christian, confirmation is the exclusive function of bishops, as it was then the prerogative of the apostles. Therefore, this particular text deserves careful discussion.

First, what is the meaning of their having "only been baptized in the name of the Lord Jesus"? Clearly, something is lacking; but the text does not tell us what the deficiency is. One interpretation would be that it consisted in their having been baptized only "in the name of Jesus," and not "of the Father, the Son, and the Holy Spirit." The problem is that elsewhere in Acts baptism "in the name of Jesus" is practiced, without any apparent deficiency or problem. In 2:38, Peter tells his listeners on the day of Pentecost, "Repent, and be baptized everyone of you in the name of Jesus Christ . . . and you will receive the gift of the Holy Spirit." In 10:48, Peter again orders that Cornelius and those with him be baptized "in the name of the Lord Jesus." Finally, in 19:1–6, Paul finds some believers in Ephesus who have only been baptized "into John's baptism." Paul then baptizes them "in the name of the Lord Jesus," lays his hands on them, and they receive the Holy Spirit. Therefore, the mere fact that the baptism that the Samaritans received was "in the name of Jesus" does not seem to have been the problem.[10]

From the foregoing it follows that what was lacking to these disciples was the gift of the Holy Spirit. The obvious question after that is, why? And the only possible answer is that we do not know. In the already quoted text, 2:38, Peter seems to imply that the gift of the Spirit will come to all those who are listening as soon as they repent and are baptized. In the story about Cornelius, which appears in chapter 10, the Spirit comes to Cornelius and his friends before their baptism, and it is because that gift has already been bestowed that Peter orders that they be baptized. In the episode in Ephesus, things are even more complicated, for these believers have only received the baptism of John. It is after they have been baptized in the name of Jesus that Paul lays hands on them and they receive the Spirit. In consequence, all that can be said is that according to Acts the Spirit is absolutely free to decide where to be poured out and where to be manifested, be it before baptism, afterward, in baptism itself, at the laying on of hands, or at any other moment. One thing is clear, and that is that if any of these texts is taken as a rigid norm that the Spirit must follow, or as absolute and essential practice in the life of the Church, this contradicts Luke's wider understanding of the freedom of the Spirit.

---

10. How can this be squared with the other baptismal formula that appears in the New Testament—"in the name of the Father, the Son and the Holy Spirit" (Matt. 28:19)—which eventually became the classical formula for baptism? Here it may be helpful to point out that the Matthean formula does not commend baptism "in the names," but in a single name. If we remember that in the biblical usage the "name" is not just the sound of the word, but also the power behind it, it would seem that "the name of Jesus" and "the name of the Father, the Son and the Holy Spirit" are the same name.

It is also important to note that the text does not say a word about whether the gift of the Holy Spirit was accompanied by extraordinary manifestations such as speaking in tongues, or at any rate how it was known that they had received the Holy Spirit. Later on, in the episodes of Cornelius and Ephesus, glossolalia will appear, but not in this text.

Nor are we told whether Simon Magus was among those who received the gift of the Spirit when the apostles laid their hands on them. We might be inclined to think that it was not so, for it is difficult to see how the gift of the Spirit could coexist with Simon's spiritual obfuscation. However, the text does not tell us one way or the other. Therefore, it is too much to assert that Simon did not receive the Spirit because he was "an unacceptable candidate for the baptism of the Holy Spirit."[11] Beside the fact that the text does not tell us whether or not Simon received the Spirit, such a judgment would seem to imply that the Spirit is received on the basis of human merit—which would in turn imply grave difficulties for Christian theology.

At any rate Simon Magus offers to buy this particular gift from the apostles (not the gift of performing miracles, which he had seen before in Philip, but rather the gift of having people receive the Holy Spirit by the laying on of hands).[12] Peter's answer is both a curse and an invitation to repentance (8:20–21). In the Greek text, that in which Simon has no part is this *logos*, whose many meanings include "word," "message," "doctrine," "reason," "matter," "subject." The NRSV does not commit itself, and thus translates: "You have no part or share in this." The NIV says, "You have no part or share in this ministry." Because Simon's answer is in the plural, asking the plural "you" to pray for him, it would seem that, although Luke only quotes the words of Peter, he is implying that John is also part of this harsh word. At any rate Simon's answer seems to indicate repentance, although the text does not say explicitly that he repented, but only that he asked the apostles to pray for him.[13]

The text ends with the return of Peter and John to Jerusalem, and on the way back they use the occasion to preach in the Samaritan villages that they visit.

Few biblical characters have had as much bad press as Simon Magus. In the ancient church it was said—and it is still repeated in many history books—that he was the founder of just about every heresy of uncertain origin. At some point around the third or fourth century, an anonymous writer with much imagination wrote the *Pseudo-Clementine* literature, in which Simon Magus is the villain who goes everywhere trying to undo the work of Simon Peter. During the Middle Ages Christians wishing to reform the Church and

---

11. Ralph Earle, *Hechos* (Kansas City: Casa Nazarena de Publicaciones, 1985), p. 364.

12. On what Simon actually desired, see J. D. M. Derrett, "Simon Magus," *ZntW*, 73 (1982), 52–68.

13. Some manuscripts of the Western text, as well as the Syriac version, add that Simon "wept for a long time."

who rued the practice of buying and selling ecclesiastical positions gave that practice the name of "simony" after Simon Magus, who wished to buy the gift of the Spirit. And, so as not to be less than the rest, Hollywood in the twentieth century produced a movie (*The Silver Chalice*) in which Simon Magus is a con artist who employs tricks of magic to try to outdo the miracles of the apostles. Most commonly, it is said that Simon Magus was a hypocrite who tried to use the gospel for his own financial benefit.

The text, however, does not say such a thing. It simply says that Simon believed, and that he was "amazed" at the things that he saw happening around Philip. It also says that he was a powerful man. He was so powerful that people said of him, "This man is the power of God that is called great." That incredible prestige of Simon is confirmed by the witness of Justin Martyr, who hailed from the region of Samaria. Simon, this powerful and prestigious man, is converted. But upon seeing that the apostles have the power to confer the Holy Spirit he wishes to have the same power; and he wishes to receive it in exchange for money. He has always been powerful, and now he wishes to exchange money, a symbol of his power in Samaria, for the gift of the apostles, in order to be as powerful and prestigious in the Church as he is in Samaria. It is to this that Peter responds with harsh words, telling him that "you are in the gall of bitterness and chains of wickedness," and that therefore his money will perish with him. To this Simon responds with words that seem to indicate at least the beginning of repentance.

When thus read, the text is not about sincerity or hypocrisy, but about how power affects Christian life. Because this subject is of great importance for our churches, it should be explored in greater detail.

Simon Magus is accustomed to being powerful and therefore it is difficult for him to see the difference between the power that counts in Samaritan society—money and miracle working—and the power that counts in the Church. Simon Peter is a humble fisherman from Galilee whom Jesus and the work of the Spirit have turned into a fisher of souls. Simon Magus, accustomed to being called the "great power of God," cannot experience the power of God as Simon Peter saw it in Pentecost, as the great leveler that is poured on "all flesh," and that makes sons and daughters prophesy.

In between them, there is Philip. We are not told exactly what it was that he thought, nor can we tell on the basis of the text why his acts of baptism must be followed by the laying on of hands by Peter and John. But the text does imply that, for whatever reason, Philip did not know or could not make Simon Magus see the difference between the power of money and the power of God, between the power that makes people say about him, "this is the great power of God," and the power that turns Simon Peter into an apostle of Jesus Christ.

BETWEEN SIMON MAGUS AND SIMON PETER

This tripartite typology—Simon Magus, Simon Peter, and Philip—well describes the situation in many of our churches. Like Simon Peter, our churces have come out of relatively obscure social conditions. Even though the history of Protestantism in Latin America has generally focused its attention on the work of visionaries with significant outside support, the truth is that most of the Protestant growth on the continent has been due to an anonymous multitude of witnesses, most of them poor and with little academic training. In dark corners of the Andean jungle, the gospel has turned those who earlier were mere statistics of poverty and illiteracy into apostles. The same has happened in the equally ferocious jungles of our slums. The first worship services of most of our congregations did not take place in well-built and respected churches, but in the humble house, with cardboard walls and straw roof, of some brother or sister. The "good" society stigmatized them with epithets such as *Canuto, cultero,* and *aleluya.* They were attacked and persecuted in a thousand ways. In Colombia and other countries there was open and ferocious persecution. Throughout the continent, many churches were stoned or burned by fanatical crowds. In government schools, many of our children were told that they were not true Christians, but "heretics." In civil bureaucracies, Protestants were present only in the lower echelons, because the positions of higher prestige were generally closed to any who would speak openly of their Protestant faith. There was little access through the press, the radio, or other media. We were like those Christians in Corinth to whom Paul writes, "not many of you were wise by human standards, not many were powerful, not many were of noble birth" (I Cor. 1:26).

The same is true of Spanish-speaking Protestant churches in the United States. A few were founded by middle-class immigrants who brought their faith from Latin America. Others have been established in middle-class communities by the churches of the dominant culture. But the vast majority are in the poorer neighborhoods of large cities such as New York and Los Angeles (where today there are more than a thousand Protestant Hispanic churches), or in the small peasant communities of Texas and New Mexico. They are not churches of great prestige, precisely because they have worked among poor people who had little opportunity for education.

It is at this point that the text we are studying becomes relevant. Sometimes we are so used to being few, to being marginalized, to being considered ignorant and sectarian, that when a prestigious person joins us we imagine that this somehow increases our power or makes us better. Rather than challenging that person to understand the contrast between the power that he or she has in society and the power of the Spirit, we give the impression that power in this society can be directly and automatically turned into power and authority within the church. In some churches, if a *licenciado*—a lawyer—comes in, we say, "Come right in, *señor licenciado*; please sit here, *señor licenciado.*" In others we do the same with famous atheletes, with rich persons, and even with dictators. This problem is neither new nor unique, for it existed also in the early Church—as may be seen in James 2:1–3. But the truth is that all of this reflects a power similar to that of Simon Magus, who has "no part or share in this."

Over against this power stands that of Simon Peter: a poor fisherman who had some difficulty in understanding the message of Jesus, and who was not always faithful in spite of his good intentions, but who discovered in the presence of the Spirit a power to face people such as Simon Magus, and eventually (according to a very ancient tradition) death itself. That power still exists in our churches. As in the case of Simon Peter, quite often those who perceive it most clearly are those who have been powerless in society and who therefore can see the contrast between the two sorts of power. Over half a century ago this was clearly stated in his own unique style by Mexican philosopher, theologian and poet Alberto Rembao:

> Thus, an illiterate person or a man of scarce education will be better cultivated than a doctor in sciences or humanities, if that illiterate person knows how to receive the free gift of divine cultivation, which is not a matter of intellect and school, but of emotion and conduct. The first chief of the Christian community of Jerusalem, without any preparation, receives the science that elevates him to the level of a great transformer of the course of history.[14]

From its very beginnings, the power of the Protestant Spanish-speaking church has been precisely there: in being a church which, like Simon Peter, has received its own sense of value and direction, not from the surrounding scale of social values, but from the Holy Spirit.

Between Simon Peter and Simon Magus stands Philip. The text does not tell us exactly what it was that he taught Simon Magus. But the narrative itself seems to indicate that, even though Philip did preach the gospel to Simon, he did not communicate the contrast between the values of that gospel and the values of Samaritan society—between the values of the gospel and the value of money. Philip preached to Simon and baptized him, apparently without further ado; and, even though Simon followed him everywhere, Simon apparently was never confronted with the contrast and the contradiction between those two powers.

We Latino Protestants are also tempted with that attitude. Times have changed. Today people of prestige, money, and social standing come to us. Many of them, not necessarily out of ill will, but because they are used to it, take for granted that in the Church they will be treated with the same deference and privilege as in the rest of society. Like the Magus, they see no difficulty in employing their money, symbol of power in society, to attain special respect in the Church. Clearly, the gospel is also for them. But, are we ready to call them to repentance, as we do the rest? To make them see the radical demands of the gospel? Or do we make things easier so that they are not annoyed and leave us? A Protestant leader in Latin America has expressed this concern quite concretely:

> "Presidential breakfasts" have become the fashion, as have also all sorts of meetings with the authorities. Have Protestants ever raised their

_____

14. Alberto Rembao, *Discurso a la nación evangélica* (Buenos Aires: La Aurora, 1949), pp. 17–18.

prophetic voice in them? Are we really trying to cultivate the wealth and the privilege of unrepentant hearts among the powerful, guaranteeing for them that the gospel will produce laborers who do not strike, students who sing religious songs instead of painting graffiti with calls for social action, guardians of peace at the price of injustice?[15]

In all of this we see a process that is very similar to the Simon Magus story in Acts: a church composed mostly of dissidents, of people who do not entirely fit in the social fabric, now tempted by the change that could bring to it the addition of people such as Simon Magus. The alternative is still the same: capitulate before Simon Magus, sell the gift of the Spirit, lose the missionary and evangelizing power, or tell any Simon Magus who comes to us unrepentant to tempt us, "May your silver perish with you, because you thought you could obtain God's gift with money!"

2. The Ethiopian (8:26–40)

Philip, who was the central character at the beginning of the previous episode, but was then upstaged by the encounter between the two Simons, once again occupies the center of the narrative. An angel (which, remember, does not necessarily mean a winged spirit-being, as we now tend to think, but a messenger of God) tells him to take the road to Gaza. Different possibilities have been suggested as to where Luke placed Philip before this angelic visitation. The reference to the wilderness may be to Gaza itself, which was repeatedly deserted; but it seems to refer rather to one of the two roads that led from Jerusalem to Gaza, so that the reference to the wilderness is an indication as to which of these two roads Philip is to take.[16] If this is the meaning of that particular phrase, it would seem to indicate that Luke places Philip in Jerusalem. But it is also possible to read this passage as the continuation of the previous one, as if Philip were still in Samaria. Because much later (21:8) Luke tells us that Philip lived in Caesarea, that place has also been suggested as the starting point for this journey. Although we are not told where Philip was, we are told that he is supposed to go south (the text literally says "noon," but the meaning seems to indicate that this has to do, not with the hour, but with the direction, just as today the Spanish *mediodía* can mean either noon or south, and the French *midi* can also have both meanings).

On this journey, Philip encounters "an Ethiopian eunuch." In some ancient texts, the word "eunuch" does not necessarily mean a man who has been emasculated, but a high government functionary. The fact that Luke tells us that he was "an Ethiopian eunuch, a court official," would seem to indicate that he was in truth a eunuch, for otherwise there would be strong redundancy.

---

15. Samuel Escobar, "Responsabilidad social de la iglesia," in *Acción en Cristo para un continente en crisis* (Miami: Caribe, 1970), p. 35.

16. E. Jaquier, *Les Actes des Apôtres* (Paris: V. Lecoffre, 1926), p. 269.

"Candace" is not the name of a particular queen, but the title that was given to the queens of Nubia, south of Egypt.[17] It was one such queen that this eunuch served as a treasurer. The region that was then called "Ethiopia" was not the same as the country that now goes by that name. It was rather the area of Nubia, whose territories bordered the Nile south of Egypt, and was closer to what is today Sudan. In the Old Testament, its name is Kush. Its capital, where presumably the eunuch was going, was Meroe.[18]

That the eunuch had come to Jerusalem to worship tells us that he was one of those "God fearers" who, although they believed in the God of Israel, did not completely submit to the Law or to circumcision.[19] That somebody from such a distant country would come to Jerusalem to worship is not unbelievable, for already six centuries before Christ there was a very strong Jewish colony in the island of Elethantine, at the first cataract of the Nile, that is, at the very border between Egypt and Nubia.

This civil functionary in Candace's court was "reading the prophet Isaiah" (8:28). Philip hears him, so he must have been reading out loud, which was customary in ancient times; or he had someone reading out loud to him, which was also common among the well-to-do.

The quotation that appears in 8:32–33 is from Isaiah 53:7–8.[20] This does not mean that the eunuch was reading only these two verses. At that time there was no other way of making bibliographical references (for there were no chapters and verses), so what Luke does is to quote a well-known part of the text, in order to indicate what the eunuch was reading was approximately what we now know as Isaiah 53. Philip asks him if he understands what he reads,[21] and the eunuch invites him to enter the chariot and explain to him what the prophet is saying.[22] It is "starting with this scripture"—that is to say, Isaiah 53—that Philip announces to the eunuch the good news about Jesus. Note

---

17. See Pliny, *Hist. natur.* 6.35.

18. For some people, Ethiopia was the end of the world, and on that basis it has been suggested that the entire eighth chapter of Acts follows the outline of 1:8: "Judea" (8:1–4); "Samaria" (8:5–25); "and to the ends of the earth" (8:26–39). T. C. G. Thornton, "To the end of the earth: Acts 1:8," *ExpTim*, 89 (1978), 374–75.

19. On this point, see the commentary on 10:2.

20. On the manner in which this text was interpreted in Christian antiquity, see P. B. Decock, "The Understanding of Isaiah 53:7–8 in Acts 8:32–33," *Neot*, 14 (1981), 111–33. According to Decock, what was emphasized was not the sacrifice of the suffering servant for others, but rather the contrast between his humiliation and his exaltation. As such, this theme was the continuation of Jewish apocalyptic tradition, and became important for Christians during the first years of persecution.

21. The question, "Do you understand what you are reading?", is a play on words in Greek: *ginôskeis ha anaginôskeis.*

22. The Greek construction that the eunuch employs here is highly refined, and stands out from the style of the rest of Luke's work. With a masterly touch, Luke presents the

that the text does not say that he only explained the passage from Isaiah, but that this was his starting point.

It is then (perhaps after several hours, or even days, for Luke does not say) that, seeing water, the eunuch asks Philip if he can be baptized. The phrase employed here is parallel to similar phrases in 10:47 and 11:17. Apparently it was the formula employed before accepting someone for baptism. Verse 37 does not appear in the best manuscripts, and therefore, many scholars think that it was added later in order to round out the action by quoting Philip's answer.[23] At any rate, the narrative indicates that Philip told him that there was no impediment.

They both "went down into the water," and after the baptism they "came up out of the water." The grammatical forms employed here in Greek indicate that they actually entered the water, and that it was standing in the water that the baptism took place. This was the normal form of baptism, as may be seen in Romans 6:4, Colossians 2:12, and other places in the New Testament.[24]

After this the Spirit took Philip away, apparently placing him in Azotus, where he continued preaching until he went to Caesarea (where we will find him again in 21:8). The eunuch continued his way rejoicing.[25]

This passage is often interpreted as the beginning of the mission to a new land. The Church of Ethiopia, one of the most ancient in the world, which has millions of members, claims that its origins are precisely in this encounter between Philip and the Ethiopian eunuch.[26] Furthermore, this passage may be read as representing the beginning of the mission to the Gentiles even before

---

eunuch speaking in a way that suggests the manner in which a high functionary of a royal court would speak.

23. This addition, if it really is such, must have been relatively early, for Irenaeus, toward the end of the second century, already quotes a text that includes verse 37. All the manuscripts including it reflect the Western text. J. Heimerdinger, "La foi de l'eunuche éthiopien: Le problème textual d'Actes 8:37," *EtThRel*, 63 (1988), 521–28, defends the authenticity—or at least the great antiquity—of both the Eastern text and of the Western one with this edition.

24. The most ancient surviving reference to baptism by only pouring water over the head is in the *Didache*, a Christian document written sometime between the years 70 and 120: "If you have no running water, baptize in another water; if you cannot do it in cold water, do it with warm. If you do not have either, pour water on the head three times in the name of the Father, the Son, and the Holy Spirit" (*Did.* 7.2–3).

25. The Western text adds a few words at 8:39, between "Spirit" and "of the Lord," so it reads: "the Holy Spirit fell on the eunuch, and the angel of the Lord snatched Philip away." Although normally the Western text is not considered trustworthy, in this particular case several scholars suggest that it may be closer to the original than the more commonly accepted text.

26. Apart from this text, the earliest historical data we have about a Christian mission to Ethiopia comes from the fourth century, when two shipwrecked brothers, Frumentius and Edessius, took the Christian message to the area. Frumentius returned to Alexandria where he was consecrated as bishop of Ethiopia by Athanasius.

the Church at large authorized it.[27] It will only be after the episode of Peter and Cornelius that leaders of the church of Jerusalem will come to the conclusion that "God has given even to the Gentiles the repentance that leads to life" (11:18).

Even apart from such matters, it is important to consider the interview itself between Philip and the eunuch, and what it might mean for today. For this purpose, one must realize that the eunuch, even though he is a "God fearer," cannot become a convert to Judaism, for it is strictly forbidden by the law of Israel (Deut. 23:1). Although that law might seem obscure to us today, it must have been well known to the Ethiopian, who was sufficiently interested in Judaism to come to Jerusalem to worship, but who knew that entry to the people of God was forever forbidden for him because he was a eunuch. And also, for the same reason and for his own condition, he must have been aware of the promise that appears in the Book of Isaiah, only three chapters beyond what he was reading (Isa. 56:3–5), that the day will come when there will be in the house of Israel a place for the foreigner as well as for the eunuch.

Beginning with Isaiah 53, Philip tells him of "the good news about Jesus." What is this good news for the foreign eunuch, but that, with the advent of Jesus and the gift of the Spirit, the "last days" have begun and that the promise of Isaiah is beginning to be fulfilled? It is after hearing the good news of these last days that the eunuch, upon seeing water, asks Philip, "What is to prevent me from being baptized?" On the basis of the law that has ruled in Israel for centuries, the answer should be clear: "your condition as a eunuch." But on the basis of the good news that Philip has just proclaimed to him, that the reign of God has been inaugurated, the answer is different: there is nothing to prevent it!

On baptizing the eunuch, Philip is doing much more than we think. He is not just baptizing a new convert, nor is he only opening the way of the gospel to an entire nation or a whole continent. He is doing all of that; but he is also doing much more. He is declaring that the day of the fulfillment of the promises of the reign has arrived. He is reaffirming and applying what Peter said at Pentecost: "This is what was said by the prophet Joel: in the last days!" Precisely because the church lives in "the last days," the promise of Isaiah is being fulfilled, and the eunuch and the foreigner also have a place in the house of the Lord (Isa. 56:3–5).

On taking this step, Philip is moving ahead of the rest of the Church, which will only come to discover these implications of the gospel three chapters later in Acts. If Philip can move ahead of the Twelve, that is because, although they are "Hebrews," he is a "Hellenist" (as was explained in the comments on 6:1–7). As a person who has been marginalized within the people of

---

27. Unless as some authors suggest, Luke does not follow a strictly chronological order, but rather completes the "Acts of Philip" before moving to another subject. In such a case, although the conversion of the Ethiopian appears in chapter 8 and that of Cornelius in chapter 10, the latter preceded the former.

Israel, Philip can see that the margins have become wider, and thus begins the mission to the Gentiles even before the actual leaders of the church have sanctioned it.

WHEN THE PROMISE IS FULFILLED

What does all this have to do with us? Quite a bit—for we, too, are a community of the Spirit living at the beginning of the end. We, too, by virtue of the Spirit, live in "the last days." We, too, are called to bear witness, as did Philip, to the fulfillment of God's promises.

Philip was a Hellenist among Jews. As such, he might well have thought that his mission consisted in repeating and saying the same that the apostles, the "Hebrews," those who knew the gospel earlier, said and did. On the other hand, precisely because he is a Hellenist, he can begin opening doors to those who are even more marginalized than he is.

In studying the history of the Church and its missionary progress, we repeatedly see that the great movements, the most notable discoveries of unsuspected dimensions of the gospel and of obedience to it, usually appear not at the centers but at the margins, at the periphery. As a Hellenist, Philip is one of those marginalized in the community that until then had been dominated by "Hebrews." When that community gives him a measure of power, electing him one of the seven, he could well be content with that and continue doing what had always been done before. But that is not what happens. By virtue of the Holy Spirit, who uses Philip's condition as a Hellenist with an experience of marginality, Philip widens the margins, and dares tell the eunuch that nothing prevents him from being baptized.

Many Latinas, Latinos, and other minorities in the Church have much that is akin to the experience of the Hellenists. We are members of the Church and are accepted as such. The older churches that sent and often continue sending missionaries are proud of their "work"; that is to say, of us. We are expected to continue that work, and we undertake it enthusiastically. However, what is clearly expected is that we continue it exactly as we were taught by the "Hebrews," by those who preceded us in the faith. However, precisely because we are at the periphery, where Christianity constantly faces new situations, it is quite possible that the Spirit may be calling us, like Philip before, to new forms of obedience and new understandings of the gospel.

This has happened repeatedly in the history of Protestantism in Latin America. For instance, in some of our countries there were churches founded by North American southern whites who brought along not only the message of Jesus Christ, but also many of the racial prejudices that had been so dominant in their land of origin. As a result, there were churches in Latin America in which for a long time blacks were not well received. It was some Latin American leaders, who were conscious of the conflict between the gospel's inclusivity and what the missionaries had taught, who took definitive steps to change such attitudes.

In other cases those who first preached among us rejected all elements of the aboriginal cultures, thinking that they were anti-Christian or even demonic, without taking the time to study their true significance and value. Thus, for instance, in many cases we were taught that only "religious" music could be sung in church, always accompanied by either a piano or, in wealthier situations, an organ. They did this while ignoring that in many cases the music that they called "religious" often was as "worldly" in its origins as any of our own tunes. In following such practices, not only were we alienated from our cultural roots but we also lost contact with a significant part of our population, who did not see why our traditional instruments and musical styles had no place in divine worship. Today there is an entire new generation of Latino leaders who compose music and write words that are both profoundly theological and very much ours.

In practically all of our countries there are churches that seem to have sacralized the form of government bequeathed to them by the missionaries, often defending the thesis that such a form of government is the only one that can be justified by Scripture. The truth of the matter is that every present form of government in any church is the result of a historical process that took place in lands and cultures very different from ours, and that therefore they must all be examined in the light of our mission and our own circumstances, and corrected as necessary.

All of these various forms of exclusion we have learned from people to whom we have reason to be grateful, and whose memory we must respect. These very people brought us a message of a reign of God to which all are invited, white and black, Hispanic and Asian, all with their own cultural contributions, some with pianos and some with their guitars. To deny such contributions is a form of exclusion and is therefore a denial of the reign of God that we proclaim.

The eunuch asked Philip, "What is there to prevent?" Philip could have responded with a long theological lecture on what the Law had to say about eunuchs. He could have told him that the "Hebrew" leadership of the Church had not authorized the baptism of Gentiles, much less of eunuchs. But his answer was simply that nothing is to prevent. Today new generations and new circumstances are asking us repeatedly, "What is there to prevent?" What will our answer be?

B. SAUL'S CONVERSION (9:1–31)

1. The Conversion (9:1–19)

We come now to one of the most dramatic passages in all of Scripture. This is the conversion of Saul, which Luke describes not only here, but also in 22:4–16 and 26:12–18. Because all of these passages deal with the same episode, we shall study here all three versions that appear in Acts.[28] Up to this

---

28. There are many studies comparing the three narratives. One of the most recent and also relatively brief is that of C. W. Hedrick, "Paul's conversion/call: A comparative analysis of the three reports in Acts," *JBL*, 100 (1981), 415–32.

point, all that Luke has told us about Saul is that he was present at Stephen's death and that then he began persecuting Christians. Later we will also learn that he was a Pharisee (23:6), educated under famous professor Gamaliel (22:3), and that he was a Roman citizen by birth (22:28). Also, in the letters of Paul himself there are several passages that refer to this conversion and to various other events in his life.

This is the first time that Acts speaks of the Christian faith as "the Way" (9:2). This name will not appear again until 19:9 and thereafter in 19:23, 22:4, 24:14, and 24:22. Several of these references appear in the context of Paul's conversion, and all of them are related to his career and ministry. This is interesting, because in his own epistles Paul never refers to the Christian faith as "the Way."[29]

All three stories affirm that Saul had obtained letters from the religious authorities in Jerusalem in order to search out and arrest Christians in other places, and that this was his purpose in going to Damascus (9:2, 22:5, 26:12). This poses some historical questions, for it is not clear what authority the high priest or other Jewish leaders had to issue orders of arrest against people in other cities.[30] Most probably what Saul carried were not actually warrants of arrest, but rather letters of introduction to the synagogue leaders in Damascus. He hoped that with these letters those leaders would take steps to have Christians arrested, for at that point Christians were Jews, and therefore they would be subject to the laws of their own community, as was often the case with various minorities within the Roman Empire. It has also been suggested that, because Damascus was a place through which many pilgrims passed on their way to Jerusalem, the Jewish authorities in Jerusalem had special interest in warning their counterparts in Damascus about the dangers of the new heresy, or perhaps even that news had already arrived at Jerusalem, indicating that the new faith had already made some headway in Damascus.[31]

---

29. In the Gospels, Jesus does speak of the "way" that leads to life, in contrast to the one that leads to perdition (Matt. 7:13–14; a saying of Jesus that does not appear in Luke). In Luke's Gospel, it is Jesus' enemies who tell him hypocritically that he teaches "the way of God in accordance with truth" (Luke 20:21). And in John, Jesus calls himself The Way (John 14:6). Also, in two very ancient Christian documents, the *Didache* and the *Epistle of Barnabas*, there is a contrast between two ways, one leading to life and the other to death. Therefore, the subject of the "way" seems to have been important in early Christian preaching.

30. There is an interesting suggestion in Santos Sabugal, *La conversión de Pablo* (Barcelona: Herder, 1976), pp. 163–224. Sabugal suggests that "Damascus" in these texts as well as in the Epistles of Paul himself does not refer to that city in Syria, but is rather a symbolic name that was given to the northwestern corner of the Red Sea. In that case, this would solve a number of the chronological and political difficulties that have been posed regarding the story of Paul's conversion. The main difficulty in accepting this suggestion is that the bases on which Sabugal builds his argument are not persuasive.

31. Such is the thesis of C. S. Mann, "Saul and Damascus," *ExpTim*, 99 (1988), 331–34.

Saul's dramatic experience takes place "approaching Damascus" (9:3; confirmed by 22:6) and at noon (22:6 and 26:13; the narrative in chapter 9 does not indicate the time of day). So that he was surrounded by a light,[32] he fell to the ground,[33] and he heard the voice of the Lord. All of this is told in very similar words in the three versions. The first words of Jesus in each of them are practically the same: "Saul, Saul, why do you persecute me?" According to the version in chapter 26 Jesus adds, "It hurts you to kick against the goads." This phrase is a classical Greek proverb, usually applied to any futile endeavor.[34]

In Saul's answer the word "Lord" does not necessarily have to be interpreted in the sense in which it is employed in the Pauline Epistles. There it is a title indicating the supreme dignity of Jesus. Here it is the normal way of addressing an unknown respectfully—equivalent to the English "Sir."

In all three narratives, with slight variants, the answer is the same: "I am Jesus, whom you are persecuting." It is significant that the words of Jesus establish a close relationship between him and the Church. Saul was not persecuting Jesus, but only the Church. However, what Jesus implies is that the relationship between himself and the Church is such that the persecutor is persecuting him—which reminds us of what was said earlier, commenting on the episode of Ananias and Sapphira, that to lie to the Church is to lie to the Holy Spirit.

Jesus then gives Saul some instructions. According to the Western text, Saul has asked for such instructions: "What do you want me to do?" In the versions in chapters 9 and 22, Jesus tells him simply to continue on to the city, where he will be told what to do. Saul goes to Damascus, where he eventually has the interview with Ananias. In the third narrative (chapter 26), there is no reference to Ananias and apparently Saul receives his instructions on the very road to Damascus. Also in this third version, Saul receives more detailed instructions about his future ministry (26:26–18). The reason seems to be that in this third case Paul is telling the story of his conversion to King Agrippa, and what is important is the result of his conversion, and not how he came to that outcome. The instructions that Saul seems to receive in 26:16–18 are in fact a reflection of the ministry and vocation that he himself discovered and learned in a number of progressive steps, according to the narrative in Acts.

On the experiences of those who accompanied Saul, there are significant differences between the narrative in chapter 9 and that in 22: in one case they hear the voice, but see no one; and in the other they see the light, but do not

---

32. The reference to this "blinding light" adds interest to the reference to noon, which would make the light all the brighter, in order to compete with the sunlight.

33. It is frequently said that Paul "fell from his horse," and thus the event is often depicted in art. The text does not say a word about the party going on horseback, although given the distance between Jerusalem and Damascus (some 250 kilometers) that might have been the case.

34. Euripides, *Bacchae*, 795; Aeschylus, *Agamemnon*, 1624; Terence, *Phormion*, 7.8.

hear the voice. Another difference is that in 9:7, "the men who were traveling with him stood speechless," whereas in 26:14 Paul declares that they all fell to the ground. If they were on horseback, the two narratives could compliment each other, the image being that the riders have fallen off their horses, and as they rise they are amazed. In any case, these companions of Saul on the road to Damascus are significant for the narrative. Although they are often depicted as soldiers accompanying him and under his orders, most probably they were simply other people who had joined the same group to which Saul had attached himself, as was often customary for long-distance travel.

Saul is made blind (not necessarily as a punishment, but simply because of the light itself: 22:11), and his companions have to lead him by the hand to Damascus. This marks a sharp contrast between the earlier Saul, who was proudly "breathing threats and murder against disciples of the Lord," and the present Saul, who now must be led by the hand. This is followed by three days of total fasting.

In verse 10, Luke takes us to another scene, in order to introduce Ananias, whom God will send to Saul. This Ananias is not to be confused with the one in chapter 5, who is already dead. He is Christian. Therefore, Saul's suspicion that there were already Christians in Damascus was well founded, even though Luke does not tell us how the Gospel reached that city. Ananias is afraid of going to Saul, who is already well known for the persecution that he leads. But the Lord insists, and Ananias finally goes. (There is still in Damascus a street called Strait, which may well be the same street; but the house that is often pointed out as that of Judas, where Saul lodged after his experience, is little more than a tourist attraction.) Ananias goes to Saul, prays with him, and the blindness disappears. The same story, although omitting the conversation between the Lord and Ananias, and with more emphasis on what Ananias told Saul, appears also in 22:12–16. In the story in chapter 9, Paul's future mission is announced in the vision of Ananias: "Go, for he is an instrument whom I have chosen to bring my name before Gentiles and kings and before the people of Israel; I myself will show him how much he must suffer for the sake of my name."

It is then (apparently after receiving the Holy Spirit, 9:17) that Saul is baptized—after which he breaks the absolute fast that he had kept during the three days since his encounter with the Lord.

2.   Saul as a Disciple (9:20–31)

Luke tells us that "immediately" Saul began preaching in the synagogues. Then he went to Jerusalem. This poses the problem of coordinating it with what Paul himself says in Galatians 1:15–21. There he says that immediately after his conversion, without going to Jerusalem, he went to Arabia, and that three years later he went to Damascus and then to Jerusalem. Many scholars have concluded that Luke did not know about the trip to Arabia, and that therefore he thought that the visits to Damascus and Jerusalem took place immediately after Paul's conversion.[35]

In order to deal with these matters, it is important to look first at what Acts tells, and then to see whether it agrees with Paul's own witness. According to Luke, Saul began preaching in the synagogues, and this provoked the enmity of the Jews in Damascus, who decided to kill him. They set a watch at the city gates in order to do this. To allow him to escape, other Christians let him down in a basket through an opening or window in the wall. (In order to understand this one must remember that in ancient cities very often there were houses that backed into the walls, with windows facing outward.)

Saul then went to Jerusalem, where he had difficulties in establishing contact with the believers, who distrusted him. It seems strange that after Saul had been preaching Christ in Damascus for "some time," Christians in Jerusalem would not have learned of it. One could conjecture that, on the basis of his previous zeal against them, they feared that it was a trap. Finally, it is Barnabas who sponsors Saul and introduces him to the rest of the church. At that point Saul lets it be known that he is a believer, allowing himself to be seen in the company of Christians. One wonders why he disputed specifically with the Hellenists (9:29), and not with other Jews. Apparently, because he himself was a Hellenist, and it was the same group that had unleashed the persecution, it was from the same source that the greatest opposition now came. It is in view of this situation that the believers arranged to have Saul go to Cesarea, and from there to his own city of Tarsus.

Finally, the passage ends with verse 31, which is another of Luke's frequent summaries. This particular one tells us that the Church now had peace "throughout Judea, Galilee, and Samaria."[36] In truth, Luke has said nothing about the churches in Galilee, and very little about "all Judea," or about Samaria beyond the story of Philip and Simon Magus. Therefore, this summary is Luke's way of reminding us that he is only narrating a few episodes illustrating the events of those early years. On the other hand, this summary immediately after Saul's conversion almost gives the impression that with that conversion persecution ended. That this is not so is clear from the very fact that Saul himself had to flee first from Damascus and then from Jerusalem.

---

35. Such is the opinion of E. Haenchen, *The Acts of the Apostles: A Commentary* (Philadelphia: Westminster, 1975), pp. 334–34, and the many other scholars, mostly German, whom Haenchen quotes.

36. It has been suggested that one of the reasons the churches enjoyed peace was that Jews in general were involved in a bitter conflict with Caligula, who was attempting to place a statue of himself in the temple (Josephus, *Ant.* 18.2, 2.9). Facing such a dire threat to their own religion, the leaders of Judaism had little time to spare for Christians. Lorenzo Turrado, *Hechos de los Apóstoles y Epístola a los Romanos* (Madrid: Biblioteca de Autores Cristianos, 1975), p. 109.

However, although Luke does not explain why, he tells us that there was a period of peace for the churches after Saul's conversion.

How does all of this compare with what Paul himself tells us? In Galatians 1:17–23 the outline of events is as follows:

a. After his conversion, Saul did not go to Jerusalem, but to Arabia.
b. He later returned to Damascus.
c. Then, after three years, he did go to Jerusalem.
d. There he spent fifteen days, and the only leaders whom he saw were Peter and James, "the brother of the Lord."
e. Finally, he went "into the regions of Syria and Cilicia."
f. During all that time, he was "still unknown by sight to the churches of Judea that are in Christ," although obviously they had learned about his conversion and preaching.

On the other hand, according to Acts:

a. After his conversion, Saul was "some time" in Damascus, preaching in the synagogues, and "proving that Jesus was the Messiah."
b. Eventually, the Jews tried to kill him, and Christians saved him by letting him down from the wall in a basket.
c. Then Saul went to Jerusalem, where Barnabas believed him and took him to meet the Twelve.
d. There he preached and debated with Hellenistic Jews who resolved to kill him.
e. In order to save him, Christians arranged for him to go to Cesarea, and eventually into Tarsus.

The problem is both clarified and made even more complicated because in II Corinthians 11:32–33, Paul mentions the episode of his flight from Damascus by being let down from the wall in a basket, although he gives a different reason: it was not the Jews, but the governor under King Aretas, who guarded the city in order to seize him.[37] Aretas IV, to whom Paul refers, was king of the Nabateans from 9 B.C.E. to 40 C.E. There was not much known about Nabateans until relatively recent times, for their inscriptions had not been deciphered, and all that was known about them was found in authors such as Josephus, the books of Maccabbees, and some classical authors. During the twentieth century their writing was deciphered and historical and archaelogical work rediscovered much of their history and civilization. Thanks

---

37. This divergence is one of the arguments employed by those who claim that Acts was written in order to convince Roman authorities that Christianity was not subversive. They claim that in this passage Luke wishes to say nothing about Paul being a fugitive from authority and that he therefore blames the Jews for seeking to kill him, when in fact he was fleeing from established authority.

to this research, we know that around the year 37 Emperor Caligula ceded the government of Damascus to Aretas IV, who kept it until Nero's reign. Also, the name "Arabia" did not mean in ancient times what it means today, but rather referred to an extensive territory that included the present-day province of Arabia as well as Sinai and a good portion of Transjordania. The main people inhabiting that area were precisely the Nabateans, and therefore quite frequently when the king of the Nabateans is intended, he is called "king of the Arabians."[38] Thus, when Saul went to Damascus after his experience with the Lord, he may have been in territories belonging to King Aretas, but not necessarily part of Arabia.

On this basis, it is possible to see the connection between what Luke tells us in Acts and what Paul says in Galatians and in II Corinthians. Note that according to Acts 9:19 Saul spent some time in Damascus, and according to 9:23 he had to flee after quite a few days. Therefore, it is conceivable and even probable that after his conversion Saul did spend some time in Damascus, and that when he did leave the city, he remained in other parts of the kingdom of Aretas for about "three years,"[39] in order finally to return to Damascus. There he had conflicts, apparently both with the Jews (as Acts tells us) and with the authorities representing Aretas (II Cor.), and he had to be let down from a window in a basket.

In that case, the trip to Jerusalem mentioned in Acts 9 would be the same trip to which Paul refers in Galatians 1. The main difference would be in that Acts does not tell us how long Paul was in Jerusalem, whereas Paul indicates that it was a fortnight. The other difference would be that, whereas Luke says that Barnabas introduced Saul to the apostles, Paul himself does not mention Barnabas (which in any case would not be relevant to his argument in Galatians) and makes it clear that he only saw Peter and James.

It is after that visit that Saul spent some time in Tarsus and the surrounding area (9:30) or, which is approximately the same, in "the regions of Syria and Cilicia" (Galatians 1:21).

DAMASCUS ROADS

This episode is so well known that we often add to it elements that do not appear in the biblical narrative. Thus, for instance, we imagine Saul as we have seen him in famous paintings, dressed as a Roman soldier lying on the ground

---

38. See Josephus, *Ant.* 14.15-17.

39. The phrase "three years," as Paul uses it, does not necessarily mean thirty-six months, but one whole year and at least part of two others, one before and one after. According to this manner of counting time, for instance, the fifteen months between the first of November of 2000 and the first of February of 2002 would be "three years." It is for the same reason that from the crucifixion on the afternoon of Friday to the resurrection on Sunday morning there are "three days" (part of Friday, the entire day of Saturday, and part of Sunday).

beside his horse. In fact the text says nothing about whether Saul and his companions were on horse or foot, and the soldier's garb is no more than a product of the imagination of an artist seeking to make his paintings more colorful.

There is, however, another important consequence of our familiarity with the text: we miss much of the dramatic impact of Saul's conversion. It clearly is a surprising conversion. Up to this point, Luke has presented Saul as the archenemy of Christianity. If we were reading Acts as we read a novel for the first time, on coming to 9:2 we would be convinced that the rest of the book will deal with the conflict between Saul and Christians. But suddenly everything changes. The one who seemed to be a powerful and unflinching enemy rises from the ground weak and blind. Anyone who does not know the end of this story will decide that God has punished him by blinding him. The same God whom Luke has already depicted healing the sick and striking Ananias and Sapphira dead, now has struck this Saul who was "breathing threats and murder against the Christians." Were we reading this story for the first time, upon seeing him spend three days blinded, we would say, "He got his just desserts!"

But the story does not end there. God has other plans for Saul, and sends reluctant Ananias to him. Ananias, instead of coming with recriminations, addresses him as "brother Saul" (9:17). At this point all that we have is a glimpse of the further plans that God has for this Saul. But at least we are told quite clearly that the Jesus who prayed for those who crucified him is still ready to forgive and to receive the enemies of his Church—those, who like Saul, by persecuting it persecute him.

This is a very different vision of human relations from what we find in the movies or in television programs. There the "good guys" struggle against the "bad guys" and usually the victory of the "good guys" consists in crushing and destroying the bad ones. It is also a vision very different from the one that sometimes reigns in our churches, where we see ourselves as the "good" and the rest as the "bad." It is rather a vision of the transforming power of the Lord, who has transformed and continues transforming those who are already disciples, but can also transform even his most bitter and determined enemies.

Earlier we noticed the contrast between the "people" and their leaders. In Acts, it is usually the latter who persecute and oppress Christians, not only for religious reasons, but also because of issues having to do with power and control. At the beginning of chapter 9, Saul is the representative of those spheres. What one would never have imagined is that he would soon become one of those whom he had recently persecuted. However, that is exactly what happens. What this means is that Christians must always see even their most determined enemies as potential brothers and sisters in Christ. That is why, when the martyrs of the early centuries faced their judges, they made every effort to do so, not condemning those judges, but calling them to faith. And let us not forget that Paul himself, after his speech to King Agrippa in Acts 26, where he retells his own story of conversion, ends by expressing his desire that those who stand in judgment of him will follow his path of conversion: "I pray to God that not only you but also all who are listening to me today might become such as I am—except for these chains!" (26:29).

The situation that Luke describes in the early chapters of Acts is still the situation of many of us today. There are still countries where the powerful persecute Christians who question their power or who call for a justice they do not desire. In other places, although Christians are not persecuted unto death, means are found to silence their voices. Christians organizing the tenants in one of our barrios soon have to deal with slum lords, banks, politicians, and often also the police. Those who preach against vice, and especially those who organize effective programs to struggle against vice, soon clash with those who become rich by exploiting vice. In such situations, it is no wonder that we are tempted to think that such people are the irreconcilable enemy whom we have no alternative but to destroy before they destroy us. For such people—abusive, exploiting, disbelieving, blasphemous, murderers—we have no other word than stark condemnation.

It is at that point that this ninth chapter of Acts breaks into our set ways. When it was least expected, this Saul, who was breathing threats and murder against the disciples of the Lord, becomes a brother to Ananias and to those very disciples whom until then he persecuted. Likewise, that unbeliever who now scorns us, that inordinately wealthy one who lives it up while the people suffer, that journalist who lies about us because someone pays him to do so, and even that sergeant who tortures one of our sisters or brothers—any one of them may one day fall to the ground "on the Damascus road." In such a case, even though our natural inclination, like that of Ananais, may be exactly the opposite, we have no other alternative than to call them "brother" or "sister," and treat them as such.

This is a harsh word, for in the polarized situations of extreme suffering where many among our people find themselves, what is natural is to hate those who are evil and to convince ourselves that for such there is no hope of salvation. However, if we reject this word, we shall also be rejecting the transforming power of the gospel, which has reached us and may also reach them.

The nature and the immediate consequences of Paul's conversion must be taken in this context. As we saw in the case of Simon Magus, there are powerful ones who wish to become Christians without giving up their power, and who even believe that their power should give them some advantage in their new life. There are also dictators and presidents of great nations who claim to be born again, but use this only as a political strategy to bring about immediate dividends. There are in Latin America petty dictators who use their power to oppress others and who, when the army kills or "disappears" someone, look the other way. There are politicians who, like Simon Magus, wish to employ their "faith" in order to increase their power. But a true conversion turns everything upside down. Saul arises blind and disabled. When he falls to the ground, also his own sense of importance and authority fall. Saul has to become a disciple of Ananias, who compared to him is a mere nobody.

Likewise, while we keep the door open for the conversion of those who to-day use their power to oppress the people or to oppose the faith, when such conversion comes about we must invite them and insist that this be truly a new birth, a radical transformation such as that of Saul, who finds himself asking for strength and direction from the same one whom three days earlier he sought to kill. The other option, a "conversion" without change, is a cheap imitation of the true thing.

RENEWED CALLS

Verse 6 invites another reflection. When Saul asks the Lord for direction, the an-swer of the Lord is simply, "Get up and into the city and you will be told what you are to do." Once in Damascus, he has to wait three days before his inter-view with Ananais. In Acts 9, Ananias only tells Saul a few words about God's purposes of turning him into a preacher of the gospel. In 22:14–15, he says a bit more; and the same is true in 26:16–18. It is only as we read the rest of the Book of Acts, as the action unfolds, that we see a series of new calls from God to Saul, who at each step discovers a new dimension of his ministry, or a new place where he is sent. In Antioch, the Spirit will give instructions that Barnabas and Saul be set aside for a special task, but will say very little about the nature of that task. Later will come the vision of the Macedonian youth, inviting Paul and his companions to new fields of witness. And the story goes on.

What this means is that when God calls us, rarely are we told more than we need to know at the time. If God gives us a vision of what we are to do, that vi-sion is clarified precisely as we do it. Conversion, or the call to a specific minis-try, are not normally the last call from God, but rather day by day, step by step, we discover what God desires from us.

It is important to remember this, because too often we refuse to respond to God's call until we have clarified every detail and every future step along the way. If those details are not clear, we do nothing. Quite often we use that lack of clarity as an excuse not to respond to situations that seem difficult or controver-sial. However, all the great figures in the history of the Church received partial calls and answers whose meaning was clarified in the very course of their own obedience: Saul on the way to Damascus, Augustine in the garden of Milan, Luther studying the Epistle to the Romans, Las Casas in liberating the natives that had been entrusted to him, Wesley in Aldersgate, and so on. God's call to us today may seem insignificant (such as "get up and enter the city"), but may well be the beginning of an unexpected adventure of faith.

C. PETER'S WORK (9:32–11:18)

The narrative now brings us back to Peter, whom we had left upon his re-turn to Jerusalem after the episode of Simon Magus (8:25). What follows is a series of events in which we will see the gospel expanded geographically while also making greater inroads among the Gentiles. These events begin with two miracles.

1. Two Miracles (9:32–43)

a. The Healing of Aeneas (9:32–35)

Peter is going about visiting all "the believers." This is another of those phrases with which Luke signals that he is not about to tell us all that Peter did, but just some examples. Peter goes about preaching and teaching. In one of those occasions, he visits Lydda (in Hebrew "Lod"). This was a small town some forty kilometers from Jerusalem, on the way to Joppa. Today it is a fairly good-sized city, where the main international airport of Israel is situated. Although the name of Aeneas is Greek, most likely he was a Hellenistic Jew. The text does not explicitly say that he was a believer, but the context of Peter's activity in Lydda would seem to indicate that this was the case. He was visiting "the saints living in Lydda" when he met Aeneas. The phrase the NRSV translates as "for eight years" could also mean that Aeneas had been paralyzed since he was eight years old. Likewise, what the NRSV translates as "make your bed" could also be a way of telling someone to set the table. Given the context, the translation in the NRSV makes most sense. Finally, Sharon is a plain that extends along the coast from Lydda and Joppa to Mount Carmel. Clearly, the "all the residents" of 9:35 is a hyperbole, for Luke does not mean that every inhabitant of that entire area was converted.

b. The Resurrection of Dorcas (9:36–43)

Joppa is the present Jaifa by the sea, some fifteen kilometers from Lydda. The name "Dorcas" is the Greek translation of "Tabitha" and means "gazelle." The text does not say whether the disciples sent for Peter so that he could accompany them in their mourning, or so that he could do something about Tabitha. The widows mentioned in 9:39 were impoverished women for whom Dorcas had been providing clothing.[40] Now they wear the clothing that Dorcas has provided, and show it to Peter as a sign of her good works.

Peter orders everyone out of the room. The miracle that is about to take place is not a spectacle. The phrase that Peter uses in 9:40—"Tabitha, get up"—is very similar to what Jesus says in Aramaic in Mark 5:41: "Talitha cum."[41] For that reason, some scholars suggest that it may be the same story that sometimes has been attributed to Jesus and others to Peter. At any rate, it is significant to note that here, as so often in Acts, Luke conjoins a story about a man and another one about a woman.

Finally, Luke tells us that Peter remained in Joppa "for some time," lodging in the house of a certain Simon, a tanner. This will be the address that the angel will give Cornelius in the following chapter, so that he may send for Pe-

---

40. Later, there will appear within the Church the office of "widow." This was a woman consecrated to the service of the Lord (see I Tim. 5:9–10). In the case of the narrative in Acts, the women seem to be literal widows; that is to say, women whose husbands had died and who therefore were left without support or protection.

41. In the parallel passage in Luke 8:54, the phrase appears in Greek. In Mark 5:41 Jesus addresses the girl in Aramaic.

ter (10:6). It is also significant that the occupation of tanner was considered unclean by many Jews, because tanners had to work with dead animals (see Lev. 11:39), and that it was precisely at the house of this Simon that Peter had to face the vision of the unclean animals.

2. Peter and Cornelius (10:1–48)

Chapters 10 and 11 comprise one of the critical points in the entire narrative, for it is here that the Christians in Jerusalem come to the conclusion that the gospel is also for Gentiles, and this is a fundamental thesis throughout the book of Acts.[42]

a. The Vision of Cornelius (10:1–9a)

While Peter is still in Joppa, at Simon's home, the scene changes. We now find ourselves in Caesarea, the great city built in Roman style by Herod the Great to honor Augustus Caesar (hence the name of "Caesarea"). Although there were Jews there, it was generally disliked by the more orthodox and nationalistic Jews, for it was the seat of Roman government, and many of its inhabitants practiced pagan customs. The name of "Cornelius" was very common, for in the year 82 B.C.E. Sulla had freed ten thousand slaves, who took Sulla's family name, Cornelius. The fact that this Cornelius was a centurion means that he was a Roman citizen, a requirement to hold such a rank. The "Italian cohort" seems to have been an auxiliary body of archers.[43] One of the difficulties that historians pose is that there were no Roman troops stationed in Caesarea until after the death of Herod Agrippa in the year 44, and the events that Luke narrates seem to have taken place before that time. Does that mean that it is necessary to place the Cornelius episode later than usual? Was Cornelius in the city under some special commission, without his own cohort? Is Luke mistaken in his data? All that can be said about this question is that we simply do not know.

At any rate, Cornelius is "a devout man who feared God." What this means is that, like the Ethiopian eunuch in chapter 8, he was a Gentile who believed in the God of Israel, but who was not ready to be circumcised and obey all the law.[44] As early as chapter 6 we have found "proselytes" in the church in

---

42. Some have suggested that Luke is working here with two separate traditions that he has interwoven into a single story: Peter's vision and the conversion of Cornelius. That theory has been ably disputed by K. Haacker, "Dibelius und Cornelius: Ein Beispiel formgeschichtlicher Überlieferungskritik," *BibZeit*, 24 (1980), 234–51.

43. There are indications that the "second Italian cohort of Roman volunteers" was stationed in this area during the first century. They were not legionnaires, but auxiliary troops. Legionnaires had to be Roman citizens, and fought in the traditional Roman style, whereas auxiliary troops were armed in various ways according to their origins and traditions (archers, light cavalry, etc.) and became citizens upon completing their tour of military duty.

44. J. A. Overman, "The God-fearers: Some neglected features," *JStNT*, 32 (1988), 17–26, supports this traditional understanding of the "God-fearers." There is a different inter-

Jerusalem—that is, Gentiles who had become converts to Judaism and then to Christianity, such as Nicholas (6:5). Also in 8:2–13 we are told of the conversion of many Samaritans. But to this point, with the sole exception of the Ethiopian eunuch, there is no mention of a Gentile converted to Christianity.

Cornelius has a vision. Luke tells us that "he clearly saw." This may mean simply that he was awake when he had the vision, and that it was not a dream. But it is most likely a manner of contrasting the clarity of the vision of Cornelius with the ambiguity of Peter's vision and the perplexity in which he is left. At any rate, this vision took place in mid-afternoon, at one of the appointed times for Jewish prayers, and therefore it is possible that Cornelius, a God-fearing man, was praying when he had his vision. What the angel tells him is absolutely clear, giving him exact directions as to what to do, and the exact address where Peter may be found.

In response to that vision, Cornelius sends for Peter in Joppa by means of two servants and another God-fearing soldier who, like him, belonged to the group of Gentiles who had been approaching Judaism. His trust in these messengers is manifest in that he tells them all that he has seen (10:8).

b. The Vision of Peter in Joppa (10:9b–23a)

It is the following day that Peter has a parallel vision, which will help him to respond correctly to Cornelius's. In contrast with Cornelius's vision, Peter's is confusing, and takes place while he is in a trance. Luke even seems to establish a relationship between Peter's hunger at the time of the vision and the fact that what he sees is food. It has been suggested that there is a connection between the sails of the ships that Peter would see from the roof and the "large sheet" in which the animals of the vision descend.[45] Whatever the case may be, Peter sees all sorts of animals, both clean and unclean, and the voice tells him that he is to eat of all of them.[46] Peter refuses, and the voice insists three times before "the thing"—that is exactly what the text calls it—is taken up to heaven.

Thus ends Peter's vision. In contrast with the vision of Cornelius, it is confusing and indecisive. Its interpretation will be in the rest of the story. But

---

pretation in M. Wilcox, "The God-fearers in Acts: A reconsideration," *JStNT*, 13 (1981), 102–22. According to him, the "God-fearers" obeyed the law more closely than has usually been supposed.

45. William Neil, *The Acts of the Apostles* (Grand Rapids, Mich.: Wm. B. Eerdmans, 1973), p. 138.

46. Peter refuses to eat because he has never eaten anything "profane" (*koinos*) or "unclean" (*akathartos*). Technically, there is a difference between the two. The profane is that which has not been consecrated. The unclean is that which can contaminate the believer. By the time of the New Testament, the distinction had almost disappeared. It is interesting to note that in verse 15 the voice combines both things by telling Peter "what God has made clean, you must not call profane." See C. House, "Defilement by association: Some insights from the usage of *koinos/koinoo* in Acts 10 and 11," *AndUnivSem*, 21 (1983), 143–53.

Peter does not understand this, and he is simply perplexed when Cornelius's messengers arrive at Simon's home, and the Spirit tells Peter to receive them and go with them.[47]

The fact that the vision takes place in Joppa is significant. It was in Joppa that Jonah, when God ordered him to go to Nineveh, took a ship in the opposite direction, towards Tarshish (Jon. 1:3). Peter's true name is "Simon, son of Jonah" (Matt. 16:17). Now this Simon son of Jonah, like the earlier Jonah, and in the very city of Joppa, will hear the call sending him beyond the limits of the people of Israel.[48]

An interesting detail is that in verse 23 Peter acts as if the house were his. This may be an indication of his own personal authority or a sign of the manner in which Christians place their possessions at the service of others.

c. The Events in Caesarea (10:23b–48)

The next day Peter goes to Caesarea with the two messengers, the soldier, and "some of the believers." Later (11:12) Luke will tell us that these were six. Some suggest that Peter took them with him to serve as his witnesses, for he was going to visit a Gentile, and he may have felt that he needed someone to attest to his behavior as a good Jew. Eventually this will indeed be their function, although in a different context. However, in the manner in which Luke tells his story, especially if we read it as someone who does not know what follows, it is apparent that Peter has no idea why he is going to Caesarea, nor what awaits him there. Therefore, there seems to be no reason for him to think he will need witnesses, and apparently he simply takes these six brothers as company.

Cornelius, on the other hand, is certain that Peter will come, and is expecting him "together with his relatives and close friends." Their first encounter is not very successful, for Cornelius worships Peter and Peter rebukes him (10:25–26).[49]

Peter enters the house and does not show great tact. His interest is not in winning the good will of those who are present. On the contrary, his first statement is that from his own religious perspective it is "unlawful" for him to

---

47. In 10:19, several very trustworthy ancient manuscripts say "two men" instead of three. It is possible that Luke originally wrote "two," referring to the two servants who were truly Cornelius's messengers, for the soldier came as an escort, and that later a copyist, seeing the contrast between verse 7 and verse 19, may have said "three" where the original said "two." That is why some versions say "three men," others "two," and still others "some."

48. See R. W. Tall, "Peter, 'Son' of Jonah: The conversion of Cornelius in the context of canon," *JStNT*, 29 (1987), 79–90.

49. However, what Cornelius does is not strictly to worship Peter. The *proskynein*, which Luke employs here, means to prostrate oneself before another as a sign of respect. It was certainly done before the gods, but also before superiors, and especially rulers. Therefore, the episode is not to be understood as if Cornelius had become an idolater, but rather in the sense that Peter is not superior to him, and does not expect such ceremonies.

visit Cornelius, and that he has acceded to this only because he has had a vision in which God has told him "that I should not call anyone profane or unclean"—in other words, that if it were up to me that is precisely what I would call you!

Cornelius's answer seems to surprise Peter.[50] It is at this point that Peter declares that he now understands "that God shows no partiality, but in every nation anyone who fears him and does what is right is acceptable to him." Up to that point, his interpretation of the vision of Joppa was simply that he should go with the messengers and even go as far as to enter a Gentile home. But now, upon learning of Cornelius's vision, he comes to the conclusion that God has indeed spoken to Cornelius.

Peter then begins his speech—one could almost say, his usual routine—about what God has done in Jesus. But he is suddenly surprised by the result: the Holy Spirit falls upon those who are listening, and they begin to speak in tongues and to extol God. This causes great amazement among the Jewish Christians from Joppa, for they did not believe it was possible for the Spirit to come upon Gentiles. "The circumcised believers that had come with Peter were astounded that the gift of the Holy Spirit had been poured out even on the Gentiles."

It is then that the final surprise comes. Peter, who two days before would never have dreamt of doing such a thing, now asks himself whether there is any reason not to baptize these believers. The question is very similar to what the Ethiopian asks Philip in 8:36, and may even reflect early ritual practices. The answer is in practical terms the same: "He ordered them to be baptized in the name of Jesus Christ" (10:48).

And, as a further surprise, which does not seem such to us but would have been astounding to any orthodox practicing Jew of the time, for whom contact with Gentiles should be assiduously avoided, Peter stays with Cornelius "for several days" (10:48).

3. Reporting to the Church in Jerusalem (11:1–18)

It is precisely this last point that most disturbs some of the believers in Jerusalem.[51] The phrase that the NRSV translates as "the circumcised believers" could be understood also in the sense of believers who insisted on circumcision. In this latter case, Luke would be beginning to speak about a party within the Church that formed as a reaction to the growing openness toward Gen-

---

50. The "four days" refer, as in the case of the "three years" of Paul in Arabia, to two complete days and portions of two others. The messengers left Caesarea the first day, arrived at Joppa on the second, began their return journey on the third, and arrived with Peter on the fourth.

51. Verse 11:2 is much longer in some manuscripts of the Western text. Some scholars argue that this longer text may come from Luke's own hand: E. Delebecque, "La montée de Pierre de Césarée à Jérusalem selon le Codex Bezae au chapître 11 des Actes des Apôtres," *EphThLov*, 58 (1958), 106–10.

tiles. This group, sometimes called "Judaizers," insisted on the need to obey the Law, and in the case of males, to be circumcised, in order to be a Christian. Because such a group does not appear until later, and because in 10:45 Luke has spoken of the believers in Joppa as "circumcised believers," it is most likely that he simply is referring to Jewish Christians, as the NRSV translates the text.

At any rate, these people called Peter to account, although apparently not so much for having preached to Gentiles, or for having baptized them, as for having gone into their house and eaten with them.

Peter's answer is a retelling of what we have already seen in chapter 10, except that in verses 16 and 17 he tells them something of what he thought when he saw the Holy Spirit being poured upon Gentiles. He remembered the promise of Jesus about baptism with the Holy Spirit, and he asked himself, "Who was I that I could hinder God?" The reaction of those present is one of positive surprise. They are surprised: "then God has given even to the Gentiles the repentance that leads to life!" And they are positive: "They were silent. And they praised God." At this point the feelings seem so positive that if we did not know the rest of the story we would imagine that this was the end of the debate about the place of Gentiles in the Church.

WHAT GOD HAS MADE CLEAN, YOU MUST NOT CALL PROFANE

The enormity of what Peter has done escapes us, because we think as Gentiles and it is difficult for us to see matters from Peter's perspective. It is natural for us to see that event through the lens of almost twenty centuries of mission among the Gentiles. But in order to understand what is actually taking place we must look at it through the lens of many other earlier centuries of insistence on absolute obedience to the Law, for that was Peter's perspective. He was convinced that contact with Gentiles must be avoided. To join Gentiles was, as he himself says, "unlawful" (10:28). The last thing Peter would have expected the day he abandoned his fishing nets by the Galilean lakeshore was that as a result some day he would visit a Gentile and dwell in his house. Yet now, as the result of a long journey from Galilee to Jerusalem, then to Lydda and eventually to Joppa, Peter accepts such Gentiles as his brothers and sisters, and he has them baptized.

The enormity of the entire episode becomes even greater when we remember that this particular Gentile was a Roman centurion. We know nothing of Peter's political opinions, but we know that among the more pious Jews it was customary to steer as far away from Romans as possible, for these particular Gentiles had conquered practically the entire known world and thanked their gods for it, while at the same time inviting their subjects to mingle their religions. It was precisely because of that profound dislike of Jews toward Romans—particularly toward Roman troops—that the representatives of the empire had their seat in Caesarea, and not in Jerusalem.

Although this entire episode is usually called "the conversion of Cornelius," it is just as much the conversion of Peter himself. Note that the vision that Cornelius has is clear, giving him detailed directions, whereas all that Peter has is a dim and confusing vision that leaves him perplexed. In this case, as in so many others, God does not speak most clearly where we would most expect, among the "insiders," but even calls the apostle Peter himself to obedience by means of the vision of a pagan.

Without knowing why, and perhaps even unwillingly, Peter goes to Cornelius. He does not have the least interest in gaining the good will of Cornelius and his family. Actually, at the first encounter he rebuffs Cornelius (10:28). If it were up to him, he would say that Cornelius and his kin are unclean; but God has told him not to call them such, and he will obey God's command.

Then, in the midst of a situation that for him must have been at least uncomfortable, the unexpected happens: by pouring out the Holy Spirit, God shows Peter and later the church in Jerusalem that "God has given even to the Gentiles the repentance that leads to life."

Time has gone by, and thanks to God and to that experience that Peter had, we and others who otherwise would be far have been made near (Eph. 2:13).[52] But now we are the ones who have laws, rules, and principles that, no matter how good, sometimes run the risk of being obstacles to our mission. It is no longer a matter of not entering a Gentile household. Now it is a matter of keeping ourselves pure by not attending certain kinds of celebrations, not participating in certain social activities, not joining people who are drinking, or whatever else the various churches have listed as norms of conduct. In order to save that purity, we often limit our circle of contacts, so that we are always among believers, and we avoid rubbing shoulders with those who do not believe as we do. There certainly is some value in this, for the community of faith has a very important role in Christian life, strengthening us when we are weak and helping us to discover God's will. But when we carry this to the extreme, we run the risk of so limiting ourselves to that community that we forget that Christ died, not only for ourselves, but also for all those others whose company we avoid: the irresponsible, the immoral, the amoral, the unbelieving, and so on.

In such circumstances, we must remember that, as Peter declares, "God shows no partiality," and that Christ died for sinners. If we serve a Christ who came to seek us in our own state of being lost, are we not obliged to go and seek others no matter what state they may be in? Let us not forget that Peter went to the house of a *centurion*. He went to the house of an officer of the army that was occupying his own native land and of the empire that oppressed it with heavy taxes. He went not because he wished to gain the support of this powerful man, but because it was God who told him to do so. Are we equally ready to undertake equally risky and unprecedented mission?

---

52. There is a study of the episode of Peter and Cornelius from a missionary point of view: D. Lotz, "Peter's wider understanding of God's Will: Acts 10:34–48," *IntRevMiss*, 77 (1988), 201–7. On its application to a Latin American context, with a number of examples and valuable reflections, see the chapter "Mirad los campos," in G. Cook, *Profundidad en la evangelización* (San José: Publicaciones INDEF, 1975), pp. 68–84.

In a way, this episode is similar to Saul's conversion, although now from the opposite perspective. There we saw how the one who until then persecuted Christians is converted, and God uses him for great deeds. Now we see how an obedient church, in the person of Peter, lives that gospel that is good news even for people such as Saul when he was persecuting Christians, or this official of an occupation army. The result is that the entire church in Jerusalem is converted to a wider view of the gospel.

We live in a world that is full of corruption, vice, injustice, and oppression. As Christians, we have to condemn all of this with a clear and prophetic voice. But at the same time we have to be careful not to fall into the trap of acting as if the Church were only for people "like us." When in any of our churches people are rejected because "they are not decent," or because "they practice vices," or because they do not share our political ideology, it is time for us to stop and reflect on this episode of Peter and Cornelius, and ask ourselves what is the meaning for us today when we declare that "God shows no partiality." There is no doubt that in our churches there is much talk of evangelization and of the need to take the "good news" to the rest of the world. Let us not forget that the good news includes precisely the proclamation that those who were far away have been made near. The "good news," like medicine, is not for those who are healthy, but for the sick.

D. The Church in Antioch (11:19–30)

Although what is told in this section seems to be a parenthesis within the narration of a series of actions by Peter, what Luke is interested in is not the actions of Peter or of any other of the apostles, but how the Spirit calls the Church to new forms of obedience. For this reason, now that he has told us that Peter baptized Cornelius and his friends—that is, that there was a Christian church of Gentile origin in Caesarea—he moves on to tell us about a similar church, this time in Antioch. The chronological order of events is not clear, for in 11:19 we go back to what was said in 8:4, and therefore it might seem that these events took place at the same time as the others that are told in chapter 8.[53] Some commentators suggest that the narrative does follow a chronological order, for its logic would seem to indicate that what Luke tells us about Antioch happened after the conversion of Cornelius, as it is only then that the church in Jerusalem is ready to accept the existence of a partly Gentile church such as the one in Antioch. It would seem that 11:19 refers to events that took place right after the death of Stephen, and that what we are told in 11:20 took place either after or practically at the same time as the conversion of Cornelius. This would explain why the believers in Jerusalem were not scandalized when they learned that there were Gentiles in the church in Antioch. On the other hand, it may be best not to insist too much on the linear nature of a chronology such as this, for possibly what Luke is trying to show his

---

53. The Greek grammatical construction of this verse, very similar to that of 8:4, implies that Luke indeed wants the reader to relate the two episodes.

readers is that the mission to the Gentiles was the work of the Holy Spirit, who was acting along the same lines through various parallel events: the conversion of the Ethiopian eunuch by the witness of Philip, that of Cornelius and his friends by the preaching of Peter, and now the founding of a community that is partly Gentile in Antioch.

Antioch itself was a great city, the third largest in the entire Roman Empire. It had been founded on the shore of the river Orontes by Seleucus Nicator around the year 300 B.C.E. and named "Antioch" in honor of Seleucus's father Antiochus. By the first century, it had some five hundred thousand inhabitants. It was a hub for the interchange of ideas, cultures, customs, and religion. The Jewish community there was numerous, and it had a beautiful synagogue, which attracted many pagans.[54] Therefore, the contrast between the cultural and religious atmosphere in Antioch and that in Jerusalem was stark. It is not surprising that there were in Antioch significant numbers of pagans interested in listening to the gospel, or that the church there was willing to preach to them.

The narrative in 11:19–20 is terse. We are told that some of those who fled after the death of Stephen went directly to Antioch, and others to Phoenicia and Cyprus. This list does not intend to be complete, for in the very next verse Luke will speak of others who came from Cyrene. At any rate, Phoenicia is a narrow coastal plain that extends from Samaria to the Orontes, and it therefore makes sense to imagine that some of those who scattered after the beginning of the persecution went from Jerusalem to Phoenicia, and then to Antioch. However, Luke does not tell us that among those who first preached in Antioch were people coming from Phoenicia. Cyprus is a nearby island, which had maritime communication both with the seaport of Caesarea, the gateway to Jerusalem, and with Antioch. Barnabas, who will soon reappear on the scene, was from Cyprus (4:36), and it was to that island that Barnabas and Saul first went in their missionary journey. Therefore, by the end of verse 19 all that we have been told is that, at least in Phoenicia, Cyprus, and Antioch, the gospel has been preached, although exclusively among Jews.

It is in verse 20 that the radically new appears. "Some men of Cyprus and Cyrene" came to Antioch and began preaching to the Greeks.[55] Cyrene was a city in Libya on the northern shore of Africa, where there was a strong Jewish community. Cyrenean Jews are mentioned in the episode of Pentecost (2:10), and among the Hellenists who opposed Stephen's preaching (6:9). Luke himself in his Gospel mentions Simon of Cyrene, who carried the cross of Jesus (Luke 23:26; see Matt. 27:32 and Mark 15:21). Later, in 13:1, when listing leaders of the church in Antioch, Luke would mention "Simon who was called Niger" (that is, "Simon the Black") and Lucius of Cyrene. It is possible that these

---

54. Josephus, *War.* 7.3.3.

55. The NRSV translates "Hellenists." In this particular case, it is clear that Luke refers to actual Gentiles, and therefore a better translation, less likely to cause confusion, would be "Greeks."

two were among those who first preached the gospel among the Gentiles in Antioch.

At any rate, the radically new thing is that these people from Cyprus and Cyrene begin preaching also to the Gentiles. Luke affirms that "the hand of the Lord was with them," as a way of letting us know that the proclamation to the Gentiles was blessed by God. It is important for him to emphasize this, for one of the matters that was still bitterly discussed at his time was the conversion of Gentiles. Luke rejects the opinion of the "Judaizers," that converted Gentiles must obey the entire Law (and, in the case of men, be circumcised). The Gentiles of Antioch became Christians without first becoming Jews, and God blessed this development.

Barnabas, whom the church in Jerusalem sent to Antioch, is one of the most attractive characters in the entire book of Acts. We have already been told that the apostles called him "son of consolation," and that he was generous with his goods (4:36–37). We have also been told that after Saul's conversion it was he who received Saul in Jerusalem and introduced him to the rest of the Christian community (9:27). Finally, Barnabas will be an important character from 12:25 to 15:39. It is only in Galatians 2:13 that Paul says something negative about Barnabas, and this in a tone of surprise, as if Barnabas were the last person from whom he would have expected such behavior. In the text we are studying, Luke tells us that the church in Jerusalem sent Barnabas to Antioch. It is interesting to note that Barnabas receives his commission from the church in Jerusalem, and not from the Twelve. Were the Twelve not in the Holy City? It is impossible to know. Nor does the text tell us whether Barnabas was sent in order to inquire about what was taking place and then bring a report back to the church in Jerusalem, or was sent rather in order to support those in Antioch. Whatever may have been the reason he was sent, the fact is that he remained in Antioch, without returning to Jerusalem for quite some time.

Upon arriving in Antioch, Barnabas rejoiced in what he saw,[56] and he exhorted the faithful. (The NRSV does not give the sense of a continuing action of exhortation, which does appear in the Greek. What Luke says is not that he exhorted the congregation once, but that he continued exhorting them.)

Barnabas then "went to Tarsus to look for Saul." This would seem to indicate that Barnabas had already spent some time in Antioch, and by then was one of the leaders of that church. It would then appear that Barnabas went looking for Saul to help him in that work. This would seem to be during the time when, according to Paul's own witness, he was preaching in "the regions of Syria and Cilicia" (Gal. 1:21). Tarsus was the capital of Cilicia. The Greek text gives the impression that Barnabas had to look actively for Saul, until he found him.

Back at Antioch, they spent an entire year working there. Luke tells us little about that year, which must have been crucial for the history of Christian-

---

56. Here there is a beautiful play on words in Greek, telling us that when he saw the grace (*charis*) Barnabas rejoiced (*echarē*).

ity, for one can imagine that it was there and at that time that the fundamental characteristics of the Gentile Church, to which most of us Christians belong today, were shaped.

An indication of the ferment that existed in Antioch at that time is the fact that it was there that for the first time the disciples of Jesus were called "Christians." On the original meaning of that term there are several theories. The most common is that it was mockingly given by pagans to the disciples, perhaps in imitation to the name given to the fanatical followers of Nero.[57] Others suggest that the word means "slaves of Christ," and that the disciples were the ones who took it up as a sign of who they were.[58] The latter theory, which is perhaps the most likely, claims that the disciples took this name in order to indicate that they were agents of the Anointed King, of the "Christ"—which gave them an important sense of dignity both in their difficult present situation and in the coming reign of God. It may also be worth mentioning that the first person known to have employed the word "Christianity" to refer to the new faith was a bishop of Antioch, Ignatius, early in the second century.

While Barnabas and Saul were working together in Antioch, some prophets arrived from Jerusalem. This is not extraordinary, for it is clear that in the ancient Church there were itinerate preachers who visited the churches exhorting and edifying believers, and thus serving as a link between congregations at a time when the Church did not have many other means of communication.[59] One of these prophets, Agabus, announced that there would be a great famine over all the inhabitant earth (the entire *oikoumenē*, that is to say, the entire inhabited world or at least the whole Roman Empire).[60] Agabus is also mentioned in 21:10–11, where he foretells Paul's arrest. History records at least five different famines during the reign of Claudius (41–54 C.E.), when

---

57. H. B. Mattingly, "The origin of the name 'Christiani,'" *JTS*, 9 (1958), 26–37. The main difficulty with this theory is that most of the examples that Mattingly offers are later than the name "Christians."

58. B. J. Bickerman, "The name of Christians," *HTR*, 42 (1949), 109–24, and J. Moreau, "Le nom des Chrétiens," *Nouvelle Clio* (1950), 190–92. The verbal form employed in the Greek text can be translated both as a passive voice ("Christians were called") and as a reflexive verb ("Christians called themselves").

59. See M. de Burgos Núñez, "La comunidad de Antioquía: Aspectos históricos y papel profético en los orígenes del cristianismo," *Comm*, 15 (1982), 3–26. Soon the existence of these itinerate prophets created difficulties, for it was necessary to distinguish between the true and false prophets. This may be seen in the *Didache*, which tries to offer guidelines on the matter. *Did.* 11.6–9.

60. At this point (11:28), the Western text says, "While we were gathered, one of them whose name was Agabus." This is the first place in which the first person plural (we) appears in the Book of Acts. If it is part of the original text, it would indicate that the very much debated "we" includes either one of the believers from Antioch or one of the prophets from Jerusalem. However, this is most likely a later addition on the part of a copyist who was convinced that the "Lucius" in 13:1 was Luke, the author of Acts.

there were poor harvests in various parts of the empire. As a whole, Claudius's reign was a period of famine and want. However, it is difficult to go beyond this general assertion. Josephus speaks of a famine in Palestine in the years 47 and 48, when Cuspus Fadus and Tiberius Alexander were Roman procurators.[61] If we are to take literally the words in Acts 12:1—"about that time King Herod"—we will have to place the events in Antioch at the same time as the persecution of Herod Agrippa, that is between 41 and 44 C.E.[62]

The believers in Antioch collected an offering and sent it to Jerusalem by means of Barnabas and Saul, although the text does not tell us whether the offering was in response to the prophecy of Agabus or in response to the famine itself. It is interesting to note that, although Acts does not mention the collection for the poor in Jerusalem, which has such an important place in Paul's Epistles, it does assert that from an early date Paul was involved in the efforts to provide support for the disciples in Jerusalem.

It is not clear who are the "elders" or the "presbyters" in Jerusalem to whom the offering was sent. By the time that Luke was writing, there were in each church such persons who served as pastors and leaders of the congregation. The problem is that Luke has not mentioned any "elders" in Jerusalem. They certainly are not the apostles. Some interpreters suggest that these are the "seven" elected in Acts 6, or their successors, arguing that their function was to manage what was collected for the poor, and the same seems to be the function of these "elders."[63]

This passage, like so many in Acts that refer to Paul's career, presents once again the problem of how to coordinate the data presented here with what Paul himself says in his letters.[64] Briefly stated, the problem is that in Galatians 1 and 2, in summarizing his own career, Paul speaks only of two trips to Jerusalem, the second of them to attend the so-called "apostolic council" described in Acts 15. What can we make then of this "offering trip"? Some scholars suggest changing the order in which Luke presents matters, and claim that this particular trip took place after the apostolic council. Others suggest that perhaps Luke erred, and Paul did not go to Jerusalem with the delegation that took the offerings from Antioch. Probably the most acceptable solution is that Paul does not mention this very brief trip in Galatians simply because it has nothing to do with the matter at hand, and because at that time he did not even talk to the Twelve, and in any case he went only as a companion to Barnabas (whose name therefore appears first in 11:30).

---

61. *Ant.* 20.101.

62. See A. M. Tormes, "La fecha del hambre de Jerusalén aludida por Act 11,28–30," *EstEcl*, 33 (1959), 303–16.

63. See Turrado, *Hechos de los Apóstoles*, p. 123.

64. The problem this passage poses, as well as the various suggested solutions, are very well summarized in Alfred Wickenhauser, *Los Hechos de los Apóstoles* (Barcelona: Herder, 1973), pp. 200–203.

THE GREATNESS OF THE SMALL

If we did not know the rest of the story in Acts, we would wonder why Luke now tells us about a church that has just been founded almost five hundred kilometers away from Jerusalem. He does not mention the names of those who founded this church, nor of those who took the gigantic step of beginning to preach to the Gentiles. The truth is that as we read these verses we are inclined to boredom: the fact that there is one more church is not surprising after Luke has told us so much about so many new communities, and of believers scattered all over Galilee, Samaria, Cyprus, Phoenicia, and elsewhere. We want him to get back to Jerusalem, where the center of action is, and to tell us more about what the apostles were doing.

Luke has placed these verses here because later on as the narrative unfolds the center of action will move from Jerusalem to Antioch. After these short words he will take us back to Jerusalem, but after that he will say almost nothing further about that very first church. The old center will no longer be such, and another church, which until then was quite peripheral, far away from the center, will become the focus of attention and action.

This makes sense. The church in Jerusalem had its moment and its mission. Now a new time dawns. It will be necessary to respond to the challenge of mission to the Gentiles. Who can respond to that challenge better than this church in Antioch, itself at the edge of the earlier Jewish church? Beginning with chapter 13, Luke will deal almost exclusively with the church in Antioch and its missionary work, not because it was the most ancient, the richest, or the most powerful, but because it was the one that responded to the new challenges of the time.

The same has been true throughout the history of the Church. Those who until a certain moment have been at the periphery, precisely in part because they have been in the periphery, are those who most often prove to be ready to respond to the challenges of a new age. As Paul says in I Corinthians 1:27–28, "God chose what is foolish in the world to shame the wise; God chose what is weak in the world to shame the strong; God chose what is low and despised in the world, things that are not, to reduce to nothing things that are."

The Spanish-speaking church, Catholic as well as Protestant, has been at the periphery for a long time. This may discourage us or create in us a feeling of inferiority, leading us to believe that the best always comes from the north, from Europe, from another culture, and that our task is simply to receive what those other centers and those other cultures give us. Certainly, too often that has been the attitude of many among us.

But there is another possibility. Precisely because we are at the periphery of the Western world—cultural, religious, and economic periphery—it is quite possible that our church is particularly prepared to respond to the new challenges of the day.

Let us take an example. Throughout the world there is much talk about the need for better and greater evangelization. In the traditionally rich churches in Europe and the United States ambitious programs are developed, with all sorts of technical and economic resources, to promote evangelization. But in most cases such programs lead to meager results, and the churches that are still growing are our own Latino churches, working without many resources, but with great enthusiasm and conviction. Therefore, if the evangelizing work is to continue, most probably it will start not from the centers (the Jerusalems) of the rich churches in the North Atlantic, but from the Antiochs, from churches such as the Hispanic churches, which have been founded in rural and urban zones throughout the hemisphere. Today there are active churches, giving witness to the gospel by word and by action, practicing love and justice, in Chile as well as in Peru, and in many of the poorest neighborhoods of New York and Los Angeles. The origins of such churches are probably as little known as the origins of the church in Antioch. Their future impact no one can tell.

However, in order for these churches, Catholic and Protestant, to be responsible at this time, it will not suffice to continue repeating what has been received from Jerusalem. That important year of which Luke only gives us a glimpse, which Barnabas and Saul spend working in Antioch, has to be repeated in our own communities. What happened during that year was that the church in Antioch acquired an understanding of itself, and assimilated the gospel in such a way that it became able to share it under new terms, better adapted to the mission that God had entrusted to it. Likewise, it is necessary for our churches, through their own reflection, prayer, and even financial management, to discover the manner in which the gospel speaks to us and to our communities today. Perhaps the difficult times through which many of our churches are going, times of debate and polarization, are the process by which we are being prepared by God's Holy Spirit for a mission such as that out of Antioch, without precedent. Antioch did not simply repeat what it heard from Jerusalem.

Two-Way Mission

In the very same passage in which Luke gives us the first news about the church in Antioch he also tells us that the believers in that church collected an offering for the church in Judea. Up to this point, the center of mission seems to have been Jerusalem, as if impelled by a constant centrifugal impulse. In Samaria there are some believers, baptized by Philip, and the church in Jerusalem sends Peter and John to see what is happening. Another church appears in Caesarea, thanks to the visions of Cornelius and Peter, and the latter has to go to Jerusalem to render an account of what he has done. Now in Antioch another church appears, and once again those in Jerusalem send an emissary—Barnabas.

In this case, however, things take a different turn. Other prophets arrive from Jerusalem, and one of them proclaims that the mother church will find itself in difficulties. The result is that the church in Antioch gathers its resources in order to help the mother church. Antioch will not be content with simply receiving from Jerusalem, but rather, at the proper time it too will contribute to the previous center.

Once we notice this, it is not surprising that the church in Antioch became a missionary center, sending Barnabas and Saul, and possibly others, on a series of travels that took the gospel to distant lands. These Antiochene Christians are not passive believers, waiting to see what comes from Jerusalem, but rather active believers, conscious of their own missionary responsibility, not only toward the Gentiles, but even toward their sisters and brothers in Jerusalem.

What this means for the Latino church should be obvious. Many of our churches are the result of missionary efforts from other latitudes or other cultures. Some are content with receiving and are constantly asking for more help, more economic resources, more personnel. Others have taken responsibility for themselves and their own work, and eventually have become missionary centers. The difference is not in that some have more resources than others. In fact, some of the churches that have taken their own missionary responsibility most seriously include among their members some of the poorest people in our own communities. The difference is rather in the vision the Church has of itself and its mission. The difference is in that, like the church in Antioch, these new missionary churches of today take their own responsibility quite seriously.

E. Herod's Persecution (12:1–24)

1. Introduction: James Is Killed (12:1–2)

Having mentioned the delegation from Antioch, Luke returns with them to Jerusalem, where he tells us about the death of James and Peter's imprisonment. He says that this took place "about that time" (12:1). The exact meaning of this is not clear. The simplest interpretation would be that these events took place at the time when Barnabas and Paul were visiting Jerusalem; but one would expect that if Luke thought that Barnabas and Saul were in Jerusalem during this time of persecution, he would have mentioned them. Perhaps "that time" refers to the period before Barnabas and Saul were sent to Jerusalem. To complicate matters, when eventually, in 12:25, Luke tells us again about the two envoys from Antioch to Jerusalem, the ancient manuscripts do not agree, some saying that Barnabas and Saul returned *to* Jerusalem, and others that they returned *from* Jerusalem.

The reference in this entire section is to Herod Agrippa I, grandson of Herod the Great and nephew of Herod Antipas, to whom Luke refers in the context of the birth of Jesus. He received the title of "king" in the year 37. From that time on, partly due to his political ability and partly to his manipulation of both Roman and Jewish authorities, he added to the territories under his rule, which eventually included an area similar to that which his grandfather governed. However, while Herod the Great had almost constant conflict with the Jews, Herod Agrippa knew how to win the favor of the Jewish leadership and the principal priests, and thus count on their collaboration.[65]

Luke gives us no further indication as to who were the "some who belonged to the church" whom Herod arrested nor as to what eventually became of them. As in many other cases, Luke simply describes the general condition

---

65. See Josephus, *Ant.* 18.6–7; 19.5.

and then offers one or two examples. The James who was killed by Herod was the brother of John, and is not to be confused with another James, a brother of Jesus who also played an important role in the church in Jerusalem (see 12:17).[66] His death "with the sword" indicates that this was an official execution, after a formal trial.[67] The fact that Herod chose this particular apostle as his first victim indicates that he was actively engaged in leadership in the church, perhaps preaching or "disturbing the peace" in some other way. Thus, although Luke only tells us of the activities of two of the Twelve, Peter and John, this does not mean that all the others remained inactive. We simply do not know.

2.   Peter Imprisoned and Freed (12:3–19a)

What the NRSV translates as "to bring him out" (12:4, 6) is a verb that tends to denote formal presentation before a court (*anagagein*), even though the further explanation "to the people" would suggest that the purpose of this trial was to seek popularity rather than justice. At any rate, what we have here is the persecution of believers, no longer by Jews and particularly their leadership, but now by officials representing Roman power and authority—in this case King Herod Agrippa. Herod acts this way in order to please "the Jews" (which probably should be understood in the sense of the Jewish leaders), but his authority comes from Rome, and it is as an official authorized by Rome that he executes James and has Peter arrested.[68]

Possibly he wishes to make sure that, after the festival of Unleavened Bread, the trial and death of Peter will be the center of popular attention, and that pilgrims who have come to Jerusalem for the religious celebrations will return to their lands telling about how Herod defends Jewish orthodox beliefs. Up to this point there are in the narrative several phrases and circumstances paralleling what Luke tells us about the passion of Jesus, and this seems to be intentional. The reader is led to expect that Peter will die after a trial, some time around the feast of Passover, as did Jesus.

---

66. It is about this other James, or Santiago, that legend claims he preached in Spain, and that his body was taken to Compostela, where it is buried. Although this is only a legend, it became very important for the later history of Spain and its colonies, for pilgrimage to Santiago de Compostela was one of the elements that helped develop a Spanish sense of unity and nationhood and resistance against the Moors. According to legend, Santiago fought with Christians against Moors, and later in the Americas, against the natives. There are in the Western Hemisphere now more than fifty cities and towns named after Santiago.

67. Eusebius of Caesarea tells of a tradition about the death of James that was already circulating late in the second century, because Eusebius took it from the writings of Clement of Alexandria. According to that tradition, the one in charge of bringing James before the court was so moved by the witness of James that he was converted, and the two were beheaded together. *H.E.* 2.9.2–3.

68. Josephus, *Ant.* 19.6–7, shows how Herod sought to please the Jewish leadership.

Herod takes all sorts of precautions in order to prevent Peter's escape. The squads that are to guard Peter were usual in the Roman Empire, where a group of four soldiers took turns at each post, each standing guard for a period of three hours before being relieved.[69] Herod assigns four of these squads (*tessarsin tetradiois*, a total of sixteen men) to the task of guarding Peter. Then, for greater security, Peter is tied with two chains between two soldiers (12:6). It was customary in order to retain or control a dangerous prisoner to tie him to a soldier with a chain (much as is done today with handcuffs).[70] In the case of Peter, this extra precaution is doubled, for each of his hands is tied to a soldier. Then, other guards (probably two more, one from each of the other two squads) guarded the door.

Over against all these precautions there is another power: the church prays without ceasing. The last night before the trial ("the very night," 12:6) an angel appears in prison. The shining light is a sign of the divine presence. Peter still sleeps, and the angel has to wake him up. The NRSV translation for the angel's action, "he tapped Peter on the side," is too mild to convey the meaning of the Greek text. The word employed here implies a hard blow, and perhaps we should understand that the angel "shook him awake," or that he "poked" Peter. Throughout this narrative, there is a slight undertone of humor. Even after being poked by the angel, and all the way through verse 10, Peter is still half awake. He thinks he is dreaming, and the angel has to give him detailed instructions as to how to get dressed (12:8). Together they go by the other two guards. Although the text does not say so, it is to be understood that they too are asleep. The angel and Peter finally come to the door itself, which opens for them on its own accord. It is then, out on the street, that the angel leaves Peter, apparently without any further explanation. Then Peter "came to himself" and realized that he was actually free.

The slight touch of humor in the first part of the story now becomes stronger. Peter goes to a house where he knows that Christians will be praying. Luke tells us that this was the home of "Mary, the mother of John whose name was Mark." That she is identified by her son indicates that John Mark would eventually be a better-known person in the ancient Church. Traditionally, the second Gospel has been attributed to him. We shall meet him again in Acts (12:25; 13:5, 13; 15:37–39), as well as elsewhere in the New Testament (Col. 4:10, where we are told that he was Barnabas's kin, II Tim. 4:11, Philem. 24, I Pet. 5:13).[71]

---

69. Vegetius, in his *De re militari*, 3.8, says that "since it is impossible for one person to remain alert all night, the night is divided into four vigils, so that it is not necessary to remain awake more than three hours."

70. See, for instance, Josephus, *Ant.* 18.6.6.

71. In spite of the importance of John Mark, there seems to be much exaggeration and daring in the thesis of Josep Rius-Camps, "Qüestions sobre la doble obra lucana, II: Qui és Joan, l'anomenat 'Marc'?", *RCatalT*, 5 (1980), 297–329. According to Rius-Camps, Mark

According to a later tradition, it was at the house of Mary and her son John Mark that the Last Supper and Pentecost took place. It seems to have been a fairly large home, not only because of the number of people who could gather there, but also because it had a front yard with an outer gate through which one gained access to the house. Peter knocks and "a maid named Rhoda" answers.[72] She recognizes Peter's voice and, instead of opening the gate, she runs joyfully to tell the others, apparently forgetting Peter at the gate. These others, although they have been praying ardently for Peter's liberation, do not believe what they are told, and tell her that she is deranged. She insists, but they tell her that she must have seen a ghost.[73] Meanwhile Peter is standing outside knocking. He is a fugitive, liable to arrest at any time, and while his friends discuss who he might be, he is left outside. Finally they open, and the first thing that Peter does is to tell them to be quiet—perhaps so they will listen to him, or perhaps so they will not draw the attention of the authorities. He then tells them what has happened, sends word to James and the rest of the church, and simply leaves and goes to "another place."

Luke does not tell us where Peter went. All that he says is that Peter left, apparently to hide, without telling us where. From that point on, Peter will disappear from the story, only to reappear briefly, with no other explanation of where he has been, in 15:7.

At the end of the passage, Herod blames his soldiers for Peter's escape. The Greek simply says that he ordered them to be "taken out." But the NRSV correctly translates the meaning by saying that he ordered them "to be put to death."[74]

This entire story of Peter's imprisonment and liberation is written with more graphic detail, and even humor, than appears in much of the rest of Luke's writing. It is possible that he is recording a story that he has heard circulating among others already, with a bit of the same touch of humor.

3. Herod's Death (12:19b–24)

The second half of verse 19 is ambiguous, for the Greek says that someone ("he") went to Caesarea. The NRSV says "Peter," probably trying to fill the void left by verse 17, where Luke says that Peter "went elsewhere." But the

---

the evangelist is the guarantor of the true preaching of the gospel, and therefore from this point on in Acts wherever Mark is with Paul, Paul's work is in accordance to the divine will; but when Mark is absent, that absence is a negative judgment on what Paul is doing.

72. The name "Rhoda" is an adaptation of a diminutive form of Rose, and therefore it could be said that her name was "Rosie."

73. Literally, the text says "his angel." This refers to the belief among Jews at that time, that each person has an angel that is that person's double, a combination of what today is understood by a guardian angel and a spirit. It was believed that sometimes the angels of the dead appeared to the living. Possibly Mark 18:10 refers to this.

74. The verb employed here, *apagō*, means "to take," but in situations such as this one it is often used in the sense of taking to the scaffold.

sense of the text, which is speaking of Herod's actions, would seem to imply that "he" is Herod—even more so, as Herod died in Caesarea. Although technically Caesarea was in Judea, for Luke it was a foreign and Gentile land, as it was for many of his Jewish contemporaries. That is why he says that "he went down from Judea to Caesarea."

The exact nature of the dispute between Herod on the one hand and Tyre and Sidon on the other is unknown. Even though the text literally says that they stood for peace (12:20), there certainly could not have been an armed encounter, for they were all subjects of the Roman Empire, which would never have allowed it. Apparently it was an economic conflict. Whatever might have been its nature, finally the Phoenician cities asked for a reconciliation, "because their country depended on the king's country for food" (12:20). This seems to refer to the Galilean wheat that Tyre and Sidon required to feed their population. The mention of these events, and more specifically of "Blastus, the king's chamberlain," points to Luke's interest, both in the Gospel and in Acts, in relating his narrative to the general history of the empire and of Palestine. Unfortunately, no more than this is known about this Blastus, who seems to have played an important role in Herod's court, and certainly in his negotiations with Tyre and Sidon.

It is while celebrating this peace that Herod dies. His appearance and voice were so impressive that the people kept shouting "the voice of a god, and not of a mortal!" Luke's narrative is sharp and even harsh. Because Herod had not given glory to God, God simply struck him down. His death, being eaten by worms, is an apparent way of showing that he is anything but a god.

Jewish historian Flavius Josephus, in his telling of these events, confirms and clarifies much of what Luke says.[75] According to Josephus, Herod was dressed in clothes of pure silver, and the reaction of those who praised him was partly due to his dress. These are probably the "royal robes" to which Luke refers. The year was 44, and therefore it is thought that the events of Peter's imprisonment and liberation as Luke tells them should be placed around the Passover of 43.

Finally, Luke ends this entire section with another summary: "the word of God continued to advance and gain adherents."

FAITH AND PERSECUTION

It is almost in passing that Luke mentions James and others whom Herod arrested. He does not even tell us what happened to these others. It is important to notice, before we turn to the joyful story about Peter and his liberation, that here Luke tells us about two apostles: James and Peter. One dies; the other is freed. We are not told that one had more faith than the other. It is to be supposed that, during the time between the arrest and the death of James, Christians prayed for him with as much fervor as they did later for Peter.

---

75. Josephus, *Ant.* 19.8.2.

It is important to remember this, for there is a common notion that faith and prayer will solve all problems one has and will make everything turn out all right. If someone is ill and after prayer the person is not healed, some say that this is due to a lack of faith. If someone gives daring witness in difficult circumstances and dies for it, some will say that it was because he or she did not have faith or because God did not really want such action to take place. There are even preachers who claim that for those who have faith everything turns out rosy and prosperous.

That is not what the Bible says. The Bible says indeed that the Lord can free, and sometimes does free, those who trust in God. The Bible also says that the lack of faith leads to destruction, both in the present and in the future. But the Bible clearly says also that faith does not always produce the most agreeable results, and sometimes what faith does is not to alleviate our sufferings and difficulties, but to make them worse. This may be seen in Hebrews 11:33–38. There we are told first of those who by faith worked wonders and attained incredible victories: "conquered kingdoms, administered justice, obtained promises, shut the mouths of lions, quenched raging fire, escaped the edge of the sword, won strength out of weakness, became mighty in war, put foreign armies to flight"; but we are told also of "others" who, by the same faith, had the opposite results: "were tortured, refusing to accept release, . . . suffered mocking and flogging, and even chains and imprisonment. They were stoned to death, they were sawed in two, they were killed by the sword. . . ."

The entire passage in Acts 12 is a clear example of this. James died for his faith. Peter was freed. This does not mean that James had less faith than Peter, or that the church prayed better and harder for Peter than for James, or that James's preaching was more offensive to Herod than was Peter's. Actually, all historical indications are that eventually Peter also died for his faith. If in that year 43 God did free Peter, and with that gave a sign of divine power, later on, in the year 67 or 68, God did not free him, and with that also was God's power made manifest. Christians must not forget even for an instant that the center of our faith is in the cross of Jesus, who suffered not because he lacked faith nor because he was a sinner, but exactly the opposite.

This has enormous pastoral importance among our people. This lies, first, in that the idea—that if God does not give us what we ask it is because we lack faith—can have disastrous consequences. Imagine, for instance, a paralyzed seven-year-old girl who is told that, if she has faith, she will walk. People around her pray and even cry out loud; but she is not healed. At the end of the service, that girl who entered with a serious physical handicap now leaves also spiritually and mentally wounded, for now she believes that if she cannot walk it is her own fault, for she lacks faith. Now she must carry the burden, not only of a body that will not obey her commands, but also of a soul that apparently does not obey her either, for she truly does wish to have faith. Perhaps to those who preach such a "gospel" do the words of Jesus apply (Luke 17:2): "It would be better for you if a millstone were hung around your neck and you were thrown into the sea than for you to cause one of these little ones to stumble"!

Even apart from such extreme cases, this is important because sometimes the notion that faith solves all problems prevents us from attaining a more mature faith. Such mature faith does not consist in being able to manipulate God, but rather in placing one's self in God's hands, in such a way that we may be at the divine disposal in every circumstance. As Mexican poet Amado Nervo said, "Shepherd, I bless thee for all that thou givest; but if thou givest not, still do I bless thee." Or, as Paul put it, "I have learned to be content with whatever I have" (Phil. 4:11).

On the other hand, in claiming this, one must be careful. This does not mean that Christians are to lead a passive life, allowing events to succeed each other without attempting to intervene in them. We have already referred to the danger of using Gamaliel's advice in this fashion. The entire book of Acts tells us how obedience leads to action. In the next chapter we shall see Saul and Barnabas undertake a missionary trip because that is God's will. In Damascus, Saul does not simply say, "Let God's will be done," but collaborates with those who lower him in a basket from a hole in the wall. The seven-year-old who is not cured by a miracle must still seek to be cured by all means possible. Christians must actively and efficaciously oppose all that is against the will of God. That too is faith. Truly mature faith plunges into active obedience, no matter what the cost, trusting in God's fidelity.

The text also tells us about Herod's death. According to Luke, that death is an act of God just as much as was Peter's liberation. The manner in which the two stories are juxtaposed leads us to understand that Luke believes these to be two sides of the same coin: God intervenes in history. What this text affirms is what was also affirmed for a long time by the prophets and preachers of the Old Testament: God does not ignore political powers, nor does God simply let them act. God is against injustice and tyranny. Certainly in the case of tyrants something similar happens to the opposite case of the righteous. Just as some by faith avoided the edge of the sword and others by the same faith died by the sword, so is it also true that sometimes God punishes and overthrows tyrants and other times not—at least, in the present order. Yet, it is still true that "the Lord watches over the way of the righteous, but the way of the wicked will perish" (Ps. 1:6). Just as God calls us to obedience, either freeing us from the edge of the sword or letting us die by the sword, so also does the Lord call us to obedience amidst political and social strife in our day, and whether tyranny and injustice are overthrown or not is no absolute measure of our obedience.

Finally, the text reminds us of something that is a common experience among Christians: those believers in Mary's home pray for Peter's liberation, and when their prayer is answered they do not believe it. First they think that the maid is crazy. Then they say that she has seen a ghost. It is only when they can no longer deny it that they finally believe that Peter has been freed. This shows how needful faith is, not only to ask, but also to receive. Here, God did exactly what Christians were asking, but even then it was difficult for them to believe. How much more difficult it is to believe when God does not do exactly what we ask, or does it in an unexpected way!

All of these issues come together in the common experience of our churches and our people. We are constantly asking God's help for the poor and the needy. Some among us not only ask, but also act. Some act by participating in programs of direct assistance to the needy. Others act taking political options that they hope will help the needy. In many of the circumstances in which the Latino church finds itself, both groups risk marginalization and perhaps even persecution. When such difficulties come, there are Christians who see in this a sign that what those others were doing was not God's will—as if the death of James were an indication that for some reason God did not look upon him with favor. Or exactly the opposite happens in some other circumstances: some other person or agency comes to help the needy for whom we were praying. Seldom are we ready to see in this the answer to our prayers. All of this should not surprise us, because already those early Christians in the first century, who had seen so many signs of God's action and whose prayer God answered by giving them exactly what they requested, were no more ready to believe than we are.

5

The Mission Is Defined
(12:25–15:35)

We now come to a very different section in Acts. For one thing, from this point on Peter and the Twelve practically disappear from the narrative, and Saul/Paul becomes increasingly important. Also, the center of attention ceases to be Jerusalem and is now clearly Antioch and the mission out of it. Therefore, at the beginning of this new section, it is important to insist that Luke is not seeking to write an entire history of the life and expansion of the Church in its first decades. Just as in many cases earlier he offers a summary, and then tells one or two incidents that illustrate that summary, now what he has to say about Paul and his work should be seen as the story of one of many missionaries and preachers that must have existed. Luke does not say a word, for instance, about how Christianity expanded toward the south, and yet we know that somehow the new faith reached Alexandria, the capital of Egypt. Nor does he say anything about expansion toward the east, and yet we know that this was rapid and extensive, and that soon there were churches within the Persian Empire. Likewise, when Paul reaches Rome he finds Christians in that city and even in the nearby port of Puteoli (28:13–15), and Luke gives no hint of how the new faith reached the capital. Clearly, Paul was the most important of all those early missionaries. But this was not because he was the only one, nor even the most daring. His importance lies in his letters, which came to form part of our New Testament, and therefore in the impact Paul's interpretation of the gospel and of the mission of the Church has made throughout the history of Christianity. The way Luke presents the story, Paul is important as an example of the manner in which the Holy Spirit progressively clarifies its mission to the early Church; and this is precisely the main subject of this section in Acts.

One should also note that, even though the section that we now enter is traditionally called "Paul's first missionary journey," that name is not quite accurate, for it is clear that his mission to "the regions of Syria and Cilicia," near his own city of Tarsus to which he refers in Galatians 1:21 must have taken place before this other journey. Actually, it is reasonable to suppose that when Barnabas was looking for Saul in Tarsus, and had to search for him, this was because Saul was out on some sort of a missionary journey.

At any rate, the tendency to read the rest of Acts as a series of "missionary journeys" of Paul comes, not so much from a careful reading of the text, as from the interest of missionary societies and movements in the nineteenth and the twentieth centuries in finding in Acts guidelines for their own work, and in Paul and his journeys the paradigm that modern missionaries should follow. It is interesting to note that the very notion that this section of the book can be outlined in terms of three "missionary journeys" of Paul is not to be found in any ancient or medieval commentary, but is rather the creation of the modern missionary movement.[1]

A. THE SENDING (12:25–13:3)

The narrative now returns to Antioch (where it had been in 11:19–30), with the return of Barnabas and Saul, bringing John Mark with them.[2] The text does not say how much time elapsed between that return and the sending that takes place in chapter 13. It is to be supposed that there was enough time for Barnabas and Saul to report on their mission, and for them to gain their place as leaders in the community in Antioch.

In 13:1 we are told that there were "prophets and teachers" and are given a list of five names with no indication of who among these were prophets and who were teachers, and perhaps without distinguishing between these two functions. Those interpreters who believe that there was a distinction between the two think that the first three are prophets, and the last two teachers.[3] Barnabas heads the list, and Saul is the last. About the other three, all that is known is what is said here. It has been suggested that "Simon who was called Niger" may have been from Cyrene like Lucius, and on that basis some think that he was the Simon of Cyrene who was forced to carry the cross of Jesus (Luke 23:26). The NRSV translation, "Manaen, a member of the court of Herod the Ruler," does not convey all the meaning of this reference. The Greek text clarifies that this was Herod "the tetrarch" meaning Herod Antipas, the one who had John the Baptist executed. Also, the Greek implies that Manaen grew up with Herod, and therefore it has been suggested that it was probably

---

1. See J. T. Townsend, "Missionary journeys in Acts and European missionary societies," *AngThRev*, 68 (1986), 99–104.

2. On John Mark, see commentary on 12:12.

3. Josep Rius-Camps, *El camino de Pablo a la misión a los paganos* (Madrid: Cristiandad, 1984), p. 33, supports such a distinction, based on the prepositions separating the various names. Most other interpreters, however, think either that there was no difference between the two functions or that, if there was, it is impossible on the basis of this text to determine who belonged to each of the two categories. On "prophets" in the ancient Church, see the commentary to 11:27–28.

he who provided Luke with the information that he had regarding Herod and his actions.[4] Finally, on the basis of the similitude between "Lucius" and "Luke," it has been suggested that this "Lucius" is the author of the Gospel of Luke and of Acts. This is no more than an interesting conjecture.[5]

The word that the NRSV translates as "worshipping" is the same word from which we get the English "liturgy," and it was originally employed for the public service that the empire required of its subjects. By extension, it was used also for the service to God. Its use here seems to indicate that it was during the act of worship that the word came from the Spirit. The urgency of the Spirit's command is not apparent in the English versions, for here Luke employs a Greek particle that is difficult to translate, but which conveys a sense of energy. Its meaning is similar to our "Hey!" Note also that the Spirit does not clarify what is "the work" for which Barnabas and Saul have been chosen. This will be discovered step by step, as the narrative unfolds.

The laying on of hands in 13:3 is not an indication that the other three—who apparently are the ones who performed this act—had more authority than Barnabas and Saul, but appears to be rather an act whereby the entire community authorizes, blesses, and sends the two whom the Spirit has called.

CALLING AND COMMUNITY

At this point, it may be helpful to consider the manner in which Saul receives his missionary calling. Back in chapter 9, the first announcement comes to him, not directly in the vision that leads to his conversion but through Ananias, who is the one who receives word from the Lord as to how Saul is to serve him. Now, when the calling comes to undertake this missionary journey, the Holy Spirit does not speak privately to Barnabas and Saul, but rather tells all the "prophets and teachers" (or perhaps the entire church, for the Greek is ambiguous at this point) saying, "set apart for me Barnabas and Saul."

Due to a series of historical circumstances, and to the manner in which the gospel has been preached to us, in many of our churches it is thought that a calling always comes to a person directly. It is true that the vision of the Macedonian young man came to Paul privately (16:9). But it is also true that in the

---

4. Luke says that he was *syntrophos* with Herod, which literally means that they grew up together. This was the name usually given to young men who were placed next to princes in order to grow up with them and provide them with company. Therefore, Manaen must have been part of the local aristocracy (E. Haenchen, *The Acts of the Apostles: A Commentary* [Philadelphia: Westminster, 1975], p. 395; F. F. Bruce, *Commentary on the Book of Acts*, 2nd ed. [Grand Rapids: Eerdmans, 1954], p. 253). His name, which means "comforter," is Hebrew in origin. Another Manaen, who may have been a relative of this one, prophesied to Herod the Great when he was still young that he would become a king (Josephus, *Ant.* 15.373–9). It is possible that the Manaen in Acts may have been placed as a companion for Herod Antipas as a reward from his relative's prophecy.

5. Apparently the first one to suggest it was Ephraim the Syrian (fourth century), in his commentary on this passage.

case we are now studying the missionary calling came through the church. And, in order to complete the picture, in 13:45–48 we shall see that the more specific calling to the mission among the Gentiles comes to Paul and Barnabas through a series of events that take place in Antioch of Pisidia, and where an important agent in their own calling is the negative reaction of those who will not listen to them.

What all this means is that the will of God is revealed to us at least through three complementary means: our own personal relationship with God and willingness to be guided (the case of the Macedonian young man), the discernment of the community of faith (the case we are now studying), and the outward events that lead us in one direction or another (what happens to Barnabas and Paul in Antioch of Pisidia).

As we today seek to hear our calling and fulfill our mission, these three must be allowed their particular roles. Personal devotion and the quest for God's will in our lives are of fundamental importance. However, to this must be added the discernment of the community of faith, which very often can see in us gifts or deficiencies that we ourselves do not recognize, and whose judgment therefore should be taken into account. Finally, we also need a clear understanding and analysis of what is happening around us. The challenges of our time and of our hemisphere may be to us as much a call from God as the challenges in Antioch of Pisidia were a call for Barnabas and Paul. However, that comes later in our story.

B. Cyprus (13:4–12)

Although the church in Antioch "sent out" the missionaries (13:3), Luke emphasizes that they were "sent out" by the Holy Spirit (13:4). Seleucia, where they took ship, was the port serving Antioch, some twenty-five kilometers away. The city of Seleucia had been founded in 301 B.C.E. by Seleucus Nicator, and in Paul's time was a "free city" within the structure of the Roman Empire. About the activity of the missionaries in Salamis, where they landed in Cyprus, Luke only says that they preached in the synagogues. In the city there was a good number of Jews, and therefore there may have indeed been more than one synagogue there. There were frequent contacts between Cyprus and Judea. Some years earlier Emperor Augustus had granted to Herod the Great half of the profit of the famous copper mines on the island, and as a result the contacts between Cyprus and Judea increased.

From Salamis, Barnabas and Saul, jointly with John Mark, went on to Paphos. The word that the NRSV translates as "to assist them" may mean either that John Mark was a secretary or assistant, or also that he was a fellow worker in the missionary enterprise, perhaps instructing those who were converted.[6]

---

6. As was said (12:12), the thesis of Rius-Camps is that John Mark is the "guarantor" of the gospel, and that when he and Paul part the Spirit also leaves Paul. This is hardly convincing, and has not been well received among scholars.

Not a word is said about the trip from Salamis to Paphos, the Roman capital of Cyprus. The verb employed here seems to indicate that they traveled by land, although not necessarily so.[7] At any rate, as may be seen throughout the voyages of Paul, his centers of operation were always the cities, and very little is said about his activities while traveling from one city to the next. This may be the result of Luke's own narrative style, centering his attention on the highlights. But another reason may well have been that away from the cities the ancient languages of the various conquered peoples were still spoken, and Paul and his companions did not know those languages.

The name of the false prophet, "Bar-Jesus," means "son of Jesus." In contrast to that name, Saul calls him "son of the devil" (13:10). There has been much discussion about his other name, "Elymas," for such a name is not known in Greek. An ancient manuscript says "Etoimus," and this has led to conjectures trying to identify him with another known magician, also a Jew in Cyprus, whose name was "Atomus."[8] Clearly, Luke's words, "Elymas (for that is the translation of his name)" cannot be taken to mean that his name is a translation of "Bar-Jesus." Some have suggested that it is rather a translation of "magician" in the language of the area.[9]

About proconsul Sergius Paulus all that is known is what Luke says here, although some inscriptions have been found that might refer to him.[10] As in so many other cases, Luke signals his attention to historical detail by giving this man the title of "proconsul," for at that time Cyprus was a senatorial province, and that was the title of the Romans governing such provinces.

It is in 13:9 that for the first time the name of Paul appears: "Saul, also known as Paul." Because this was also the proconsul's name, this has led to speculations about whether Saul took this name in honor of the proconsul.[11] There is no basis for such speculations. The fact is that it was customary for every Roman to have at least three names: his own, that of his clan, and his family name.[12] Besides this, parents often gave their children another name, called "signum" or "supernomen," which was employed by family and friends. In this particular case, "Paul" was his Roman family name (today we would say his last name), and "Saul" seems to have been the "signum" that was given him in honor of the ancient king from the tribe of Benjamin (which was also Paul's tribe). About his other names nothing is known. At any rate, "Saul" was

---

7. The Western text, rather than saying that they went "through the whole island," says that they "went around" from Salamis to Paphos.

8. Whom Josephus mentions: *Ant.* 20.7.2.

9. L. Yaure, "Elymas-Nehelamite-Pethor," *JBL*, 79 (1960), 297–314.

10. David John Williams, *Acts* (New York: Harper & Row, 1985), pp. 215–16.

11. Thus, for instance, Rius-Camps, *Camino*, p. 46: "the surname of the pagan, Paul, was immediately adopted by Saul as his missionary name."

12. See the study regarding this manner of naming, as well as its implications for the name of Paul, by G. A. Harrer, "Saul who is also called Paul," *HTR*, 33 (1940), 19–34.

the name that he used among Jews and friends, and "Paul" was his name among Gentiles. It is precisely at the moment of beginning his mission to the Gentiles, and later in writing his letters, that Saul uses the name of "Paul."

Because Bar-Jesus/Elymas seeks to prevent the proconsul from listening to Barnabas and Saul, the latter speaks harsh words, and the magician is blinded "for a while." On seeing this, the proconsul "believed." It is not clear whether this means that he was converted or that he believed in Paul's power. Significantly, nothing is said about his being baptized, even though up to this point baptism has followed immediately after conversion. This may be due to his being the first Gentile convert who was not even a "God-fearer," that is to say a student of Scripture. Such people, who had no notion of Judaism before they believed in Christ, would require more time of preparation for baptism, so they could learn what distinguished their new faith from their ancient beliefs and customs. Whereas a Jew or a "God-fearer" who became a Christian was already a believer in a single God and had been instructed in the moral principles of Judaism—which were also those of Christianity—such was not the case with converted pagans, who therefore were not immediately baptized. This is why as time went by and the Church became increasingly Gentile, the period of preparation for baptism was extended.

SAUL, ALSO KNOWN AS PAUL

It is often said that "Paul" was the name that Saul took after his conversion, as a sign of the radical change that had taken place in him. This is blatantly false, as has already been explained. In fact, Luke continues calling him "Saul" until the very beginning of the mission to the Gentiles. The truth is that Saul/Paul is a bridge personality, and that this function is manifest in his two names. He is a Jew, as he himself says, "circumcised on the eighth day, a member of the people of Israel, of the tribe of Benjamin, a Hebrew born of Hebrews; as to the law a Pharisee" (Phil. 3:5). But he is also a Roman citizen as well as an eloquent writer and speaker in the Greek language. As a Jew, although at first he persecuted the Church, he was able to understand the message of Jesus and of God's reign, which was the culmination of the hopes of Israel. (As he himself says in 28:20, "it is for the sake of the hope of Israel" that he does what he does.) However, as a Jew from the diaspora, as a Roman citizen who has been educated in Hellenistic culture, he can interpret that message to Gentiles in a way that could not be done by Peter or the other apostles. It is precisely because he is a bridge that Paul can be at the vanguard of the mission of the Church, and open the way to the future.

"Saul, who is also Paul," reminds us of the situation of the millions of Hispanics living in the United States, a country whose Spanish-speaking population is now the fourth in size in the entire hemisphere. The fact itself of a name change happens every day. A boy whom his parents called "Jesus" is told by his teacher that he cannot have such a name and is immediately "rebaptized" as "Jesse." Anyone entering as an immigrant from Latin America into the United

States immediately finds it practically necessary to drop one of his or her two family names. However, all of this is a symptom of a greater reality: the Latino people in United States live in two realitites. As Virgil Elizondo would say, to be Latino in the United States is to be "mestizo."[13] The word "mestizo" originally referred to a person of mixed blood, and was used pejoratively. Elizondo uses it in the sense of the "in between-ness" in which Hispanics live in the United States. In that situation, they find that they are neither Latin Americans nor Americans, and are often discriminated against by both groups as also happened to Hellenistic Jews, discriminated against by Gentiles and Judean Jews. However, this very painful situation also allows Hispanics in the United States to serve as a bridge between the two main cultures that share the Western Hemisphere. Saul opened the way to the future because he was also Paul. Perhaps the Latino Church in the United States may open the way to the future precisely because it finds itself in the difficult space between two cultures—or, in other words, because it is a mestizo church.

The same may be said about the entire Latin America, a mestizo continent almost by definition. Many years ago an old friend—later "disappeared" in Argentina—affirmed that "no culture is called to be a province." Latin American culture (or rather, cultures) is the result of the mestizaje of several cultures, some native, and others imported from Africa and from Europe. Cultures live only as they engage in dialogue with each other and are renewed.

What is true of cultures is even more true of the Church. The Church, being incarnate in human reality, must be incarnate also in those cultural encounters. The Church is not here in order to defend "pure" cultures, just as it is not here in order to promote "pure" races. It is only as it participates in this dialogue—and even in this clash—among cultures that the Church can truly be visionary, and can therefore truly be the Church.

In our Latino churches in the United States, there are some who wish to make the Church an exact copy of the churches in the dominant culture; and over against these there are others who believe that the Church is to be an instrument for the preservation of Hispanic culture. The truth, however, lies in neither of these positions. The Latino Church in the present circumstances in the United States, precisely because it has, so to speak, a foot in each culture, has a particular opportunity and responsibility, just as did "Saul, who is also Paul."

In Latin America something similar happens. There are those who think that the function of the Church is to "promote culture," but what they understand by that is to promote that part of the culture that is European in origin, as if the other currents that adjoin to form our identities had no culture. Thus, the "best music" for worship is that composed by Bach and Beethoven, but not the *danzón,* nor the *cueca,* nor the *tango,* nor the *corrido.* Given such positions, it is not surprising that such churches find it difficult to reach the people.

---

13. Elizondo's two main works on this subject are *Galilean Journey: The Mexican-American Promise* (Maryknoll, NY: Orbis Books, 1983; rev. ed. 2000), to which I have already referred, and *The Future Is Mestizo* (Bloomington, Ind.: Meyer & Stone, 1988).

"Saul, who is also Paul," lived simultaneously in several realities. Our Church also lives in several realities. The Evangelical Methodist Church of Bolivia, for instance, is "of Bolivia," but is also Latin American; it is Hispanic and it is *aymara*; it is Latin American and Methodist, but it is also part of the universal Church; it is guardian of the faith delivered to the apostles, but it also has to live that faith in present-day Bolivia, with problems and challenges very different from those faced by the first Christians. We wish everything would be clear and simple, and therefore we imagine that this multiplicity of realities and contexts is a burden; but the truth is that, as in the case of "Saul, who is also Paul," it is an opportunity for mission and for obedience to the gospel.

C. ANTIOCH OF PISIDIA (13:13–51a)

Most of what Luke tells about this missionary journey takes place in Antioch of Pisidia. In order to get there, "Paul and his companions" (from here on Paul becomes the main character) went to Perga in Pamphylia, and from there to Antioch. In Pamphylia (as we are told in 15:38) and without Luke giving us any explanation, John Mark left them and returned to Jerusalem. Later (15:37–40), this caused a disagreement, which led Barnabas and Paul to go separate ways.

The region of Pamphylia was in the southern coast of Asia Minor, and Perga was some eleven kilometers inland, going upstream along the river Cestrus. They probably would have landed at the port of Attalia, which Luke mentions in 14:26, when Paul and Barnabas are on their way back. The text does not tell us how long the missionaries remained in Perga—which has provided opportunity for speculations that, because this was a swampy region, Paul became ill and that this was the reason they went inland, to the much healthier Antioch.[14] This is an interesting theory, but hardly more than that. Given the manner in which Luke tells his story, it is very possible that the missionaries remained in Perga for a significant time. However, there are no archaeological or other signs that there was a synagogue in Perga. Because Paul and Barnabas usually seem to have begun their preaching at the synagogue, that may have been the reason that made them move on to Antioch.

Antioch "of Pisidia" was not really in Pisidia, but in Phrygia. It was commonly called "of Pisidia" in order to distinguish it from the larger city by the same name, in Syria, from which the missionaries had started. It was an important city, for it was at the very heart of Asia Minor, and the road that led from Ephesus toward the east went through it. Administratively, it was part of the province of Galacia, jointly with Iconium, Derbe, and Lystra, and it is quite likely that Paul's epistle to the Galatians is addressed to Christians in that region.

---

14. W. M. Ramsay, *St. Paul the Traveller and the Roman Citizen* (London: Hodder & Stoughton, 1897), pp. 94–97.

The detailed story of the early mission in Antioch of Pisidia begins on a Sabbath. The "officials of the synagogue"[15] invite Paul and Barnabas to speak. This may be an indication that they had already spent some time in Antioch, and that Luke, as is his custom, has summarized his story without letting us know about the time elapsed. This could also be the first visit of the missionaries to the synagogue, and they may have been invited because Paul was a rabbi, or perhaps because both have let it be known that they had something to tell the congregation.[16] At any rate, such an invitation was part of a usual service, in which, after reciting the summary of the Law (Deut. 6:4–9, 11:13–21; Num. 15:37–41), portions of the Law and the prophets were read, and then there was a sermon or an exhortation on the basis of the last reading.[17]

Paul opens his speech after the manner of a classical orator, standing and with a gesture requesting silence.[18] Even though his speech is relatively long (13:16–41), what we have is a summary of Paul's preaching according to Luke. From here on, whenever Paul finds himself in a similar situation, speaking in a synagogue, Luke will be very brief in his description of the contents of Paul's speech. In this particular case, Paul shows himself aware that there are in the audience both Jews (by birth or by conversion) and "God-fearers" (13:16).[19]

The first part of the speech (vv. 16-25) is a summary of the history of Israel, taken mostly from what we now call the Old Testament. This is very similar to the earlier speeches by Peter and Stephen. However, in contrast to the latter, Paul does not say anything about ingratitude or disobedience on the part of Israel.[20] The specific reference to King Saul (13:21) may reflect Paul's personal interest, for he carried that king's name, and like him was a member of the tribe of Benjamin. (The "forty years" of Saul's reign are not attested in

---

15. In Palestine, there only was one "archsynagogue" (*archisynagōgos*) in each synagogue. Luke's use of the plural in this context would seem to indicate that at least in this case this title was given to more than one of the members of the synagogue. It is also possible that the title includes those who have previously held such functions, just as today we employ the term "governor" for all who have held that office.

16. It is interesting to note that the officials of the synagogue request from the visitors a "word of consolation" (*logos paraklēseōs*), and that the one who responds is not Barnabas, the "son of consolation," but Paul. See Rius-Camps, *Camino*, p. 52.

17. It has been suggested, on the basis of Paul's speech, that the reading for the day would have been Deuteronomy 1 and Isaiah 1 (Ramsay, *Paul*, p. 100).

18. It was customary to be seated when speaking in the synagogue (see Luke 4:20–21). Perhaps here the custom was different, or perhaps Luke wishes to emphasize the solemnity and formality of Paul's speech.

19. On the "God-fearers," see the commentary on 10:2.

20. The only place where there may be a suggestion along such lines is verse 18, "he put up with them in the wilderness." On this text, the manuscripts do not agree, for while some say *etrophorēsen* (he put up with them) others say *etrophophorēsen* (he supported or fed them).

the Hebrew Scriptures, but there was a tradition that affirmed that Saul had indeed reigned for forty years.)[21]

It is in verse 23 that Paul introduces a subject that would be new to the audience. Up to this point he has been retelling a history well known by all. Now comes the new: "God has brought to Israel a Savior, Jesus, as he promised." That promise refers both to the ancient promises and to the preaching of John the Baptist.

In the second part of his speech (vv. 26–37), Paul clearly states that his message is both for the "descendants of Abraham's family" and for "others who fear God" (13:26)—that is to say, both for Jews and for Gentiles. What then follows is very similar to the speeches that Luke has already placed on the lips of Peter and Stephen. Even some of the biblical references are repeated (compare, for instance 13:35–37 with 2:27–31). However, in these different circumstances the message is also slightly different. The subject of the rejection of Jesus is now employed not to accuse the audience, as in the speeches before the Council, but rather to declare that, because the leaders of Judaism in Jerusalem have rejected the promise, the good news is now for this audience in the diaspora. Notice the logic of this argument in verses 26–27: "to you the message of this salvation has been sent. Because the residents of Jerusalem and their leaders did not recognize him or understand the words of the prophets that are read every Sabbath, they fulfilled those words by condemning him."[22] After that affirmation, verses 27–37 amplify and corroborate what has just been declared: Paul tells about the death of Jesus, and above all about his resurrection, as having been announced in the Hebrew Scriptures.

The third part of the speech (vv. 38–41) invites the audience to accept what they have just been told. Paul announces to them the forgiveness of sins and invites them to believe. In 13:39 he expresses the typically Pauline subject of the impossibility of freeing oneself from sin by obedience to the Law, and the only viable option being faith in Jesus. This is significant, because even though quite possibly Luke is composing most of the speeches he puts on the lips of his speakers, he is trying to be faithful to the particular emphasis of Paul's preaching.

Verses 42 and 43 have been interpreted in various ways. Taken literally and in chronological order, Luke seems to be saying that Paul and Barnabas left the synagogue before the end of the service and that the people who were outside asked them to continue speaking to them on the next Sabbath (13:42).[23] Then, after "the meeting in the synagogue broke up," many Jews and

---

21. Josephus, *Ant.* 6.14.9.

22. In this quotation, some manuscripts say "to you," as quoted above, whereas others say "to us," as the NRSV translates.

23. What tends to reinforce this interpretation is the reading in some manuscripts indicating that those in verse 42 who asked them to continue preaching were "Gentiles." The NRSV avoids this difficulty by accepting the probably better reading, which does not include the word "Gentiles."

"devout converts" continued following the preachers, and asking them to say more.[24] To further complicate matters, the phrase that the NRSV translates at "the next Sabbath" in verse 42 can also be understood as "between Sabbaths"—that is to say, during the week. Most probably, the details in these two verses are not to be taken strictly in the order in which they appear. Luke is simply telling us that, upon leaving the synagogue, many of the Jews and the Gentile God-fearers continued listening to the missionaries, and that they were joined by other Gentiles as they learned that the message was not only for Jews, but also for them.

Whatever the case may have been, by the following Sabbath "almost the whole city gathered to hear the word of the Lord" (13:44). On seeing such a crowd, the Jews "were filled with jealousy." The text does not tell us why they were jealous, but one surmises that they were disturbed that what up to that point had been their exclusive property (which they shared with a few prose-lytes who adjusted to what they said) was now open to the entire city. If such a thing were to continue, they would lose control over the synagogue and over its message. Therefore, they begin to argue with Paul "and blaspheming, they contradicted what was spoken by Paul." (What is translated as "blaspheming" can also mean "insulting," although we are not told whether they insulted Jesus, Paul, or whom.)

It is in response to this situation that both Paul and Barnabas utter words that would increasingly mark the character of the Pauline mission. The message was first of all for Jews; but because they reject it, the missionaries say, "we are now turning to the Gentiles." This is the narrative expression of what elsewhere Paul expresses in more general terms: "I am not ashamed of the Gospel; it is the power of God for salvation to everyone who has faith, to the Jew first and also to the Greek" (Rom. 1:16). This does not mean, however, that from this moment on Paul and Barnabas will address only Gentiles. On the contrary, throughout the rest of the book we shall see that their normal practice will still be to begin their teaching at each new place in the synagogue, and then to approach the Gentiles.[25]

---

24. The phrase "devout converts" is also confusing. Normally, the "converts" or "proselytes" were those who had completely accepted Judaism in a formal manner, whereas the "devout" or "God-fearers" were those who although they accepted the truth of Judaism, had not embraced the Law, and therefore had not been formally converted. Therefore, if both terms are employed in the strict sense, it is impossible to be a "devout convert." Some suggest that the word "converts" or "proselytes" was a later comment added by a copyist. However, the existing manuscripts do not support such a conjecture. Most probably, Luke is not speaking here of "proselytes" in the technical sense of the term. At any rate, the general sense of the text is clear: both people of Jewish descent and others of Gentile origins followed Paul and Barnabas.

25. The thesis of Rius-Camps in *El Camino* is precisely that Paul did not see clearly that the priority of Jews had been abrogated, and that therefore his tactic of addressing first the Jews in each city was mistaken. This very doubtful thesis, Rius-Camps expresses suc-

As usual, Luke does not say how long Paul and Barnabas remained in Antioch of Pisidia. One could suppose that verses 48 and 49 summarize at least several months and perhaps even years of work. It must have taken some time for "the word of the Lord" to "spread throughout the region."

In reaction to the success of the mission, "the Jews"—meaning those Jews who did not believe the preaching of Paul and Barnabas—promote action against the missionaries. The "devout women of high standing" in verse 50 seem to be Gentile women who were however "God-fearers"—that is, who participated in worship in the synagogue. Most interpreters think that these women would influence their husbands, who were "the leading men of the city," in order to have the missionaries expelled. Note that in this case, in contrast with other earlier cases, the missionaries do not flee, but are officially expelled. Note also that, even though their leaders are expelled from the city and shake the dust off their feet in protest (see Luke 10:11), the disciples who remain behind are "filled with joy and with the Holy Spirit."

THE POWER OF THE GOSPEL

A phrase that is frequently used in our churches, but on which we reflect little, is the "power of the gospel." In this passage we see that power acting in two ways. First, what we immediately note is that this power convinces and attracts people. What Luke tells is surprising: two missionaries arrive at a city and their announcement of the good news attracts the majority of the population. This is due only in a secondary way to the oratorical skill of Paul and Barnabas, or to the strength of their arguments. It is really due to the power of the gospel, which is none other than the power of the Holy Spirit, promised by Jesus in 1:8. This we have seen so frequently in the Book of Acts, that there is no need to insist on it.

There is however another dimension of the power of the gospel (and of the power of the Spirit) that we do not remember as frequently, but is equally important: this power breaks all molds and preconceptions. It is not a power that we can manipulate at whim, and on which we can count whenever and however we wish. This is what happens to those Jews in Antioch of Pisidia who refuse to hear the message. It is important to remember that the very fact that there were Jews was because they had received the revelation given in ancient times through Moses and the prophets, and that this was by the power of the Spirit. The Spirit who supported and strengthens Paul and Barnabas is the same Spirit who spoke by the prophets. But these particular Jews in Antioch apparently considered themselves the exclusive owners of that revelation. It is all right for a

---

cinctly: "The tactic adopted by Paul of addressing the Jews as a privileged people and only secondarily addressing pagans will weigh like a heavy stone throughout the mission and will lead to disastrous consequences. The only one responsible for this deviation of the mission in the direction of Jews is Paul" (*El Camino*, p. 55).

few "God-fearers" to come to the synagogue. It is all right for some of them to be converted, to submit to circumcision, and to become proselytes. What is not all right is for the doors to be open so wide that the Gentiles will flood in, and the Jews will lose their ancient position of privilege. The text seems to indicate that they were jealous, not of Paul and Barnabas, nor of the few "God-fearers," but of the enormous number of Gentiles to whom these Christians were opening the door. It is then that, impelled by the same Holy Spirit who gave rise to Judaism, Paul and Barnabas say "we are now turning to the Gentiles."

This is of utmost importance for us, for it is true not only of Jews in the first century, but also of us today. The text can be directly applied to the present task of evangelization and to the growth of the Church. In some of our churches one hears complaints that our numbers do not increase, and we are told that we need more evangelizing zeal. That may be true; but we must also acknowledge that too often we only want those people to join who are "like us." This we see often in many denominations in the United States, where one constantly hears complaints about how the denomination is no longer as evangelistic as it used to be, but where at the same time there is fear of the "excessive" presence of Latinos, other minorities, undocumented aliens, drug addicts, and so on. It is also seen throughout the hemisphere, where there are so many churches constantly speaking of carrying the good news to others, but at the same time do not wish to risk their own economic and social status. Let more people come, certainly; but only as long as they are like us. Let other churches serve the homeless, the uneducated, those whose smell is not pleasant. But not us. Sometimes we hide these feelings behind supposedly theological arguments, saying, for instance, that the Church is to be a special community, and that it must not allow room within itself for those whose witness is not good. The problem is that then we identify a "good witness" with what the surrounding society considers good and decent. In such a case, this text in Acts comes to us as a word of judgment, just as the words of Paul and Barnabas were judgment for those Jews in Antioch.

Worse still, the text continues. Those Jews who out of jealousy would not listen to nor accept the preaching of Paul and Barnabas now go to the magistrates of the city, to functionaries of the very Roman Empire that held Jerusalem in subjection, in order to rid themselves of these two fellow Jews whose words they find irksome. Unfortunately, the same has happened repeatedly throughout the history of the Church, and continues happening in the Americas today. In the history of the Church, there are abundant examples of cases in which a prophet or preacher was too bothersome for ecclesiastical authorities. Instead of trying to convince him or her by the power of the word, or trying to see if there is any truth in what is being said, the Church authorities appealed to the state—to the "secular arm" as was then said—to quiet the annoying prophet. In Latin America we all know cases in which this has been done and is still done. The best-known example is that of those who began declaring that biblical faith requires Christians to be involved in the social and economic problems of their community, and suddenly were accused by other Christians of being subversive Communists. No matter how much that particular person quoted the Bible, nor how honestly his or her words were based on the words of Jesus himself, if what the person says is not to my liking, it is subversive. And, if the political power at hand happens to be one of our frequent dictatorships, there are even those who bring the complaint before the authorities and the supposed subversive has to go into exile or shows up dead by the roadside.

While those jealous Jews were plotting to have the leaders of the city expel Barnabas and Paul, "the word of the Lord spread throughout the region." Probably when they saw the missionaries leave the city, the leaders of the synagogue thought that they were rid of the problem. But by the power of the Spirit what had begun continued, and when we read that story today it is clear that those who end up being excluded are not the expelled ones, but those who promoted their expulsion. How will the future read the story of our plots, our trials, and our expulsions? Let us take care; let us take care with fear and trembling, lest those whom today we silence turn out to be the messengers whom the Spirit is sending in order to call us to ever-renewed obedience, for it might well be that in rejecting them we provoke our own rejection.

D. ICONIUM (13:51b–14:6a)

The last two verses in chapter 13 serve as a bridge between Antioch of Pisidia and Iconium. What is summarized at the end of verse 51 with the words "went to Iconium" is a trip of more than 150 kilometers. Verse 52, although appearing after the missionaries have left Antioch and reached Iconium, seems to refer to the disciples in Antioch, for Luke gives no hint that the gospel had been preached in Iconium before.

Iconium, in the province of Galatia, was a rich and prosperous city. Today it is called Konya. What happened there regarding the initial success in the synagogue and the opposition of those who did not accept the preaching of the missionaries is very similar to what happened before in Antioch of Pisidia, although in this case Luke summarizes it in two verses (14:1–2).[26] As in Antioch, the opposition promotes the ill will of the Gentiles toward "the brothers." However, because they were not expelled as in Antioch, the missionaries remained in Iconium "for a long time," and the conflict came to the point where the population was divided between those who were "with the Jews" and those were "with the apostles" (14:4).

This is the first time that Luke calls Paul and Barnabas "apostles" (see also 14:14). This is historically accurate, for there are many indications in the New Testament that in early times the title of "apostle" was not limited to the Twelve, but many others also held it. (It is also possible that Luke is employing

---

26. Because these two verses seem to repeat and summarize the more detailed story about Antioch, one may suppose that the "Greeks" in 14:1 are both "God-fearers" and pagan Gentiles.

the term, not as a title, but rather in the sense of "sent ones," or "missionaries.") In the end all led to a project to stone the missionaries, who fled.

GOSPEL AND POLARIZATION

Because this passage summarizes events that are very similar to those in the previous section, the reader is invited to review what has been said about that other text, under the heading "The Power of the Gospel." Practically all that was said there about the events in Antioch of Pisidia applies equally to those in Iconium.

However, the story in Iconium adds another dimension, which is particularly relevant for our present situation. In Iconium, it is not only a matter of the Jews, jealous over the new openness that the missionaries proclaimed toward Gentiles, conspiring against them. What is added here is the polarization of the city itself, whose residents "were divided; some sided with the Jews, and some with the apostles."

This is a well-known phenomenon among us. When the gospel is preached in such a way that it threatens existing privileges, those who enjoy those privileges are disturbed (as Luke would say, they are filled with jealousy) and do all they can in order to put an end to such preaching.

This happened in times past in several Latin American countries where Roman Catholic leaders, upset over Protestant preaching, joined forces with the more conservative elements, so that the conflict between liberals and conservatives in many cases became a religious conflict—one that quite frequently involved physical violence. As in the case of Iconium, the people were divided, for some persecuted Protestants and others, while not quite defending them, at least tolerated them.

Similar situations exist in our day, although it is no longer usually a conflict between Protestants and Catholics. One of the salient notes of Latin American life in the last decades of the twentieth century was polarization. The old conflicts between liberal and conservative parties had been eclipsed by the much more violent confrontation between the extreme right and the radical left. Protestant churches that a few years before worked in relative harmony, today attack each other, and are even divided within themselves, for reasons similar to those that divide the society. Even the matter of being "ecumenical" or not has become a party issue, and new movements of unity and collaboration have appeared with claims not to be ecumenical!

What can one say about such polarization? It certainly is deplorable. The gospel message is about reconciliation, and a Church that is divided and polarized will hardly be able to witness faithfully to such a message. However, the solution is not, as some suggest, in preaching a message that is not "polarizing," that does not threaten anyone. Such is not the solution of Paul and Barnabas. Their preaching is a "word of grace" (verse 3). They do not seek to produce jealousy nor polarization. However, the very word of grace is such that it leads to jealousy among those who see their privilege threatened. In response, the latter polarized the city. Therefore, if we are to deal with the problem of polarization in our own situation, this passage offers the following guidelines: (1) Our message must not seek to polarize or to threaten, but simply to announce the grace of God. (2) However, because God's grace destroys every human privilege and claim, we are not to be surprised if some do hear it as a threat. (3) In such a case, the ensuing polarization should also not surprise us. (4) Even in the midst of the most acute polarization, our responsibility is to make certain that our message is still "word of grace," and not of hatred or revenge.

E. Lystra and Derbe (14:6b–21a)

The missionaries "fled to Lystra and Derbe, cities of Lycaonia, and to the surrounding country" (14:6).[27] What this implies is that for quite some time they preached about the region, going from one place to another. It is during that period that the incident in Lystra takes place.

A miracle occurs in Lystra, which leaves the crowd amazed. In order to underscore the wonder of the miracle, Luke describes the condition of the paralytic in three phrases that are basically the same: "he could not use his feet . . . had never walked . . . had been crippled from birth" (14:8). The man was listening to Paul preach, and the apostle, "looking at him intently" (the same verb that was used in the healing of another lame man, that other time at the Temple gate: 3:4), saw that he had faith and he ordered him "in a loud voice" to stand up.[28] The miracle occurs, and the lame man "sprang up and began to walk" (the order of the two verbs is interesting, for it is the reverse of what would be expected).

However, the crowd that witnesses the miracle interprets it in its own fashion. Speaking in their own tongue, which Paul and Barnabas cannot understand, they comment that the missionaries must be gods. Barnabas must be Zeus, and Paul, who seems to be the spokesman, must be Hermes the messenger god. Even the priest of Zeus is convinced that the gods are visiting and prepares to offer them sacrifices.[29] Therefore, it is not surprising that now the people identify Barnabas and Paul with those two gods. Luke does not tell us where Paul and Barnabas were, or what they were doing, while the priest made preparations for the sacrifices. Apparently, after the healing of the lame man, some time elapses as the word gets around and enthusiasm grows for the visit of the "gods."

---

27. I. H. Marshall, *The Acts of the Apostles* (Leicester, England: Inter-Varsity Press, 1980), p. 235, is correct in pointing out that Haenchen is not consistent when first he complains that the narrative in Iconium is too brief, and the one about Lystra is too detailed, to be authentic.

28. The Western text adds: "in the name of the Lord Jesus Christ I say unto you . . .," whose purpose seems to be to underline the parallelism between this passage and the healing of the lame man at the Temple (see 3:6).

29. In some manuscripts of the Eastern text, it is "the priests," in the plural.

The apostles [30] finally learn what is happening, and they tear their clothes in sign of pain and shame, going out among the people trying to dissuade them with shouts. Luke summarizes their arguments. Note that here they do not appeal to Scripture, for the hearers are not Jews. Rather, they appeal to the order of nature, declaring that the "living God" is the creator of all that exists, and that even though in times past this God has allowed people "to follow their own ways," that did not mean that there were no witnesses to the truth, for all good things—rains on time, sustenance and joy—come from the hand of God. But the most important point that they make, which stands as the foundation of their entire argument, is that they "are mortals just like you" (the Greek says *homoiopatheis*, of similar sentiments or feelings). With these arguments, and with difficulty, they finally dissuade the crowd.

Luke then tells us that some Jews came from Antioch and Iconium, where Paul and Barnabas had been preaching before, and persuaded the crowd that earlier wished to worship the missionaries to stone Paul and leave him as dead at the outskirts of the city. It is there that the disciples find him, and he gets up and returns to the city. The text does not imply that Paul's getting up had any miraculous significance; but it certainly underlines Paul's valor in returning to a town where he had just been stoned. It is also ironic that the ones who now persuade the people in Lystra to stone Paul share the same convictions that Paul held before his conversion. Just as Paul, in his religious zeal, went out from Jerusalem in order to persecute the disciples in Damascus, now these Jews leave Antioch of Pisidia and Iconium in order to persecute Paul.

THE MESSENGER AND THE MESSAGE

The events in Lystra that Luke describes show the human tendency to idolatry, and the ever-present danger that the messenger be confused with the message. On two earlier occasions, almost in passing, we saw Peter facing that danger. The first was at Solomon's porch after the healing of the lame man at the entrance to the Temple, when Peter rebukes those who listen for looking at them— Peter and John—as if it were by their own power or piety that the miracle took place (3:12). The second is when Cornelius goes out to receive Peter and worships him, to which Peter responds, "Stand up; I am only a mortal" (10:26). In the first of these two cases, those who seem inclined to idolatry are Jews. In the second, it is a "God-fearer." In the case we are now studying, they are pagan worshippers of Zeus and Hermes. In all these cases, what happens is that people attempt to transfer the admiration and worship that are due only to God to those other people whom God uses as messengers or instruments.

---

30. Normally, Luke reserves the title of "apostle" for the Twelve. However, in the ancient Church the title was employed in a wider sense, including any person who was properly sent and commissioned by the Holy Spirit and by the Church. Here Luke seems to use the term in that wider sense.

The same phenomenon appears frequently in our churches. There are people who attend a particular church because they like the pastor; and if another pastor comes, they will possibly go to another church, or simply go to none. There are pastors who promote such feelings and build small empires in which they rule. There are radio and television preachers who attract followers, not so much of Jesus Christ, as of themselves. They speak of their great enterprises as "my ministry," and they have thousands of followers who listen to them regularly and send in their offerings. Frequently the competition between such "ministries" is as ferocious as that between any two companies trying to sell the same product.

It is not difficult to see the harm this does. Part of the harm is in that, when such idols fall, people are disillusioned and their faith falters. Another consequence, sometimes less dramatic, but much more pernicious, is that in the competition among such enterprises much of the love that must be at the very heart of the Christian witness is lost. However, the worst of all the evils of this kind of situation is that an idol is placed where only the supreme God should be. The reason Peter first, and then Paul and Barnabas, refused to be worshipped is that such worship is a negation of the message they preach. What is really important is not that people believe. What is important is that they believe in God and in Jesus Christ. If they believe in Peter or in Paul, this is not to be seen as a victory, but as a failure. That is why Barnabas and Paul rend their clothes. The task of the messenger certainly requires being faithful to the message and reflecting it; but reflecting it in such a way that it may be clearly seen that between the messenger and the message, between the preacher and Lord, there is an unbridgeable difference. With reference to that difference, the greatest and holiest preacher stands on the same side as the most humble and hesitant believer. Whoever seeks to hide that truth, no matter how eloquent a preacher, is not faithful to the message of the apostles.

F.   THE RETURN (14:21b–28)

These few verses very quickly summarize the return trip. We are told first of all that Paul and Barnabas preached in Derbe, where they made many disciples. Paul would later return to Derbe (16:1–4). However, now Luke leads us in a dizzying return trip: Derge, Lystra, Iconium, Antioch of Pisidia,[31] Pamphylia, Perga, Attalia (which was not mentioned in the trip in the opposite direction) and finally Antioch of Syria. Although the narrative is rapid this does not mean that the return journey was equally fast. On the contrary, in verses 22 and 23 Luke tells us that in each church the missionaries strengthened and encouraged the disciples, calling them to persevere. Their message on such oc-

---

31. Although the authorities had expelled Paul and Barnabas from Antioch, it was customary in such cities for magistrates to change annually. Because, in all probability, several years had gone by since the first visit, the missionaries could now return to Antioch of Pisidia and remain in the city unless the new magistrates agreed with the earlier ones that they should be expelled.

casions, as Luke summarizes it, was the need to suffer in order to enter the reign of God (which is closely related to what has already been said in the earlier chapters of Acts). They also worked on the organization of the churches, appointing "elders." These were to be the leaders of the church or their pastors. Our modern word "presbyter" comes from the Greek word that is employed here and elsewhere in the New Testament to refer to these "elders." As to how they were selected, Luke simply says the apostles "appointed" them. However, the verb employed here leaves room for their having been elected by the congregation.

Once back in Antioch, the missionaries render a report to the church that has sent them. The verb that the NRSV translates as "related" in verse 27 is in the imperfect tense, and therefore the implication is that this was an ongoing activity. Possibly the report took several sessions, given that probably the missionaries had been absent for more than four years. After finishing this journey, the missionaries stayed in Antioch for "some time."

MISSION TO ANTIOCH

It was the church in Syrian Antioch that sent Barnabas and Saul as missionaries to Cyprus and Asia Minor. We are now told that at their return the missionaries brought their report to the church that had sent them. That is to be expected. However, what is remarkable is that as a result of that mission—and probably of many others that Luke does not mention—the church in Antioch was also enriched. When Paul and Barnabas return, their experiences and discoveries in the missionary enterprise were shared with the church that sent them. This is why, as will be seen in chapter 15, the church in Antioch played an important role in the entire discussion regarding the inclusion of Gentiles, and what was to be required of them. After that fifteenth chapter, Luke will say little about the church in Antioch. But Church history tells us that this church was a center of missionary activity for centuries. Why? Partly because it was strengthened by its own mission. If Gentiles in Pisidian Antioch were able to hear the gospel thanks to the efforts of believers from Syrian Antioch, the latter were able to hear from Saul and Barnabas "all that God had done with them, and how he had opened a door of faith for the Gentiles" (14:27). In the mission of the Church as in every other realm of life, God's word never returns empty.

When today we say that our Hispanic American church must be missionary, this is important not only because it would lead to the founding of new churches, but also because thereby the already existing church—as happened earlier to the church in Antioch—will be strengthened in faith and will discover new dimensions of the gospel. Mission is always a two-way street, so that those who give also receive.

On the other hand, it is crucial that we do not limit our understanding of "mission" to the purely geographic dimension. Mission takes place wherever, impelled by faith, Christians cross the border between belief and unbelief, and beyond that border they witness to their faith. Mission takes place when a student, gathered with her fellow students who do not know the gospel and who live according to other principles, witnesses to her faith. Mission takes place when Christians, moved by the pain of those who suffer, go to the neediest places in our hemisphere, to the impoverished barrios and the remote villages with scarce resources, and there live their faith. Mission takes place when Christians participate in the cultural, political, and economic life of society, and there show their compassion and the power of their faith. Mission takes place wherever God leads us, because, after all, the mission is not ours, but God's!

All Christians who are struggling and giving witness to their faith in all these various environments are missionaries. What the rest of the Church must then do, as did earlier the church in Antioch, is twofold: First of all, we must bless all those who will take the risk of mission—as Luke would say, "lay our hands on them." Second, we must listen to them when they gather with us, and learn from them and their mission.

Unfortunately, this is not what is done in many of our churches. On the contrary, when some of our members participate in spheres of life where all are not believers such as labor unions, student movements, cultural salons, musical groups, and so forth, what we do is to criticize them. "They are being lost," we say. "They have gone to the world." Sometimes we even shun them. Rather than strengthening them for their mission and exhorting them to give witness wherever they are, we give them to understand that it is not legitimate to witness in such an environment. On the second point our reaction is even worse. If they come to the church telling us of what God is doing in those "worldly" places, they are told in a myriad of ways that the church is not the appropriate place to speak of such matters. With such attitudes, what is at risk of being lost is not only the missionaries but also the Church itself, whose vision dims.

G. THE COUNCIL IN JERUSALEM (15:1–35)

1. The Problem Is Posed (15:1–3)

Luke does not clarify the chronological relationship between chapter 15 and the preceding narrative. Although the NRSV translation begins with "then," a more literal translation would say simply: "certain individuals." Because the previous chapter ends letting us know that Paul and Barnabas remained in Antioch for some time with the disciples, it would seem that the conflict was not the immediate result of their own travels and preaching but actually developed some time later.

Nor does Luke tell us who "came down from Judea."[32] In Galatians 2:12 Paul speaks of people who "came from James," and who also insisted on

---

32. Greek verbs do not need explicit subjects as do English verbs. Therefore, even the words "certain individuals" is an addition required by the character of English grammar. Some manuscripts do add that those who came from Judea were Pharisees. Luke uses the phrase "came *down* from Judea" because Jerusalem was higher than the surrounding area, and therefore it was customary to talk about going down from Judea and up toward Jerusalem.

the need to keep the Jewish Law. If both passages refer to the same episode, it would seem that Luke is softening the edges of the conflict between the Twelve, particularly James, and Paul. This is one of the many points at which scholars debate the historical accuracy of Luke, and whether part of his agenda is precisely to make it appear that there was more unity and agreement between Paul and the church in Jerusalem than there actually was.

At any rate, what these people from Judea taught is clear: "Unless you are circumcised according to the custom of Moses, you cannot be saved." Certainly, circumcision was not all that was at issue, for the Law of Moses also included many regulations on diet, religious celebrations, and so on.[33] The traditional opinion, probably correct, is that these "Judaizers" were Jews, possibly Pharisees, who had converted to Christianity and now wished for all Christians to submit to the Law of Moses.[34]

Such teaching provoked significant dissension and discussion in Antioch, where apparently its main opponents were Paul and Barnabas. As a result, the church in Antioch decided to send these two "and some of the others" to Jerusalem "to discuss this question with the apostles and the elders." The very fact that they decided to send to Jerusalem to clarify the matter would seem to indicate that the Judaizers claimed to have the support of the mother church. That may be the reason Paul says that they have come "from James." In Galatians 2:1–2, Paul tells about a visit to Jerusalem that may very well be the one to which Acts refers, although Paul offers a different reason for the trip: "after fourteen years I went up again to Jerusalem with Barnabas, taking Titus along with me. I went up in response to a revelation." Thus, it would seem that Titus was among the others who were sent with Paul and Barnabas to Jerusalem.

Along the way, as they passed through Phoenicia and Samaria, they "reported the conversion of the Gentiles and brought great joy to all the believers." Luke has probably included this detail in order to let us know that the position of Paul and Barnabas regarding the admission of Gentiles had wide support, not only in Antioch but also in Phoenicia and Samaria, where they had not worked.[35]

---

33. Some manuscripts of the Western text, in describing what the people from Judea taught, add "and walk on the way of Moses." This seems to be an attempt to include these wider issues and not limit the conflict to the matter of circumcision.

34. Although this is a traditional opinion, which is still held by most New Testament scholars, some have suggested that these Judaizers were not themselves Jews, but Gentile converts to Christianity who now wished not to be less than Jews and therefore insisted on the keeping of the Law. This opinion is held by J. Munck, *Paul and the Salvation of Mankind* (London: SCM Press, 1959).

35. Such is the interpretation of E. Haenchen, *The Acts of the Apostles: A Commentary* (Philadelphia: Westminster, 1975), p. 144.

2. Events in Jerusalem (15:4–29)

a. First Reception and Difficulties (15:4–5)

When the Antiochene delegation reaches Jerusalem, it is well received "by the church and the apostles and the elders," and tells them what has been taking place—particularly, one would imagine, the results of Paul's and Barnabas's journey. It is at that point that difficulties emerge, for "some believers who belonged to the sect of the Pharisees" begin arguing that the people who had been converted must be circumcised and must also keep the Law. In order to understand their position, it is important to remember that for these early Christians Christianity was not a new religion. It was rather the fulfillment of the promises made to Israel, of all that they had long been expecting. Therefore, a Pharisee who accepted Jesus as the Messiah or Christ did not thereby cease being a Jew nor a Pharisee. It is not, as we would tend to read the text today, that some former Pharisees still remained attached to their earlier beliefs, but rather of practicing and sincere Pharisees who, while still keeping their close observance of the Law, are also Christians. It is ironic to note at this point that Paul, one of the main promoters of a new openness toward Gentiles, was himself a Pharisee. His own missionary work, as the narrative has made clear, forced him to become ever more open toward Gentiles in a way that was not necessary for Christian Pharisees in Jerusalem.

Some interpreters claim surprise at finding that the church in Jerusalem once again has to discuss the question of the admission of Gentiles, as the matter had already been discussed after the conversion of Cornelius and his friends, and even after a new church had been founded in Antioch, which had a large number of Gentiles in its midst. Human reality, however, is not always logical, and human groups faced with new ideas quite often waver. What Luke tells us on this point is much more realistic than some reconstructions of events that try to place them in absolute logical order. According to Luke, the question of the admission of Gentiles was discussed repeatedly. Although the discussion surrounding the conversion of Cornelius should have settled the matter definitively, that was not the case. The same could be said about the founding of the church in Antioch. And, even though after this fifteenth chapter Acts speaks almost exclusively of the mission among the Gentiles, and does not discuss in detail the matter of their having or not having to accept the Law of Moses, the fact is that through Paul's letters it is clear that the matter was far from resolved. What Luke tells us here, just as what he told us before, is just one of many episodes that little by little opened the door to the Gentiles.

b. The Assembly (15:6–29)

In order to deal with the debate caused by the conversion of Gentiles and the resistance of the "Judaizers," an assembly takes place. Perhaps there is more than one session, for although at the beginning those who are gathered are "the apostles and the elders" (15:6), later we are told that "the whole assembly" kept silence (15:12); and eventually the decision was taken by "the apostles and the elders, with the consent of the whole church" (15:22). Thus, perhaps we should not think in terms of a single session, but rather of an entire process out of which Luke chooses certain moments and interventions that he considers particularly significant. In Galatians 2:2, Paul says that he communicated his ideas privately to the leaders of the church in Jerusalem. Apparently, Luke is dramatizing the entire process by condensing it into what at first reading appears to be a single session, but apparently took much longer.

i. Peter Intervenes (15:6–11)   In these few verses Peter retells his experience in connection with the conversion of Cornelius (10:1–11:18). The phrase in verse 7, "in the early days," would seem to indicate that it is already some time since those events. This would help explain why it is necessary to discuss once again the question of the admission of Gentiles. From the point of view of Christians in Jerusalem, the conversion and baptism of Cornelius and those with him would seem to be a remarkable episode, but not something that had happened with sufficient frequency to set the direction in which the Church was to move. It is now, through the results of the missionary work of Barnabas and Paul (and perhaps others), that the question becomes urgent as to how Gentiles are to be admitted into the community, and what is to be demanded of them.

However, in this brief speech Peter does go one step beyond what he had said in the case of Cornelius. Now he offers a theological reason why the "yoke" of the Law is not to be imposed on Gentiles: this is a yoke "that neither our ancestors nor we have been able to bear," and at any rate the important point is that all, Gentiles as well as Jews, are "saved through the grace of our Lord Jesus" (15:10–11).[36] This has been used to claim that what we have here are not Peter's words, but an expression of Luke's theology.[37]

ii. James Intervenes (15:12–21)   Upon hearing Peter's words, "the whole assembly kept silence." We have not been told that there was any particular noise or disorder. What Luke indicates with these words is that there was an attitude of attentiveness and reflection. Barnabas and Paul[38] make use of this moment to tell once again (according to 15:4, they had already done so) what had

---

36. The order itself of verse 11 is interesting: Peter does not say that the Gentiles will be saved, just as the Jews, by grace, but the opposite: that the Jews will be saved by grace, just like the Gentiles.

37. Thus, for instance, Haenchen, *Acts*, p. 446, n. 3: "This assertion corresponds neither to Jewish nor to Pauline theology. The Jew saw in the law a privilege and a help: the idea of 'the yoke' (of the law) denoted the religious duties and contained no complaint that the law was hard or intolerable. . . . Here however we have the law seen through Hellenistic Gentile Christian eyes, as a mass of commandments and prohibitions which no man can fulfill. Luke here is obviously speaking for himself and transmitting the view of his age and milieu."

38. It should be noted that within the context of Jerusalem the name of Barnabas appears before that of Paul. Barnabas had been one of the first and most respected leaders of

taken place in their mission among the Gentiles. It is to be supposed that what they said was seen as a confirmation of Peter's experience in the case of Cornelius.

Then James intervenes. Throughout the Book of Acts, and up to this point, this James, who was not one of the Twelve, gains in importance. In 12:17, which was the last time we heard about Paul before this particular passage, we are told that when Peter prepared to flee from Jerusalem he sent word to "James and to the believers." Now that we are back in Jerusalem, we find that Peter has also returned, although we are not told how nor when, and that James is one of the leaders of the church.

James begins by referring to what "Simeon has told us." The name "Simeon" is the Aramaic version of "Simon." Therefore, Luke is hinting that James spoke in Aramaic.[39] The manner in which James summarizes Peter's speech includes a remarkable assertion: God has "looked favorably on the Gentiles, to take from among them a people for his name" (15:14). Luke usually uses the term "people"—*laos*—in order to refer to the "people of God." Therefore, what James is saying is that God is raising a new people, or an extension of Israel.[40] And in order to uphold this position he offers a biblical argument that seems to continue what Peter has just said. According to a text in Amos, God will carry forth a work of restoration, "so that all the peoples may seek the Lord—even all the Gentiles over whom my name has been called." On this basis, James offers his solution, which is eventually adopted.[41]

The quotation from Amos presents a problem. As is usually the case, the text that Luke places on the lips of James is taken from the Septuagint—the Greek translation of the Hebrew Scriptures that most of the early Greek-speaking Christians employed. In this particular passage, the Hebrew text differs from the Septuagint and could not have been used to support James's argument.[42] It would seem very strange for James, speaking Aramaic in Jerusalem, to quote Scripture, not from the Hebrew text but according to the Septuagint, and that he would dare do this in a case in which it would be very easy to contradict him by simply quoting the Hebrew text. Those who insist

---

the church in Jerusalem, and he enjoyed the respect of the Twelve, who had given him the name he bore.

39. Another explanation that has not been generally accepted is that this Simeon is not the same as Simon Peter. That is the opinion of D. W. Riddle, "The Cephas problem and a possible solution," *JBL*, 59 (1940), 169–80.

40. J. Dupont, "Un people d'entre les nations (Actes 15:14)," *NTSt*, 31 (1985), 321–35.

41. What the NRSV translates as "I have reached the decision" is a verb that can be interpreted both in the sense of determining the course that has to be followed and in the sense of offering an opinion. Given the ambiguity of the verb, it could be translated, as does the NRSV, in the sense that the decision was up to James, and in the sense that he is merely offering his view.

42. See the translation of Amos 9:12 in the NRSV, where what is announced is that the people of Israel will "possess the remnant of Edom and all the nations who are called by my name."

on the absolute historical accuracy of the speeches in Acts have had to develop strange theories to solve this difficulty. Some have suggested that the Septuagint text is the original, and that it was circulating in the first century in an Aramaic translation, which James quotes.[43] This is mere conjecture whose only basis is the desire to safeguard the historical accuracy of the speeches supposedly quoted by Luke. It would seem simpler to say that, although James probably supported Peter's position, and perhaps even offered biblical arguments for it, what Luke is doing is placing on James's lips an argument that circulated somewhat later among Gentiles, when the Septuagint was already the commonly used Bible.

At any rate, what James either suggests or decides becomes also the decision of the meeting. The main thrust of this is that Gentiles "who are turning to God" should not be troubled but should be required to observe four points. There is also much discussion about this decision, both in terms of the actual words of the text and in terms of their meaning.

The textual issues arise because at this particular point there are different readings in various manuscripts. The most ancient that has survived[44] includes only three things from which the Gentiles must abstain: idolatry, that which is strangled, and blood. However, because it is only that particular manuscript that limits its lists to these three points, most scholars agree that what we have here is simply an omission by the copyist. The Egyptian text, accepted by most scholars, reads as does the NRSV, and therefore refers to four points: "that you abstain from what has been sacrificed to idols and from blood and what is strangled and from fornication." The Western text omits "what is strangled," and therefore its list is limited to idolatry, fornication, and blood. The same text then adds the golden rule in its negative form: "not doing to others what you do not wish done unto you."

This discussion about the text is important, for much of the theological meaning of the decision depends on the particular list of observances given. The Western text seems to imply that the prohibitions are moral in character, whereas the Egyptian, which is most likely the original, seems to indicate that they are ritual in nature.[45] This is particularly clear in the case of "blood." What is the meaning of abstaining from blood? If, as in the Western text, nothing is said about the "strangled," abstaining from blood will seem to mean not killing or otherwise committing violence.[46] If, on the other hand, "blood" ap-

---

43. Such is the position of Th. Zahn, *Die Apostelgeschichte des Lucas* (Erlangen: A. Deichert, 1919–21), vol. 1, p. 521.

44. The Chester Beatty papyrus.

45. This is the manner in which most scholars contrast these options. However, C. K. Barret, "The apostolic decree of Acts 15:29," *AusBibRev*, 35 (1987), 50–59, claims that the theological contrast is not as stark as has usually been thought.

46. It was thus that the entire text was interpreted in the Western Church. Therefore it was the basis for the theory that there are three major sins (sins that some would call unforgivable): idolatry, fornication, and homicide.

pears next to that which is "strangled," as it does in the Egyptian text, the implication is that the prohibition refers to the ancient Jewish law of not eating blood, be it from animals that were not bled when killed or as an ingredient of a dish.

The problem then posed is that, if the Egyptian text is the original, James seems to contradict himself, for he is saying that he agrees with Peter that the Gentiles are not to be subjected to the Law, but then he tells them that there are indeed four points that they must observe, and that these include not eating blood nor any animal that has not been bled. This is the main argument in favor of the Western text, which otherwise would have been rejected outright by most scholars.

In spite of this difficulty, it would seem that the Egyptian text is the original and that in fact the provisions do refer to ritual and dietary matters more than moral. The reason for this is that these four prohibitions are precisely those that, according to the Law of Moses, were to be imposed on Gentiles living in Israel (Lev. 17:8–18:26).[47] Thus read, what James is doing is not really imposing rules onto Gentiles who wish to become Christians. Rather what he is doing is telling them that, in order to be able to commune with Jews, and in order to be as the Gentiles who in ancient times dwelled in the midst of Israel, they only have to follow the same directions that in ancient times were applied to those Gentiles.

In order to understand all of this, we must place ourselves at that time, and look at matters from the perspective of that early Jewish Church. As they saw matters, what was taking place was not, as we tend to think today, that some Jews were abandoning Judaism in order to become Christians. What was happening was rather that some among the Gentiles were now being added to Israel, thanks to the good news of Jesus Christ. Therefore, the question was not, as it is for us today, how much of the Law must be obeyed in order to be a Christian? It was rather, how much of the Law must one obey in order to live in the midst of Israel? The answer to this question was clear, for the Law itself established it in Leviticus 17 and 18. These are the principles that James now suggests as the basis on which Gentile Christians can commune with Christian Jews.[48]

Taking all of this into account, we see that the purpose of the decision is not to tell Christians that the Law is no longer valid except in these four points. The purpose is rather to find a means whereby Gentile Christians can join Jews without violating the conscience of the latter. This is why, as the

---

47. As far as I know, the scholar who first pointed out this relationship, and especially the fact that the order of the prohibitions in Leviticus is the same as in the "official" text of the "decree" from Jerusalem (15:29), was H. Waitz in his article "Das Problem des sogennanten Aposteldecrets," *ZKgesch*, 55 (1936), 227.

48. C. Perrot, "Les décisions de l'Assemblée de Jérusalem," *RechScR*, 69 (1981), 195–208, holds that what was at stake was also the legal status of the new community as part of Israel.

Church became more Gentile and less Jewish in its membership, this prohibition lost importance. It was no longer necessary to think constantly about Jewish brothers and sisters with whom one had to keep communion. It is for this reason and in the same spirit that in I Corinthians 8 Paul tells his readers that, although in the final analysis eating meat sacrificed to the idols will neither help nor hinder them, if there is someone who will be scandalized by their doing so, they must abstain.

Finally, before the decision itself, verse 21 does not seem to relate with the subject at hand. Why are these words included, and what do they mean in this context? Among the many interpretations and explanations,[49] the most likely is that James means to make two points: (1) Gentile Christians, even though they are not in Palestine, live in the midst of Israel, for there are synagogues and Jews everywhere, and that therefore the rule of Leviticus 17 and 18 applies to them, and (2) because there are synagogues everywhere where the Law of Moses is read, Christians are not obliged to witness to that Law by obeying it.

iii. The Decision (15:22–29) The apostles (although we are not told exactly which of them were present),[50] the "elders" (about whose origin and function we have not been told), and "the whole church" decide to write a letter and send it by means of Silas and Judas Barsabbas. No more than the name is known about Judas Barsabbas. (Could he be a brother of Joseph Barsabbas, the other candidate to the apostleship when Mathias was elected?) About Silas much more is known, both through Acts and through the rest of the New Testament. In Acts itself, we shall find him again traveling with Paul in his journeys through Philippi, Thessalonica, and Berea, until he disappears from the scene in Corinth (18:5), without another word being said about him.[51] Under the Latin form of his name, "Silvanus," he appears also in II Corinthians 1:19, I Timothy 1:1, II Timothy 1:1, and I Peter 5:12.

The letter, although brief, has the characteristic structure of letters at that time, which is the same that appears repeatedly, although more extensively, in Paul's epistles. It begins by indicating the identity of the writers: "the brothers, both the apostles and the elders," and then naming the addressees: "to the believers of Gentile origin in Antioch and Syria and Cilicia." Then follows a brief salutation ("greetings"), after which comes the main body of the letter, and finally a farewell, which is usually a blessing or an expression of goodwill ("fare well"). Regarding the addressees, it is important to note that the letter is not addressed only to the Gentiles in Antioch, but also to others who have been

---

49. Summarized in Haenchen, *Acts*, p. 450, n. 1.

50. Luke only mentions Peter and James—who was not one of the Twelve. Paul (Gal. 2:9) also mentions John.

51. B. N. Kaye, "Acts' portrait of Silas," *NT*, 21 (1979), 13–26, suggests that the reason Silas seems to leave Paul in Corinth is that from that point on Paul no longer continues his earlier practice of basing his mission on the synagogue of each city.

converted thanks to the Antiochene missionary work, in Syria as well as in Cilicia. As to the message of this brief epistle, in essence it is what James said before: that the Gentiles are not to be troubled by anything beyond the four points already mentioned (three of which have to do with dietary practices)— that which has been sacrificed to idols, blood, the strangled, and fornication.[52]

3. Return to Antioch (15:30–35)

This brief passage does not require much explanation. As had been agreed, Judas Barsabbas and Silas go to Antioch. Those who were "sent off" may refer not only to these two, but also to those who had come earlier from Antioch to Jerusalem: Barnabas, Saul, and others (15:2).

The meeting that Luke describes seems to be rather official. The verb that the NRSV translates as "delivered" was employed at that time for the formal presentation of a letter or any other document. The letter was read in the congregation, and received with joy, apparently because Gentile Christians in Antioch were worried about the possibility that those in Jerusalem would tell them that it was necessary to be circumcised and to obey all the Law, and about the possibility of schism this would bring about.

As the prophets they were, Judas and Silas preached before the congregation, and their preaching encouraged and strengthened the believers. The "some time" during which they remained there could be anything from a few weeks to more than a year—the text does not say. After that time, as they prepared to return to Jerusalem, the church in Antioch gave them a formal farewell, for this is the meaning of verse 33.

Verse 34 appears only in the Western text. That is why the NRSV and other recent versions omit it. Scholars suggest that it was possibly introduced at this point in order to avoid the apparent contradiction between verses 33 and 40, for the former seems to imply that Silas returned to Jerusalem, and the latter places him at Antioch when Paul begins his next journey. Apparently the earlier reading, which is in the common or Egyptian text, is to be understood in the sense that the church of Antioch sent back the two delegates from Jerusalem (verse 33), and not as an attempt to explain how Silas got back to Antioch before Paul's next journey.

Mission and Vision

Much could be said about this text. Let us however begin by looking at the contrast between the Pharisees who are disturbed because Gentiles have been added to the Church without demanding that they be circumcised, and that other Pharisee, Paul, who is one of the main defenders of the opposite position.

---

52. This second list offers the same variations between the Western and Egyptian texts as were pointed out in the discussion of 15:20.

Why is it that Paul can see what God is doing among the Gentiles, and be open to it, and the other Pharisees cannot? Certainly, it is not because these Pharisees in the church of Jerusalem are less sincere than Paul. They, just like him, have accepted Jesus as the Messiah and have joined the Church, probably even at great personal sacrifice and by severing many important relationships. Where, then, is the difference?

The answer, although simple, is profound: these Pharisees have received the gospel and have accepted it; but Paul, beyond accepting it, has joined God's mission in the world. One may suppose that the Christian Pharisees in Jerusalem, as all the church in that city, "devoted themselves to the apostles' teaching and fellowship, to the breaking of bread and the prayers" (2:42). Paul and Christians in Antioch would do the same. However, the church in Antioch, and Paul within it, did more: they joined God's mission in the world. The Pharisees in Jerusalem had not had Paul's experience in Antioch of Pisidia, in Iconium, or in Lystra. The Spirit was certainly active in Jerusalem; but where the Spirit was doing new things, opening new ways, widening horizons, was in those other far-flung places. Paul and Barnabas had accepted the call of the Spirit, and in those distant cities had joined what God was doing. Therefore, when the problem is posed in Jerusalem, those who have a vision of what God is doing in their day are precisely people such as Paul and Barnabas—or Peter because of his encounter with Cornelius—who have participated in the mission of the Spirit.

Throughout its history, the Church has had to face similar situations. The old centers, like those Christian Pharisees in Jerusalem, sometimes appear inflexible, and therefore incapable of responding to the challenges of the moment. It is at the edges, where Christians have to face such challenges continuously, and where they see God's action in those very challenges, that the great awakenings take place, the adventures of faith, the discoveries of heretofore unsuspected dimensions of the gospel. This is certainly what takes place throughout the life of Paul, and not only in this episode. The Epistles of Paul, which are such an important part of the New Testament, are not works of speculative theology, but are rather responses to the missionary challenges of the moment.

The Hispanic Church is a result of missionary adventures of the past. Some of them were more violent than others, and some more benevolent than others. But in all of them we learned to receive. We received missionaries. We received doctrines. We received ideas. We received money. In the midst of so much receiving, we are tempted to believe that we are somehow inferior: the important church is elsewhere, the place where the missionaries come from; the books worth reading are only those that come from over there; the models that we should imitate are the ones that have proven valuable in that other place. We, poor little folk, must forever be receiving.

But no! The case of Paul, a Pharisee of Pharisees (23:6) and his contrast with these other Christians, equally Pharisees from Jerusalem, presents the matter in a different way. The place where we are, at this apparent edge, is where God is doing new things. And those who daily see the new things that God is doing in the world have the obligation toward God and toward the rest of the Church to go back to the old centers, which often have lost much of their vision, taking to them our renewed vision of what God is doing today.

What is true at the global level is also true in the more limited circle of our own nations and conditions. Here too we find problems similar to those discussed in Acts 15. God is acting today in our hemisphere. It would be easy—it is easy—to remain comfortably seated in our church pews and from there, like those Pharisees in Jerusalem, to say "that is not the way things ought to be." There are Christians—sincere Christians like those Pharisees in Jerusalem—who would wish for things not to change, that the same hymns would be sung, that the same sermons be preached, the same activities be held, and nothing more. In fact, to a lesser or greater degree we all suffer from that temptation. But that is not where God is calling us. Like Paul, God is calling us, not only from the church—be it in Jerusalem, Antioch, Los Angeles, or Buenos Aires—but also, as earlier Barnabas and Saul, from all those other places and spaces where faith does not reign, but where the divine mercy also reaches. Because they were instruments of the work of God in those places, Saul and Barnabas could also be instruments so that God was able to speak to the church in Jerusalem. If the Church today is to hear a similar word, it will hear it, not from its own centers, but rather from those who, like Barnabas and Saul, have heeded the call to venture beyond the edges of the Church itself.

6

Mission to Europe
(15:36–18:22)

It is at this point, after the "council" of Jerusalem, that the Pauline mission takes flight. We are now precisely at the point in Paul's life on which his letters shed most light.

A. THE CALLING (15:36–16:10)

1. Paul and Barnabas Part (15:36–41)

The mission to Europe is not the outcome of great vision or foresight. On the contrary, it all begins with an idea which in itself is not very original: "After some days Paul said to Barnabas, 'Come, let us return and visit the believers in every city where we proclaimed the word of the Lord and see how they are doing.'" The "some days" to which Luke refers may have been no more than a few weeks, although most probably they were at least a few months, and perhaps even years, as seems to follow from verse 35. At any rate, Paul's purpose is not to expand the mission further, but simply to visit the churches previously established and see how they are doing.

Nor does the new mission begin on a very inspiring point, but rather with a serious disagreement between Paul and Barnabas. Luke tells us that the basis of the disagreement was that Barnabas wanted to take John Mark again, and Paul refused, because Mark had abandoned them in the previous journey (13:3). The clash was strong. What the NRSV and NIV translate as a "sharp disagreement" (JB: "violent quarrel") is *paroxysmos*, from which the English word "paroxysm" derives. From Paul's letters we learn that the matter was more complicated than Luke tells us. To begin with, John Mark was kin to Barnabas (Col. 4:10). In Galatians 2:13, Paul lets us know that his disagreement with Barnabas went far beyond the mere matter of taking Mark with them or not. Apparently, Paul understood the decision made at Jerusalem in wider terms than did Barnabas. For Paul, what had been decided in Jerusalem meant that Gentile and Jewish Christians could eat together—that is, could participate jointly in the Lord's Table. However, when a dispute arose in Antioch regarding this matter, both Peter and Barnabas took the stance of those who insisted that Jews should eat separately, in order to keep their ritual purity. The dispute became bitter, and Paul even accuses both Peter and Barnabas of hypocrisy.[1]

The outcome of such disagreements was that Paul and Barnabas parted company. Barnabas and John Mark left for Cyprus—Barnabas's native land—while Paul and Silas took the land route through Syria and Cilicia. It is important to note that the purpose of both missionary teams is still to visit the churches previously founded, and that Paul and Silas traversed Syria and Cilicia "strengthening the churches."

The breach that had occurred in Antioch between the two missionaries was eventually healed. Although the believers in Antioch commended Paul "to the grace of the Lord," from that moment on he acted more as an independent missionary than as a representative of the church in Antioch. Barnabas does not appear again in Acts. However, in I Corinthians 9:6 Paul indicates that Barnabas continues his missionary labors and that, just as Paul, he supports himself with his own work. This reference, as well as Colossians 4:10, indicate that Barnabas was widely known and respected, not only in the churches that he had earlier visited with Paul, but also in others.[2] Mark appears later in Rome as Paul's companion (Col. 4:10, Philem. 24, II Tim. 4:11) as well as Peter's (I Pet. 5:13).[3]

2.   Timothy Joins the Mission (16:1–5)

The three cities mentioned here—Derbe, Lystra and Iconium—had already witnessed the missionary labors of Paul and Barnabas in their earlier journey (14:1–21). Verse 1 begins in the singular (NRSV: "Paul went"; JB: "he traveled"; NIV: "he came") because it is the continuation of the end of chapter 15, where Paul is the subject. It is clear that Paul and Silas are together in Derbe and Lystra.

---

1. There is a good study of this subject, trying to outline the spiritual journey of Barnabas: W. Radl, "Das 'Apostelkonzil' und seine Nachgeschichte dargestellt am Weg des Barnabas," *ThQ*, 162 (1982), 45–61.

2. According to an ancient legend, Barnabas died as a martyr in Salamis in the year 61. Another legend claims that he founded the church in Milan. Tertullian, toward the end of the second century, affirms that Barnabas wrote the epistle to the Hebrews (*On modesty*, 20).

3. According to Papias, bishop of Hierapolis in the middle of the second century, Mark was the "interpreter" (*hermēneutēs*) of Peter: "Mark, who was Peter's interpreter, carefully set down in writing, although not in order, all the things that he remembered about the sayings and actions of the Lord." Eusebius of Caesarea affirms that it was Mark who took the gospel to Alexandria: "It is said that this Mark was the first to be sent to Egypt, and that there he preached the gospel and founded churches, beginning with Alexandria itself" (*C.H.* 2.16.1).

It is in the latter city that Paul meets Timothy, who is well known and re-spected among the leaders, both in Lystra and in Iconium. Timothy must have been very young, for much later, in the pastoral epistles, a tradition is reflected that he was still relatively young when Paul was already quite old (I Tim. 4:12, II Tim. 2:22).

Timothy was the son of a Jewish mother and a pagan ("Greek") father. According to Jewish law, the children of a Jewish mother were considered Isra-elites. Paul wished to take Timothy with him but feared that his condition of being an uncircumcised Jew would create problems with other Jews. The phrase "they all knew that his father was a Greek" implies that it was generally known that he had not been circumcised. Therefore, Paul decided to circum-cise Timothy. (Compare this with Gal. 2:3, where Titus, who is of pagan birth is not circumcised.)

Although the Jerusalem decision regarding Gentile converts was ad-dressed strictly to "the believers of Gentile origin in Antioch and Syria and Cilicia," Paul seems to have understood that it was to be applied to all Chris-tian communities, and therefore he travels around delivering the "decisions" (*dogmata*) of Jerusalem.[4]

Finally, verse 5 is another of Luke's "summaries," in which probably sev-eral other churches as well as a significant length of time are condensed.

3. The Vision of the Macedonian Man (16:6–10)

The general direction of the route described here is northwest. In a few words a long trip, which must have taken at least several months, is summa-rized. Galatia was both a province of the Roman Empire and a region that was somewhat smaller. The Roman province of Galatia, created by Augustus Cae-sar in 25 C.E. included, besides Galatia proper, which was inhabited by Gala-tians, other lands inhabited by Phrygians, Lycaoneans, and others. Because later Paul wrote an Epistle to the Galatians, the matter of what region the apostle actually visited is closely related to the debate among scholars regard-ing the actual addressees of that Epistle. Although Acts does not say so, Paul tells us that it was an illness that forced him to go to Galatia (Gal. 4:13–14).

It may be to that infirmity that Acts refers when declaring that the Holy Spirit would not allow the missionaries to speak in either Asia or Bithynia. On the other hand, the hindrance of the Spirit to which Luke refers may have been a vision, similar to the one that then called Paul to Macedonia.

The JB translation in verse 8, "they went through Mysia," is less accurate than the NRSV, "passing by Mysia." The Greek implies that they skirted that region, and that they traveled to Troas by sea.

---

4. Verses 3 and 4 are significantly expanded in the Western text. The details given there, which seem believable and historically accurate, have provided an argument for those who hold that, at least here and in other portions of chapter 16 (16:3–4, 9–10, 35–40), the Western text reflects a revision made by Luke himself. É. Delebecque, "De Lystres à Philippes (Ac. 16) avec le *codex Bezae*," *Bib*, 63 (1982), 395–405.

It is at Troas, "during the night," that Paul has the vision, which may be an indication that it came in the form of a dream. In that vision, a Macedonian man begs Paul to "come over to Macedonia and help us"; that is that he cross over to Europe and come to their aid.[5] The Greek text makes it very clear that the Macedonian was a male, "a man."

It is in verse 10, in response to that vision, that the "we" first appears in Acts (that is, not counting the dubious text of 11:28): "we immediately tried to cross over to Macedonia, being convinced that God had called us to proclaim the Good News to them." These sections where the verbs are in the first person plural (16:10–17, 20:5–15, 21:1–18, 27:1–28:16) have been much discussed. Why is it that in some passages, and only there, Luke speaks as "we"? Some scholars think that in writing the Book of Acts Luke used for this section some material written by one of Paul's companions—or perhaps even by someone totally unrelated to Paul—a sort of travelogue.[6] The main difficulty in that suggestion is that it does not explain why Luke did not take the trouble—which would have been quite simple—of transposing the narrative to the third person, to agree with the rest of the book. He would have been aware that in these passages the narrative is presented from a different perspective, that of an eye witness.

Others suggest that Luke used the first person plural as a stylistic resource, in order to make a particular point. Thus, for instance, Haenchen claims that "the 'we' has the same effect in this instance as the chorus of admiration confirming a miracle elsewhere."[7] This argument also is not convincing, for not all the passages in which Luke speaks as "we" seem worthy of such particular emphasis.

Still others suggest that the "we" is a sort of secret theological key.[8] It seems best simply to accept that the author of Acts was a participant at least in

---

5. W. P. Bowers, "Paul's route through Mysia: A note on Acts XVI.8," *JTS*, 60 (1979), 507–11, points out that the earlier route that Paul followed was already leading him toward Macedonia, and on that basis claims that Paul had already decided to go there, and that all that the vision did was to confirm that decision.

6. For instance, S. Dockx, "Luc a-t-il été le compagnon d'apostolat de Paul?," *NRT*, 103 (1983), 385–400, and U. Borse, "Die Wir-Stellen der Apostelgeschichte und Thimoteus," *StNTUmv*, 10 (1985), 63–92, suggest that it was a travelogue written by Timothy.

7. E. Haenchen, *The Acts of the Apostles: A Commentary* (Philadelphia: Westminster, 1975), p. 491.

8. For instance, Josep Rius-Camps, *El camino de Pablo a la misión a los paganos* (Madrid: Cristiandad, 1984), p. 96, claims that it is "a literary-theological procedure whose purpose is to tell the reader, after the breach between Barnabas and Paul, which is the route which the Spirit follows, and of which actions on the part of Paul and his entourage the Holy Spirit approves or disapproves." It is difficult to believe that Luke would write a book in code, in such a way that whoever did not have the key to the "we" would misunderstand the meaning of the book. And it is even more difficult to believe that it was necessary to await the twentieth century until someone would be able to unlock the code.

those episodes that are told in the first person plural, and that if he does not tell us where or how he joined or left the group, this is simply because that is the manner in which his narrative always proceeds, so that characters disappear and appear again without the author ever telling us when they left the group or joined it again.[9] However, even this does not solve the problem, which is quite complex.[10]

MISSIONARY LESSONS

The passage that has just been studied carries several missionary lessons that may be significant for our present situation.

The first is the need to nourish, supervise, and admonish the community of the Church. In reading the Book of Acts, many receive the impression that Paul spends all his time running from one place to another, always seeking to preach the gospel in new places. The reason for this is that, as has been pointed out repeatedly, Luke often summarizes in a few lines what may well have taken months and even years. In this passage, Paul's initial purpose is to "return and visit the believers in every city where we proclaimed the word of the Lord and see how they are doing." Although the Spirit will widen that vision and lead the missionaries to new lands, this takes place only after they have visited those churches that have been founded earlier. In a few verses, Luke summarizes a long itinerary, which is almost the same as in the earlier journey by Paul and Barnabas.

It is important to emphasize this point, because in many of our Hispanic churches quite often a poor reading of Acts has led to a questionable missionary strategy. We imagine that what the Spirit required of Paul, and now requires of us, was simply that he go from place to place preaching and founding churches. The result has been a vast number of local churches in which persons who have been recently converted, and with scant knowledge of Scripture or of the implications of faith for daily life in these complex times, lack the necessary help to mature in the faith. In some circles it is thought that the vocation of the evangelist is higher than that of the pastor. There is much talk of how many churches were founded, how many people were converted; but little attention is paid to the much more difficult task of nourishing, comforting, and challenging all those new churches and new believers. We forget that Paul, besides sometimes spending even more than a year in a city, returned as often as he could, and that his letters, which are so highly valued today, are the result of his pastoral interest—of that very interest that led him to suggest to Barnabas that they undertake a new journey to visit the churches "and see how they are doing."

---

9. For instance, C. J. Hemer, "First person narrative in Acts 27–28," *TynBull*, 36 (1985), 79–109, claims that, at least in the events told in the last two chapters of the book, Luke was present.

10. The various aspects and dimensions of this problem are well summarized in S. M. Praeder, "The problem of first person narrative in Acts," *NT*, 29 (1987), 193–218.

Among Protestants in Latin America, as well as among Hispanic Protestants in the United States, the consequences of an erroneous reading of the text have sometimes been tragic. There are people who allow themselves to be carried by "every wind of doctrine," because no one has taught them to test the spirits. Anyone who shows up with a new interpretation of Scripture makes easy prey among such believers. Others have simply learned by rote what they have been taught, and even though they do not allow themselves to be moved by every wind of doctrine, they have not developed the necessary maturity to face the unexpected challenges of each new day.

We need, besides evangelists and missionaries, pastors and teachers, people who study and teach Scripture in congregations, and who join them in asking how we are to respond to today's challenges as faithful Christians.

The second lesson is in Timothy's joining the missionary team. He was certainly well spoken of; but he was young and inexperienced. Although we are told elsewhere that both his mother and his grandmother were believers (II Tim. 1:5, 3:15), it is also true that he had not even been raised as a good Jew, and that his youth and inexperience could have led Paul to doubt, especially after his sad experience with John Mark. However, part of Paul's mission consists in recruiting those who will continue and expand his work. In many of our Latino churches we suffer from the attempt on the part of certain leaders to control everything. Those who have held positions of authority for some time seem to think that they should hold them permanently. Thus, instead of preparing new generations to assume responsibility, and allowing them to occupy those positions as soon as they are ready, conflicts arise in which the older generation seeks to retain control, while the young either struggle against their elders in order to share in the leadership, or simply leave the church and move to other spheres where they are better received.

The third lesson can also be found in the episode of Timothy. Paul had championed the position that converts among the Gentiles should not be forced to be circumcised nor should be burdened with the obligations of the ritual laws of Israel. However in this particular case, before taking Timothy with him, he decides that Timothy must be circumcised, "because of the Jews who were in those places." Rigidity and intransigence plague our churches and often hinder our mission. We are not ready to work or to cooperate with anyone who is not in absolute agreement with all that we believe. In some churches those who dare pray without kneeling are excommunicated. In others a woman who wears a wedding band is too ostentatious, and not a good Christian. On the other hand, there are churches where it is thought that anyone who is not as revolutionary as the rest is reactionary, ignorant, and apostate. We are all so certain and firm in our own opinions and convictions, that we cannot find common fields of action nor give way in the least. The result is that, while we engage in such discussions, mission is forgotten.

There is an ancient fable in which some hares are running away from a pack of dogs. One of the hares shouts, "Run, the dogs are coming!" The other answers, "They are not dogs, they are hounds!" And in the discussion about whether they are dogs or hounds, the pack arrives and kills the hares.

Paul is well aware—probably much more than most of us—of the dangers inherent in legalism, and therefore he has insisted that it is not necessary to be circumcised. But when the time comes when he must choose between mission and a concession to those who do not see things as he does, he is ready to make such a concession.

Finally, the text gives us some insight regarding the difficulties encountered in mission. Besides the tensions with Barnabas, which were already quite a burden, now Paul and his companions find that they cannot preach in Asia. The Epistle to the Galatians seems to indicate that one of the difficulties that Paul encountered was an illness that somehow forced him to change his itinerary, but whose result was his mission among the Galatians. Then, because he could not preach in Asia, Paul planned to go to the province of Bithynia, where there were important cities. However once again the Spirit would not allow it. It is quite often that we say, quite correctly, that the Spirit goes ahead of us, opening doors for the gospel; but the opposite can also be true. Sometimes the Spirit closes doors in order to lead us along routes we had not thought of following. Difficulties in the path of the Church are not always the work of the Evil One. Sometimes they are the work of God, who like a shepherd leads us where we should go. Actually, in reading this passage that image comes immediately to mind, for it will seem that the Spirit is shepherding Paul and his companions to Troas, in order there to grant them a new vision.

When difficulties arise, and alternatives seem to disappear, our common inclination is to give up. At such times, we will do well to remember how it was that the Spirit directed Paul toward Europe. We might also take as an example William Carey, the famous missionary to India, who in one of his letters says, "My position is now untenable. . . . There are difficulties everywhere, and even more ahead; therefore, we have no other alternative but to continue."[11]

Protestant churches in Latin America are facing enormous difficulties. Some have long been dependent on funds that are no longer coming as abundantly. Others begin to realize that the methods of preaching and witnessing that worked a few decades ago are rapidly becoming obsolete. Others are perplexed by political, economic, and social crises in their countries. Others are clashing with the government. Some wonder how they will keep their younger generations, often tempted by options that their elders did not have. There are doubts, difficulties, and dangers everywhere. Therefore, we have no other alternative, we must go forward!

---

11. Quoted in A. H. Oussoren, *William Carey: Especially His Missionary Principles* (Leiden: A. W. Sijthoff, 1945), p. 66.

B. Philippi (16:11–40)

The narrative continues in the first person plural up to verse 17, where the narrator begins to become distinct from Paul ("Paul and us"), and finally in verse 18 returns to the third person.

1. The Beginning of the Mission in Europe (16:11–15)

The journey from Troas to Neapolis took the travelers two days. At that time mariners avoided sailing at night, and therefore in this particular case they stopped in the island of Samothrace, approximately halfway in their journey. The distance is some 250 kilometers, which indicates that the winds were favorable. On another occasion, in the opposite direction, the same journey will take five days (20:6). Neapolis (which means "new city") was a seaport some fifteen kilometers away from Philippi. The phrase "which is a leading city of the district of Macedonia," can be interpreted in various ways. It could mean simply that Philippi was the first city in the route that the missionaries were to follow—"the first city in the district of Macedonia." Codex Bezae, a manuscript representing the Western text, says that Philippi was "the capital city of Macedonia." This is not true. Other interpreters, suggesting the possibility of a slight variation in the text, and the fact that Macedonia was divided into four districts, suggest that the phrase actually means that Philippi was in the first of these districts. At any rate, Luke is quite correct in calling Philippi "a Roman colony," for that was precisely the legal standing of the city.[12]

The "some days" in verse 12 refer to the time before the Sabbath to which verse 13 alludes, for evidently the missionaries remained in Philippi much longer that that. At any rate, that Sabbath they went to the outskirts of the city, by the river, where they supposed[13] that there was a "place of prayer." Apparently they had made no contact with the Jews in the city, or they had not found any whom they could contact. The term *proseuxe*, translated as a "place of prayer," was sometimes used as a synonym for "synagogue." Therefore, the missionaries are looking for the place where Jews gather to pray, or for the synagogue.

---

12. The title of "colony" was conferred by the emperors to certain cities. These were originally places where groups of poor Roman citizens, often veterans from the legions, had settled in quest of lands. In Philippi, Caesar Augustus had settled veterans of the war with Mark Anthony, which ended in the year 31 B.C.E. The city had the privileges of *jus italicum*, that is to say, the same legal principles applied in it as did on Italian soil. F. F. Bruce, "St. Paul in Macedonia," *JnRyl*, 61 (1979), 337–54, offers a number of details showing that Luke is quite accurate in his description of the geographic and political conditions of each place of which he speaks. The full name of Philippi was "Colonia Julia Augusta Philippensis."

13. This is a better translation than the JB, which does not take into account the expectation of the missionaries.

What they find is a group of women. This was not a formal service in a synagogue, which would require ten men. But they do seem to have found the place for which they were looking, for the women had gathered there in order to pray. It was there that they met Lydia of Thyatira, "a worshiper of God," that is to say, one of the "God-fearers," who sold purple cloth. Because Thyatira is in the region of Lydia, it is possible that "Lydia" was not really her name, but rather a reference to her place of origin—just as today someone from Texas might be called "Tex." Some have speculated that Lydia was in fact one of the two women to whom Paul later refers in Philippians 4:2. Purple was a dye obtained from the ink sacs of tiny mollusks and was highly prized. Therefore, one can surmise that a dealer in purple cloth had significant economic resources. The narrative does not have to be understood in the sense that Lydia was converted when Paul and his companions first spoke to her. On the contrary, the verbal tenses seem to indicate that the process continued for some time, and culminated in the baptism of Lydia and her household. According to the use of the time, the "family" or "household," especially in the case of a wealthy person, included all the persons—relatives as well as servants and others—connected to the family in various ways. Therefore, the "household" of Lydia may well have included quite a few people.[14]

After her conversion, Lydia invited the missionaries to live in her house. We know that Paul avoided receiving money or material goods from his disciples or converts (see 20:33–35). That is why Acts says, "she prevailed upon us." Paul would not forget this gesture, nor the continued generosity of the Philippians, to which he refers in Philippians 4:15–16: "You Philippians indeed know that in the early days of the gospel, when I left Macedonia, no church shared with me in the matter of giving and receiving, except you alone. For even when I was in Thessalonica, you sent me help more than once" (see also II Cor. 11:9).

MISSION, CHALLENGE, AND OPPORTUNITY

The passage tells us much about the flexibility required in order to be faithful to the mission. We have already seen that Paul was able to have a wider vision than that of his fellow Pharisees from Jerusalem, precisely because of his missionary experience. Here we see another dimension of the flexibility that mission requires and produces.

The first thing to be noted is that the missionaries go seeking a synagogue or place of prayer, apparently expecting to find there some men with whom to share their message, and what they find is a group of women at prayer. Paul's custom and strategy was to begin his contacts in each new city through the synagogue. Now he finds that there is no synagogue, but only a group of

---

14. Are children included in the baptism of Lydia and her household or in the baptism of the jailer and his household? The text does not provide any basis on which to either affirm or deny it.

women who gather in order to pray. The contrast between this and what the missionaries expected is sharpened if we remember that the vision at Troas had been of a "Macedonian man," and what they now find is a group of women. This does not stop Paul, who shares his message with the women, and the result is the conversion of Lydia, whose household will be the first nucleus of the church in Philippi, and will provide the missionaries with a center of operations.[15]

Lydia is not only converted, but also brings her entire household to the Lord, and then insists that Paul and his companions should lodge with her. This was contrary to Paul's normal missionary practice, for he sought to support himself through his tent-making (to which we shall return later on), and insisted on not receiving material help from his converts. In spite of this, Paul accepted that generous offer, and from that point on counted on the support of the Philippians, not only when he was in Philippi, but also later in the continuation of his mission.

Such flexibility in mission is urgently necessary today. Too often churches are still tied to policies and missionary structures that were quite useful half a century ago, but no longer. In some cities, Paul began his work in the synagogue; but elsewhere he began in other ways. What once worked does not always work in the same way. Evangelistic campaigns for a while were quite successful among Latin Americans. However, it is important to remember that new methods may be necessary in new circumstances. How are we to evangelize students? industrial laborers? the masses who have been uprooted from their lands, many of them now living in the cities of Latin America and the United States? The same methods do not fit all.

Another important point is that Lydia, as soon as she was converted, put her resources at the service of the mission. Some of us became accustomed to receiving resources from outside, and thus dependent churches were created whose main concern is how to continue receiving those outside resources that now seem necessary for their survival. Matters of stewardship have to be reexamined, not only dealing with how much each individual should give, but also dealing with how our churches can become full partners in the total mission of the Church of Jesus Christ. That was what Lydia and the Philippians did, for even though they themselves did not travel with Paul, they did participate with the apostle by means of their resources.

---

15. In spite of what is commonly said, Paul seems to have overcome much of the prejudice of his time against women. This may be seen in Acts, where women such as Lydia and Priscilla play important roles, and also in the Epistles of Paul himself. This is particularly true if, as is commonly held, Ephesians and the pastoral Epistles are deuteropauline, and the passage on women keeping silent in I Corinthians is indeed an extrapolation from the pastorals. A very valuable book regarding Paul's position vis-à-vis women is Dennis R. MacDonald, *The Legend and the Apostle: The Battle for Paul in Story and Canon* (Philadelphia: Westminster Press, 1983).

2. The Girl with a Spirit of Divination (16:16–24)

This episode probably takes place long after the previous one, for it leads to the end of Paul's ministry in Philippi. In the story about Lydia, Luke tells us about the beginning of that ministry. In the episode of the girl and its sequel, that of the jailer, he tells us about the end of that ministry. Between the two some time must have elapsed.

Apparently the place where the missionaries are going when the slave girl meets them is the same place of prayer where they had earlier met Lydia. Now this girl with "a spirit of divination" meets them.[16] Luke understands this phrase in a pejorative sense—the spirit of divination is in fact a demon.

That demon, as often happens in the New Testament, sees what humans cannot see, and therefore declares, "These men are slaves of the Most High God who proclaim to you a way of salvation." This she does, not once, but rather for many days, following Paul and his companions. After a while, Paul intervenes, addresses the spirit in the name of Jesus Christ, and the spirit leaves the girl.

One may imagine that, because the girl had been healed from what was an obvious case of demon possession, all would rejoice. But that is not what happens. The owners of the girl, who made "a great deal of money" from her condition (v. 16), are enraged, and in revenge for what they have lost they take hold of Paul and Silas (the text does not tell us what became of Timothy, or of the former protagonist of the "we" portions), and bring charges against them. Because they cannot accuse Paul and Silas of having cast out a spirit of divination, they accuse them of disturbing the peace (v. 20) and of corrupting the good customs of the Romans (v. 21).[17]

The trial is not really such, but is rather a riot. The magistrates do not even give Paul and Silas an opportunity to defend themselves, but have them stripped and beaten with rods, after which they are jailed. Their imprisonment "in the innermost cell" and with their feet in the stocks will make their deliverance even more surprising.

WHEN EVIL PRODUCES GOOD, AND GOOD PRODUCES EVIL

The passage is quite interesting, for here we have a demon witnessing to the gospel. And then, when Paul heals the girl, the good that he does, rather than yielding admiration and gratitude, earns him a flogging and imprisonment. Let us look at these two elements in order.

---

16. What most English versions translate with this phrase or something similar is literally "a Python's spirit." According to ancient tradition, in Delphi there had existed a famous snake called Python who pronounced oracles. Apollos killed it and took its place, and therefore he was called Apollos Python, and the woman who pronounced oracles in Delphi was called a "python." Sometimes ventriloquists, who often used their skills in order to appear as soothsayers, were also called "pythons."

17. With historical exactitude, Luke calls the magistrates *stratēgoi* (in Latin, *duumviri*), which was the title of such magistrates in a Roman colony such as Philippi.

(1) The demon (or "pythonic spirit") gives witness to the gospel. Paul does not accept that witness, but rather scolds the spirit and casts out the demon.

This contrasts sharply with what happened in Europe when Hitler was ascending in his power. The Pope and the curia received news of the atrocities being committed against the Jews and against enemies of the German regime. But, in order to avoid creating problems for the Church, and because in any case Hitler was not attacking the Church, they decided to remain silent.

However, let us not speak only of the errors of the papacy. There are similar situations also among Protestants. There are among us many "demons" who give verbal witness to the gospel. I shall never forget when I visited the former palace of the late dictator Rafael Leónidas Trujillo and saw there, on the dining room wall, a sign saying, "Jesus is the invisible guest at our table, a silent witness to our conversation." Nor will I forget that, before the dictator's death, I heard Protestant brothers speak of how they had visited him, and had been positively impressed by that "witness." It was indeed a "witness"; but, a witness to what? To accept such a witness simply because it is convenient, or to justify it saying that after all what is important for us is that people believe, would be a false witness, not only on the part of the dictator himself, but also on our part. In such a case it would be much better, after the example of Paul, to reprove the evil spirit rather than accept a witness that, although verbally correct, is marred by its own evil.

There are other "demons" who give similar witness. In some of our agricultural zones there are large enterprises that have taken possession of vast extensions of land, to such a point that the peasants who before were able to produce enough for their own families and even have something left over to sell, now have no alternative than to work for the company at whatever salary the company itself determines, and under whatever conditions the company imposes. There are cases in which such corporations have granted a piece of land for the building of a Protestant church, or have even paid for the building itself. And then we imagine that this is enough to forget everything else, and that the company is "witnessing" to Jesus Christ. Possibly Paul would have said what he said to the girl's spirit of divination: "I order you out in the name of Jesus Christ."

In summary, not everyone who says "Lord, Lord" will enter the kingdom of heaven, and we are not to accept the witness of any who, like that spirit of divination, calls us "servants of the most high God, who proclaim to you a way of salvation."

(2) Paul heals the girl; however, that good, instead of bringing him glory and gratitude, produces a flogging and imprisonment.

There is a popular saying in Spanish, "There is no evil that does not bring about some good." Perhaps we should also say the opposite, "There is no good that does not bring about an evil." This may be somewhat exaggerated, but it is often true. We live in a fallen world, which is therefore dominated by structures of sin. Thus, when we oppose sin, we are opposing someone's interests. Paul heals the girl; but in so doing, he harms the economic interests of her owners, who then accuse him and have him flogged and imprisoned.

Not understanding this point may inhibit our obedience, for we somehow imagine that the Church can be faithful without being controversial. As was already stated, the word "controversial" serves as a break against many of our best attempts. Without being controversial, it is impossible to be faithful. This does not mean that we should go out seeking conflicts for their own sake; but it does mean that we must be ready to understand that our obedience and fidelity will inevitably lead to conflict, and therefore we must be ready not to be discouraged nor to doubt when those conflicts become apparent.

Let us see two examples. The first comes from a Hispanic church in the United States. The leaders of that church became aware that many people in the barrio could not work because the public transportation was inadequate, and began organizing so that a bus line would come through the neighborhood. They thought they were doing good. But they soon discovered that several important people in the neighborhood—including two church members—made a living by offering transportation at inflated prices to those who urgently needed it. Soon the controversy exploded: "The church has no business in these matters."

The second example comes from a slum in a city in Latin America. The church, seeing that many of its members and neighbors did not make enough in order to eat, and that the prices in the nearby markets were high, organized a consumer's cooperative. Twice a week they bring food but at wholesale prices, and sell it with practically no profit. But opposition is already beginning to surface, for among the merchants in the neighborhood there are several who have contributed to the programs of the church on various occasions, and now claim that the church is undermining their business. Should the church close its consumer's cooperative, which has suddenly become controversial? Or does its own faithfulness to the gospel require it to continue along the path it has taken?

3. The Jailer in Philippi (16:25–34)

The passage is one of the best known in the Book of Acts. In spite of having been flogged, and being sore and tied in the stocks, Paul and Silas are singing at midnight. The other prisoners hear them, which is included in the narrative in order to make them witnesses of the miracle that will follow. Suddenly there is an earthquake. That it is a miracle, and not a mere natural phenomenon, is underscored by affirming that not only are the doors open, but also the chains are loosened. However, no one escapes, even though Luke does not tell us why. The jailer, believing that the prisoners have escaped and that he has been dishonored, is ready to take his own life when Paul tells him that no one has fled.

Then comes the famous question from the jailer, who trembling before Paul and Silas asks, "Sirs, what must I do to be saved?" Possibly the question itself does not have all the theological dimensions that later preaching has given to it. The jailer is scared by the earthquake, which is clear proof of the divine wrath about the manner in which the missionaries have been treated. What he wishes is to flee from the punishment, whatever it may be, which such a powerful God may have prepared for him. How is he to be saved from such a punishment? Verse 31 gives the famous answer of the missionaries: "Believe in the Lord Jesus, and you will be saved, you and your household." The fact that Luke tells us that both Paul and Silas said this is an indication that this is not a mere short formula that both repeated in unison. It is rather that, in answer to the jailer's question, the missionaries spoke to him about the gospel. In response to that message, the jailer washes their wounds and is baptized with "his entire family."[18]

A Radical Conversion

The passage about the jailer in Philippi is well known. The phrase that is usually underlined when preaching about this passage is, "Believe in the Lord Jesus, and you will be saved, you and your household." Certainly this phrase is the center and high point in the narrative. However, on studying the entire passage we see some dimensions that are often overlooked.

Most remarkable is the change that takes place in the jailer as a result of his conversion. Here is a man whose career and personal prestige are so important that, when he thinks that the prisoners have escaped, he is ready to take his own life. For him life is worthless without that prestige and respect. Now, after his conversion, he takes those prisoners who had been entrusted to him with such insistence, and it is he who takes them out of the jail, washes their wounds, and takes them to his home to feed them. Apparently, now his career and professional prestige no longer have their former importance, to the point that he is ready to risk them in order to care for Paul and Silas and to offer hospitality.

Such is the character of true conversion. In Hispanic churches throughout the Americas, there has been much preaching of a toothless "conversion." On the basis of this particular text, we say "in order to be saved all that is necessary is to believe in Jesus." What we do not say, and often do not even see, is that belief in Jesus implies much more than mere assent. It is also a radical change, not only in the manner in which we live, but also in the values by which we measure success in life. For the rich person who used to think that money was everything, conversion must include a new life in which his economic resources are put at God's disposal. For the professional who used to think that success in life was in prestige, and in the respect that others granted her, conversion must lead her to seek ways in which her profession may truly be of service to all. And, if such means cannot be found, perhaps conversion should lead to a quest for another occupation or means of service. (In this context I am thinking of a young woman whom I met in Argentina, a violinist of great promise, who on a certain

---

18. As in the case of Lydia and her household, here also there has been much discussion as to whether those baptized included children or not. The text does not say a word about it, and whatever a particular interpreter might say in one direction or the other is a mere reflection of that interpreter's preconceived views.

day simply told her teacher with whom she was studying abroad that, as a Christian, it was becoming increasingly difficult for her to devote her life to "playing pretty music for the rich." She returned to her country, where she devoted herself to seeking employment for the poor young people in a slum.)

The gospel includes the good news that our life can be useful in God's reign. It also includes the good news that the value of our life does not depend on the manner in which society evaluates it. For the jailer in Philippi, it is no longer necessary to measure life in terms of whether he fulfills his duty of retaining the prisoners. For us, if we truly have received the gospel, the good news includes the freedom to be obedient, to be authentic, in spite of all that society may expect of us.

4. The Missionaries Are Absolved and Expelled (16:35–40)

The following day, the magistrates sent the "police"[19] with the order to release Paul and Silas. The text does not tell us why that order was given. Codex Bezae, and with it much of the Western text, attribute this to the earthquake, implying that the magistrates knew that it had been caused by the God of the missionaries. Some suggest that Lydia or some other influential Christian may have intervened. From the text it is apparent at least that the magistrates have ordered the accused flogged and imprisoned in the midst of a riot, yielding to the pressures of the moment, and that they probably had no interest in following a formal judicial process against them.

It is then that Paul surprises the authorities telling them that both he and Silas are Roman citizens. The *Lex Julia*, an ancient Roman legal principle, prohibited the flogging of a Roman citizen.[20] The magistrates want Paul and Silas to leave the city surreptitiously, which might bring about shame to the gospel they proclaim. Therefore, now Paul demands that the magistrates themselves come and free them. This causes great fear among the magistrates, who go to jail to offer apologies, and beg Paul and Silas to leave the city without creating any more problems for them.[21]

Apparently the missionaries agreed, although they did not abandon the city before visiting Lydia and taking leave from the church. Years later, Paul would remember the entire episode in I Thessalonians 2:2.

---

19. Here again Luke employs the correct term for those who did this kind of work in a Roman colony.

20. According to Cicero, "Whoever ties a Roman citizen commits an iniquity, and whoever flogs him commits a crime" (*In Verrem* 2.5.66). Why did Paul and Silas not invoke their rights before they were flogged? Once again, the text does not tell us. If it all happened in the midst of riot, it is conceivable that they had no opportunity to assert their rights.

21. Shortly before, in the year 44, Emperor Claudius had punished the city of Rhodes for having disregarded the traditional privileges of Roman citizens, crucifying one of them (Lorenzo Turrado, *Hechos de los Apóstoles y Epístola a los Romanos* [Madrid: Biblioteca de Autores Cristianos, 1975], p. 172).

HUMILITY AND DIGNITY

On reading this passage, it almost seems that Paul behaves like a spoiled child. He complains that after flogging them publicly the magistrates want to be rid of them secretly, and he appeals to his Roman citizenship in order to intimidate the magistrates and force them to come in person to beg him to leave the city. However, what is at stake is much more than Paul's wounded pride. What is at stake is the dignity of the gospel. If Paul and Silas simply accept the order to leave without even meeting again with the church, they will leave the impression that they are slippery characters whose message is not worthy of credit. How will the believers react? Will their faith waiver? For that reason they appeal to their Roman citizenship, thus forcing the magistrates to take them seriously, and also gaining the opportunity to meet with the church before leaving the city.

Later in this commentary (22:25–29), we shall have occasion to return to Paul's use of his Roman citizenship. At present, however, it is important to note that Paul does not employ it among the church membership in order to claim greater importance, whereas he is quite ready to employ it beyond the confines of the church, in order to demand respect for Silas and for himself and, by implication, for other believers.

This distinction is of great importance and merits some reflection. In many of our churches there are increasing numbers who enjoy a certain social prestige. How is this to be employed? Unfortunately, most frequently it is used in order to make certain that "respectable" people receive special treatment within the Church. Instead of building up the body, this underlines distinctions that soon lead to resentment and division. Those who are not professionals, who have no property, or who have scant education, are less privileged than the rest. Would it be possible to employ whatever social prestige our members have, not in order to create distinctions within the community of faith, but rather to promote a unity and fellowship that may be a sign to the surrounding community?

C. THESSALONICA (17:1–9)

The narrative continues in the third person. Therefore, if the "we" includes Luke, it would seem that he remained in Philippi. The text does not say a word about Timothy or what he did, for his name is not mentioned again until Berea (17:14). On the other hand, Luke usually deals only with the central characters of his narrative and mentions others only when it is necessary. Furthermore, in the greeting of Paul's two letters to the Thessalonians Silas ("Silvanus") and Timothy are mentioned jointly with Paul, and both of these letters would seem to imply that Timothy was among the founders of the church in Thessalonica. Thus, one may suppose that Timothy left Philippi with Paul and Silas, or that he joined them slightly later in Thessalonica.

The route described in 17:1 follows the great *via Egnatia*, one of the main roads of the Roman Empire. The distance between each of the cities mentioned (Philippi to Amphipolis, Amphipolis to Apollonia, Apollonia to Thessalonica) is some 50 kilometers, so that the total distance is approximately 150 kilometers. The mention of Amphipolis and Apollonia might imply that these were stops along a route followed on horseback, for otherwise it would be too far to travel from one city to another in a single day.[22] There is no indication that they stopped to preach in these other cities, which are not mentioned again in the New Testament. Thessalonica was the main city in the area, and the residence of the Roman governor—whom Luke does not mention. On its ruins now stands the modern city of Salonica.

There are few difficulties in the text. In Thessalonica, Paul simply follows his custom of beginning his preaching at the synagogue, where he presents his message on three Sabbaths. That message is summarized in three points (17:3): (1) the suffering of the Messiah; (2) his resurrection; (3) that Jesus is the Messiah.

Those who accepted this message are described in verse 4. "Some of them" refers to the Jews who believed. The phrase "devout Greeks" presents some difficulties. As it appears in the NRSV, and in the manuscripts on which this version is based, it seems to refer to those who are elsewhere called "God-fearers," that is, Gentiles who had approached Judaism. However, there are several manuscripts of the Western text that say "Greeks and devout persons." This is supported by the Vulgate. In such a case, the text refers to two different groups: some who were "God-fearers" and others who were simply pagans. The reference to the "leading women" points to a situation that would become permanent in the first centuries of the Christian Church: there were distinguished women who joined the Church, many of them without the consent or participation of their husbands or fathers.

Luke does not tell us why the Jews became "jealous." In 13:45 it would seem that such jealousy referred to the great number of converts, which seemed to overwhelm the Jewish population in the synagogue. Here we hear again of "a great many of the devout Greeks and not a few of the leading women." Therefore, the jealousy may once again be due to the number of Gentile converts. However, as we are not told that the missionaries preached beyond the confines of the synagogue, one could also suppose that these many converts were actually people who attended the synagogue and probably supported it. At any rate, these jealous Jews seek the support of the free-floating population that existed in Thessalonica as in every city, and who apparently had no other occupation than to join the latest riot. These are the "ruffians in the marketplaces."

Up to this point Luke has not even mentioned Jason, who suddenly appears in verse 5.[23] Obviously, it was there that Paul and his companions

---

22. See K. Lake and H. J. Cadbury, *The Beginnings of Christianity* (London: MacMillan and Co., 1933), vol. 4, p. 202.

23. The name Jason was relatively common. Some Jews named Joshua used it as the Greek equivalent to their Jewish name. (Just as Saul used the name Paul.) Given the frequency with which the name appears in ancient documents, it is not certain that this Jason is the same as Paul's relative mentioned in Romans 16:21.

lodged. In order to find the missionaries, the mob seized Jason and some believers, and dragged them before the authorities.[24] The believers are accused of
being subversives, "who have been turning the world upside down" and who
contradict the decrees of the Emperor "saying that there is another king
named Jesus." Jason is also implicated for having offered them hospitality. Because the main accused did not appear, the authorities take bail from Jason
and the others and let them go. The text does not tell us what happened later
to Jason and the rest, although in I Thessalonians Paul speaks of the "persecution," which believers there have suffered (I Thess. 1:6).

A SUBVERSIVE MESSAGE

As we advance in our reading of Acts, we see that accusations against Christians
become increasingly serious. At first they were limited to debates among Jews.
Such accusations will remain throughout the book. Then, in Philippi, the owners of the girl who had been healed accused the missionaries of teaching "customs that are not lawful for us as Romans to adopt or observe." Now, in Thessalonica, they are accused of being disloyal to the emperor, proclaiming another
king.

Such accusations are partly false, but also partly true. They are false inas-
much as they do not reflect the real motives behind the missionaries' being
taken before the authorities. But they are true in that the missionaries were indeed calling their converts to practices that were forbidden (for instance, refusing to burn incense before the emperor or the gods), and also in that the absolute lordship of Jesus puts a parenthesis around the lordship of the emperor,
which also claims to be absolute.

Later, when the Roman Empire begins persecuting Christians, the same situation will exist. At first persecution may have been due to a misunderstanding.
But as time goes by, the more the Romans understand the Christian message the
more violent and thoroughgoing will the persecution become.

There is no denying that there is indeed a subversive element in Christian
faith. The accusers were right in saying that the missionaries were turning the
world upside down. A crucial aspect of Christian faith is the claim that there is a
radical difference between the world as it is and the world as God wills it to be.
The reign of Caesar is not the reign of God. Where God is king, there can be no
other absolute ruler. Therefore, every absolute claim is undermined. Neither nationalist absolutism, nor ideological absolutism of the right or the left, nor military absolutism, nor ecclesiastical absolutism, are compatible with Christian
faith. If we faithfully preach the gospel message we will also be accused of act-

---

24. Once again, Luke shows his interest in historical accuracy when he calls these
authorities *politarchas*. Such a title does not appear anywhere in ancient literature. However, a number of inscriptions show that this was precisely the title given to non-Roman
authorities in Greek cities.

ing contrary to the decrees of the present world, claiming that there is another ruler, Jesus.

Unfortunately, in many of our churches the opinion exists that it is possible to preach or to live the gospel of Jesus Christ without including this element that turns the world upside down, that subverts every absolutism, that questions every present order, judging it, not on the basis of a preconceived ideology, but on the basis of the coming reign of God. In fact, the full preaching of the gospel must subvert the existing order, and must also subvert subversion itself. Is this the message we are proclaiming?

D. BEREA (17:10–14)

The missionaries, who apparently were hiding in Thessalonica, leave that night toward Berea. This was a city somewhat distant from the main thoroughfares, and approximately 80 kilometers from Thessalonica. Possibly the believers in Thessalonica encouraged the missionaries to go to that city because they had contacts there, or perhaps because, being away from the main routes of trade and travel in the empire, it was a better place for hiding from their enemies.

There once again the missionaries began their work in the synagogue. Luke tells us that the Jews there were "more receptive" than those in Thessalonica—literally, of better birth, or "more noble," as the NIV translates. They were quite open to studying Scripture and to judging the truth of what Paul was saying.

The success was remarkable, as is shown in verse 12. Once again there is explicit mention here of "not a few Greek women of high standing." (The adjective would seem to apply only to the women, rather than to both the women and the men. Therefore, rather than translating as the RSV does, "not a few Greek women and men of high standing," we should translate as the JB does: "many Greek women from the upper classes and a number of the men."[25]

Somehow the news of what was happening in Berea reached Thessalonica, and those Jews who had incited the mob in Thessalonica repeated their actions in Berea. The result was that Paul had to leave "immediately,"[26] while Silas and Timothy (who we had not been told was with the group) remained in Berea.

---

25. For some unexplained reason, on this point the NRSV seems to favor the Western text, whose anti-feminine prejudice is evident, and which therefore seeks to dilute the significance of these upper-class women. A translation of the Western text would be, "Some of them believed, but others not, and from among the Greeks and the people of high standing many men and women believed."

26. In verse 14, where the NRSV says that Paul was sent "away to the coast," some manuscripts say "as if he were going towards the coast," giving the impression that this was done in order to throw pursuers off the track, and that in fact Paul traveled by land.

THE ZEAL OF THE OPPOSITION

In reading this text, one is struck by the manner in which those Jews, who began their persecution in Thessalonica simply for reasons of jealousy, and who presented false accusations before the authorities, now persecute the missionaries as far as Berea, a city several days' journey away.

This is what often happens when passions are aroused. The accusation of being subversive, which was made in Thessalonica, and which is still so often made in Latin America, although at first employed to cover up other motivations, eventually gains its own impetus, and continues even when the initial motives have been forgotten. In a certain country in Latin America a situation occurred in which a medical doctor, who was embittered (perhaps rightly so) because an ecclesiastical institution had not dealt justly with his father many years before, began employing his economic resources to accuse that institution and all who had anything to do with it of being subversive, even though they had not been present when his father was mistreated. When he published his first accusations, he was quite conscious that he was doing this to avenge his father. But as time went by, he himself was convinced by his accusations, and became one of the spokespersons for a group that was using his resentment for its own purposes. Unfortunately, in such cases, as also in Thessalonica and Berea, dialogue becomes impossible.

What are Christians to do in such a case? Probably what Paul and his companions did: to continue preaching, teaching, and living what they consider to be the gospel.

E. ATHENS (17:15–34)

Paul did not travel alone from Berea to Athens, but was conducted there by some of the believers. This supports the conjecture that he traveled by land, for in order to go by sea such company would not be necessary. When these believers returned, Paul sent instructions that Silas and Timothy were to join him in Athens as soon as possible.

According to verse 16, Paul's purpose in Athens was not to preach, but merely to wait for his companions. However, as he waited, being a good Jew and a Christian, "he was deeply distressed to see that the city was full of idols."

Athens had seen better times. Greece was now one of the most impoverished zones of the Roman Empire.[27] The population of the city had declined. However, much of the ancient glory remained. The marbles of the Acropolis still shone, with its famous portals, its Parthenon—the temple to Athena the virgin (*parthenos*)—and its other minor temples: the Erechtheum, the temple to Athena Nike, and others. In those temples and in many other less famous ones, the ancient worship of the gods continued. Therefore, in a city in which

---

27. See M. Rostovtzeff, *Historia social y económica del Imperio Romano* (Madrid: Espasa-Calpe, 1981), vol. 2, pp. 465–66.

population had declined, but which still had such magnificent temples, it is not surprising that Paul was distressed by the prevailing idolatry (v. 17).

However, Athens' fame was not limited to its temples. Even more famous were its philosophers and its writers. There had flowered persons such as Socrates and Plato, Aristophanes, Euripides, and Phidias, the peerless sculptor. The Academy of Athens, founded by Plato, still existed, and was still an intellectual center with few rivals—until it was closed in the year 529 C.E. by order of Emperor Justinian. This intellectual activity is what Luke refers to when he says rather pejoratively that the people there "would spend their time in nothing but telling or hearing something new" (17:21).

In that situation, Paul was fighting on two fronts, for "he argued in the synagogue with the Jews and the devout persons, and also in the marketplace every day with those who happened to be there." The "devout persons" in the synagogue are also the "God-fearers" that have been discussed elsewhere (see the commentary on 10:2). The "marketplace" was probably the ancient *agora* in the middle of the city, although it could also have been one of the smaller squares. On Paul's witness in the synagogue, and the possible conversion of Jews, Luke says no more. He is interested in telling us what happens at each place that is new, and for that reason the rest of the chapter is devoted to Paul's efforts among the Greeks.

The two philosophical schools mentioned in verse 18 were indeed the ones that were vying for hegemony at the time. Both sought to offer, more than a metaphysics, an entire philosophy of life. Stoics held that life must follow the natural law that rules the universe, and that when one conforms to that law and reaches the estate of "apathy," in which one no longer suffers nor is subject to passions, one is truly wise. Epicureans, on the other hand, held that the purpose of life is pleasure; but not mindless pleasure, but rather pleasure wisely managed and directed, so that it does not lead to pain and despair. It is the philosophers of these two schools who show some curiosity about Paul's teachings—curiosity, not respect. The word that the NRSV and NIV translate as "babbler" ("parrot" in the JB) is *spermologos*, which originally referred to birds that went about searching for food. Then it began to be employed for people who lived by rummaging through waste dumps. Eventually it was used to refer to any charlatan or dilettante who went about collecting ideas and joining them to each other with no particular sense or wisdom. It is in this latter sense that it is applied to Paul. The second part of verse 18 implies that some thought that Paul was preaching two new gods: Jesus and "resurrection."

It is these philosophers, out of curiosity, who take Paul to the Areopagus. That was the name of a hill north of the Acropolis, and separated from it by a small stream. From ancient times it had been the meeting place of the city court, which therefore was also called the "Areopagus." The text does not clarify whether Paul was taken to the hill or to the court, which still existed in Roman times, although with limited authority and convening elsewhere. As the reason to give Paul a hearing was mere curiosity and there is no hint that there was an accusation or a trial, it would seem that Paul spoke on the hill and not before the court.[28]

Paul's speech begins as was then customary, with some words praising his audience—as when we today begin a sermon in a church where we are visiting by saying that "it is a pleasure and a privilege to be with you." In the rhetorical theory of the times, this sort of introduction was called the *captatio benevolentiae*. That is the purpose of verses 22–23a. Rather than beginning by attacking their idols, Paul tells the Athenians that they are very religious people, for he has even found an inscription "to an unknown God."[29]

This introduction has often been interpreted as if Paul meant that the Athenians already knew something about God. This, however, misses the fine irony in Paul's speech. Paul tells them that he has seen this inscription to "an unknown God" (*agnostos theós*).[30] Already in the second part of this verse Paul's tone begins to change, for he subtly accuses the Athenians, who believe themselves to be so wise, of being ignorant: "What therefore you worship as unknown [*agnoountes*, in ignorance] this I proclaim to you."

As a sign of the ignorance of the Athenians, Paul then moves on to a description of the work of God, partly based on Isaiah 42:5. This God, unknown to the Athenians, has created all humankind "from one ancestor" (or, as other manuscripts say, "from one blood") with two purposes: "to inhabit the whole earth" and "so that they will search for God and perhaps grope for him and find him." In verse 28 the pill is sugarcoated with some slightly altered quotations from poet Epimenides of Crete: "In him we live and move and have our being," and of Stoic philosophers Cleanthes and Aratus: "For we too are his offspring." Immediately, verse 19 moves further to the attack by rejecting the idea that this God "is like gold, or silver, or stone, an image formed by the art and imagination of mortals." This too was not new for the Athenians, for their own philosophers, from as far back as Xenophanes (sixth century B.C.E.), had leveled similar criticisms to traditional religion.

In verse 30 Paul finally gets to the core of his message: all that has gone before were "the times of human ignorance (*agnoia*)." Now we see that the *agnostos theós* (unknown God) whom the Greeks worshipped *agnoountes*

---

28. On the other hand, John Chrysostom in the fourth century, and Theophylact in eleventh, held that Paul spoke before the court. Such is the opinion of W. M. Ramsay, *St. Paul the Traveller and the Roman Citizen* (London: Hodder & Stoughton, 1897), pp. 242–45. An argument that would seem to favor the court rather than the place for public discussion is that one of the converts seems to have been a member of that court: Dionysius the Areopagite (v. 34).

29. See D. Zweck, "The exordium of the Areopagus speech. Acts 17:22, 23," *NTSt*, 35 (1989), 94–103. This author concludes that what we have here is a speech that strictly follows the rhetorical canons of the time.

30. On the meaning of these words, and similar ones, in the literature of the times, see H. Kulling, "Zur Bedeutung des Agnostos Theos: Eine Exegese zu Apostelgeschichte 17, 22–23," *TZ*, 36 (1911), 65–83.

(without knowing him) is a sign of this *agnoia* (ignorance). The true God, who has decided to overlook such ignorance even among these Greeks who believe themselves to be wise, *now commands* all to repent. Here Paul comes to the heart of the matter. It is not a question of static truths or theories that philosophers may discuss. It is rather a matter of this particular historical moment. The time of ignorance is over. Now is the time of judgment (v. 31). The proof of this is the resurrection of Jesus.

At this point, the audience will take no more. Some scoff openly. Others tell him, "we will hear you again about this," very much the way someone today says "some day," meaning never. The session ends, and Paul has not even been able to finish his speech.

In spite of the fiasco, some are converted. Among them Luke mentions two: the most famous of them is Dionysius the Areopagite (that is, the member of the court called Areopagus), about whom later many influential legends were woven,[31] and Damaris.[32]

PREACHING AND POPULARITY

Compared with many of his other sermons, Paul's speech at the Areopagus was a failure. Not only were there few converts, but also there is no record in the New Testament that a church developed in Athens as a result of Paul's mission.

Perhaps Paul could have avoided such a failure. At the beginning of his speech he gave signs of knowing the rhetorical principles of the time, and later he was able to quote some of the poets known and respected by his audience. All that was necessary in order to avoid failure was to have omitted what he says in verses 30 and 31. Up to that point, all seemed to be going quite well. However, in the matter of proclaiming the gospel, can everything be measured on the basis of success? Certainly Paul knew that what he was about to say in verses 30 and 31 would not be well received. But even so he said it, for had he not done so his preaching, although perhaps successful, would have been false.

This is a very important lesson. The true proclamation of the gospel must not be measured only by its results, but also and above all by its faithfulness. In Latin America, as well as among Hispanics in the United States, it has become quite easy to gain quite a following by preaching an unincarnate gospel, as if it were merely a matter of going to heaven, and God had no concern for earth, or

---

31. In the fifth century C.E., a pious Christian of Neoplatonic mystic tendencies wrote a series of books that claimed to have been written by this Dionysius. Because they were soon taken as genuine, they were thought to have been written by an immediate disciple of Paul, and therefore enjoyed great prestige and profoundly impacted medieval religion, piety, and theology. Also during the Middle Ages it was widely believed that Dionysius the Areopagite had gone to France as a missionary, and that he was the founder of the monastery that bears his name in the outskirts of Paris—St. Denis.

32. Of whom no more is known than the name. Codex Bezae, perhaps due to an error, or perhaps reflecting its anti-feminine prejudice, omits her all together. Chrysostom believed her to have been the wife of Dionysius.

as if instead of human beings we were angels floating in the clouds. There is also much successful preaching of a false gospel according to which God will always do what believers wish, and all problems will be solved according to one's desires. Furthermore, there are many who admire evangelists, who, through their preaching in the media, live in luxurious mansions, for it is thought that such mansions are a reward for their faithfulness. All of this is false gospel. Yet, because it is successful it is still preached. We count the numbers who come to church or to the stadium to listen to such preaching, and, although we know that the message of the Bible has been twisted, we rejoice in the numbers. From that point of view, a good preacher is anyone who manages to attract crowds, no matter what they hear.

Paul's example is quite different. Paul preaches the truth. He tries to gain the good will of his audience, as may be seen in the first verses of his speech. But he does not wish to have such good will at the price of not being faithful to the message. Sometimes, as in Athens, his success is minimal. Other times, his preaching leads to persecution. Yet without that firmness in the apostle's witness, the churches he founded would have been unable to resist the persecution that soon followed—people who join the church because it is successful will most likely not be around when persecution or any other signs of apparent failure appear.

It is impossible to know what the future will bring to the Latino Church. There are indications that it will be a difficult future, in which the Church will have to respond to unexpected challenges. There will be enormous political, social, and economic convulsions in our lands. It is possible and even probable that in some places Christians will be persecuted. It is also likely that in some other places authorities will try to cultivate the support of the Church. In such circumstances, the Church's obedience will depend on the degree to which it has prepared itself through a deep and correct understanding of the gospel. Will we know, like Paul, how to offer to our people that teaching and preaching, even though they may not always be well received?

THE PURPOSE OF THE HUMAN CREATURE

In this passage, Paul also says that God created humankind with two purposes: to inhabit the earth and to seek God (vv. 26–27). The very fact of inhabiting the earth is part of God's will for us. God is not interested only in our religion. God is also interested in our dwelling on earth. God is offended when idolatry is committed, as in the case of Athens and in so many aspects of today's religious life. Therefore, we do well in attacking idolatry and superstition. That is what many have done repeatedly from our pulpits and in all our teaching. This is good.

But God is also offended when the land is hoarded, and when for that reason some do not have land on which to dwell. In Latin America today, it is not enough to attack idolatry and superstition; one must also attack the unjust practices that impede the double purpose of God for human creatures, that they seek God, and that they inhabit the earth.

On the other hand, to inhabit the earth does not mean only to occupy it physically, but also to care for it in such a way that it continues being habitable. One of the greatest collective sins of humanity in our generation has been the manner in which we have offended God by destroying the land. Lake Aral, in the former Soviet Union, which until recently was the fourth largest in the world, is rapidly drying up, and what remains is a dead sea where almost no life is possible because the water is highly contaminated with pesticides and other chemicals. The jungle in the Amazon basin is rapidly disappearing, and the carbon dioxide that is produced as it burns is one of the main factors that lead scientists to fear a significant and tragic warming of the earth. The deserts in Africa are growing at a rate of several kilometers a year. In the industrialized nations, the enormous production of contaminants is a threat for all humankind. In Mexico City the air one must breath is highly toxic. Countless animal and vegetable species disappear every year. Clearly, the reasons leading to such conditions are also social and economic. Is it not high time that the Church, which believes that God has placed us here so that we may seek God and inhabit the earth, take decided action for the salvation of the earth itself?

F. CORINTH (18:1–17)

Athens is one of the few cities from which Paul did not have to flee as a result of his preaching. Luke does not even tell us whether the journey to Corinth was by land or by sea. By land it would be a little bit more than 80 kilometers. If traveling by sea, Paul would have boarded a ship in Piraeus (Athens' seaport) and landed in Cenchreae, a seaport some 14 kilometers from Corinth.

Corinth was a rich city. It dominated the isthmus of Corinth, so that all land traffic between the Peloponnese and the rest of Greece had to go through Corinth. Also, sea traffic between the Aegean and the Adriatic often avoided circumnavigating the Peloponnese by carrying goods and passengers over land between Cenchreae, on the Aegean, and the Gulf of Corinth in the Ionian Sea. This saved a distance of some three hundred miles in navigation.[33] Although Corinth had flourished centuries before, in the year 146 B.C.E. it was completely demolished by the Romans as a punishment for its important role in resisting Roman occupation. In 44 B.C.E. it was rebuilt by order of Julius Caesar, who settled a large number of Italian colonists there. Thanks to its great commercial activity, it soon attracted thousands of inhabitants whose main occupation was trade. In 27 B.C.E. Caesar Augustus created the senatorial province of Achaia, and made Corinth its capital.

The new city, which had existed for less than a century when Paul visited it, was bustling with activity. As often happens in such cases, much of that ac-

---

33. A system of pulleys had been constructed, which allowed small vessels to be transported over land from one side of the isthmus to the other. Shortly after Paul's visit, Nero began building a canal from one side to the other. The project was abandoned soon, and was not completed until 1893.

tivity consisted in licentious living. Already in ancient times Corinth's fame along those lines had been proverbial, to the point that a verb had been invented, to "corinthicize," as a synonym of easy and licentious living.

As Paul himself says (I Cor. 2:3), he was in Corinth "in weakness and in fear and in much trembling." This may refer, at least in part, to the illness he had suffered earlier. Given what we know about first-century Corinth, it is not surprising that the Christian apostle felt overwhelmed upon arriving to the city.

It was in Corinth that Paul established contact with Priscilla and Aquila. The text does not tell us how that contact began, but simply that Paul "found" Aquila. Aquila was a Jew, originally from Pontus (on the southern coast of the Black Sea), and shortly before that time he and Priscilla had arrived at Ephesus from Rome. The decree from Claudius, to which 18:2 refers, is known also by the witness of Roman historian Suetonius, who says that Claudius "expelled the Jews from Rome, because they were constantly involved in riots at the instigation of Chrestus."[34] Historians tend to agree that this "Chrestus" is none other than Christ, and that what happened was that, as in so many other places, Christian preaching in the synagogues produced riots that eventually led to the expulsion of those held responsible.[35]

Luke does not say a word about the conversion of Priscilla and Aquila. Most likely they were already Christians when they lived in Rome, before the edict of expulsion. Otherwise it is difficult to explain how a Jew who had been forced to abandon Rome because of the disturbances caused by Christian preaching would now offer lodging to a Christian missionary. Shortly thereafter, in Ephesus, Priscilla and Aquila were sufficiently respected in the Christian community to correct the preaching of Apollos (18:26).

Verse 18 is the only place in the entire New Testament in which Aquila is mentioned before Priscilla (see 18:18, 26; Rom. 16:3; II Tim. 4:19).[36]

In this case, both the grammatical construction and the need to explain that Aquila was a Jew (was Priscilla also a Jew?) are the reasons he is named first. The fact that everywhere else Priscilla is named first would seem to indicate that she was more important in the life of the Church than her husband.

It is in 18:3 that we learn that Paul was a "tent-maker."[37] Apparently, his economic requirements were such that he could only be free to preach on the

---

34. *Claudius,* 25.

35. Most likely the expulsion was not absolute, as both Acts and Suetonius seem to imply, for there continued existing a Jewish community in Rome. Dio Cassius, a Roman historian of the third century, says that what the decree did was to forbid Jews to continue meeting (*Historia Romana* 60.6). Josephus, in a quotation conserved only by fifth-century writer Orosius, gives the date of that edict: 49 C.E.

36. "Priscilla" is the diminutive form of the name "Prisca," and therefore all of these passages refer to the same person.

37. The Greek term is *skēnopoios.* Literally, this means, as the NRSV translates, a maker of tents. However, what does this mean? Some have suggested that what Paul did was to

Sabbaths (18:4), which he did in the synagogue,[38] until Silas and Timothy arrived with support from the believers in Macedonia, which allowed Paul to be "occupied with proclaiming the word." In his second Epistle to the Corinthians, Paul reminds believers that "when I was with you and was in need, I did not burden anyone, for my needs were supplied by the friends who came from Macedonia" (II Cor. 11:9).

Luke does not always keep the reader informed regarding the movements of Timothy and Silas, for they are not central characters in the narrative. Apparently Timothy joined Paul in Athens, but he soon left again for Macedonia. As to Silas, no more has been said about him since he was in Berea (17:14). Furthermore, this is the last time he will be mentioned in the entire book. As has already been stated, he does appear in the rest of the New Testament under his Roman name, "Silvanus" (see the commentary on 15:22).

Apparently, now that Paul was more persistent in his mission,[39] opposition within the synagogue grew, and Paul left them with a dramatic gesture ("he shook the dust from his clothes") and an imprecation ("your blood be on your heads"). Shaking one's clothes was a sign of disgust, leaving them as unworthy of his presence (much as today someone would turn up their nose). The blood over their heads means that they, and not Paul, will now be responsible for whatever happens to them. (Compare this expression with Matt. 27:25.)

Abandoning the synagogue, Paul established his center of activities at the home of a certain Titius Justus, next door to the synagogue. The Western text implies that Paul himself moved there from his lodging with Priscilla and Aquila. The meaning of what is said here is that Paul established his teaching center at the home of Titius Justus, and no longer in the synagogue. Although some ancient manuscripts call this man "Titus Justus," this does not suffice to claim that he is also the Titus of the Pauline Epistles. (It is strange, however, that throughout the entire Book of Acts, Titus is never mentioned.)

Among the Jews who accepted the preaching of the gospel was Crispus, "the official of the synagogue" (JB, "president of the synagogue"; NIV, "the synagogue ruler"; the Greek says *ho archisynagōgos*). The definite article in the Greek text implies that there was only one such official, and that if later Sosthenes is given the same title, it must be because he succeeded Crispus. Al-

---

weave the cloth of goats' wool out of which some tents were made. Such cloth was known as *cilicium*, because it had originally been produced in Cilicia—Paul's own province— which makes it plausible that such cilicium was what he actually made. However, most scholars think that the tents to which reference is made here were made out of leather, and that therefore Paul's occupation, rather than weaving, was one of the many occupations having to do with the working of leather for tents.

38. The definite article implies that there was only one synagogue in Corinth.

39. The Greek text is much stronger than the NRSV implies: "Paul was occupied with proclaiming the word." More literal are the translations of JB, "Paul devoted all his time to preaching," and NIV, "Paul devoted himself exclusively to preaching."

though Acts does not say so, Paul informs us (I Cor. 1:14) that he baptized Crispus. According to Acts, Crispus believed with his entire household, and the same was true of many other Corinthians who became believers and were baptized. Because Paul did not baptize them, one may surmise that they were baptized by members of the Christian community that Paul already found when he arrived at Corinth and whose nucleus seems to have been the household of Priscilla and Aquila.

The vision in verse 9 and 10 becomes particularly important when one remembers the words of Paul quoted above, regarding his attitude of fear at the beginning of the mission in Corinth. It becomes more significant when one takes into account the episode that follows, which is the trial (or attempted trial) before Gallio.

This latter episode (18:12–17) is sandwiched between two declarations about the time that Paul remained in Corinth: "a year and six months" (18:11) and "a considerable time" (18:18). There is some doubt whether the year and a half refers to the period before the appearance before Gallio, or whether it is the total time that Paul spent in Corinth. At any rate, he was there for at least a year and a half.

Gallio, "proconsul of Achaia," is also known through other sources in Roman history and literature. He was born in Spain, and was a brother of the famous philosopher Seneca. His birth name was Marcus Annaeus Novatur; but he had been adopted, as was common among Roman aristocratic families, by a friend of his father, and therefore his official name was Lucius Junius Gallio Annaeus. Like his brother Seneca, he was a friend of Nero, but eventually fell from his master's grace and had to commit suicide at Nero's order. Thanks to an inscription found early in the twentieth century, it is now known that Gallio was proconsul of Achaia from July of 51 to the same time the following year. (The position of proconsul, much sought after by Roman aristocrats, usually was held only for a year.) Thanks to this fact, and to the date of the edict by Claudius (18:2), it is possible to affirm that the period that Paul spent in Corinth was approximately from the autumn of 50 to the spring or the middle of 52. This is one of the few episodes in Acts that can be dated with relative accuracy.

What takes place before Gallio can hardly be called a trial. The accusation itself is ambiguous, for it is said that Paul "is persuading people to worship God in ways that are contrary to the law," but there is no indication whether this refers to the law of Rome or the law of Moses. Gallio, however, will not allow himself to become involved in the matter. Before Paul can even defend himself, Gallio responds with somewhat supercilious words, and ends with the official formula that a judge employed to declare that he would not hear a case: "I do not wish to be a judge of these matters." The pejorative tone of his words probably reflects the attitude of a large part of Roman aristocracy toward Jews. The same attitude is found in the writings of Seneca, Gallio's brother. Therefore, it is not that Gallio is a just judge or that he fears that Paul's party may be powerful, but simply that he is not interested at all in the accusers nor in the accused, who for him are no more than despicable Jews. The same attitude is manifested when he immediately orders them all expelled from the tribunal, but then allows Sosthenes to be beaten right in front of the tribunal while Gallio pays no attention.

Verse 17 is difficult to understand. Most manuscripts, like the NRSV, do not say who it was that seized Sosthenes. Some manuscripts say that it was "the Greeks," but this may well be the guess of a copyist who felt that more clarity was needed. Who was it that seized and beat Sosthenes? There are several possibilities: (1) those who beat him were the city mob, scoffing at him on the basis of the attitude the proconsul had shown toward Jews, and knowing that Gallio's attitude granted them immunity; (2) they were Jews who were angry because their chief had failed them and shamed them in the presence of Gallio; (3) they were Jews, but they did this because Sosthenes, like the previous ruler of the synagogue, was inclined toward Christianity or had already become a Christian. This last possibility finds support in the fact that Paul later refers to a "Sosthenes" who was with him in Ephesus, and that he does this precisely when writing to the Corinthians (I Cor. 1:1).

THE ACTS OF THE SPIRIT AND THE ACTS OF HISTORY

In the introduction to this commentary it was stated that this book of the Bible, rather than "Acts of the Apostles," should be called "Acts of the Spirit," for its subject is not what the apostles did, but rather what the Spirit does. We have repeatedly seen the Spirit's action in the community of believers, or in the work of Paul and his companions. In this particular text, however, we see another very significant dimension of the action of the Spirit: the Spirit is also active in history, sometimes in such mysterious ways that we do not ever suspect them.

There are two examples of this in the present passage. The first is the edict issued by Claudius, expelling the Jews (or at least some of them) from Rome. It is because of that edict that Priscilla and Aquila are in Corinth when Paul reaches that city. The entire work of this couple, first in Corinth and then in Ephesus, is the result of that edict by a pagan emperor. The second example is the trial before Gallio. Gallio had no intention of protecting Paul. Apparently what he actually felt was contempt both for him and for those who accused him. However, that very contempt on the part of a powerful person provides Paul and other believers with the necessary space to continue their work.

What is the significance of all of this for us today? Sometimes we think that the Spirit of God is active only in the Church, where that action is manifested in various ways. To think that the Spirit acts only in the Church is to limit the power and work of the Spirit. Before Paul ever reached Corinth, the Spirit of God was already preparing the way by taking Priscilla and Aquila there. God does not act only in the history of the Church and in the lives of believers, but also in the history of the world and even in the lives of unbelievers. It is important to remember that repeatedly in the history of Israel, when the people were not faithful, God employed not only their own prophets, but also their enemies (the Philistines, the Amorites, Cyrus, and many others) to fulfill the divine will. It is important to remember also that according to the biblical witness God not only brought the children of Israel out of Egypt, but also the Philistines from Caphtor and the Arameans from Kir (Amos 9:7). God is present in the history of Latin America. God is present in the pilgrimage of the Hispanic peoples in the United States. To deny that presence is to deny the power of God.

Part of the message of the prophets of the Old Testament was precisely that: the presence of God in the historical events of their time. The same may be said about Luke. In his gospel, he relates the birth of Jesus to the political circumstances of the time: King Herod, the edict by Augustus Caesar, and the rule of Quirinius over Syria. The same is true in Acts, as may be seen in this passage. Likewise, our message today must be related to the action of God in the events of our time and among our peoples. If there happens to be a dictator, that fact is not alien to the will and the judgment of God. If there is injustice in our lands or among our peoples, if some are homeless, if peasants lack land, if there is repression, if there is justice, if there is freedom, if there is need, if there is prosperity . . . all of this is closely related to the Christian message and the work of the Spirit.

Naturally, it is not always easy to discern the work of God in the historical events of our time. We can imagine Paul, lodging with Priscilla and Aquila and learning from them how the preaching of the gospel had created difficulties in Rome. Now he himself is preaching in Corinth, and he has ample experience of how such preaching might lead to difficulties. Therefore, it is not surprising that he feared and trembled, and that he would need a vision to give him greater courage. We too are discouraged when we see so much injustice around us. In the Church itself there are some who become upset if other Christians denounce the injustice of our societies. Therefore, sometimes because we fear making a mistake and sometimes because we fear the consequences, we hesitate in clearly naming such injustice and declaring that it is against the will of God. In such cases, the words of the Lord to Paul are highly relevant: "Do not be afraid, but speak and do not be silent." When God commands us to speak, silence is sinful.

Then there is another sort of difficulty that is less dramatic, but equally present: the contempt of the powerful. Gallio could not care less about Paul and his followers. However, even without Gallio knowing it, God is still Lord even of his contempt. Similar situations often obtain today. We live in a world where we are often looked upon with contempt or at least ignored. The great movie and television stars, famous athletes, and even criminals, receive much more attention and public interest than does the preaching of the gospel. There are deeply committed Christians who devote their entire lives to serving the needy, often with enormous sacrifices, who are however ignored by the same society that eagerly inquires into every detail of the life of someone who has become enormously wealthy by exploiting others. In any one of our countries, more resources are invested in cosmetics and cigarettes than in the preaching of the gospel or in works of justice. That is one of the reasons preachers are so often tempted to imitate the publicity and marketing methods employed for selling cosmetics or cigarettes. Gallio must have been proud of the inscription celebrating his proconsulate in Achaia, which was then the equivalent of our television programs. How sad a situation for Christians in Corinth—despised, ignored, while no one wrote inscriptions in their honor! But today we know that even that contempt provided an opportunity for the work of the Spirit. Will we be able to see the same in today's contempt? Or will we try to be like Gallio by seeking recognition, appearing in television programs and in newspapers, being photographed with dictators or magnates, even at the cost of our own faithfulness? The temptation is real and severe.

G. THE RETURN (18:18–22)

Paul's sojourn in Corinth was prolonged ("a considerable time," 18:18). It is quite possible that during that time other churches in nearby cities were founded. In Romans 16:1, Paul refers to the church in Cenchreae—which, as stated above, was Corinth's port on the Aegean. In II Corinthians 1:1 he addresses his letter "to the church of God that is in Corinth, including all the saints throughout Achaia."

At any rate, the time came to return to Antioch, and Paul "sailed for Syria." In the geography of the time "Syria" included both Syria proper and Judea. As will be seen later on, Paul went first to Caesarea, which was the seaport serving Jerusalem, and then to Antioch. At the beginning of the journey he was accompanied by Priscilla and Aquila. They were traveling to Ephesus, possibly for business reasons, and Paul, who had been lodging with them, traveled with them. As to Silas and Timothy, not a word is said, and one may suppose that they remained in Corinth, working with the church in that city and the surrounding area.

The end of verse 18 is difficult to interpret. The first question it raises is who was it that had his hair cut because he was under a vow. In a strict grammatical sense, this seems to refer to Aquila, who is the last person mentioned before. However, Luke seldom gives such details about secondary characters, and the flow of the narrative itself, whose main subject is Paul, would seem to indicate that this particular phrase refers to the apostle.[40]

The other difficulty posed by this particular phrase is independent from the first: what was the vow itself? The cutting of one's hair brings to mind the vow of the nazirites, described in Numbers 6:1–21. Upon fulfilling his vow, a nazirite would shave his head and offer his hair in sacrifice to God. However, this was normally done in the Temple, and whoever made those vows away from Jerusalem would then plan to spend the last days before their fulfillment in Jerusalem. According to the school of Shammai, which was the most flexible in such matters, one should spend at least thirty days in Jerusalem before having one's head shaved. On the other hand, a rather ambiguous text

---

40. Some manuscripts of the Western text, as well as the Vulgate, affirm that it was Aquila who had made a vow.

in Josephus seems to imply that a nazirite who was away from Jerusalem could have his head shaved, and later bring his hair to offer as a sacrifice in the Temple.[41]

Whatever the case may be, it seems likely that Luke mentions this vow on Paul's part in order to underscore his continued fidelity to Jewish religious practices. Paul was not anti-Jewish, nor did he advocate abandoning the practices of his ancestors, but simply insisted that those who were not Jews did not have to follow such practices in order to accept Christ and join the Church.

From Corinth, Paul went to Ephesus. Looking at a map it may seem strange that, in order to go from Corinth to Caesarea, one would go first to Ephesus. This may have been partly due to Paul's desire to accompany Priscilla and Aquila, who were traveling to Ephesus.[42] But it can also be explained on the basis of the preferred methods of travel by sea at the time. Sailors always sought to remain within sight of the shore, or at least to avoid long crossings over the high seas. Therefore, people going from Cenchreae eastward frequently crossed the Aegean first toward Ephesus, and then followed a southerly and eastward route.

Ephesus was an important seaport in Asia Minor.[43] Its temple of Artemis (or Diana) was one of the seven wonders of the ancient world.[44] In the middle of the city there was a wide avenue more than thirty feet wide, with another fifteen feet of portals on each side. That avenue led from the seaport to the theater. The theater itself, which could seat 24,000 people, gives an idea of the size of the city.[45]

From this moment on, Ephesus will play an important role in the history of the Church in the first century. That city and its church will occupy the center of the stage in Acts until the end of chapter 21. Later, it is found again in the Book of Revelation.[46]

---

41. Josephus, *War* 2.15.1. David John Williams, *Acts* (New York: Harper & Row, 1985), p. 315, defends this interpretation of Josephus, whereas Haenchen, *Acts*, pp. 543–546, rejects it. Others have proposed, without great success, the theory that this was some other kind of vow, more private in nature.

42. In Romans 16:3–5a, Paul sends them greetings, thus implying that Aquila and Priscilla were at that time living among the addressees of that letter, for he refers to the church in their house. This would seem to indicate that at a later date the couple returned to Rome. However, some scholars suggest that the last chapter of Romans is really a letter addressed to another church, perhaps in Ephesus. In such a case, Priscilla and Aquila could still have been in Ephesus.

43. Due to fluvial deposits, the sea has receded, and the ruins of Ephesus are now several miles away from the sea.

44. See the commentary on 19:23–41.

45. On the theater, see 19:29.

46. Although among the Pauline Epistles there is one addressed to the Ephesians, the question of the actual addressees of that letter is much debated. The best manuscripts of that letter do not include the reference to Ephesus (Eph. 1:1).

What is the meaning of the phrase "he left them there" in 18:19? The immediate reading of the text would seem to indicate that the synagogue was outside the city itself, and that Paul, after leaving his companions in Ephesus, went to the synagogue. However, the rest of the passage, where the verbs are in the imperfect tense, would seem to indicate that Paul visited the synagogue repeatedly. Therefore, perhaps in verse 19 Luke is simply getting ahead of himself. Paul left Priscilla and Aquila in Ephesus when he continued his journey toward Judea. Meanwhile, while he remained in Ephesus, he had several discussions with the Jews in the synagogue, who asked him to stay longer.

The KJV includes in verse 21 a phrase not found in the best manuscripts, and therefore omitted in the NRSV and other modern translations: "I must by all means keep this feast that cometh in Jerusalem." In verse 22, the Greek text says only "he went up and greeted the church." However, throughout the Book of Acts and also elsewhere in the New Testament the phrase "going up" often refers to Jerusalem, which was atop a hill. In Acts itself, there are frequent references to "going up" to Jerusalem, and of "descending" from Jerusalem to Antioch. If one were to understand the phrase "went up to greet the church" as simply going up to the city itself of Caesarea, one would have difficulty explaining why Luke then continues telling us that Paul "went down" to Antioch. From Jerusalem to Antioch one does descend; but not from Caesarea to Antioch. Furthermore, the reason for sailing from Ephesus to Caesarea, and not directly to Antioch, must have been Paul's desire to go to Jerusalem. Therefore, even though Jerusalem does not appear in the best manuscripts of verse 22, and even though Luke does not mention it by name, the NRSV correctly translates the meaning of the phrase.

Finally, Paul returned to Antioch, from which he had departed a long time before.

MISSION AND CONNECTION

Luke does not tell us much about what Paul did in Jerusalem or in Antioch. Furthermore, already in the very next verse he is leaving on a new journey. However, the very fact of returning to these two cities is crucial to understanding Paul's vision of his own mission. He has no need to return to these two cities. His situation is not that of today's missionary, who must periodically return to the churches that provide his or her support. On the contrary, Paul supports himself by making tents, or by whatever he receives from the churches he has founded, such as that in Philippi. Whenever there are economic transactions between himself and Jerusalem, it is the latter that is receiving contributions from the Pauline churches, not vice versa.

Paul's purpose in returning to Jerusalem and Antioch has nothing to do with missionary support, but is fundamental for the nature of his mission. His mission is not only preaching the gospel, converting people, and founding churches, but also creating and strengthening the ties among Christians and among churches. When someone is converted as a result of his work, he joins that person to the church. When Paul founds a church in Philippi, what he has created must be

closely linked to the rest of the body of Christ. That church may have its auton-
omy, and even some sort of independence, but it cannot be a church of Christ
by itself, isolated from the rest of the body. That understanding of the connection
and nature of mission is crucial for the Latino Protestant Church. Partly as a reaction to a dominant Church, which was highly hierarchical, often we have
gone to the opposite extreme. The connection among Christians, and among believing communities, then becomes secondary. What is important is "believing
in Jesus Christ," we say; the Church is a matter of convenience, of support in believing, and not part of the gospel itself. In the biblical vision, to believe in Jesus
Christ implies and requires joining the community of the faithful, the *koinônia*
that was so important in the early chapters of this commentary. To believe in Jesus Christ is indeed a very personal matter, but not a private one.

When that vision is lost, several consequences follow. The first is that for the
believer, the Church becomes optional. I partake in the life of the Church if I
feel like it, or if it somehow supports my faith. After all, what is important is my
own personal relationship with the Lord. That is why in our pastoral visits so
often we are told, "Don't worry, pastor, I can be a Christian without attending
church."

The second consequence is that we limit the function of the Church. The
Church is there to fill *my* spiritual needs. If what is said or done at the church on
a given day does not respond to those needs, I might just as well abstain. Quite
often we hear that the Church is like a service station where we come to receive
energy for the rest of the week. That may well be true; but the Church is much
more than that. The Church is part of the gospel, of the good news; the Church
is the community that lives in expectation of the reign of God, and in which
therefore that reign makes itself present, difficult though it may seem for us to
believe at times. The Church is there to respond, not only to *my* needs, but also
to the needs of all believers, and to the needs to this entire world for which Jesus
Christ died.

The third consequence is that, because the Church is optional and is there
in order to meet my own needs, it is mostly a matter of personal taste. That is
why some people change churches as often as they change shirts. I don't like
the pastor. That other church is more active. The music over there is better. That
one has a more active program for young people. We thus become spiritual
tourists and, like any tourist, we never really get to know the country we visit.

The fourth consequence is that any excuse suffices to divide the Church. If,
after all, the community of believers is of no great importance, any disagreement or strife suffices to divide us. If a group does not agree with the pastor, they
simply leave and find another. Or, if a pastor has difficulties with a particular
congregation or with a denomination, he simply declares himself "independent," becomes an "evangelist," and that is that.

Finally, as a consequence of all this, we become a series of splinter groups,
which spend more time competing and debating among ourselves than witnessing to God's reign and being a sign of God's work in our world.

Over against such a truncated view of mission, there is what Luke presents throughout the entire Book of Acts, and what Paul shows in this passage. The Church is an essential part of Christian life. Its purpose is not only to respond to my needs, but to respond to the needs of the world, and to be a sign of the work and grace of Jesus Christ. In carrying forth the mission, believers must remain in contact with each other. They may not always be in total agreement, as seen repeatedly in the Book of Acts (remember the need for the meeting in Jerusalem, and the disagreement between Paul and Barnabas). But when there are disagreements, every possible effort must be made to preserve the ties of love and communion. Thus, and only thus, will the world believe. It was both for us and for the sake of the world that the Lord prayed, "that they may all be one . . . so that the world may believe that you have sent me" (John 17:21).

7

At and around Ephesus
(18:23–20:38)

Paul begins a new journey in verse 23. Although in this journey he will visit several other places—some of them for at least the second time—Luke will pay special attention to Ephesus and to events in that city and the surrounding area.

A. DEFICIENT DISCIPLES (18:23–19:7)

1. Apollos (18:23–28)

a. A Summary (18:23)

The brevity of verse 23 summarizes much. Paul spent "some time" in Antioch. How long? It is impossible to know. However, given the conditions of the roads that he had to take to reach Galatia and Phrygia, one would imagine that he remained in Antioch at least until the following spring. The passes through the mountains were closed during winter. Furthermore, "the region of Galatia and Phrygia" includes several cities that Paul had visited before: Derbe, Iconium, Lystra, and others. Because Luke tells us that he went about "strengthening the disciples," it stands to reason that he spent at least a few weeks in each of those cities. Therefore, what stands behind the brevity of this verse is a fairly long journey. Once again, Luke gives us a very short summary of what must at least have taken months and perhaps even years.

b. The Preaching of Apollos (18:24–28)

Luke now introduces a new character in his story, who will disappear again at 19:1. Apart from Paul's references in I Corinthians, these few verses are all we know about Apollos.

His character and person are described in verse 24. The name "Apollos" is an abbreviated form of "Apollonius." He was a Jew from Alexandria. Alexandrian Judaism had been characterized, even from before the time of Jesus, by its sages and philosophers, many of whom had built bridges between Judaism and the best of pagan culture. Therefore, when Luke tells us that Apollos was an Alexandrian Jew, this immediately brings to mind that entire intellectual tradition, of which Apollos was most probably an heir. The word that the NRSV translates as "eloquent" (*logios*) can also be translated as "learned" (NIV), "erudite," or "intelligent." He was also "well versed in the Scriptures" (literally, "powerful in the Scriptures"), which seems to refer to his ability to refute his adversaries on the basis of Scripture, as may be seen in verse 28.

Apollos was already a Christian, fervent in spirit (literally, "boiling in the spirit"), and he taught "accurately" about Jesus. All of this agrees with what Paul tells us in I Corinthians.

However, the preaching of Apollos was deficient, for "he knew only the baptism of John." It is difficult to know the exact nature of this deficiency. On comparing this passage with the one that follows (19:1–7), it would seem that knowing only the baptism of John means not knowing or not having received the baptism of the Holy Spirit. However, if this were the case it would not have been sufficient for Priscilla and Aquila to take Apollos aside and explain "the way of God to him more accurately." Here there is no indication that, after such instruction, Apollos received the Holy Spirit. Therefore, it would seem that what is at stake is a theological deficiency. What makes the interpretation of the entire passage most difficult is that verse 25 tells us that he taught "accurately," and that the very next verse tells us that this teaching was deficient. Some scholars try to solve this difficulty by claiming that the sources Luke employed praised Apollos, but that Luke himself, being a follower and admirer of Paul, tried to minimize the ministry of this rival to Paul, and therefore introduces the suggestion of a theological deficiency.[1] However, reading the text as a whole, one reaches the conclusion that, although Apollos knew quite well and accurately the life of Jesus, he had not followed the consequences of that life beyond a calling to repentence (the "baptism of John"). In that case, what he preached in the synagogue, and led Priscilla and Aquila to call him aside, would be simply the life and teaching of Jesus, and the injustice that had been committed in having him crucified (perhaps even also his resurrection); but not the inauguration of the "last days," as Peter had said at Pentecost. This would explain why in 19:1–7 the matter of the Holy Spirit is contrasted with the baptism of John.

Having been instructed "more accurately," Apollos left for Corinth, with a letter of recommendation from the believers in Ephesus, and there he was a considerable help to the church.[2]

---

1. See E. Haenchen, *The Acts of the Apostles: A Commentary* (Philadelphia: Westminster, 1975), pp. 554–55, and M. Wolter, "Apollos und die ephesinischen Johannesjünger," *ZntW*, 78 (1987), 49–73.

2. According to the Western text, it was at the request of some Corinthians who were at Ephesus that Apollos went to Corinth.

A WOMAN WHO TAUGHT THEOLOGY

In the text, the name of Priscilla appears before that of Aquila. However, by the second century the Western text had inverted the order saying that it was "Aquila and Priscilla" who called Apollos aside. This tendency to minimize the importance of Priscilla as time goes by may be seen elsewhere. For instance, one of the ancient churches in Rome in the fourth century was called "church of St. Prisca"; later it became "of Prisca and Aquila"; and by the eighth century it was the "church of Saints Aquila and Prisca."

For a number of reasons, in the second century an anti-feminine reaction developed in the Church, and as part of that reaction, which limited the authority of women in the Church, the tradition of women who had been significant leaders was obscured. One of these women was Priscilla.[3]

The Protestant Church in Latin America is part of that tradition. Furthermore, in a strange way the history of the ancient Church, which was at first quite open toward feminine leadership, and then became more closed, has been reenacted in our churches. When Protestant missionary work began in Latin America, there were women as well as men among the missionaries. Women traveled to remote places, created new opportunities, founded churches, taught theology. Thus, just a few decades ago the Spanish-speaking Protestant churches were quite used to having women in positions of authority, and as pastors and preachers. Then other currents came from abroad that sought to limit the ministry of women. Today there are many who are convinced that such ministry is an innovation, a recent invention, when the truth is quite the opposite.

Priscilla—as well as the four daughters of Philip who preached, whom we shall meet further on in this narrative (21:9)—is an indication of what Peter said in his Pentecost speech, that the gifts of the Spirit are poured out upon young and old, men and women. Before the acts of such a Spirit, all the limitations that we humans impose on each other must give way. The Latin American Church has a valuable resource in its women, and those who refuse to allow the proper use of those resources must take care lest they be found resisting the Spirit.

2.   The Twelve Disciples in Ephesus (19:1–7)

This episode is closely related with the previous one. It takes place after the departure of Apollos, but apparently there are still in Ephesus some disciples who know no more than "the baptism of John" (19:3). Because this is the same phrase that appears in 18:25 in reference to Apollos, the text would seem to imply that there was some relationship between these twelve (or, "about twelve," 19:7) disciples and Apollos. Were they people who had been taught by Apollos before he received his lesson in theology from Priscilla and Aquila? Or

---

3. It has been suggested that she was the author of the Epistle to the Hebrews, and that her name was eliminated as part of that anti-feminine reaction.

were they simply people coming out of the same circle as Apollos? It is impossible to know.

In any case, now we find a clear explanation of the deficiency, if not of Apollos, at least of these disciples. Paul adds two elements to what they already knew: first, that the preaching of John the Baptist pointed to the one coming after him, Jesus the Christ (19:4); and, second, that there is a Holy Spirit (19:2, 6). Apparently these disciples were followers of Jesus as a teacher, but not as the Christ, the expected Messiah, the fulfillment of the promise. (Could this also have been the deficiency of Apollos, that is, that he could accurately speak of the teachings and miracles of Jesus, but did not know that he was the fulfillment of the promise?) What Paul tells them is that this was actually the message of John himself. Then, on the basis of the joint witness of Paul and John, these disciples are baptized and when Paul lays his hand on them, they receive the Spirit.

JESUS AND THE SPIRIT

Although this is not a treatise on the doctrine of the Holy Spirit, there are two important points that follow from this narrative that are particularly significant for the Protestant Spanish-speaking Church, where there is so much discussion about the Holy Spirit.

The first point is that there is a very close relationship between having the Spirit and being able to confess fully who Jesus Christ is. This is seen in the narrative itself. The Twelve do not know about the Spirit, and Paul responds to this situation by letting them know that Jesus is the Christ. Then they are baptized "in the name of the Lord Jesus" and they receive the Spirit. In this case, when Paul learns that someone does not know the Spirit, he tells him or her about Jesus. There is a necessary connection between knowing and confessing Jesus as the Christ and having the Holy Spirit. As Paul himself says elsewhere (I Cor. 12:3), "no one can say 'Jesus is Lord' except by the Holy Spirit."

The second important point is that the manner in which these various things are related is not always the same. We like to have everything in black and white, to know exactly how and when the Spirit acts. Particularly in our churches, there are some who claim to know about the Holy Spirit and its action more than it is given for humans to know. This is to attempt to limit the power and the freedom of the Spirit. Here, as in most other passages in Acts, the Spirit comes after baptism, with the imposition of hands by the apostles (see, for instance, 8:17). However, in the episode of Cornelius, the Gentiles receive the Spirit first, without any laying on of hands; and it is later, as a consequence of having received the Spirit, that Cornelius and his companions are baptized.

The importance of all of this for our churches should be clear: let us not claim to know more than we really know, nor try to limit and to control the action of the Spirit.

B. MIRACLES IN EPHESUS (19:8–22)

1. Paul's Teaching (19:8–10)

These verses are a brief summary that includes, first, Paul's preaching in the synagogue; second, his breach with the synagogue; and finally, Paul's continued teaching in the lecture hall of Tyrannus. After two years of preaching, the word had spread throughout the area, "so that all the residents of Asia, both Jews and Greeks, heard the word of the Lord." Perhaps because he is simply summarizing Paul's activities, Luke does not mention a visit to Corinth that must have taken place at this time, as can be deduced from Paul's Corinthian correspondence.

The only point here that may need clarification is the reference to the lecture hall of Tyrannus. The Western text says "of a certain Tyrannus, from the fifth to the tenth hours"—that is, from eleven o'clock in the morning to four in the afternoon. The Alexandrian text, which is probably the original, and which the NRSV follows, simply says "the lecture hall of Tyrannus." No more is known about this person, nor about his lecture hall or school. Perhaps he was a teacher who had lectured or still lectured in the same place, and whose fame was such that the place was known by his name. Perhaps he was simply the owner of a building used for lectures. He could also have been its architect or builder. At any rate, by the time the Western text came about, probably in the second century, the scribe copying it did not know who Tyrannus was, and that is why the text says "a certain Tyrannus."

2. False Miracles (19:11–16)

The entire section deals with miracles that took place in Ephesus through the ministry of Paul. Luke does not normally present Paul as a miracle worker. According to Acts, Paul's main function is preaching, teaching, and strengthening the faith of the churches. In the Pauline Epistles we also see that he was collecting an offering for Jerusalem. In Luke's narrative, the miracles that take place in connection with Paul's ministry are numerous, but are not normally the center of the narrative, but rather the occasion for some other event that becomes important. Thus, for instance, the healing of the girl with a spirit of divination in 16:16–18 serves as an introduction for the jailing of Silas and Paul in Philippi.

Here, the miracles that take place "through Paul" serve as an introduction, not to an episode in the life of Paul, but rather to an episode that shows the failure of those who seek to imitate him, with the hope of being able to accomplish miracles such as those attributed to the apostle.

a. A Summary about Miracles (19:11–12)

Luke introduces the episode of the sarcastic demon (19:13–17) with a summary about the miracles that God did "through Paul." Upon reading this passage, we immediately think that all the miracles mentioned took place in Ephesus. But it is possible that the text should be read in more general terms. Luke is about to tell us about an event that took place in Ephesus, which shows the weakness of false miracle-workers, and introduces that narrative with a general commentary about the many miracles that took place in connection with Paul's ministry.

The reference to Paul's handkerchiefs and aprons has provided some supposed evangelists with an opportunity to make money by selling handkerchiefs and other items they have blessed. Note however that here the text implies, not that Paul gave away or proclaimed the power of his handkerchiefs and aprons, but rather that people took them away without the apostle's knowledge. It is not, as some would claim today, that Paul blessed handkerchiefs so that through them miracles would be accomplished.

b. The Sarcastic Demon (19:13–16)

Paul's fame, manifested in people's eagerness to take his handkerchiefs and aprons in order to perform miracles, also leads some exorcists to imitate him. The reference to Jewish exorcists should not be surprising, for among Jews in the first century exorcism was a common practice.[4]

The narrative itself, however, poses some problems. In the first place, the relationship between verses 13 and 14 is not clear. In verse 13 the reference is to "some itinerant Jewish exorcists," and in 14 the reference is to "seven sons of a Jewish high priest named Sceva." Are these two different groups, or are those in verse 14 a particular instance of what is mentioned in 13? Second, among those who served as high priests among the Jews there was no one named Sceva. Third, it is difficult to explain why Luke would refer to such an important person as if he were an unknown, which is the implication of the Greek grammatical construction. Finally, in verse 14, Luke speaks of *seven* sons of Sceva, whereas in verse 16 he tells us that the evil spirit jumped over "both of them"—the NRSV avoids this difficulty by simply saying "them." In all of these cases, the Western text seems to solve the difficulties.[5] Therefore some scholars believe that this was the original version, whereas others insist that it is only a very well crafted revision of the original, precisely seeking to solve the difficulties that the original presented.[6]

---

4. Josephus, *Ant.* 8.2.5. On the fame of Jewish exorcists, see B. A. Mastin, "Scaeva the chief priest," *JTS*, 27 (1976), 405–12.

5. In the Western text, there are two different groups of exorcists. The first, in verse 13, are Jewish. The second, those who appear in verse 14 and in the rest of the story, are pagans. Sceva is a high priest, but we are not told that he is a Jew, and therefore he seems to be the high priest of some particular form of worship that existed in Ephesus. Then the "both" in verse 16 seems to refer to both groups, and not to two exorcists. There are also many other details (such as the use of the singular and the plural in various dialogues) in which the Western text appears more coherent than the Alexandrian.

6. W. A. Strange, "The sons of Sceva and the text of Acts 19:14," *JTS*, 38 (1987), 97–106, holds that the Western text is the original, whereas E. Delebecque, "La mésaventure des

The difficulties in the Alexandrian text are not insurmountable. First of all, verse 14 may be a particular example of what verse 13 says in more general terms. There were Jewish exorcists who sought to cast out demons in the name of Jesus. Among them were the seven sons of Sceva, about whom the narrative speaks more specifically. Second, the title of "high priest," which is given to Sceva, may be interpreted not as that of the head of the priesthood but rather as being an important person among the priests.[7] Finally, in some writings of the time the term "both" (*amphoterōn*) is used in the sense of "all."[8]

At any rate the general trend of the narrative is clear: some exorcists tried to cast out demons with the formula, "I adjure you by Jesus whom Paul proclaims." It is a rather strange formula, in which the exorcist distances himself from Jesus in whose name he claims to cast out the demon. He does not say "in the name of Jesus," but "by the Jesus whom Paul proclaims."

The demon's response is rather sarcastic: "Jesus I know, and Paul I know; but who are you?" In the Greek text two different verbs are employed, and therefore the JB translates the demon's response as, "Jesus I recognize, and I know who Paul is, but who are you?" Although perhaps the difference between these two verbs should not be overstressed, they do indicate that the demon acknowledges Jesus and Paul in two different ways: the first more directly, as when one knows someone; the second as a matter of information, as when one knows something.

Immediately, this demon who seems to scoff at the exorcists adds injury to insult, for the man jumps on them and gives them a sound thrashing.

3. The Reaction of the People (19:17–20)

These four verses summarize the reaction of various groups to all that took place, and especially the beating received by the sons of Sceva. Verse 17 indicates that when all of this became known in Ephesus, all were awestruck, "both Jews and Greeks." Verse 18 affirms that the news also affected Christians, who "confessed and disclosed their practices." The next verse clarifies what some of those practices were, including magic. It is not clear whether all those who practiced magic and burned their books were Christians who had not abandoned their former practices, or whether they were other people who had heard of what had taken place. Perhaps the text should be read as referring to both, so that at least one of the sins that Christians confess (verse 18) was continuing with their ancient superstitions.

---

fils de Scévas selon ses deux versions," *RevScPhTh*, 66 (1982), 225–32, believes that it is only a very well crafted revision.

7. It could be translated "chief priest," thus keeping the possibility of both interpretations. At other places in Acts, Luke himself employs the same title in plural, which shows that at least there he does not intend it in the sense of "high priest," but rather in the sense of "important priest": 4:23; 5:23; 9:14, 21; 22:30; 23:14; 25:2, 15; 26:10, 12.

8. There is an ample bibliography on this matter in J. Renié, *Actes des Apôtres* (Paris: Pirot-Clamer, 1951), p. 265.

It is particularly important that this event took place in Ephesus, for that city was known for the books of magic produced there, which were often called "Ephesine writings."[9] It is also important to point out the value of the books that were burned. Fifty thousand silver coins would be the rough equivalent of a good salary for an equal number of days, that is, roughly 150 years of a good salary. It is possible that Luke mentions this figure in order to mark the contrast between what happens here and the next episode, in which economic interests will seek to hinder the preaching of the gospel. In this case, the impact of the gospel is such that it overcomes economic interests.

Finally, verse 20 is one of the many summaries that Luke includes in his book.

4. An Outline of the Future (19:21–22)

These two brief verses are an outline of what is still to come, a summary of the future. Especially in verse 21, we are told that Paul will travel through Macedonia and Achaia, in order then to go to Jerusalem and finally to Rome. This is the outline of the rest of the book. However, what we have here is more than an outline; it is an indication of a radical shift in the nature of the narrative. The phrase "after these things had been accomplished" implies that something has now been fulfilled. In a way, Paul has now fulfilled the missionary task that the Spirit has entrusted to him. What is now lacking is to go to Jerusalem and then to Rome, places not so much of missionary work as of suffering and persecution. In Paul's career, this passage is parallel to what Luke says about Jesus, that "he set his face to go to Jerusalem" (Luke 9:51). The verb "to fulfill," which appears at that point in the gospel, also appears in this verse in Acts. Just as it may be said that the passion of Jesus begins in Luke 9:51, so does Paul's life now become one of increasing suffering and official opposition.

In verse 22, Paul begins making arrangements for the journey he proposes by sending Timothy and Erastus to Macedonia. Timothy we have met before (16:1, 17:14–15, 18:5). This is the first time that Erastus is mentioned in Acts, although the same name appears in II Timothy 4:20 (where it clearly refers to the same person mentioned in Acts) and in Romans 16:23. Because this was a relatively common name, it is impossible to know if the Erastus mentioned in Romans and called "the city treasurer" (of Corinth), is the same as the one who appears in Acts. Although Acts does not speak of the offering for Jerusalem, from Paul's letters we know that the offering was very important for him, and therefore it is possible that he sent two colleagues to promote it in Macedonia, or perhaps to collect what had already been gathered.

---

9. Such books were still called "Ephesine," even though by that time more were produced in Egypt than in Ephesus.

VICTORY OVER TODAY'S DEMONS

The present commentary seeks to read the text in Acts in the light and within the context of the current reality of Latin America and of the Latino population in the United States. When we look at that reality, we become aware of the mysterious and overwhelming power of evil. A few decades ago, one might have thought that our problems could be solved with relative ease. It was said, for instance, that the root of all our difficulties was ignorance or lack of education, and that by founding schools and promoting public education most of our tragic circumstances would disappear. As years have passed, we have seen how frequently education is being employed, not to help the people solve their difficulties, but rather to exploit others. Physicians, lawyers, accountants, engineers, and even ministers of the gospel, use what they know to gather wealth and power, while the people at large are still living in disease, injustice, misery, and sin. Quite correctly did a speaker at a graduation at one of our universities declare that the degrees to be given that afternoon were as many "privateers' licenses." Certainly, education is not the cure-all that it was thought to be. Others would argue that what we need is more economic development. Repeatedly we see how as bridges and roads are built, and our hinterlands are open to national and international markets, there are more and more peasants losing their lands, and the population in our slums bulges. Therefore, economic development is not the solution we used to think it would be.

The same may be said even of the preaching of the gospel. It is frequently said that, if everybody would accept the faith, our problems would be solved. But statistics show that some of the countries in which general church attendance is highest—and, for those who think that it is a matter of preaching the Protestant message, where Protestant Christianity counts with most adherents— are also the countries with greatest economic misery, agricultural crises, and political oppression.

What all of this means is that the last years of the twentieth century forced us to face the power of evil, and to confess that it is indeed a mysterious power that we cannot comprehend and we know not how to subject or destroy. In other words, that the events of our nations, as well as those throughout the contemporary world, are leading us back to what the Bible calls "demons." The power of evil is not something that we can explain, nor comprehend, nor control, nor destroy by ourselves. It is mysterious, overpowering, inexplicable. It is precisely there that its terrible perversity lies. If we could explain it, we would be well along the way to overcoming it. But, because we can neither explain nor understand it, its evil is immensely greater. Therefore, in the face of the ills affecting our people we must declare that the Bible is justified in speaking in terms of demonic powers, and that it is these demonic powers that subject our people.

This does not mean that we should jump back twenty centuries and forget all that, with God's help, humankind has learned about viruses, psychoses, and hormones. Knowing all of this, and knowing also about the economic and political manipulations that stand behind the suffering of our peoples, we cannot pretend that the cause of our difficulties is just a small group of little devils floating around with horns and pitchforks.

What it does mean is that, if it is true that the world vision that explains all ills on the basis of such little devils is naive, just as naive is that other world vision, often called "modern," according to which our ills and problems can be easily solved, if we simply apply the best of contemporary knowledge.

When we look at it this way, then the conflict that the New Testament describes in terms of demons is not all that different from what we today mean when we speak about "injustice" and "oppression." Actually, the demon of economic oppression is much more fierce, much more demonic, than any little devil whispering in our ears, like those we see in cartoons. If this is the case, it follows that a study of what the New Testament tells us about victory over such powers will also tell us something about the manner in which we today are to face the twin demons of injustice and oppression—or any others of the many demons that have taken possession of our people.

Read in this manner, the passage about the sarcastic demon relates to our situation in various ways. First, the demon says that it knows Jesus and is also acquainted with Paul: "Jesus I recognize, and I know who Paul is" (JB). This knowledge of Jesus is much more than having heard about him. It is the knowledge of one who has met Jesus, and therefore knows and even acknowledges his power. This is a matter that may be difficult for us "moderns" to understand, but is central in the message of the New Testament. What the New Testament says about Jesus is not simply that he was a great teacher, that he performed miracles, and that he died for our sins. The New Testament certainly says all that; but it says much more. It says also and above all that throughout his life and death Jesus faced the most powerful and fearsome forces of evil and came out victorious. Even though evil is still quite manifest and even overpowering, its power has been destroyed, for there is One who has conquered it and in that One we are all conquerors. Therefore, the central message of the New Testament is that in Jesus a new day has begun, and that the culmination of that new day will be the final destruction of all powers of evil.

The powers of evil know the power of Jesus. What this means is that the final word does not belong to those powers; that evil will be (and in a certain way already has been) conquered; that in mysterious ways that the eyes of faith can merely glimpse we are already enjoying the first fruits of the new creation. As Paul says elsewhere, "So if you have been raised with Christ seek the things that are above . . . for you have died, and your life is hidden with Christ in God. When Christ who is your life is revealed, then you also will be revealed with him in glory" (Col. 3:1, 3–4). This trust in the victory of Jesus initiated in his resurrection and to be completed in his final triumph is an essential part of the faith of the New Testament. Unless we put our trust in this victory of Jesus, our supposed faith is really distant and secondhand, like that of the exorcists who sought to cast out demons "by the Jesus whom Paul proclaims."

This leads to the second important point in this text: the demon acts as if it does not know who the exorcists are; but therein lies its sarcasm, for it does know about them all that really matters: that they have no authority to invoke the power of Jesus. The remark, "but who are you?" implies much more than a lack of knowledge. Actually what it implies is a disconcerting knowledge. The demon is telling these people that, although it does know the power of Jesus, it also knows that there is a vast distance between that power and those who now seek to invoke it. The powers of evil do not acknowledge the power of the exorcists precisely because they know that their relationship with the power of Jesus is distant and secondhand.

This also we see today in our struggles against the powers of evil. The Church makes a pronouncement against social injustice and soon hears the voice of today's sarcastic demons: "You are combating oppression, when your churches are ruled by chiefs who command as if they were feudal lords? You complain of economic injustice, when among yourselves there are similar injustices? You preach the joy of salvation, when in your church everybody has to be long-faced, as if the entire world were in mourning?" What such voices tell us is very similar to what the sarcastic demon told those itinerant exorcists: "Jesus I recognize, and I know who Paul is, but who are you?" Those who control the world today know, no matter how dimly, that the teachings and the life of Jesus have something to do with human injustice. Perhaps they even suspect that their own works oppose the power of Jesus. But they also know that it is quite easy to place a wedge between ourselves and that powerful Jesus.

This leads to the third point: it is much better not to invoke the name of Jesus than to invoke it secondhand. The power of Jesus, convoked from a prudent distance and from a secure position, does not work. The exorcists not only fail, but are also beaten and have to flee naked. When Christians are quite ready to attack today's evils in the name of Jesus, but not to claim the power of Jesus over themselves, they often end up in a sorry state. The demons know us in the same disconcerting way in which the sarcastic demon knew the itinerant exorcists. No matter how much they invoked the power of Jesus, they were doing this from afar, without commitment, and therefore it was quite useless. If we are to cast out the demons that today possess our people, we will only be able to do it if when invoking the name of Jesus we do that within the context of a true commitment to Jesus.

It is here that things get difficult. A real commitment to Jesus implies much more than attending church, praying, and reading the Bible. The Jesus whom we follow went to the cross and tells us that to follow him one has to take up the cross. Commitment to Jesus is not only a matter of a confession of faith; it is also a matter of joining him in facing the powers of evil. The demon sees that it knows Jesus. Why? Because Jesus faced evil, entered its dwellings, walked with the sick, the lame and the sinners, was criticized, insulted, and eventually killed by the powers of evil, and through all this he came out victorious. The demon knows Jesus because Jesus knows the demon. The demon knows about Paul because Paul follows Jesus along the same path. Earlier, in the same Book of Acts,

Paul had told the disciples that "it is through many persecutions that we must enter the kingdom of God" (14:22). He has already set his face to go to Jerusalem and eventually to Rome, even though he knows that what awaits him there are difficulties and sufferings. It is for all of this that the demon knows who Paul is and respects him. Paul walks along life facing the powers of evil, and therefore those powers know that he does indeed have the authority to invoke the name of Jesus. The powers of evil will acknowledge our power only when we acknowledge—truly acknowledge—the power of Jesus. And, strange though it may seem, in order to know that power of Jesus one has to know also the power of evil; one has to follow Jesus in facing those powers, in receiving and even suffering all the worst they can throw upon us, and coming out "more than conquerors" by virtue of the one who has already conquered.

The old gospel hymn puts it quite well: "There is power in the cross." There is indeed power, but it is in the cross of confronting evil, which he carried and which he invites us also to carry.

C. THE RIOT AT EPHESUS (19:23–41)

Here we come to the clash between the preaching of the gospel (or, as Luke would say, "the Way") and the economic and religious interests of people in Ephesus. Those interests centered on the great temple to Artemis. (Some older translations say "Diana," because from ancient times the goddess Artemis of Ephesus was identified with the Roman Diana. The Greek actually says "Artemis," and therefore the NRSV and other contemporary versions have returned to that name.) The first temple to Artemis built on the site was destroyed by a fire, which according to tradition took place the very day of the birth of Alexander the Great in 356 B.C.E.[10] Almost immediately thereafter, the Ephesians began rebuilding their famous temple, whose foundation was more than 150 meters long and 50 wide, and which was considered one of the great wonders of the ancient world until it was destroyed by the Goths in 262 C.E. The goddess was worshipped there in the form of a stone statue with a battlement on its head and multiple breasts, and therefore called *polymastos*. This was not really the ancient Artemis of the Greeks, but was rather a fertility goddess known elsewhere in the neighboring area as the "Great Mother." Its high priest was always a eunuch and was called the *megabyzos*. Under him there was a large retinue of priests and priestesses.

The temple, besides being the pride of the city, was also a source of income, for pilgrims throughout the Mediterranean basin traveled to it. Also, as was customary in ancient times, it served as a bank that held the treasure, both of the city and of individuals. Finally, there are indications that in the popular mind the worship of Artemis was conjoined with service to the emperor, espe-

---

10. Plutarch, *Alexander* 3.3.

cially because Empress Agrippina was particularly identified with this temple and its worship.[11]

The story that Luke tells is relatively simple.[12] It all begins with the business of a silversmith named Demetrius and the artisans working with him. His business[13] consisted in making small temples of silver, replicas of the great temple of Artemis, for the pilgrims to take with them on their return.[14] Concerned about the economic loss that Paul's preaching could bring about, Demetrius calls a meeting of the artisans who work in the business, and delivers to them a speech where economic motivations are dressed up in religious fervor. According to Demetrius, Paul's preaching has drawn people away from the worship of the gods, and "there is danger not only that this trade of ours may come into disrepute but also that the temple of the great goddess Artemis will be scorned, and she will be deprived of her majesty that brought all Asia and the world to worship her." Those who hear take up the shout, "Great is Artemis of the Ephesians." Confusion ensues, and the mob marches toward the theater, the place best suited for assemblies and popular meetings. Along the way they seize two of Paul's companions, Gaius and Aristarchus, and take them to the theater.

This is the first mention of Aristarchus in Acts. He will appear again in 20:4, 27:4, and in Colossians 4:10 and Philemon 24. The case of Gaius is more complex. He is mentioned again in 20:4 jointly with Aristarchus, where we are told that he was from Derbe. Here we are told that he was from Macedonia. Does 20:4 refer to another person of the same name, or is there some other reason he is said to be from both Macedonia and Derbe? Furthermore, Paul mentions a certain Gaius in Corinth (Rom. 16:23 and I Cor. 1:14), and the third Epistle of John is also addressed to Gaius. It is impossible to know the relationship among all these people, especially as the name Gaius was quite common.

The theater in Ephesus, whose ruins visitors may still see, was imposing. It was a vast semi-circle built on a natural hollow in the land, facing the seaport,

---

11. L. J. Kretzer, "A numismatic clue to Acts 19:23–41. The Ephesian Cistophori of Claudius and Agrippina," *JTS*, 30 (1987), 59–70.

12. As in so many other cases in Acts, here again there are significant variants in the Western text. These seem to be an attempt to clarify elements that might be confusing in the original narrative. See Delebecque, "La révolte . . . ."

13. The word that the NRSV translates as "business" can also mean profit. It is the same word employed for the profit which the slave girl's owner derived from her spirit of divination in 16:16.

14. Archeologists have not found a single such silver temple, although several made of clay have been found. Probably part of the reason for this is that when the religious significance of these temples was lost, those who had them melted them in order to use the silver of which they were made.

and with marble seats for 24,000 people. At the time it was under reconstruction, part of a long program that began during the reign of Emperor Claudius (41–54 C.E.) and continued until the beginning of the second century.

When Paul learned what was happening, he wished to go to the theater, but he was prevented from doing this by the disciples. In Romans 16:3–4 Paul says that Priscilla and Aquila risked their life for him. Is he referring perhaps to something that took place during this riot at Ephesus, and is it possible that the couple were among those who kept Paul from going to the theater? Also "some officials of the province of Asia" sent a message to Paul to stay away from the theater. The word that Luke employs for these officials is "asiarchs." Asiarchs were the religious leaders of the province of Asia, in which there was a sort of league of cities, each represented by its own asiarch. Therefore, the asiarchs were religious rather than civil officials, even though they did carry some political weight.

Meanwhile, at the theater the riot continued. In verse 32 Luke describes the situation quite vividly: ". . . some were shouting one thing, some another; for the assembly was in confusion, and most of them did not know why they had come together."

Verses 33 and 34 are part of the same confusion, to such a point that the modern reader has difficulty making sense out of all that we are told. Who is this Alexander, who suddenly appears without explanation? Luke says that the Jews pushed him forward so he would speak. Perhaps these Jews were afraid that the reaction against Paul would overflow into a reaction against them, as they also refused to worship Artemis. Or perhaps they wished to make use of the riot to make certain that the people took action against Paul and his followers. At any rate, when the Ephesians saw that this Alexander was a Jew, they did not let him speak, probably because they knew that the Jews did not believe in their goddess. Pandemonium was such that for almost two hours they continued shouting, "Great is Artemis of the Ephesians."

Finally, the "town clerk" intervenes. That title does not reflect the authority of this person, whose responsibility was to implement the decisions of the city assembly, and who therefore was one of the main administrators of the city. He was the intermediary between the Roman government and the assembly of the citizens. It is on the basis of that authority that now he manages to quiet the crowd. He begins by telling them that they have no need to insist on the greatness of their goddess with their disorderly shouting, for, "who is there that does not know that the city of the Ephesians is the temple keeper of the great Artemis and of the statue that fell from heaven? Since these things cannot be denied, you ought to be quiet and do nothing rash." The town clerk's claim that the statue fell from heaven appears to be his response to what Demetrius has said in verse 26 about Paul's preaching against "gods made with hands." Artemis, fallen from heaven, is not vulnerable to such critique. Therefore, the town clerk tells the people that it is not necessary to take rash action. Up to this point, he has been telling the crowd that it is right. But now the tone of his speech changes. Precisely because the crowd is right, and their goddess is as great as they say, it is not necessary to defend her with riots and shouting. Then comes his strongest blow: the seizure of Gaius and Aristarchus, who have not committed any crime against the goddess, is not according to law. If Gaius and Aristarchus have done anything illegal, there are courts open, as well as proconsuls, and Demetrius and his friends can bring a formal accusation against these people. With these words the town clerk goes back to the original cause of the riot, reminding us that Demetrius, after he began the process, does not seem to have come forward. Finally, the town clerk reminds the people that above them is the power of Rome, and that "we are in danger of being charged with rioting today, since there is no cause that we can give to justify this commotion." With these words of warning, which threaten dire consequences on the rioters, the town clerk dismisses the assembly.

SERVING THE POCKET

The riot at Ephesus could well have taken place today, even though Artemis is forgotten and among the ruins of Ephesus all that is left of her famous temple is a single column. Most remarkable is the manner in which Luke interweaves religious and economic motivations. Demetrius begins by telling his colleagues about the implications of Paul's preaching for their pockets, and then covers everything under the mantle of devotion to Artemis. The artisans, moved at first by their possible economic loss, end up shouting, "Great is Artemis of the Ephesians." Here one sees two remarkable facts, which are still present in similar situations today. The first is that eventually the silversmiths seem to be convinced that their shouting is the result of pure religious fervor. The second is that soon there is an entire crowd shouting the same, without the slightest idea of the reason for the riot, nor of the manner in which their shouting supports the interests of Demetrius and his colleagues.

Economic and political interests are shrouded in religion, and thereby find justification both before themselves and before the eyes of the world. What happened with Artemis in Paul's time has happened and continues happening more recently with Christianity in our hemisphere. When Columbus first arrived in these lands, the queen and king of Spain ordered him to "diligently seek to encourage and bring the people of said Indies to all peace and quiet, so that they may serve us and be under our lordship and subjection."[15] The result was that, as Gonzalo Fernández de Oviedo said, "Our converters took from them their gold and even their women and children and whatever goods they had, and gave them the name of baptized Christians."[16] The same happened in Brazil, where Manoel da Nóbrega wrote to the king of Portugal: "If the Indians were to have a spiritual life, to know their creator and their subjection to your majesty

---

15. In an instruction to Christopher Columbus, dated May 29, 1493. *Colección de documentos inéditos relativos al descubrimiento, conquista y organización de las antiguas posesiones españolas de América y Oceania*, 42 vols. (Madrid, 1864–84), 30:146.

16. Gonzalo Fernández de Oviedo, *Historia general de las Indias*, reprint (Madrid: Biblioteca de Autores Españoles, 1959), 4:58.

and their obligation to obey Christians . . . men [that is, Portuguese men] would have legitimate slaves captured in just wars, and they would also have the service and servitude of the Indians in the missions. The land would be full of colonizers. Our Lord would gain many souls, and your majesty would receive great income from this land."[17]

Worst of all is the fact that the queen and king of Spain, the "converters" to whom Fernández de Oviedo and Manoel da Nóbrega refer, as well as the colonizers who exploited the Indians, were all sincere Christians. They were not people who simply sat down and calculated, coming to the conclusion that it was to their advantage to convert the natives of these lands. For them the service of God and the service of their own interests were one and the same. That is precisely why the episode about Demetrius is so relevant: the text does not give the slightest indication that Demetrius and his colleagues were hypocrites who consciously used the existing devotion to the goddess to protect their interests. On the contrary, throughout the narrative the two motivations are confused and what begins as a business discussion ends as a religious riot.

What happened at the time of Paul and at the time of the *Conquista* still happens in our hemisphere, where all sorts of religious and political interests are disguised as religion. A few years ago, while teaching in Puerto Rico, I received a long, strange, and unexpected letter containing all sorts of pseudo-theological arguments against cremation and in favor of embalming and waterproof vaults. The author was convinced that any good Christian would wish to be embalmed and buried in a vault, "while expecting the final resurrection." I found the letter intriguing, but did not quite understand its significance until I read the last paragraph, where the author claimed that he was quite qualified to discuss such matters, as he was himself an undertaker! Had he been a silversmith in the first century, that good gentleman would probably have shouted with equal sincerity and fervor, "Great is Artemis of the Ephesians."

That particular case bordered on the ridiculous; but others are tragic. If one among us dares insist that justice must be done toward the needy, affirming that this is what Scripture commands, there are some who do not even bother to consider whether this is true or not. They simply accuse this particular person of being a communist or a heretic. They insist that what the Bible tells us to do is simply to preach the "gospel" (as they understand it), and they excommunicate or at least shun those who disagree. Even worse, there have been cases in which, even beyond excommunication, a particular person has been denounced before the authorities. And the greatest tragedy of all is that it would seem that people who take such actions sincerely believe that they are doing so as Christians! What frequently happens in such cases, as in that of Demetrius, is that someone whose interests are threatened creates the necessary atmosphere, arousing religious fervor against those who seem to produce the threat, and from that point on the blind sincerity of many believers takes care of the matter. "Great is Artemis of the Ephesians!"

---

17. *Monumenta Historica Soietatis Iesus. Monumenta Brasiliae* (Roma, 1965ss), 2:122.

There is more. The intervention of the town clerk of Ephesus reminds us that the Ephesians do not stand alone in the world, nor are they masters of their own destiny. Above them there is the Roman Empire. Among us, those who take the actions just described are not their own masters. About them there are other interests and powers. There are mission boards. There are individuals, societies, and enterprises that provide financial resources for the Church. There are political relationships that must be respected. In order to understand what really takes place when people are declared to be heretical because they threaten someone's interest, it is necessary to understand that complex web of relationships, just as in order to understand the intervention of the town clerk one must remember the relationship between the Ephesians and the empire.

In the case of the riot in Ephesus, the intervention of the town clerk benefits the Christians, for the riot is dissolved. But that is not always the case. In John 11:48 we have a situation with the oppostie outcome. Jesus has just raised Lazarus from the dead. One would expect that the leaders of the people would acclaim and acknowledge his power. However, what they do is to gather and come to the conclusion that they must seek to kill Jesus, because "if we let him go on like this, everyone will believe in him, and the Romans will come and destroy both our holy place and our nation." The leaders of Israel, just like the town clerk in Ephesus, and just as many leaders in our hemisphere and churches, are not really their own masters. Therefore sometimes they act in one way, and sometimes in another, not according to truth but as best serves the interests above them.

What are we to do in such a situation? First of all, we must examine ourselves. Could it be that in some matter on which I am convinced that my attitude is simply the expression of my sincere faith I am in truth serving my own interests or the interests of those whom I wish to please? Second, we must be "wise as serpents." If something is obvious in this passage, it is that Luke was wise. Here, as in the early chapters of Acts, he shows that he understands the complex situation in which the gospel is being proclaimed in his time. Like Luke, we must try to understand what is happening around us, and to understand it in the profound sense of analyzing the powers and interests that are at play. Third, and most important, we must be faithful in the midst of all those interests. Paul was a Roman citizen. We have already seen him appeal to that citizenship, but that does not lead him to defend the empire. No matter how much protection Caesar and his order may provide for him (although in the end it would be at the hands of Caesar's servants that he would die), Paul's task is not to defend Caesar, but to proclaim Jesus. His task is to proclaim Jesus as sovereign ruler, before whom every other rule must yield. If the result is that he is accused of being subversive, that is the price to be paid for obedience.

D. JOURNEY TO MACEDONIA, GREECE, AND TROAS (20:1–12)

1. The Journey (20:1–6)

These six verses summarize a long trip. Although Paul has decided to go to Jerusalem, he does not travel directly to that city, which is toward the east, but rather goes in the opposite direction, toward Macedonia and Greece. Luke does not give the reason for this detour. From Paul's Epistles we know that a significant part of his mission was promoting and collecting the offering for Jerusalem, and that one of the reasons for his extensive travel through Macedonia and Greece was precisely to gather that offering. It would also seem that several of Paul's companions, whom Luke mentions here, were representatives of those churches who were to go with Paul and the offering to Jerusalem.

There is not much to be said about these companions. Sopater and Secundus are never mentioned elsewhere. Trophimus appears again in 21:29, and then in II Timothy 4:20. Tychicus is only mentioned in this verse in Acts, but appears quite often in the Epistles (Eph. 6:21, Col. 4:7, II Tim. 4:12, Tit. 3:12). We have already encountered Aristarchus in 19:29 and will meet him again in 27:2. Paul also mentions him in Colossians 4:10 and Philemon 24. Timothy is one of the better known characters in the New Testament. The one who presents a problem is Gaius. In 19:29 he was mentioned together with Aristarchus, as both being from Macedonia. Here we are told that he was from Derbe. Because Derbe is not in Macedonia, it would seem that we are dealing here with a different person (see also Rom. 16:23 and I Cor. 1:14). However, here the Western text does not read "Gaius from Derbe," but "Gaius from Doberes." Doberes was a small town in Macedonia, and if this is correct this Gaius is the same as the one in 19:29. What is not clear is whether the original reading is that of the Western text or whether "Doberes" is simply an attempt to correct the inconsistency implied in Gaius's being from Derbe.

Verse 5 does not make very clear who went ahead. It could be only Tychicus and Trophimus, or all seven who are mentioned in verse 4.

Paul's route takes him from Ephesus across the Aegean to Macedonia, then overland to Greece. It would have been normal then to return by sea to Asia, and then to Jerusalem. However, Paul decides to return by land to Philippi, where he and his companions (exactly which among them is not clear) celebrate Passover, in order then to cross the sea. The five-day voyage to Troas is the same that earlier, in the opposite direction, had only taken two days (16:11–12).

2. Eutychus (20:7–12)

In Troas Paul spends seven days, and it is toward the end of that stay that the episode regarding Eutychus takes place. The "first day of the week" to which the text refers could have been Sunday evening, but it could also have been Saturday at the same time, for according to the Jewish way of counting the new day begins at dusk. Therefore, what to us would be Saturday evening to them would be the first day of the week. There is ample evidence that at least by the second century Christians celebrated the resurrection of the Lord by gathering in a long vigil that began Saturday night and ended with baptisms and the breaking of the bread early Sunday morning. This was usually done on Easter Sunday, but parallel to it every other Sunday was a small Easter, and every Friday was a small Good Friday. At any rate, the disciples in Troas are gathered "to break bread," but Paul addresses them at length. This also was customary in ancient worship, in which first there was a rather extensive exposition of Scripture and then communion itself: the service of the word, and the service of the table. It is in the middle of this gathering, because of Paul's long preaching, and perhaps also because of the heat and the stale air produced by the "many lamps," that young Eutychus falls asleep while he sits at a window on the third floor.[18]

The story is clear, and does not need much comment. Overcome by sleep, Eutychus falls from the window to the street and dies. Paul goes out to the street, picks up the young man, proclaims that he lives, and simply returns to the third story, where the believers break bread and Paul continues preaching extensively. It is only after all of this and Paul's departure that Luke tells us that in fact "they had taken the boy away alive and were not a little comforted."

THE GREATEST MIRACLE

The more one studies this passage, the more surprising it becomes. First of all, one may be surprised at the freedom with which Luke affirms that Paul, his hero, preached so long that people went to sleep. Luke has no intention of exalting Paul, praising him as the greatest preacher of all times. Here, one almost reads between the lines an undertone of criticizing Paul because he is too long-winded. That alone would suffice to see the importance of this text in our context, where so often we so exalt our leaders—including our religious leaders—that we act as if to find any defect in them were a sign of disloyalty. There are preachers who like to present themselves as almost superhuman characters, the most eloquent of all time, the holiest, those with the greatest faith, those who perform most miracles, and so on. But here Luke presents us a human Paul, capable of putting his audience to sleep, as can happen to any of us any day.

However, the most surprising twist in the text itself is the course of its narrative. When we first read this story, what stands out is the resurrection of Eutychus—whose name means "fortunate." As Jesus did before with Lazarus, and Peter with Tabitha, now Paul snatches Eutychus from the hands of death. However, when we continue studying the text, that is not the most surprising. More surprising is the manner in which Luke deals with the young man's resurrection, and how he describes the reaction of the church to this event. At other times, after telling us about a miracle, Luke adds that those who witnessed it were awed, or that they rejoiced, or that they in some other way expressed their surprise. Here, however, things go on as if the raising of Eutychus were simply a parenthesis in the midst of something of greater importance.

The story evolves in two stages. First of all, when the young man falls and dies, Paul interrupts his preaching, goes to the young man, and announces that he is to live. He does not say simply that nothing must interrupt the service or that the solemnity of the occasion requires that he keep on preaching, but rather

---

18. A third floor according to the American, rather than the European way of counting stories. See D. F. Deer, "Getting the 'story' straight in Acts 20.9," *BibTrans*, 39 (1988), 246–47.

stops what he is doing, goes to the young man, and responds to his need. The church interrupts its inner life in favor of the needy.

Unfortunately, that is a lesson that we have not always learned. Sometimes we give the impression that the internal life of the Church is what is most important, and that all the needs of the world that we see are only interruptions or, in the best of cases, opportunities that we have to present the message of the Church and to invite others to join us. In the case of Eutychus, it becomes clear that Paul's God is not only the God of the Church, but is the God of life, who responds to the powers of death. We live in a continent where the powers of death seem to have camped. Hunger, illiteracy, malnutrition, lack of land, the exploitation of labor, and a thousand similar situations give the impression that death has the last word. In such circumstances, it is urgent and necessary that the Church be ready to interrupt its own agenda in order to serve the God of life.

However, even more surprising is the second moment of the narrative: Paul and the believers return and continue their worship. The miracle of the resurrection of Eutychus certainly causes them great comfort (v. 12); but it is not a reason to boast nor to abandon the worship of God and going out on the streets shouting and announcing the great miracle that God has performed. Why is this? Certainly not because the miracle is small, but rather because there is an even greater miracle: the life itself of the Church, and the presence of God in its common life and in the breaking of bread. It is not that they do not perceive the miracle of raising Eutychus; it is rather that they are listening to the word of God, and the activity of that word is more miraculous, more powerful, more surprising, more awe-inspiring, than the resurrection of a dead person.

The Book of Acts speaks of a God who performs wonders. There is ample proof of that in the book itself. But what we must never forget is that God's greatest wonder is redemption in Jesus Christ, and having created a Church out of people such as ourselves (or such as the first disciples, or the Christians of Troas). Certainly, God's power is manifest in the raising of Eutychus. But it is even more manifest in the raising of each of us, born anew, torn away from a life devoted to the powers of death and born to a life of service to the living God. And born again to a new community of love and of sharing, such as the one gathered that night at Troas in order to break bread. That is the greatest miracle in the entire Book of Acts. Without it, the rest makes no sense. Next to it, the rest pales in comparison.

The Church is a miracle. That is the central theme of Acts. It is a miracle of Jesus through the Spirit. If the Church itself is not a miracle, if the life and action of the Church are so routine that we need other miracles in order to confirm our faith, perhaps we need to rediscover what Acts tells us about the activity of the Spirit in the Church.

E. FAREWELL AT MILETUS (20:13–38)

1. From Troas to Miletus (20:13–16)

In a few words, Luke summarizes the trip to Miletus, some fifty kilometers from Ephesus. The Western text adds a stop at Trogylion, which is why some English versions also add it. Luke also tells us that the reason Paul did not return to Asia and to his beloved church in Ephesus was that he was in a hurry to reach Jerusalem before Pentecost. It is not clear whether this means that Paul feared that if he stopped at Ephesus his friends there would force him to remain longer, or if it was simply a matter of taking the first ship available sailing east, and that this particular ship did not stop at Ephesus.

2.   Farewell to the Ephesian Elders (20:17–38)

Paul sends a message to Ephesus, so that the elders from that church could come to see him at Miletus. Because between Miletus and Ephesus there are fifty kilometers, the round trip of the elders must have taken at least three days, and probably much more. Therefore, one may suppose that the ship stopped at Miletus, and that Paul made use of the occasion, while the ship was being unloaded and reloaded, to meet with the elders.

This speech appears between two "we" sections, but one is to suppose that the narrator, perhaps Luke himself, was present. There is no doubt that there are here several phrases and theological perspectives that have a clear Pauline flavor, and therefore it would seem that although Luke has summarized a conversation that must have taken hours and perhaps even days, the essence of what he tells comes from Paul himself.[19] The speech may be divided into four parts:[20]

a. Paul's Past Work (20:18–21)

The first few verses of the speech are devoted to a review of Paul's previous work. Apparently this review is here to assert Paul's authority to speak to the elders as he does.

b. Paul's Present Situation (20:22–24)

"Now" says Paul, and this brings his speech to the present moment. He is on the way to Jerusalem "a captive to the Spirit." This may be understood in various ways. First, it may mean that Paul feels an inner impulse to go to Jerusalem. In that case, the "spirit" is his human spirit. Second, it may mean that Paul already knows that he will be a captive in Jerusalem. In this case, the phrase is an announcement of what will happen in Jerusalem: he already "in the spirit" lives what will be his future. Finally, and most likely, the "spirit" may here refer to the Holy Spirit. (In ancient Greek manuscripts there is no distinction made such as capitalizing "Spirit" when the word refers to the Holy Spirit, and not when it refers to the human spirit.) In this last case, what Paul means

---

19. William Neil, *The Acts of the Apostles* (Grand Rapids, Mich.: Wm. B. Eerdmans, 1973), pp. 213–15, lists a series of parallelisms between this speech and Paul's Epistles. Because Luke does not appear to have known those Epistles, or to have used them in writing Acts, this would seem to indicate that he actually heard Paul say similar words.

20. There is a somewhat different outline in F. Zeilinger, "Lukas, Anwalt des Paulus: Überlegungen zur Abschiedsrede von Milet. Apg. 20, 18–35," *BibLitur*, 54 (1981), 167–72.

is that it is the Holy Spirit who compels him to go to Jerusalem. Certainly in the next verse Paul declares that he has already been warned by the Holy Spirit about what awaits him there, and that this warning has come repeatedly—"in every city." Because such repeated warnings have not appeared in the earlier chapters of Acts, this reminds us once again that Luke does not seek to tell us every detail of what happened in each place.

At any rate, in spite of such warnings, Paul has decided to continue his trip to Jerusalem, which leads us back to the parallelism between this resolve on Paul's part and what Luke tells us elsewhere, that Jesus "set his face" to go to Jerusalem (see commentary on 19:21). According to some manuscripts of verse 24, if all of this is fulfilled, Paul will finish his career "with joy."

c. The Future (20:25–31)

This section of the speech begins like the previous one: "and now" (the same phrase that appears in verse 22). Paul begins by giving them the sad news that he will not see them again.[21] In consequence, no longer will he be responsible for their spiritual well-being: "I am not responsible for the blood of any of you." That task will now belong to these elders whom Paul has called together: "Keep watch over yourselves and over all the flock."

The word in verse 28 that the NRSV translates as "overseers" is literally "bishops." Later, as the hierarchy of the Church develops, there will be a distinction between a bishop and an elder. However, that distinction does not appear here yet. In this case, it would seem that the term "elder" refers to the office, whereas the "episcopate" or overseeing is the function of these elders.

The reason these elders must be particularly attentive is that there will be "savage wolves." Continuing with the image of the flock, Paul now speaks of those who destroy that flock or steal its sheep as wolves. Those mentioned in verse 29 seem to be coming from outside, whereas the false teachers in verse 30 will rise up "even from your own group." There may be a reference here to the two heretical movements that most frequently afflicted Christianity in its early years: the "Judaizing" tendencies against which Paul frequently wrote, and the beginnings of Gnosticism, to which he also seems to refer in some of his letters.

d. Conclusion (20:32–38)

Finally, Paul takes leave of them, commending them to God and to the message of grace, which "is able to build you up and to give you the inheritance among all who are sanctified." What this means is that once Paul is no longer with them, they will still have the power to continue being built up on the foundation that the apostle has placed and to resist the false teachers that will arise.

---

21. This seems to contradict the pastoral Epistles, which indicate that Paul did return to Ephesus after his imprisonment in Rome. This is one of the many reasons numerous scholars believe that the pastorals were not penned by Paul himself.

Verses 30 to 35, which at first reading seem to be out of place, point to a fundamental concern on Paul's part. The economic life of the Church is not a peripheral or secondary matter. On the contrary, it is an essential part of the life of the Church. That is why Paul reminds these elders who will soon lack his direction that he himself has not sought after "silver or gold or clothing." Clothing is listed because at that time, before weaving machines or synthetic products were invented, clothing was expensive, and having several outfits was a sign of wealth. Paul himself, instead of asking for money, has "worked with my own hands," and with them has earned sustenance, not only for himself, but also for his companions. The consequence of all of this is that "by such work we must support the weak." And it all ends with words that Paul attributes to Jesus, but which may not be found in any of our present Gospels: "It is more blessed to give than to receive."

Finally, having concluded his speech, Paul kneels to pray. In the ancient Church, prayer was normally done standing, with extended hands. Kneeling was a sign of a solemn and deeply felt petition.

The ensuing farewell is highly emotional. There is much weeping, and the elders embrace and kiss Paul, finally going with him to the ship.

MINISTRY TODAY

Paul's speech in Miletus has frequently been used as a model for successive generations of ministers. There is ample reason for this, for here we hear both about Paul's ministry, summarized in a few lines, and about the ministry of his successors.

Following that line of interpretation and applying it more directly to the situation of churches in Latin America and among Hispanics in the United States, two points are worth making:

The first regards the function of these elders, presbyters, or bishops who are to make certain that there is correct teaching within the Church. Just as in the generations that immediately followed Paul the Church had to face doctrines that threatened the integrity of the gospel, so today in our churches we are threatened by similar doctrines. In the ancient Church those doctrines were essentially two: Judaizing Christianity and Gnosticism. In our churches today, the doctrines threatening us are similar to those two.

Judaizing Christianity insisted that, although Jesus had come to save the world, salvation really depended on believers keeping the Law. This would seem to be no more than an addition to the message of the gospel, and therefore a rather innocuous suggestion. But Paul saw things differently, for he was convinced that this was in fact a threat to the very heart of the gospel. If in order to be saved what one has to do is to obey the Law, the death of Christ was unnecessary, and the grace of God is useless.

One does not have to be very observant to realize that today similar teachings threaten our churches. One often hears that "yes, the grace of Christ suffices, but one has to. . . ." At that point each one adds what is imagined one has to do in order to be a true Christian. Some insist on the dietary rules of the Old

Testament. Others say something about dress, about adornment in women, about alcoholic beverages, or about social action. The fact is that all of these doctrines, no matter how called—"conservative" or "liberal," "reactionary" or "radical"—if they somehow add requirements to the grace of God, are similar to the Judaizing tendencies against which Paul wrote. Grace certainly does impel us to behave in a certain way; but such behavior is not a prerequisite for grace. We do not receive grace because we behave as we ought, but rather we behave as we ought because we know the grace of God.

Gnostics, the other doctrine that threatened and twisted the gospel in ancient times, claimed to be more "spiritual" than common Christians. Gnostics believed that material things were evil, or at least contemptible. What was important was the "spiritual." Truly spiritual Christians are not to be interested in the body—neither theirs, nor the bodies of others, nor their physical needs—but rather should be concerned only about their spiritual lives. In the end, this world is not our concern, but only the coming one that is purely spiritual. Ancient Christians had to struggle firmly and mightily against such teachings, which questioned not only fundamental aspects of Christian life, but also doctrines such as creation, the incarnation of God in Jesus Christ, and the resurrection of the body.

Such doctrines, which have appeared repeatedly in the history of the church, have become particularly attractive in Latin America and in Hispanic churches in the United States in recent years. As social, economic, and political circumstances become more difficult and violent, increasing numbers of Christians have found refuge in such doctrines and attitudes. If what is important is the salvation of the soul, and God is not concerned over the body, I do not have to worry much if in my country the bodies of people deemed subversive are tortured, or peasants lose their lands, or ethnic minorities do not receive education. In countries suffering growing social and economic tensions, or even civil war, the Church then becomes a spiritual refuge, where one need not worry or even be concerned over such matters. Furthermore, these tendencies sometimes are supported with economic and personal resources provided by people interested in keeping peace and order at all costs, and thus a false Christianity is promoted that does not deserve the name of the incarnate Lord Jesus Christ.

The second point at which this particular speech is relevant for our situation is the economic matter that Paul brings up at the end of his speech. Here three points are evident: first, Paul has not requested gold or silver; second, the elders are to follow his example; third, the purpose of all of this is to help the needy.

The first thing that this text tells us is that the economic life of the Church is not a peripheral matter, nor is it a mere utilitarian process whereby the Church meets its expenses. It is not simply a matter of the Church's having to have a budget, because otherwise it could not manage in the world in which we live. It is also and above all that such a budget, like the entire life of the Church, must reflect the gospel and its values. Unfortunately, this is not always true in our churches. For instance, there are in Latin American churches foreign missionaries who receive a higher salary than do national workers, and the difference is such that the natives live in misery, whereas the missionaries live much better than their own congregations. There are denominations where it is thought that in order truly to be a church it is necessary to be able to pay the salary of a full-time pastor, and then the entire economic effort of the church is devoted to sustaining the ordained ministry. In such cases, the possibility should be considered of having pastors who, like Paul, earn at least part of their sustenance in a different way, and serve the church during their free time. There are also evangelists who, thanks to radio and television, build vast economic empires, and then live in an opulence in which myriad poor and naive believers support them. Furthermore, no matter what the size of our churches and congregations, the fact is that in most of them most economic resources are devoted to the life of the church itself: a pastor's salary, the building and maintenance of buildings, furniture, and so on.

What Paul suggests in this passage is very different from all that. Helping the needy must be an essential part of the economic life of the Church. Frequently, in collecting an offering, we quote verse 35: "It is more blessed to give than to receive." But when we come to the point of managing the funds of the Church we forget those words. For the Church, as well as for individuals, it is more blessed to give than to receive, and the fidelity of a church, like the fidelity of each believer, must be measured, not on the basis of how much it receives, but on the basis of how much it gives.

8

Paul's Captivity
(21:1–28:31)

We now come to the last main section of the Book of Acts. Here what Paul indicated earlier will be fulfilled, that he was going to Jerusalem in spite of the chains awaiting him there. But much more than that is also fulfilled, for Paul, who had always wished to go to Rome, finally reaches the capital, although now as a prisoner.

A. FROM MILETUS TO JERUSALEM (21:1–16)

The narrative continues in the first person plural, "we." Who is included in this group is not altogether clear. In the rest of the narrative, besides Paul and the narrator himself, Trophimus and Aristarchus will be mentioned. Nor is it clear whether the others mentioned earlier are still part of the group, or have parted from it. At any rate, the journey continues, apparently in the same ship, along the coast, sailing from Miletus to Cos, then to Rhodes, and finally to Patara.[1] There they take a different ship, probably larger, which sails more directly toward Palestine. They sail south of Cyprus and eventually reach Tyre.

In Tyre the group meets with "the disciples," that is, the believers in that city. (Acts does not tell us how the gospel reached Tyre, and the verb that the NRSV translates as "looked up" implies that they had to be sought.) There the believers tell Paul "through the Spirit" that he should not go to Jerusalem. The farewell is emotional (vv. 5–6), and reminds us of Paul's leave-taking from Miletus.

From Tyre, after a stop of a day in Ptolemais and a visit to believers in that city, the group continues to Caesarea. The manner in which Luke describes the trip from Ptolemais to Caesarea ("the next day we left and came to Caesarea,"

---

1. The Western text takes the group to Myra, eighty kilometers further east, and it is there that they take a ship toward Tyre.

verse 8) seems to imply that they landed in Ptolemais and then went on to Caesarea either by land or in another ship.

In Caesarea, Paul and his companions lodge at the house of Philip, whom Luke calls "the evangelist" in order to distinguish him from the apostle. This Philip is the same one we met in chapter 8, evangelizing Samaria and the Ethiopian eunuch. Luke tells us that he "had four unmarried daughters who had the gift of prophesy"—that is, who interpreted the word and preached. Contrary to what is often thought, in the primitive Church there were indeed women in positions of leadership and, as shown in this case, women who did preach and prophesy.[2]

In verse 10 Agabus is introduced as if we had not heard of him before, in 11:28. After the style of the prophets of the Old Testament, Agabus illustrates his prophecy through action (see, for instance, Jer. 13:1–11, where the prophet, like Agabus here, uses a belt). Paul's "belt," which Agabus takes, is probably not a leather belt, but rather a long cloth that was usually worn by wrapping it around the body several times, and which was also used for carrying money and other small objects.[3] Tying himself with the belt, Agabus announces that the Jews will tie Paul and "will hand him over to the Gentiles." This is the theme of the rest of the book.

Even though the prophet speaks through the Spirit, Paul's companions, including the narrator, try to dissuade Paul from going to Jerusalem. It is only when Paul insists on doing so that they finally say, "The Lord's will be done." The group spends eight days in Caesarea, and then leaves for Jerusalem. What the NRSV translates as "we got ready" may refer to obtaining mounts for the trip to Jerusalem, a distance of one hundred kilometers. They are accompanied by the Cypriot Mnason, at whose home they plan to lodge. It is not clear whether this means that during the trip they will stop at Mnason's place, on the road to Jerusalem, or Mnason actually lived in the city, and it was there that they would lodge with him.[4]

THE MANDATES OF THE SPIRIT

This passage, apparently so simple, actually involves a serious difficulty. Already in verse 4 we were told that Christians at Tyre, inspired by the Spirit, told Paul that he should not go to Jerusalem. Before, Paul has already declared that he is

---

2. Some have speculated that it was perhaps from these daughters of Philip, or from Philip himself, that Luke heard much of what he tells in the early chapters of Acts, especially what refers to the election of the "seven" and Philip's ministry (William Neil, *The Acts of the Apostles* [Grand Rapids, Mich.: Wm. B. Eerdmans, 1973], pp. 216–17).

3. E. Haenchen, *The Acts of the Apostles: A Commentary* (Philadelphia: Westminster, 1975), p. 601.

4. The Western text clarifies the matter indicating that Mnason lived in a village halfway between the two cities, and that it was there that he offered them lodging. See E. Delebecque, "La dernière étape du troisième voyage missionaire de saint Paul selon les deux versions des Actes des Apôtres," *RevThLouv*, 14 (1983), 446–55.

going to Jerusalem under the guidance of the Spirit. Then, in verse 11, Agabus tells him what will happen in Jerusalem, although he makes no attempt to dissuade Paul from going there. The disciples, on the other hand (including the narrator himself), seek to convince Paul that he should not go to Jerusalem (v. 12).[5] Does the Spirit then give contradictory messages? Some scholars simply conclude that "Luke did not see the difficulty in which he was here entangled."[6]

Perhaps there is another answer. Perhaps Luke is suggesting that the Spirit acts differently from how we might imagine. The commonly held view is that the Spirit acts in such a way that every doubt disappears, letting us know exactly what we are to do. But perhaps Luke, while insisting on the importance of taking the direction of the Spirit seriously, is also telling us that the Spirit must not be taken as a crutch on which to rest and thus avoid making difficult decisions. In Acts, the Spirit does not tell Paul exactly what he has to do, and then confirms this with a series of prophecies that all clearly agree. On the contrary, the Spirit impels Paul to go to Jerusalem, but then also uses other people to warn him about the price of going there. The final decision is still in Paul's hands.

This would seem to lessen the importance and authority of the Spirit, but in truth it is the opposite. If Acts were to depict a Church in which the Spirit tells Christians exactly what they are to do at each step, that in itself would make it less relevant for us, for our frequent experience is that, even though the Spirit speaks to us and guides us, all of our decisions have the sign of risk and of ambiguity that is characteristic of every human action. We cannot hide behind the Spirit and simply say "the Spirit told me to do it." But, for the same reason, nor can we hide behind the lack of clear directions in order to do nothing.

Not understanding this is one of the reasons that in many of our churches we hesitate to take action. We idealize the work of the Spirit in Acts and throughout the New Testament. We imagine that when the Spirit speaks humans always know exactly what they are to do. Therefore, when there are doubts about which action to take, we convince ourselves that we must do nothing, because the Spirit has not spoken, or because we have heard contradictory voices. Had Paul done this, he would not have gone to Jerusalem. The fact is that practically all decisions that Christians and the Church must make occur in such situations. There is unemployment in our city. What are we to do? Certainly, we are to pray and to ask for the direction of the Spirit. But, does this mean that we ought not to do anything as long as we do not receive a clear revelation, telling us what we are to do at each step? Certainly not. The Spirit, by means of the Scriptures, by means of the teachings of Jesus, by means of the new life inspired in us, has already given us sufficient direction so that we at least know that we must take action. To sit around waiting until we receive a detailed and clear mandate is a mere excuse not to do what we know we ought.

---

5. This was already pointed out in the nineteenth century by W. M. L. de Wette, *Kurze Erklarung der Apostelgeschichte* (Leipzig: Weidmann, 1870), p. 356.

6. Haenchen, *Acts*, p. 602.

B. TURNED OVER TO THE GENTILES (21:17–22:24)

1. Arrival at Jerusalem (21:17–25)

In this section of the book we are told about Paul's arrival at Jerusalem, his arrest at the Temple, his defense, and how he was finally turned over to the Romans. The use of the first person plural in the narrative ("we") ends at verse 18, and does not reappear until Paul leaves for Rome (27:1). This could be explained as a theological key;[7] but the simplest explanation is that throughout the process in Jerusalem the author is interested in what happens to Paul, and not to the rest of the group. Although the narrator quite likely was present throughout these events, he was a spectator or a witness rather than a participant, and for that reason the subject of the narrative, rather than the former "we," is Paul.

Apparently, the "brothers" who received Paul and his companions "warmly" in verse 17 do not include James and the elders, who do not appear in the narrative until the next day, when Paul and his companions visit them (v. 18). Therefore, it is possible that upon arriving at Jerusalem Paul contacts first the more Hellenistic elements in the church (on these elements and their conflicts with the "Hebrews," see the commentary on 6:1–6), in order to visit the leaders of the old church of Jerusalem the next day. Apparently among the latter the "Hebrews"—that is, Palestinian Jews whose language was Aramaic—were still dominant.

Luke makes no mention of the offering that Paul was bringing, but one may suppose that at the time of this visit he handed it over to James and the leaders of the church in Jerusalem, the "elders." Who these elders were is not known, and there is no indication as to how they were selected or what authority they held. Two things are apparent: First, the "Twelve" are no longer in Jerusalem, or at least Peter, who is such an important character in the early chapters of Acts, is no longer there. Otherwise, Luke would have mentioned him. Second, there were several of these leaders, for Luke tells us that "all the elders" were there.

When James and the elders learn from Paul about the mission among the Gentiles, they praise God. But immediately they tell Paul of the problem posed by his presence. There are in Jerusalem large numbers of Jews who have believed the gospel, but who are "zealous for the law." Among them the rumor is running that in Paul's mission among the Gentiles, he has told the Jews that they no longer have to obey the Law of Moses nor to circumcise their sons. The leaders of the church fear their reaction—some manuscripts even imply a possible riot or commotion. In order to avoid this, they suggest the actions

---

7. For instance, Josep Rius-Camps, *El camino de Pablo a la misión a los paganos* (Madrid: Cristiandad, 1984), pp. 228–36, claims that the disappearing of the "we" throughout most of Paul's sojourn in Jerusalem is an indication that the Spirit does not agree with his attitude of compromise with the Judaizing elements within the Church. This is hardly convincing.

Paul should take in order to show these Jews who are "zealous for the law" that he himself is still a good Jew, faithful to the customs of Moses.

What James and the elders suggest is spelled out in verses 23 and 24. Paul is to join four men who have made a nazirite vow, and to cover their expenses, thus showing that he is still respectful of the Law. However, difficulties arise when one seeks to reconcile what is said here with what is known from other sources about the nazirites' vow.[8] Certainly, Paul cannot join the nazirites in their vows, for this would require at least thirty days of residence in Jerusalem.[9] Most probably Paul is not being told to join the nazirites in their vows, but simply to follow the rites of purification (as he has just returned from Gentile lands), and also to pay the expenses of the four nazirites. It was hoped that by having Paul show that he still sought purification after returning from other lands, and that he even went beyond the required, rumors would be quieted. Verse 25 repeats the decision of the so-called council of Jerusalem regarding what was to be required of Gentiles converted to Christianity.[10]

2. Paul's Arrest at the Temple (21:26-36)

Paul begins to do what has been suggested. Having gone through the purification rites with the nazirites and entering the Temple—actually, its outer courts, which were considered part of the sacred enclosure—he announces his purpose of following the necessary rites for his own purification, which will take seven days (to which v. 27 refers), and also to present the offering that was due from the four nazirites.

All goes well until shortly before the seven days are up, when the storm breaks. The cause is a group of Jews from Asia—that is, from one of the areas in which Paul had worked most intensively. Their presence in Jerusalem might indicate that Paul had indeed reached the Holy City before Pentecost, for these Jews from Asia may be pilgrims who have come for the feast. Paul is accused of teaching against three things (v. 28): "our people, our law, and this place." But, worst of all, he is accused of having profaned the Temple by bringing Greeks into it. Luke explains that they said this because they had seen Paul with Trophimus in the city, and they believed that he had also taken Trophimus to the Temple. Soon there is a riot that involves "all the city"—in what is probably a Lukan hyperbole. The mob seizes Paul and drags him out of the Temple, which is immediately shut. Because in Greek the subject of a verb is not necessarily expressed, in this particular case it is not clear whether those who seized Paul were actually the mob, or the Levites who guarded the Temple.

The news of the riot and of the proposed lynching reaches "the tribune of the cohort"—literally, the "leader of a thousand"—who commands the Ro-

---

8. See also the commentary on 18:18.

9. Some suggest that Luke simply did not know the details of nazirite practices, and therefore errs. See, for instance, Haenchen, *Acts*, pp. 610-14.

10. See the commentary on 15:22-29.

man garrison in Jerusalem. We will be told later (23:26) that his name was Claudius Lysias. It would not take much for the tribune to learn of the riot, for the headquarters of the Roman cohort in Jerusalem were in the Antonia tower, just above the corner of the Temple, and from it one could see most of what took place in the holy enclosure. Actually, in order to reach the site of the disorder from their own tower, Lysias and his soldiers only had to walk down the steps mentioned in verse 35.[11]

The tribune acts promptly. He arrests Paul and has him tied with two chains,[12] in order then to inquire about the identity of the prisoner and the reason for the riot. The crowd gives him contradictory answers, apparently because, as often happens in such situations, even those participating in the disorder are not quite sure of the reasons for it. What is quite clear is that they are enraged against Paul, who is carried away while the crowd shouts, "Away with him!"

3. Paul's Dialogue with Lysias (21:37–39)

Paul not only addresses the tribune in Greek, but does so in elegant and polished language. The tribune is surprised, for he had confused Paul with someone else: "Do you know Greek? Then you are not the Egyptian who recently stirred up a revolt and led the four thousand assassins out into the wilderness?" Jewish historian Flavius Josephus[13] has preserved some information about the nationalist movements that arose in Palestine at the time. Among them, Josephus refers to the "Sicarii," whose name is derived from "sica," or dagger. This is the name that the tribune gives to the "assassins" in Greek. The Sicarii stabbed their victims, often right in the middle of the crowds gathered for religious festivities, and then melted away among the crowd. Therefore, most of the Sicarii did not flee to the desert, but simply lived as apparently average persons in Jerusalem.[14] Josephus does speak of a certain "Egyptian" whom Lysias seems to have confused with Paul:

> In those days, a certain man from Egypt reached Jerusalem saying that he was a prophet and urging the multitudes of the people to go with him to the Mount of Olives, facing the city. . . . But when Felix learned of this, he ordered his soldiers to be armed, he went out with a large force of cavalry and infantry, and he attacked the Egyptian and his followers. He killed four hundred of them and captured two hun-

---

11. See Josephus, *War* 5.5.8.

12. On this, see the commentary on 12:6. Possibly Luke describes here a similar procedure to that applied to Peter earlier. In that case, Paul would be tied to two soldiers, one on each side.

13. *War* 2.13.3-6.

14. See R. A. Horsley and J. S. Hanson, *Bandits, Prophets, and Messiahs: Popular Movements at the Time of Jesus* (San Francisco: Harper & Row, 1985), pp. 200–16.

dred. The Egyptian fled during the battle and disappeared without a trace.[15]

If, as Josephus asserts, the Egyptian disappeared without leaving a trace, it is not surprising that Lysias, on seeing the riot, would think that this was the person who was being sought by the authorities. It is also interesting to note that Lysias confused the Egyptian with the Sicarii, as so often happens even today, when authorities, especially in oppressive regimes, confuse all who oppose them, as if they were an amorphous mass. On the other hand, one wonders why the fact that Paul knew Greek told Lysias that he was not the fugitive Egyptian. Most of the Jewish community in Egypt spoke Greek. But apparently Lysias knew that the "Egyptian" whose arrest was sought did not speak Greek. Still using very refined language, Paul answers that he is not Egyptian, but rather a Jew from Tarsus, and a citizen of that city. Later he will add that he is also a Roman citizen; but at first he does not mention this matter. Having provided that information, he insists on being allowed to speak to the people.

4. Paul's Speech to the People (21:40–22:24)

Having received permission from Lysias, Paul addresses the crowd "in the Hebrew language"—that is, in Aramaic. His speech is mostly autobiographical. It is here that we learn that Paul, even though he was originally from Tarsus, had been raised in Jerusalem, and had studied "at the feet of Gamaliel"—whom we have already met, 5:34–39. This is the second account in Acts of Paul's conversion. (The other two are in 9:1–19 and 26:12–18. Because the three episodes have already been compared while commenting on 9:1–19, it is not necessary to examine this particular account in detail.)

In verses 17–21 we learn something new. In Jerusalem, precisely at the Temple, Paul had an extasis in which Jesus ordered him to leave Jerusalem, "because they will not accept your testimony about me," and "for I will send you far away to the Gentiles."

If the crowd was silent to this point, they can take no more. In a few words Paul has doubly offended them. First of all, he has dared say that it was precisely in that holy place that Jesus spoke to him. It is important to remember that this was the place where the God of Israel has spoken to some of the prophets (for instance, to Isaiah in Isa. 6). By implication, Paul is equating Jesus with the God of the Temple, and establishing a parallelism between himself and Isaiah, whose message was also addressed to a people who did not wish to hear (Isa. 6:9: "Go and say to these people: 'keep listening, but do not understand; keep looking, but do not understand."'). And second, Paul has once again mentioned his mission to the Gentiles, which is precisely the reason for the riot, and has claimed that such a mission was the result of a mandate received in the very Temple.

15. *Ant.* 20.8.6. See also Josephus, *War* 2.13.6.

Once again the crowd calls for Paul's death: "Away with such a fellow from the earth! For he should not be allowed to live." The throwing off of their cloaks and tossing dust into the air, which may seem strange to us, were a sign of wrath, mourning, and bewilderment. In Job 2:12, for instance, when Job's three friends saw what had happened to him, "they raised their voices and wept aloud; they tore their robes and threw dust in the air upon their heads." This reaction of Job's three friends includes the same three elements found in 22:23: shouting, taking off of one's clothes, and throwing dust toward heaven.

The response of the tribune, in order to calm the situation, is to order the soldiers to take Paul into the fortress (he was already on the steps leading to it, v. 35), in order to inquire about the entire matter by having Paul flogged so he will tell the truth.

POWERS OF OPPOSITION

On reading through this passage, one is immediately struck by the manner in which Paul finds himself amidst various powers and interests, and how similar they are to those surrounding us today. Paul is first of all subjected to pressure by the leaders of the church in Jerusalem, who are concerned that Paul's activities may be misinterpreted. Rumors are circulating that Paul invites Jews to abandon the laws of Moses and the customs that are at the very heart of Jewish identity. James and the elders do not seem to have believed such rumors; but they also do not seem to have done much to counteract them. They do suggest to Paul to take some measures which, they say, will belie the rumors. But they do not offer to accompany him nor even to speak in his favor. Furthermore, from this point on they will never again be mentioned in Acts, while Paul is going through all the vicissitudes of his imprisonment. Sadly, it would seem that the solidarity and partnership of which the early chapters of Acts spoke is being diluted.

One does not have to go very far to see the relationship between that situation and the life of our churches, where gossip and rumor are powerful instruments of the devil. We often think that the problem lies only with the gossipmongers, who start rumors and circulate them for the mere pleasure of doing so, or with those who hear something and repeat it without making certain that it is true. But the problem goes much further, for it reaches also those who say that they do not believe the rumors, but still repeat them, or at least do not attempt to counteract them. There are even those who come to another and say, "You know? So-and-so is saying such and such about you"; but they do not seem to believe that they should confront so-and-so with the falseness of what is being said. In fact, in such a case they too become gossips, for instead of diminishing the power of the gossip, they now add another rumor, by speaking about the one whom they accuse of spreading rumors. In a way, this is what happens in the case of Paul and the leaders of the church in Jerusalem. Those leaders, instead of facing the evil rumors about Paul, bring their own gossip about those who are speaking about him. From this point on the church in Jerusalem begins to disappear from the scene; but it may also be the case that at this point that church begins to die. Gossip and rumor have a profoundly corrosive power in the life of the Church.

These believers in Jerusalem, while they tell Paul what he is to do in order to counteract the rumors, do not take a single step to join him in that task. When the Nazis occupied Denmark, they ordered that all Jews must wear the Star of David visibly on their clothing. It was clear that the purpose of that order was to facilitate the actions the occupying forces would take against Jews. The next day, the king of Denmark went out sporting a Star of David! He did not limit his action to counseling his Jewish subjects, but rather joined them in the risk they suffered. In a certain country in Latin America, where a dictator reigned, a woman threw a shoe at the dictator's image in the movies. The lights went on, and the chief of the guard announced that at the end of the movie they would find out quite easily who had been so lacking in respect for the ruler, for she would be missing a shoe. However, at the end of the movie, most of the women walked out barefooted! If this is done between a king and his subjects, or among fellow citizens, how much more should it be done among Christians! Jesus was not content with giving us good advice, but rather became one of us and participated in our pain and strife.

There are many of us in our churches quite ready to give sound advice to those who are going through difficulties, and to tell those who are the subject of gossip what they ought to do in such a situation. But that is not enough. If we are truly a body, the body of Christ, we must bear one another's burdens.

Second, there is the crowd of Jews. In the early chapters of Acts, we saw how the chiefs among the Jews (the main priests and the members of the Council) feared the people, who tended to favor Christians. Already at the time of Stephen's martyrdom we saw that for the first time it is the "people" who attack Christians. Now it is clear that the people have taken the side of the main priests and the religious and political leaders, to such a point that the riot takes place without those leaders having to provoke it. Later on the leaders of the people will appear again, seeking to destroy Paul. But in this particular passage it is simply some Jews from Asia and the mob who try to kill Paul. We can imagine Paul's pain, not only at the physical tragedy of his imprisonment, but also seeing that the Jewish people themselves had turned him over to the authorities, when it is actually "for the hope of Israel" (28:20) that he is imprisoned.

This too is part of the tragedy of our people. Many who have come to our defense, denouncing injustices committed against us and proclaiming a message of hope, have found themselves abandoned and even betrayed by the people whom they tried to serve. Naturally, much of this is due to the manner in which those who control information twist truth in order to drive a wedge between such potential leaders and the people. Remember what was said about the control of information in commenting on 4:13–22. At the end, the people become convinced that their defenders are in truth their enemies, and then become an instrument in order to achieve the destruction of those who were actually trying to help them.

The same happens in the Church. Throughout the history of the Church, there have been many who, for love of the Church itself, have sought to reform it. Most often, such people have been condemned as heretics, and expelled from the Church they loved. Does that not happen still quite often in our Latino churches? Do we not all know of a young person who, out of zeal and fervor for the Church, began suggesting ways in which the life of the Church could be improved, and was eventually excommunicated or expelled from the community?

Third, there is the tribune, who intervenes in the situation under the false impression that Paul was "the Egyptian," a famous subversive. He is not interested in saving Paul from the mob (although, as will be seen later on, in 23:27, when it suits his purposes, he claims that he intervened in order to save Paul). His interest is rather in saving his responsibility. If there is a riot while he and his soldiers are in the Antonia tower, it will be difficult for him to explain it to his superiors. That is the reason he intervenes. As a Roman and part of the army of occupation, he does not know much about the country itself or its interior religious conflicts. His only concern is to make certain that there is not a riot or a rebellion that may stain his record. He is particularly interested in capturing the famous "Egyptian." Any Jews who do not quite fit the order that Rome has imposed are the same to him, and therefore, he confuses that "Egyptian" with Paul and also with the Sicarii, paying no attention to the vast differences among these various elements. To Lysias, Paul, the Sicarii, and the "Egyptian" are all the same.

In recent decades, Latin America has seen many "tribunes" like Lysias. These are people whose only function in life is to keep the existing order at all costs, and for whom any who in any way or measure oppose or criticize that order are "subversive." Tragically, precisely because these people, like Lysias, do not make the necessary distinctions, hundreds and even thousands of people "disappear," or are tortured to force them to confess that they are indeed as subversive as the "tribunes" of national defense claim.

Similar situations, although fortunately usually with less tragic consequences, exist also in the Church. There are inquisitors who see heretics everywhere. In Latin America, the joke is often repeated, giving their full names, about the modern inquisitor who died in a traffic accident together with two theologians of more questionable opinions. Upon reaching the pearly gates, they were all told that they had to appear before the throne of the Most High in order to be examined as to their orthodoxy. The first theologian went in, was examined for half an hour and came out saying very sadly, "I did not pass." The second also went in, spent half an hour before the heavenly throne, and also came out saying very sadly, "I did not pass." The third, the famous inquisitor, entered to the Holy Chamber, was two minutes before the divine presence, and came out boasting very happily, "He didn't pass!"

Traditionally, Protestants have claimed that such attitudes existed only in the Roman Catholic Church. Yet, among Protestants similar events do take place. Instead of making the necessary distinctions, and trying to understand each person's perspective and what they are saying, we simply develop a series of labels or "intellectual sacks" in which to place people: "liberal," "reactionary," "communist," "rightist." Then we simply place each person in the sack that seems most appropriate, and we no longer have to deal with the matter. In the text we are studying, Lysias is surprised when Paul addresses him in refined Greek. He wonders, "Do you know Greek? Then you are not the Egyptian!" But too often we make certain that others do not surprise us. We already know that he is liberal, or fundamentalist, or reactionary, or leftist. However, when we lose the ability to be surprised by someone, we have lost the ability to listen, and therefore have dehumanized both that other person and ourselves.

Finally, we must look at Paul. His attitude throughout the entire narrative is interesting. He begins by accepting the advice of James and the elders, even though there is a certain risk in appearing publicly at the Temple. The church is divided because of rumors circulating about him, and he is ready to do whatever he can to counteract those rumors. Even after the riot begins, when the soldiers are carrying him toward the fortress, Paul insists in giving his witness, which deals both with Jesus Christ and with his own attitude toward Israel. His speech begins by emphasizing his connection with those who are listening. He is a Jew, raised in Jerusalem, educated by one of the greatest teachers of his time, "educated strictly according to our ancestral law, being zealous for God." He even gives those who are opposing him credit for having done this out of sincere religious motivation: "being zealous for God, just as all of you are today." It is on the basis of that relation that he offers his witness. It is on the same basis that they listen to him, until he comes to the point where he affirms something they cannot accept—that Jesus spoke to him in the Temple and sent him to the Gentiles. It is then that the multitude is aroused and Lysias orders Paul to be taken into the fort.

Paul's speech has several missiological implications. First, Paul acknowledges and underscores the ties between himself and his audience, and even gives them credit for their religious perceptions and traditions. This is contrary to much of what goes by the name of "evangelism" in many of our circles, where one begins by attacking the traditions and the culture of those who listen. It is also very different from a certain type of preaching that was quite common in many of our Hispanic communities, and is still heard, where we are told in a thousand ways that the entire Hispanic tradition and religiosity that we have learned from our ancestors have to be abandoned. No. Paul affirms the religiosity of those who listen. He does this not only to gain their good will, but also and above all because he truly appreciates that religiosity and those traditions. He certainly invites them to believe in Jesus; and in the end his insistence on the name of Jesus will renew the riot against him. But Paul does not preach Jesus by telling them first that they are worthless, that they are less than pagans, that their culture and traditions are from Satan. On the contrary, the message is one of love and of affirmation even for those who persecute him.

This is very different from what so often and in so many ways we have been taught—that in order to be true Christians we need to turn our backs on the cultural and religious traditions of our ancestors, as if they had been stubborn atheists, with no knowledge of God, or as if one could only be a Christian by accepting the foreign culture of the missionaries.

Thanks to God, the Protestant Church in Latin America is now reaching a certain maturity, and part of that maturity is precisely in being able to see the action and manifestation of God even where those early missionaries could not see it. On the basis of that vision of our culture and traditions, we begin to discover jointly with other Christians what it means to be both truly Latin and truly faithful to the gospel.

C. PAUL IN THE CUSTODY OF LYSIAS (22:25–23:33)

Up to this point, Lysias is intervening in what is after all a matter among Jews. Now, upon taking Paul as a prisoner, and especially from the moment that the apostle declares himself to be a Roman citizen, the entire Roman legal system comes into play.[16]

1. Paul Claims Roman Citizenship (22:25–29)

Paul is now tied "with thongs." This probably refers to tying him to a post in order to be flogged. It is at this point that Paul lets the centurion know that he is a Roman citizen. Immediately the centurion realizes the gravity of the situation,[17] and requests new instructions from the tribune. The latter comes to see Paul and asks him if it is true that he is a Roman citizen. His own comment about the price he had to pay for such citizenship probably implies that Paul must be a man of substance. The name of the tribune, *Claudius* Lysias, may be an indication that he bought his citizenship while Claudius was emperor, when Empress Messalina made significant profit by selling letters of citizenship.[18] In this case, Claudius would be his Roman name, taken in honor of the emperor on becoming a Roman citizen, and Lysias would be his Greek name.

There is no indication as to how Paul's ancestors acquired Roman citizenship. Perhaps one of them bought it, as did Lysias. At any rate, the result of Paul's declaration is that he is not tortured or flogged, and even the tribune fears the consequences of what he has done. Nor are we told how Paul proved that he was indeed a Roman citizen. It is known that to claim such citizenship falsely was a capital crime.[19]

---

16. On the juridical background of the entire book, and especially on items having to do with Roman citizenship and its privileges, see M. Black, "Paul and Roman law in Acts," *RestorQ*, 24 (1981), 209–18. On Paul's use of his citizenship, see R. J. Cassidy, *Society and Politics in the Acts of the Apostles* (Maryknoll, N.Y.: Orbis, 1968), pp. 100–103.

17. On this point, see the commentary on 16:37.

18. Dio Cassius, *Roman History* 60.17.

19. Epictetus, *Diatribes* 3.24, 41.

2. Paul before the Council (22:30–23:10)

The next day Lysias releases Paul, but still brings him to stand before a meeting of "the chief priests and the entire council." Such a meeting of the Jewish Council presents several difficulties. First of all, there is the matter of how Claudius Lysias, a pagan, could have been present at a session of the Council. Second, there is the matter of how it is possible for Paul not to know that the one presiding over the session was the high priest (vv. 2–5). Third, the question has been raised of how the tribune would understand the deliberations of the Council, which would be conducted in Aramaic. For these reasons, the historicity of this narrative has been questioned.[20]

These difficulties are obviated if one thinks, not in terms of an official session of the Council, but rather of a meeting of the members of that Council, convoked by the tribune, and probably taking place at his own residence or at some other Roman venue. That is why 22:30 really says that he called the members of the Council, not that he called the Council itself, or that he presented himself in one of its sessions. In that case, as it was not a meeting of the Council, but of its members gathering at the invitation of the Roman tribune, it is to be supposed that Ananias would not wear his official vestments, nor would he preside over the session, and that the discussion took place either in Greek or with interpreters, so that the tribune could follow it. After all, that was the purpose of the meeting itself.

About the high priest Ananias something is known from other sources. In Acts he appears only here and in 24:1. He was high priest from the year 48 until 58, and he owed his position to Herod Agrippa II. His cruelty and arbitrariness (shown in 23:2) were such that when the Jewish rebellion broke out in the year 66 he was killed by the people.[21]

In verse 6, Paul makes use of a stratagem in order to divide his accusers. Claiming his condition as a Pharisee, he asserts that he is on trial "concerning the hope of the resurrection of the dead." Paul does not clarify that the point under discussion is not whether the dead will rise again, but rather whether the resurrection has already begun with Jesus of Nazareth. The result is that the members of the Council are divided, and a dispute arises between the Pharisees and the Sadducees, precisely because on this point the Pharisees were closer to Christian teachings than were the Sadducees (v. 8). Apparently, the discussion rose to such a pitch that the tribune began to fear that Paul would be torn to pieces. Perhaps remembering that the prisoner was a Roman citizen, and the grave consequences his death at the hands of a rioting crowd could bring about,[22] the tribune orders the soldiers to intervene, taking Paul out of the meeting and back to the barracks.

---

20. See, for instance, Haenchen, *Acts*, pp. 639–43.

21. Josephus, *Ant.* 20.5–6; *War* 2.17.9.

22. The word that Luke employs here in order to describe the disorder is the same used in Ephesus by the town clerk, when referring to the possible accusation of seditiousness. It was considered a capital crime.

3. A Plot against Paul (23:11–22)

At night Paul receives a vision in which the Lord encourages him, telling him that just as he has witnessed in Jerusalem so will he witness in Rome. Although at first this may seem like a simple promise that everything will turn out alright, one must not forget that here there is a parallelism between what has happened in Jerusalem and what will happen in Rome. In other words, that Paul is to take courage, not because his difficulties will end soon, but rather because what has begun in Jerusalem will continue in Rome.

Luke then tells us about a plot to kill Paul. It is an intrigue worthy of a modern suspense novel. A fanatical group commits to a total fast until they manage to kill Paul, and then joins forces with "the chief priests and elders."[23] The plan is relatively simple: the priests and elders will ask the tribune to send Paul before the Council, and those who have sworn to kill Paul will fulfill their oath as the apostle is being led through the narrow streets of Jerusalem. Later, in verse 21, we are told that those making the oath to kill Paul numbered more than forty.

Paul's nephew learns of the plot. This is one of only two times in which the apostle's kindred is mentioned in the New Testament.[24] The sister mentioned here is the only sibling of whom we know. At any rate, his nephew visits Paul in the fortress and tells him what is being plotted. Paul is careful not to say a word to those who guard him, but simply asks one of them to take the young man to the tribune. When Lysias learns of the plot, he tells the young man to keep silent and takes steps to frustrate the conspiracy.

4. Paul Is Sent to Caesarea (23:23–33)

Lysias orders two centurions to prepare a strong escort to take Paul to Caesarea, where the governor resides. Apparently fearing a new riot, or perhaps that the conspirators might learn what is afoot and attack the escort in one of the desolate regions that they must traverse, the tribune takes two precautions. First, he orders them to leave during the third vigil of the night—that is, three hours after sunset or approximately at nine in the evening, as the NRSV translates. The plan is to travel all night, so that by daybreak Paul and his escort will be too far for the plotters to plan a different coup. Second, he orders a much stronger escort than would seem necessary—a total of 470 men.[25] Thus, if the plotters learn of the Roman plan, or even if they see the es-

---

23. Note that the scribes are not mentioned. It has been suggested that, because among the scribes there were many Pharisees, those who had formed the conspiracy did not trust them. Lorenzo Turrado, *Hechos de los Apóstoles y Epístola a los Romanos* (Madrid: Biblioteca de Autores Cristianos, 1975), p. 221.

24. The other is Romans 16:7.

25. The word that the NRSV translates as "spearmen" is of uncertain translation. Clearly it has a military meaning, but it is not sufficiently common in ancient texts so that its exact meaning can be determined. It refers to lightly armed soldiers. They could be arch-

cort leaving, they will not be able to create a riot and whisk Paul away in the confusion.

Lysias's purpose is to send Paul to Felix, the governor. The situation has become too complicated and risky, and the tribune—as is common among officials of any government—decides that the moment has arrived to pass the responsibility to other shoulders.[26]

The letter that Lysias writes and Luke reproduces in verses 26 to 30 is an *elogium*. According to Roman legal practice, when a lesser magistrate transferred a case to a higher one, he must send with it such an *elogium*, in which he summarized the process that had been followed, as well as the nature of the case. Claudius Lysias, as protocol demands, calls Governor Felix "his excellency." This is the same title that Luke gives to Theophilus in Luke 1:3. It is interesting to note that Lysias gives a different spin to events, trying to avoid any possible criticism of his action. In verse 27 he says that he went with his soldiers in order to save Paul, "when I learned that he was a Roman citizen." According to Luke's narrative, this is not strictly true. Lysias went for other reasons. He did not even know who Paul was. It was only much later that he learned that Paul was a Roman citizen. There is a subtle contradiction between verses 29 and 30, which hints at the tribune's hesitancy. In verse 29, he says, "I found that he was accused concerning questions of their law, but was charged with nothing deserving death or imprisonment." But then in verse 30 he says that he has decided to send both Paul and his accusers to Felix, so that he may hear the case. In other words, that Lysias believes that Paul is innocent, but still sends him to Felix for trial. It is not difficult to read between the lines the anxiety of a government official who fears the possible consequences of a situation and decides to pass the responsibility to another.

The manner in which the escort proceeded is not clear. From Jerusalem to Antipatris the distance is more than sixty kilometers. The infantry goes with Paul to that point and the next day returns to the barracks. This is possible only if "the next day" means, not the day after they left Jerusalem, but the day after they arrived at Antipatris.[27] Because they are now a good distance from Jerusalem, a smaller escort suffices. The cavalry continues with Paul, while the rest return to their base. Finally, they arrive at Caesarea, where both the pris-

---

ers or men armed with slings. Because the traditional translation has been "spearmen," the NRSV simply follows that tradition.

26. The Western text adds that Lysias did this because he was afraid that the Jews would take and kill Paul, and that then it would be rumored that Lysias had accepted money in order to allow this.

27. Haenchen, as he so often does, simply claims that Luke does not know the geography of Palestine (*Acts*, p. 648). It is also possible that the "spearmen" were light cavalry, and that the infantry soldiers only went with Paul to the outskirts of Jerusalem, so that those who returned from Antipatris were the light cavalry, and the seventy of regular cavalry continued the task of escorting Paul to Caesarea. Thus, most of the journey from Jerusalem to Antipatris could have taken place at the speed of cavalry.

oner and the letter explaining his case are handed over to the governor. From there on, Paul is the responsibility of Felix, and not of Claudius Lysias.

AMIDST THE POWERS

What is most remarkable throughout this passage is the manner in which Paul moves amidst the political and religious powers of his time, even while he is in prison. Apparently, he is not particularly proud of his Roman citizenship. Earlier, when Lysias asked him if he was not the "Egyptian," he simply told him that he was a citizen of Tarsus. However now, when the authorities are ready to flog him, as was customary then to force the accused to confess their crimes, Paul lets them know that he is indeed a Roman citizen. The result is consternation among the very Romans who until that moment thought that they were masters of the situation. The tribune who before thought that he had managed to capture the dangerous "Egyptian" now learns that his prisoner poses for him a very different threat from what he had imagined. As Luke tells us, Lysias was afraid that he had bound Paul (22:29), and at the end he finds himself planning a counterplot in order to save Paul.

However, the fact that Lysias saves Paul in that difficult situation does not lead Luke to present him, naively, as an ally. On the contrary, Luke makes the reason for Lysias's actions quite clear, and even suggests that, in his letter to Felix, Lysias gives the events a particular twist in order to make himself appear in a more favorable light. All of this is highly realistic, and reminds us of the manner in which many authorities behave today.

Then comes the episode before the members of the Council. Once again, Paul shows himself to be politically astute. Instead of entering into a fruitless discussion with them, he makes use of the disagreements that he knows exist within the Council itself, so that at the end they are arguing among themselves.

Finally we come to the plot to kill Paul. Once again Paul shows himself to be wise. He has no idea who the centurions guarding him are, nor what their interests are. But he knows that Lysias will be interested in saving him from such a plot, not because Lysias is a good person, but simply because as the officer responsible in Jerusalem he will be blamed for any irregularities taking place there. Therefore, he tells his guards as little as possible and manages to get the word about the plot to Lysias.

Throughout all of this, Luke paints a Paul who is politically astute. He is not presented, as we often imagine him, as a fiery preacher who continuously charges against the enemies of God no matter who they might be, nor what interests they might have. On the contrary, Luke depicts him here as an astute missionary, who knows how to use the interests of each of the groups and individuals involved. At the same time, he presents Paul as a person of integrity, unwilling to lie or to be silent merely to save his life.

What message could be more pertinent and urgent for our Latin American and Hispanic Church? On the one hand, the need for a realistic and sober political analysis; knowing who are the various people and groups involved, what are their interests, what motivates them, and on the other hand, employing that knowledge with integrity. Between these two poles our churches often forget Paul's example. On the one hand, there are those who claim that it suffices to "preach the gospel," forgetting that the gospel is always preached to real human beings who exist within a social and political context, and that such a context has much to do with the manner in which the message is heard and how people respond to what we say and do. The political and economic interests are quite willing to use us, and they will do so for their own purposes, if we do not know who those powers are and what their goals are. On the other hand, sometimes we seem to be too willing to "play ball" with whoever happens to be in power, or to remain silent regarding injustice and oppression as long as we are allowed to preach. Or we "sweeten the pill" for the rich so that they will give us their offerings. However, between these two unfortunate options, there is the example of Paul—wise, astute, a person of integrity.

D. PAUL IN THE CUSTODY OF FELIX (23:34–24:27)

1. First Interview with Felix (23:34–35)

Felix is known, not only throughout the Book of Acts, but also through data preserved by Roman historians[28] and by Flavius Josephus.[29] He was a freedman—that is, a slave who had been freed—whose brother had been a favorite of Agrippina (Nero's mother). Referring to such origins, Tacitus says that he "practiced all sorts of cruelty and lasciviousness, using the power of a king with the spirit of a slave." One of the means he used to advance his political career was to marry influential women, and for that reason Suetonius calls him "the husband of three queens." Later, Luke will tell us about one of them, Drusilla (24:24). He was made procurator of Judea toward the end of the reign of Claudius, who died in 54. Therefore, when Paul was brought before him (probably in 58), he had already held this position for about four years.

Apparently Felix wants to find out to what province Paul belongs because, before he decides whether to hear the case, he has to determine whether he has jurisdiction. The governors of Judea knew quite well that religious matters were thorny and could lead to riots and difficulties that would be interpreted in Rome as signs of a governor's ineptitude. Therefore, if there is any way to be rid of this difficult case in which the religious leaders of the Jewish people are confronting a Roman citizen, Felix will gladly do it. A good way to achieve this goal would be to transfer the case to another province. A criminal case could be heard before the tribunals of the province where the crime was allegedly committed (*forum delicti*) or before those of the province of the accused (*forum domicilii*). If Felix manages to transfer the case to Paul's province he will have washed his hands of a difficult matter. It turns out that Paul, hailing from

---

28. Tacitus, *Hist.* 5.9; Suetonius, *Claudius* 28. See also, F. F. Bruce, "The Full Name of the Procurator Felix," *JStNT*, 1 (1978), 33–36.

29. *Ant.* 20.8.5–9; *War* 2.13.2.

Cilicia, is a citizen of Tarsus, which is a free city within the province, and that therefore he is not subject to provincial authorities. At least this is the manner in which some scholars read verses 34–35.

"Herod's headquarters"—literally, Herod's *praetorium*—where Paul is in prison was the former palace of Herod the Great, which also served as the seat of government for the province, and therefore was called *praetorium*.

2.   The Trial before Felix (24:1–23)

The arrival of Ananias "five days later" is an indication of the importance with which the high priest and his companions regarded the case. As the total distance from Caesarea to Jerusalem was about a hundred kilometers, it is to be supposed that this Jewish group left Jerusalem no more than two or three days after they learned that Paul had been transferred. They take "an attorney" with him—that is, an expert in both law and rhetoric, which was the main discipline that lawyers studied. Although the name Tertullus is Roman, most likely he also was a Jew.

The trial revolves around two speeches, one from Tertullus and one from Paul. Both begin with a *captatio benevolentiae*, an effort to gain the goodwill of Felix. The one that Tertullus offers (vv. 2–4) is full of adulation, whereas Paul's is much briefer (v. 10b). The accusations against Paul are several: he is "a pestilent fellow, an agitator,"[30] "a ringleader of the sect of the Nazarenes," who "even tried to profane the Temple." Of all this, all that may be of interest to the governor as a Roman judge is the accusation of sedition and of profaning the Temple, for the governor had the responsibility of avoiding riots and safeguarding the Temple against any profanation.[31]

In verse 9, Felix asks and obtains corroboration of the facts from the Jewish leaders who have come from Jerusalem for the trial. Then, in verse 10, after Felix tells him that he may now speak, Paul offers his defense. Verses 11–13 deal with the two main accusations of promoting riots and profaning the Temple. Wisely, Paul ignores the accusation that he has been acting in this particular way "throughout the world," and limits his defense to the twelve days that he has just spent in Jerusalem. During those twelve days, no one has seen him debating, nor inciting the crowd, be it in the Temple or in the synagogues.

At verse 14 the nature of the speech changes, for it is no longer a mere response to accusations, but rather a positive explanation of his faith and why he has come to Jerusalem. He confesses himself a follower of "the way, which they call a sect." The word "sect" appeared earlier in the accusation by Tertullus, and now Paul responds to it. Some versions translate this as "heresy," because

---

30. Here again the same word appears, of which the town clerk in Ephesus warned the crowd and which was feared by subjects as well as by officials of the Roman Empire, for whom order was of paramount importance.

31. In this case, as in so many others, the Western text offers more details, although they are less trustworthy. See E. Delebecque, "Saint Paul avec ou sans le tribun Lysias en 58 à Césarée. Texte court ou texte long?", *RevThom*, 81 (1981), 426–34.

the Greek employed here is *hairesis*, from which our modern "heresy" derives; however, at that time the word did not have the negative connotations it does today. It rather meant a party, group, or side in a discussion. Paul adds, that while he follows this Way, "I worship the God of our ancestors, believing everything laid down according to the law or written in the prophets." He does all this in order "to have a clear conscience toward God and all people." Throughout this part of the speech, it is interesting to note that, although Paul speaks of the final resurrection, he does not mention the resurrection of Jesus, nor does he argue that this event shows that Jesus was the promised Messiah. Such a declaration would easily have been misunderstood by Felix, for much of contemporary Jewish nationalism and resistance to Rome centered on the expectation of the Messiah.

Paul continues explaining the reason for his visit to Jerusalem. Here finally Luke mentions the offering that is so important in Paul's letters, and about which Acts remains generally silent: "I came to bring alms to my nation" (v. 17). He was in the Temple, which he respects, fulfilling his religious duty, when "some Jews from Asia" found him. He was there "without any crowd or disturbance."[32] By implication, those who caused the disturbance were the "Jews from Asia," and it is they who should be before the court, giving witness of their own accusations. As to the Jews present, Paul challenges them to "tell what crime they had found when I stood before the council," except his reference about the resurrection of the dead—a matter in which Felix would have no interest.

In verse 22, after Paul's speech, we learn that Felix "was rather well informed about the Way." This probably does not mean that he felt any sympathy toward Christianity, as will become obvious in the rest of the narrative. Does it mean that Felix had already inquired about this movement that was growing in his province? Or does it mean simply that Felix learned about the Christian Way in connection with Paul's trial and eventually decided to delay the decision? It is impossible to know. What is clear is that Felix does not wish to become involved in the matter, and thus delays his decision, with the excuse that he has to wait until he hears further from Lysias.

Meanwhile, Paul was to remain a prisoner, although with "some liberty" and allowing his friends to take care of his needs.[33]

---

32. The word translated here as "disturbance" is much milder in the Greek than the accusation of "sedition" made by Tertullus.

33. There were three common types of imprisonment. The most severe was the *custodia publica,* in which the person was imprisoned and chained, as was the case of Paul and Silas in Philippi. The *custodia militaris* required the prisoner to be chained to a soldier, from the right hand of the prisoner to the soldier's left. Sometimes, if the prisoner was confined, the chain could be removed. The *custodia libera* was much milder and was similar to our present "house arrest." In this case, it would seem that Paul is placed under *custodia militaris.*

3. Interview with Felix and Drusilla (24:24–27)

Luke then tells us about another interview of Paul with Felix, although this time in the presence of Drusilla, the governor's wife. He only tells us that she was Jewish. But Josephus is more forthcoming.[34] She was the younger daughter of Herod Agrippa I (see 12:1), and therefore a sister to Agrippa II and Bernice (see 25:13). She had been married before to the king of Emesa, Aziz, but she left him in order to marry Felix. She had at least one son, Agrippa, who died with her when Vesuvius erupted in the year 79.

Felix and Drusilla have Paul brought before them and speak "concerning faith in Jesus Christ." However, when Paul begins speaking about "justice, self-control, and the coming judgment, Felix became frightened." Luke is well aware of what is said about Felix, particularly about his dissolute and cruel nature, and therefore what he paints here is the picture of a man who refuses to hear what Paul says because it actually touches him. Therefore he dismisses Paul with the vague promise to listen to him again on some future occasion when he will have more time.

In verse 26, Luke tells us that this was not the last interview between Paul and the governor, and that Felix was simply trying to obtain money from Paul to set him free. Finally, "after two years," a new governor arrived; but Felix left Paul in prison. The "two years" (in Greek *dietia*) is the technical term used in law to refer to the maximum time during which an accused person could be kept in preventive imprisonment. If Luke uses the term in this technical sense, what he means is that, after those two years, Felix should have set Paul free but that, in order to gain the goodwill of the leaders of the Jews or simply to avoid having problems with them, he left Paul in prison, so that his successor would have to deal with the matter.

POWER, PATIENCE, AND CORRUPTION

Here Luke paints a sad picture of those in authority, Jews as well as Romans. It is not necessary to add much about the high priest, Ananias. As already stated, he was a cruel man, with little support among the people. When the people finally rebelled against Rome, one of their first actions was to kill the man who claimed to be their religious leader but was in fact only concerned with his own power and authority. In this particular episode, he brings a lawyer with him, in order to present the accusation against Paul. This lawyer's adulation of a governor who is well known by his love of money and his lack of scruples is quite obvious. This is in contrast with Paul, who credits Felix with no more than having been governor for four years. The accusations brought against Paul are vague, and several of them are completely beyond the scope of Roman laws and concerns.

The Roman governor, in turn, first tries to wash his hands of the matter (like that other Roman, Pontius Pilate). Then, instead of making a decision, he delays, using the excuse that he has to wait for word from tribune Lysias. Later he brings Paul before himself and his wife; but when the apostle begins speaking about

---

34. *Ant.* 20.7.1–2.

matters of justice and righteousness, he feels accused and is frightened. But in spite of this he still seeks his own benefit, trying to find a way in which he can collect a bribe from Paul. Finally, he simply allows two years to pass, and leaves his post without having decided or resolved anything.

All of this must have called for quite a degree of patience on Paul's part. Two years in prison—probably in chains, waiting the results of a trial that has already taken place—is a very long time. It is even longer for one who knows that he is in prison because the judge does not have the courage to reach a decision or is simply waiting to be bribed. Paul must have had ample opportunity to practice what he had taught: "We also boast in our sufferings, knowing that suffering produces endurance, and endurance produces character, and character produces hope, and hope does not disappoint us" (Rom. 5:3–5).

The lesson from this passage for today is obvious. We live in times that require both a holy impatience with the present injustice and pain and a holy patience in order to persevere even when there seems to be no end in sight. It is not a matter of conforming to and accepting what exists; nor is it a matter of becoming discouraged because our efforts do not bring results. Paul was imprisoned, under the power of the most powerful empire that the Mediterranean world had ever known, and subject to the whims of a governor who was politically powerful but morally weak. It was enough to lose patience. But the years went by, and centuries went by, and of that emperor, of that empire with all its legions, nothing remains but a distant echo in the pages of history. Whereas of the poor prisoner who seemed to wilt in the prisons of the empire, the memory remains alive in every corner of the world, and his message resounds even today with as much power as when it first provoked fear in the fickle governor.

From the purely human point of view, the Latin American Church has many reasons to despair. Our peoples are mired in ever-greater poverty. The more we analyze the situation, the more we become aware that such poverty has its roots in circumstances and systems far beyond our control. Hunger, misery, political oppression, and a thousand other similar realities invite us to despair. As Christians, we know that we have to struggle against that. But at the same time, because we are realistic, we know that our struggle is not against flesh or blood, but against principalities and powers. We are subject to powers as unworthy of respect as were the high priest, Ananias, or the Roman governor, Felix. Yet in the midst of it all, thanks to the power and the presence of the Spirit (of that Holy Spirit who is the main protagonist of Acts) we have hope, knowing that suffering produces endurance, and endurance produces character, and character produces . . . hope!

E. PAUL IN THE CUSTODY OF PORCIUS FESTUS (25:1–26:32)

1. The Trial before Festus (25:1–12)

Little is known about Porcius Festus. Josephus depicts him as an energetic governor, who took immediate and wise action against the disorder that existed in the province.[35] There are some difficulties determining the exact date on which Festus reached Caesarea, but it probably was in the year 60.[36] The "province" to which verse 1 refers was the Roman province of Syria, of which Palestine was a part.

The narrative in Acts seems to confirm what Josephus says about the manner in which Festus governed. Only three days after arriving at Caesarea, he "went up" to Jerusalem. One might imagine that, being aware of the increasingly rebellious spirit of the nation, he wished to learn as soon as possible about that portion of his province that was most likely to cause difficulties.

Because Luke is only concerned about the manner in which Festus dealt with Paul, he gives the impression that the entire agenda during the visit of Festus to Jerusalem was the apostle's trial. Most likely, he went there to deal with many pending issues. Apparently, those who had plotted to kill Paul had not given up, in spite of the manner in which Lysias had frustrated them, and now they appeal to the new governor, requesting that Paul be brought back to Jerusalem. Luke informs us that the plot to kill Paul along the way was still afoot.[37] However, Festus responds, quite reasonably, that he would be leaving soon and that it would make no sense to send Paul to Jerusalem, but rather that his accusers should go to Caesarea, there to present their charges against the prisoner.

Festus continues acting with the energy that Josephus attributes to him. He remains in Jerusalem no more than ten days, and the day after Festus returns to Caesarea, Paul is already on trial. Festus had been in the province less than two weeks, and we are at the verge of the final outcome of a process that, under Felix, had languished for over two years.

We are told little about the trial itself. In chapter 24 Luke has just told us about the trial before Felix, so now he limits this aspect to two verses (7 and 8) in which he summarizes both the accusations against Paul and his defense. At the end, Festus suggests that the trial should be moved to Jerusalem, where it is to continue under his oversight. Possibly what has happened is that Paul's accusers cannot prove their charges, and Festus wants to give them the opportunity to attempt to do this in Jerusalem, where they may have access to more witnesses. Luke says that he did this "wishing to do the Jews a favor." Interestingly, this is the same motivation that Luke attributes to Felix for keeping Paul in prison, even beyond the legal limit of two years (24:27). This seems to contradict the interpretation of those who claim that the purpose of Acts is to show its Roman readers that the gospel was persecuted by the Jews, but not by the Romans, who were always its just defenders. In this passage, as in 24:27, Luke says quite openly that Roman government officials were fickle, and that

---

35. *Ant.* 20.8-9; *War* 2.13-14.

36. See Turrado, *Biblia Comentada*, pp. 227–28.

37. The Western text adds that those who were part of this new plot were the same who had earlier conspired to kill Paul.

they were more interested in gaining the goodwill of the Jewish leaders than in doing justice.

Paul's answer is one of the most dramatic moments in the Book of Acts. He appeals to Caesar and at the same time accuses the governor of not performing his duty: "I am appealing to the emperor's tribunal; this is where I should be tried. I have done no wrong to the Jews, as you very well know." Further, he denies the governor's authority to do what he proposes: "No one can turn me over to them."

On the matter of appealing to Caesar, there are several unclear points that historians of Roman law cannot clarify. For instance, it is not known whether the right of appeal pertained only to Roman citizens, whether it applied to all sorts of crime, whether one could appeal to Caesar before the governor had issued a verdict, and several other similar matters.[38] Luke seems to imply that the right to appeal was not automatic, for Festus confers with his council before granting it (25:12). At any rate, from that moment on, Paul's case is no longer in Festus's hands, and all that follows in the Book of Acts is a series of encounters and episodes of great interest to the reader, but which have nothing to do with Paul's legal standing before the authorities.

2. Paul before Agrippa and Bernice (25:13–26:32)

Although Paul has appealed to Caesar, he does not leave for Rome immediately, but remains a prisoner in Caesarea while the necessary arrangements are being made. It is during that time that Festus receives the visit of Agrippa and Bernice. This Agrippa was Herod Agrippa II, a son of Herod Agrippa I, who had ordered the death of James. He was only seventeen years old when his father died in the year 44. Although he was a favorite of Emperor Claudius, the latter did not give him his father's throne, possibly because he was still too young, but gave him more limited territories, and it was not until the year 53 that Herod Agrippa II received the title of king. His territories did not include all of Judea, which remained under Roman governors. His capital was in Caesarea Philippi. However, because he was a member of the Jewish dynasty that had reigned in Palestine until recently, he had the right to name the high priest, and he was also the custodian of the Temple treasury. At the time of Luke's narrative, he was some thirty years old. He died much later, in 92, thus concluding the dynasty of the Herods.

His sister Bernice was a year younger, and ten years younger than Drusilla, Felix's wife. She had been married to a Jewish officer in Alexandria, and then to her own uncle, from whom she had two sons.[39] After the death of her second husband, Bernice moved in with her brother Herod Agrippa II, and soon rumors were circulating about an incestuous relationship between the two. Perhaps in order to counteract such rumors, Bernice married the king of

---

38. See Haenchen, *Acts*, p. 667, n. 2.

39. Josephus, *Ant.* 20.5.2; *War* 2.11.6.

Cilicia, Polemon; but she soon abandoned him and returned to live with her brother. Later, when the Jewish rebellion was about to break out, she tried to calm the waters, without success. Then she became the lover of Titus, whom she was planning to marry; but when Titus became emperor he had to forsake her for political reasons.[40]

Bernice and Agrippa went to Caesarea, as protocol required, to greet Rome's new representative, and it was during that visit that Festus told them about Paul and his case (25:14–21). Agrippa shows an interest in the case, and Festus promises to satisfy his curiosity. Therefore, what is taking place is not a trial, which was no longer possible once Paul had appealed to Caesar, but rather an attempt by Festus as a host to entertain his guests, Agrippa and Bernice.

The next day the interview takes place, which Luke describes in 25:23–26:32. It took place "with great pomp," and among those present there were "the military tribunes and the prominent men of the city." Festus explains why Paul has been brought. Now he adds a further purpose to the interview. Festus was supposed to send to Rome, not only the accused, but also a summary of his case (the *elogium* to which reference was made when discussing 23:25–30). In this case, Festus is at a loss, saying "I have nothing definite to write to our sovereign about him."[41] One must not forget that Festus had arrived recently at his province, and that he would not be very well informed about many of the nuances of Jewish religion, and about the manner in which his predecessors had conducted themselves regarding that religion. He therefore makes use of the visit of Agrippa in order to gain a better understanding of what is at stake, and thus write to the emperor with better information.

Agrippa gives Paul permission to speak, and Paul answers with one of the longest speeches in the Book of Acts (26:2–23). As in other similar cases, this speech begins with a brief *capatio benevolentiae* (vv. 2–3), in which the speaker tries to gain the good will of his audience. Paul's speech is a combination of autobiography with theological argument. The theological argument is essentially a joining of Pharisaic doctrine, which included the hope of resurrection, with the event of the resurrection of Jesus. Paul does not touch on the actual point of contrast between the traditional belief of the Pharisees and the Christian message: whereas the Pharisees did believe in the final resurrection, Christians claimed that the resurrection had already begun with the raising of Jesus from the dead. The autobiographical material refers mostly to Paul's conversion, which we have encountered twice before. (When commenting on

---

40. Juvenal, *Satires*, 6; Suetonius, *Titus*, 7.

41. This is the earliest time in ancient literature in which the emperor is called "lord" (*kyrios*, which the NRSV translates as "sovereign"). Shortly thereafter, Christians would face persecution, and one of the main reasons for that persecution was the incompatibility between the affirmation that Jesus is the Lord and the state's claim that Caesar is the Lord.

9:1–19, the various texts in Acts where that conversion is told were discussed, so it is not necessary to repeat that here.) Finally, after telling about his conversion, Paul returns to theological affirmation. He has indeed traveled about inviting Jews and Gentiles alike to repent and to turn to God. But "saying nothing but what the prophets and Moses said would take place, that the Messiah must suffer, and that, by being the first to rise from the dead, he would proclaim light both to our people and to the Gentiles."

It is at this point that Festus interrupts Paul by exclaiming: "You are out of your mind, Paul! Too much learning is driving you insane!" (26:24). The two words that the NRSV translates as "out of your mind" and "insane" have the same Greek root—which is also the root of the English word "maniac." The opposite of this kind of "mania" is sense or wisdom, and that is what Paul claims in the next verse: "I am not out of my mind, most excellent[42] Festus, but I am speaking the sober truth." He then turns to King Agrippa, who as a Jew must be informed about the prophets and also of the events that Paul has just proclaimed, for "this was not done in a corner." Here the word "this" refers most likely both to the teachings of the prophets and to the Christian events that Paul has just told. Agrippa, as a Jew who dwells in the region, must know the prophets and must also be aware of the birth of Christianity, that has not taken place "in a corner."[43] He then challenges the king with a question: "King Agrippa, do you believe the prophets? I know that you believe."

Agrippa's answer is difficult to translate with all the nuances. Most traditional translations imply that Agrippa declares himself about to be convinced. The NRSV is closer to the spirit of the original in translating "are you so quickly persuading me to become a Christian?" Agrippa is not saying that the argument is convincing, but rather that Paul has put him in such a position as to almost make him appear a Christian. The Greek implies a role being played, almost as in a theater, and therefore perhaps a better translation would be, "You almost make me look like a Christian." Agrippa is not saying that he is almost a Christian, but that Paul has almost managed to force him to act in favor of Christianity. The answer may even have a touch of irony.

Paul's words have become classic, for they are often quoted in Christian literature and preaching: "Whether quickly or not, I pray to God that not only you but also all who are listening to me today might become such as I am—except for these chains." The last words of Paul imply that he was chained, perhaps tied to a soldier as was customary. At any rate, what he is telling the king, as well as others present, is that he does not envy their position nor their power and that, except for the chains he bears, he is actually better off than they are. This brings the audience to an end. The king rises, perhaps showing

---

42. The same title that Luke gives Theophilus.

43. On the history of this phrase, see A. J. Malherbe, "Not in a corner: Early Christian apologetic in Acts 26:26," *SecCent*, 5 (1985–86), 193–210.

disgust at the personal tone of Paul's words, and with him leave the other important people present.[44] In a conversation aside, all of these (the king, his sister, Festus, and the important people with them) declare that they have found no crime in Paul, and Agrippa affirms that the only reason they cannot let him go is that he has appealed to Caesar. Naturally, he may also be using this as a subterfuge, for releasing Paul at that point would have brought Festus significant difficulties with the Jewish leaders who were seeking Paul's death.

WITNESSING AMID POWER, INDECISION, AND CURIOSITY

Festus brings to this situation a different style of government. Felix had taken more than two years without ever making a final decision. Festus takes up Paul's case shortly after arriving at the province. However, he does this at a time when he still does not know how deep are the feelings aroused by Paul's case. Toward the end of the trial in Caesarea, even though the accusers have not been able to prove their charges, what Festus does, instead of absolving the accused, is to propose a new trial in Jerusalem, where it is to be expected that the accusers will be able to bring forth more witnesses. This is clearly a political maneuver. Festus, like Felix before him, realizes that his political career would be threatened were he to free this prisoner who is so hated by some of the Jewish leaders. It is at that juncture that Paul appeals to Caesar. This does not mean that Paul felt particular sympathy toward the emperor, who at that time was Nero. What it means is simply that Paul realizes the contradiction between the legal principles that Festus is supposed to defend and the political interests that in fact guide his action.

Parallel situations appear frequently in Latin America. In recent decades, there have been numerous Latin American church leaders who have been imprisoned by the military, and then freed through an appeal to higher authority—sometimes even to the dictator himself. In some cases someone has been arrested, and was not made to disappear only because there was a quick telephone call to the American ambassador, or a series of wires to the United Nations and other international agencies. In the cities in the United States, Hispanic pastors daily confront cases in which the police or other government agents trample over the rights of a Latino or Latina, and the only way to achieve justice is by appealing to higher authority.

In such cases, the appeal itself is often a witness. By appealing to the emperor, Paul is pointing out, even though indirectly, the sad corruption of the empire, and the need for the message he proclaims. He is not necessarily saying that Nero is good. He is rather pointing to the inner contradiction of the system and demanding that at least it follow its own rules. When we appeal to a dicta-

---

44. The word the NRSV translates as "those who had been seated with them" is also the technical word for members of a council and therefore may be the title of those who arose. See Haenchen, *Acts*, p. 690, n. 1.

tor in the name of a brother or a sister who has been unjustly incarcerated, we are not endorsing the dictator. We are rather pointing to the inner contradictions of the system that dictator heads and demanding that it adjust at least to the basic rules of justice. The same is true when a Latino in Texas or in Illinois files a complaint against a political system that seems to discriminate systematically against Hispanics. In such cases, besides calling for justice, we are witnessing, for moral integrity is in itself a witness to the Lord whom we serve.

However, the authorities and the powerful do not always try to crush the weak and those for whom they feel contempt. Sometimes oppression consists in reducing people to mere objects of curiosity. Festus uses Paul in order to entertain his guests, Agrippa and Bernice. There is deep dehumanization in turning a human being into a mere object of curiosity, a circus freak. As Agrippa and Festus eventually discover, the supposed freak is still human, and in Paul's case has also the power and conviction that comes from the Holy Spirit, so that at the end of the encounter, it is the governor and the king who are uncomfortable. The governor has no other way out than to mock Paul: "Too much learning is driving you insane!" The king also scoffs, "Are you so quickly persuading me to become a Christian?"

In this strange encounter, Paul is the winner. At the end, those who question him are not convinced, but they are certainly convicted. So strange a power is this, that makes a man in chains victor over a king and a Roman governor! Not so strange, for it is the power of the Holy Spirit promised at the beginning of the book—the Spirit who is the main actor in this story.

F. PAUL IS SENT TO ROME (27:1–28:10)

The narrative takes up the first person plural ("we"), and will continue in the same manner until the end of this section, which deals with the trip from Caesarea to Italy and eventually to Rome. Because it is told in the first person plural, and because it offers so many details, it has often been thought that this section was originally part of a travelogue that Luke incorporated into his work. However, it is easier to explain the situation simply by saying that the author of Acts is the one who refers to Paul, his companions, and himself as "we." On the other hand, the narrator does not include himself among the prisoners. This might indicate that the instructions given by Felix concerning Paul's imprisonment were still being followed (24:23): "to let him have some liberty and not to prevent any of his friends from taking care of his needs." It is on the basis of such instructions that the narrator can sail with Paul.[45] We are also told in 27:2 that Aristarcus was part of the group.[46]

---

45. Also, the law allowed a Roman citizen in Paul's circumstances to take with himself two slaves. For that reason some have suggested, although with small success, that perhaps the protagonist of these "we sections" was traveling, at least legally, as Paul's slave.

46. On Aristarcus, see 19:29 and 24:10.

1. The Beginning of the Voyage (27:1–12)

Paul and "some other prisoners" are placed under the care of a centurion of the Augustan cohort named Julius. We know that, at least during the time of Agrippa II, there was in Caesarea a cohort called *Cohors Augusta I*. Centurion Julius may have belonged to it. On the other hand, Roman historians make several references to certain praetorian soldiers who were called "Augustans," who were sent to various parts of the empire on special missions,[47] and therefore it is possible that Julius was one of these soldiers who had come to Caesrea in some particular mission and was now returning to Rome.

The group embarks on a ship from Adramyttium, a city south of Troas. Their route takes them first to Sidon, where Julius allows Paul to visit "his friends." It is only here that Luke ever refers to Christians as "friends." He is probably repeating the manner in which the centurion would speak about Christians, not as Paul's brothers and sisters, but as his friends. One may suppose that Paul made this visit accompanied by a soldier to whom he was probably chained. After this visit, sailing north of Cyprus, they reached Myra. The text explains that they followed this route "because the winds were against us." This means that the wind was blowing from the west, and that the ship sailed under the lee of Cyprus in order to be protected from that wind, and to make use of the current, which there runs westward. According to the Western text, this leg to Myra took fourteen days.

In Myra they transboarded to a ship from Alexandria, which was in route to Italy. It is to be supposed that the first ship was planning to continue along the coast of Asia Minor, towards Adramyttium. Because the new ship was sailing from Alexandria to Italy, it would be larger than the previous one. Later (27:37) Luke will tell us that there were 276 people on board.

From the very beginning, the voyage in the Alexandrian ship was slow and difficult. The wind was still contrary, and the travelers finally reached Cnidus, in the southwest corner of Asia Minor. There, instead of continuing directly westward, which they could not do because of the prevailing winds, they went toward the south, in order to sail on the lee of Crete. "Salmone" is a cape at the western end of Crete. The city of Lasea, today in ruins, is on the southern coast of Crete, halfway between the two ends of the island. Today there is, near those ruins, a bay called "Kalolimonias," which is probably the place that Luke calls "fair havens" (*Kalous limenas*). It is not a very good bay, for it is open to the winds, and that is why Luke says that it was "not suitable for spending the winter."

In verses 9 to 12 they decide not to spend the winter there, but rather to continue toward Phoenix. Probably this port, which Luke describes in 27:12, is what today is called Lutrus.[48] This was to be a short sailing of some sixty kilo-

---

47. Tacitus, *Annals*, 14:19; Suetonius, *Nero*, 25.

48. According to another opinion, Phoenix is the place today called "Phineca," which is no longer a seaport because the land has risen some fifteen feet. See Haenchen, *Acts*, p. 700, n. 7.

meters, at the end of which they would be able to anchor in a port that was well protected against the winter winds.

But it was late in the year, and the safe time for sailing was rapidly passing. Luke tells us that it was already after "the Fast" (v. 9). This was the Jewish celebration of Kippur (see Lev. 16:29–31), which took place on the tenth day of Tishri, that is, toward the end of September or early October. In the year 59, the probable date of this voyage, the fast was on October 5. Therefore, all agreed that it was no longer possible to reach Italy before winter, and they were simply looking for a good shelter to wait until a better season.

At this point there is disagreement among the travelers as to what is to be done. The experts in navigation (the pilot and the owner of the ship) say that they should go on.[49] Paul tells them that they should remain in Fair Havens. Luke does not tell us whether Paul makes this recommendation on the basis of common sense, or by some sort of inspiration or vision. The first is doubtful, for there is no indication that Paul was an expert sailor.[50] At any rate, part of what Paul announces here will come true, and part will not, for the ship will certainly be lost, but all lives will be saved.

Normally, the decisions having to do with sailing would be the responsibility of the captain and the owner of the ship. In this case, however, Luke seems to imply that it was the centurion who had the power to decide. To confuse matters a bit more, in 27:12 he tells us that "the majority was in favor of putting to sea," which implies that there were several people whose consensus was sought. Perhaps because there was considerable risk involved no matter what decision they took, Luke is implying that there was a general discussion as to what to do.

THE AUTHORITY OF THE EXPERTS

This episode invites a brief reflection. It seems rather foolhardy for Paul, who is not an expert sailor, to tell the experts what they are to do. However, the rest of the story shows that Paul was right.

Quite often today, when the Church seeks to speak a prophetic word on any of the problems being debated in the world, it is told to remain silent, for it is the "experts" who really know what is to be done, and the Church and its spokespersons are not experts in what is being discussed. When, for instance, there is discussion about the pollution of the environment, and some Church leaders warn about the dangers of doing violence to nature in order to make a profit, there are attempts to silence them by saying that after all they are experts neither in economy nor in ecology. Or when someone raises a prophetic voice

---

49. The words that the NRSV translates as "pilot" and "owner of the ship" are technical terms on whose exact meaning there is still some debate. Most likely the first is the captain and the second is either the owner or the representative of the owners.

50. One must not forget, however, that Paul had traveled frequently by sea. There is a list of his sea voyages in Haenchen, *Acts*, pp. 702–3. In total, before this last trip, Paul seems to have sailed some six thousand kilometers.

against economic injustice, those who profit from such injustice argue that, after all, the prophet is not an economist. Similarly, in recent decades, when the Church spoke about the physical damage done by the use of tobacco, the "experts" paid by the tobacco companies insisted that the leaders of the Church were not experts in health matters. Other examples abound. The point is that, in a world in which the "experts" frequently use their authority to justify evil, it is time for Christians and for the Church to reclaim their authority. That authority is not based on being experts in matters of economy, politics, ecology, or health, but in having a clear vision of the future that God has promised, of that core element in the Christian message, God's reign. Perhaps the Church and its leaders are not experts; but if they have a word from the Lord, they do have authority.[51]

2. Storm and Shipwreck (27:13–44)

The decision seems to be corroborated when a moderate south wind begins to blow, which would allow the travelers to sail northwest toward Phoenix. However, the south wind made it difficult for them to leave the bay, and therefore it appears that they had to tow the ship by rowing the ship's boat. However, they have hardly come out of the bay when the wind veers. The northeaster to which the text refers is a much-feared wind in the area. The best course in such a situation is to turn the ship around, so that the wind will hit the bow. In that fashion, the pounding of the waves would be lessened, and the ship would not be carried away by the wind as rapidly. But the wind appeared too suddenly. In order to turn the ship around, it was necessary to offer its side to the winds and the waves, which would be extremely dangerous. Therefore, the sailors decide to simply let the wind carry them, perhaps raising only a very small sail to keep the stern toward the wind, and so that the ship would have enough steering way to avoid being hit by the waves from the sides. Apparently the wind was so sudden that they did not even have time to collect the ship's boat until they found themselves under the lee of Cauda, a small island some forty kilometers west of Fair Havens.

Verses 17–19 tell of a progressive series of emergency measures. The "undergirding" of the ship has been interpreted in various ways.[52] Apparently cables were tied around the ship in order to counteract the power of the waves that would otherwise tear the ship apart. What is not clear is how and in what direction those cables were tied. The Syrtis was a sandbank on the northern coast of Africa, which was famous for its many shipwrecks. Because the ship was rapidly carried toward the southwest, and the sailors had no way of knowing how far they had gone, their fear of hitting that bank was natural. There is some debate as to the translation of the phrase the NRSV renders as "they lowered the sea anchor." If this is the correct translation, then what they low-

---

51. For a wider discussion of this topic, see K. Strachan, *El llamado ineludible* (Miami: Editorial Caribe, 1969), pp. 137–43.

52. See Haenchen, *Acts*, p. 703, n. 1.

ered was a device that would increase the resistance of the water on the ship and prevent it from being carried away as rapidly. It would usually be either a barrel or a canvas cone tied in such a way that it floats just below the surface. At any rate, on the next day, because these measures did not suffice, they began lightening the ship by throwing the cargo overboard, probably because the ship was already waterlogged. Finally, on the third day they disposed of the ship's tackle. This refers to the main mast and its sail. From then on all that they have to guide the ship is a small sail and the sea anchor.

All of this is insufficient. The storm lasts for many days, with no sun and stars, and therefore the sailors have no idea where they are. In the midst of their despair, those aboard do not even eat. It is then that Paul intervenes. He begins by reminding them that he had counseled against leaving Crete. He does this so that now they will heed his words of encouragement and hope: "I urge you now to keep your courage, for there will be no loss of life among you, but only of the ship." According to Paul, this is because an angel (that is, a messenger) of God has told him that God wants him to go to Rome to stand before Caesar, and God has granted him the lives of all who are with him.

Thus they are carried through the Adriatic for two weeks. In this context, the "Adriatic" is not what today receives that name—that is, the sea between Greece and Italy—but includes also the section of the Mediterranean south of that sea. Finally, at night, the sailors suspect that they are approaching land, perhaps because they can hear breakers. Soundings confirm it, and they decide to anchor in order not to run on the rocks. Four anchors are thrown from the stern. These could simply be thrown overboard. But, arguing that it was necessary also to throw some other anchors from the bow, and at some distance from the ship itself, the sailors lower the ship's boat and are ready to board it when Paul warns the soldiers that the sailors are actually trying to escape and leave the rest to their own devices. At that point the soldiers cut the ship's boat away, and all must now wait the outcome aboard the ship.

In verses 33–38 Paul once again encourages his fellow travelers, although this time not only with words, but also by his example. He reminds them that they have been fourteen days without eating—which is clearly a hyperbole, for in that case they would not have been able to continue struggling against the sea. He then begs them to eat for their own health (which could also be translated as their own salvation), promising them that "none of you will lose a hair from your heads." He then joins his own example to his words, takes bread, gives thanks, breaks it, and eats it. The sequence of the verbs, taking bread, giving thanks, breaking and eating it, is a clear reminder of the Lord's Supper, although the text gives no other hint that this was anything like a communion service.[53] Paul's example gives courage to his companions, who also eat. It is at

---

53. The Western text affirms that it was indeed a communion service, but this may be simply the interpretation of the redactor on the basis of the sequence of verbs mentioned above.

that point that Luke tells us that there were 276 persons on the ship.[54] Having eaten, and now apparently expecting that the ship will run aground, they continue the process of lightening it, so that it will be able to make it closer to the coast.

In the morning they saw before them an unknown land with a bay and a beach, and they attempted to guide the ship toward the beach. Because time was running out and they had no boat, they simply cut the cables off the anchors. With the help of the steering oars and the small foresail they hoped to make it to the beach. However, before they got there they struck a reef, and the ship was about to break apart.

The soldiers, who had to answer with their lives if the prisoners escaped, decided to kill them. But the centurion, whose respect toward Paul seems to have grown through the storm, forbids it in order to save the apostle. They all make it to the coast, some swimming, some holding onto planks and other floating objects.[55]

THE CHURCH, HOPE OF THE WORLD

This entire episode is so dramatic that on reading it one may miss the fact that those who travel with Paul are saved by reason of the presence of the apostle. This may seem strange, for we tend to think in very individualistic terms: each person is responsible for his or her own actions. Here, however, God grants Paul the life of his companions. Thanks to Paul's faithfulness, obeying what God has commanded him, the rest are also saved. There is in Scripture a parallel story that shows the opposite case. It is the story of Jonah, who takes a ship in order to go in the opposite direction from what God commands. As a consequence of his disobedience, the entire ship is endangered, and those who sail with Jonah have no alternative but to toss him overboard.

It is important to keep these two stories in tension, for while it is true that a faithful Church is a hope for the world, it is also true that a disobedient Church is a threat, and that perhaps the world does well by throwing it overboard.

Thanks to Paul's faithfulness, and to the mission that God has entrusted to him, those who travel with Paul are saved from the shipwreck. Furthermore, when Paul promises them that they will be spared, and invites them to eat, the very fact that he eats is a sign that his words of hope are not empty words. He is convinced that there is a future different from the one that his companions fear. With the simple action of taking bread, giving thanks and eating, he offers hope to all the despairing sailors, soldiers, and passengers.

Likewise, the Church has a word of hope for the world. The basis for that hope is that the Church has a vision of the future that is different from that of the world. But the world will not believe us if we do not already live as those who

---

54. Some manuscripts offer lower numbers, such as seventy-six or "some seventy-six."

55. The grammar at this point is strange, and it might even mean that some made it to the shore on the shoulders of others.

truly have such hope. His companions believe Paul, and decide to eat, when they see him eating. The world will believe in the measure in which it sees us being truly the people of a new hope, announcing and already living out of a different future. In the midst of a continent in a constant crisis of hopelessness, with enormous international debts, tragic political situations, and an environment increasingly polluted and denuded, the Church has no alternative but to be an announcement, with its words, with its actions, and with its own inner life, of the different future that God has promised.

Paul's actions remind us of communion: he took bread, he gave thanks, he broke it, and he invited others to eat. Perhaps what we ought to do now is similar: that our communion be such that we remind the world of the hope of its own salvation, of the reign of God. That in taking bread, giving thanks, and breaking it, our very action, and the life springing from it, be a living announcement of the new order of God's reign. Such a Church is truly a hope for the world. The opposite is also true: the Church that does not have the necessary obedience to be a proclamation of hope deserves only to be cast out, like Jonah from the endangered ship.

3. On the Isle of Malta (28:1–10)

The island where the shipwrecked land is Malta.[56] The word that the NRSV translates as "natives" is *barbaroi*, a word employed for those who did not speak Greek. The language of the Maltese even to this day is a Semitic language akin to Phoenician. Here in verse 2 there is an ironic contrast between the fact that Luke calls these people "barbarians" and his assertion that they "showed us unusual kindness."

Because those who had been shipwrecked were many—according to most manuscripts, 276—one imagines that those gathered around the fire according to verse 2 were just some among them, while others gathered around other fires or found other ways to be warmed. In stormy times in October, temperatures in Malta can drop to 12 degrees Celsius (54 Fahrenheit), and therefore those who had been saved from the ship, wet as they were, would need to be warmed.

It is here that a viper appears. The text is clear, and does not need much explanation. There are in ancient literature parallel cases of shipwrecked people bitten by snakes.[57] The main problem with this passage is that in Malta there are no poisonous snakes. The traditional explanation by the Maltese themselves is that, as a consequence of Paul's miracle, all the snakes in Malta lost their venom! More skeptical interpreters say that this simply shows that this entire story is a legend. Others suggest that, as Malta is a relatively small

---

56. Although there is an ancient legend that holds that the island was in fact Mljet, on the Adriatic facing Dubrovnik. O. F. A. Meinardus, "St. Paul shipwrecked in Dalamatia," *BibArch*, 39 (1976), 145–47.

57. Haenchen, *Acts*, p. 713, n. 5.

island and is densely populated, venomous snakes, pursued by the inhabitants, have become extinct.

At any rate, the episode of the viper, brief though it is, shows the fickleness of these people. First they think that Paul must be a terrible sinner, because he has been bitten by the snake. Then, seeing that he does not die, they come to the conclusion that he is a god. In both cases they are wrong. Luke does not tell us what Paul did in order to try to change their minds. He did tell us before about a similar episode in Lystra, where Paul and Barnabas insisted that they were not gods.

In verse 7 "the leading man of the island" offers them lodging. This seems to be an official title, and may imply that Publius was Rome's representative in Malta. As such, he offered them hospitality for three days, while they found other lodging for the three months that they had to wait for a change in the weather. Nothing is known about Publius beyond what Luke tells us here. Strangely, Luke does not even give his full name. During the three months that Paul remained there, there were miracles in the island, of which the first was the healing of the father of Publius. (This is one of the passages in which the medical terms appear that have been used in order to affirm that Luke was a physician. On this point, see the introduction to this commentary.) Not a word is said about the preaching of the gospel, but only about the miracles performed by means of Paul, and the many honors received by Paul and his companions. Later tradition does affirm that Paul did found a church there, and that Publius was its first bishop.

BEWARE OF CHEAP THEOLOGY!

The changes in the opinions of the Maltese about Paul are notable. First, when a snake bites him, they think that he must be a terrible sinner to deserve such punishment. Then, when he does not die, they decide that he must be a god. In both cases they err. As someone has said commenting on this passage, "Bad theology is equally inept in both its assessment of the meaning of tragedy and in its ascriptions of good fortune."[58] The Maltese are wrong in the first case, because the fact that the snake bit Paul did not mean that he was a worse sinner than anyone else. They were equally in error in the second because the fact that he survived did not mean that he was a god. Paul is a human being whom God has called—as God has called each of us—and to whom God has entrusted a mission, just as we too have been entrusted with a mission. In the course of following that mission, he finds difficult times: imprisonment, floggings, shipwreck; and he finds also glorious moments: conversions, healings, liberation. In Malta, he is a prisoner awaiting trial before Nero.

What Luke tells us here is much more than an anecdote about some first-century "barbarians." Sadly, the same cheap theology of these ancient Maltese

---

58. William H. Willimon, *Acts* (Atlanta: John Knox Press, 1988), p. 185.

has found its way into the Christian Church, and is particularly popular in some Latin American and Hispanic circles. According to this theology, every misfortune is a punishment for one's sin, and whoever has faith and is obedient to God's commandments will always be fortunate and even prosper economically. Not so long ago I heard a preacher in a television program in a Latin American capital giving witness to how God had enriched him, giving him two cars, a luxurious mansion, and I don't remember what else. I was standing at a street corner, looking at a public television set. Next to me, a poor woman, barefoot and with a huge basket on her head, was attentively listening to the preacher. I wondered what that woman felt and thought on listening to such preaching. Did she think that she was poor, that her children did not have food, because she was a greater sinner than I, who was standing, well dressed, next to her? Or would she think that the characters in a soap opera that she had just seen lying and cheating on each other were better than she, because they had automobiles and pretty homes? Or did she perhaps think, with that profound wisdom that comes from living, that the preacher had no idea what he was talking about?

I do not know what the woman was thinking. But I do know that what she and I were hearing was not the good news about the One who was born in a manger, who had nowhere to lay his head, and who died on a cross. What we were hearing was rather the cheap and non-Christian theology of those ancient Maltese, who believed that if the snake bit Paul, this was a sign of his sin, and if he did not die, this was a sign of his divinity.

Sadly, such "cheap theology" turns out to be rather expensive. Its price is that we do not dare speak about our pains and our anxieties, for according to this theology, they are our fault, a sign of our own corruption. Its price is the internalization of the oppression of the poor, who are told that if they are poor this must be because they have sinned. The price is a Church in which, in opposition to all that the Bible teaches, the poor, the diseased, and the brokenhearted are treated with contempt, and the rich, the powerful and the healthy are exalted. The price, in summary, is leaving aside the cross of Christ and its deepest significance.

G. PAUL IN ITALY (28:11–31)

1. On the Way to Rome (28:11–15)

Finally, after spending three months in Malta, Paul and his companions continue their travels to Italy. Luke does not tell us whether all 276 persons who had been shipwrecked earlier sailed in this other Alexandrian ship, or only a few of them. He tells us that the ship had as its figurehead "the Twin Brothers" (the Dioscuri, or, as other translators say, "Castor and Pollux"). These twin gods were patrons of sailors. The ship, which had wintered in Malta, took them first to Syracuse, then to Rhegium, on the southern tip of the Italian peninsula, and finally to Puteoli (or Pozzuoli). This was a seaport north of Naples. Although Luke does not say it explicitly, it is there that the group landed, in order then to continue toward Rome by land.

Verse 14 is remarkable for two reasons. First, it is significant that even in the relatively small port of Puteoli, so far from Judea, there already was a church. There is no indication as to how Christianity reached the place; but this in itself reminds us that what Luke tells is only a portion of the story, and that while Paul and Barnabas were performing their missionary duties there were many others who in various ways spread the gospel. Secondly, this verse is interesting because it implies that Paul had enough freedom to decide to remain in Puteoli for a week, at the invitation of the believers in that city.[59] After knowing him for half a year, it would seem that Centurion Julius had come to respect and perhaps in a certain way even to love the prisoner who had been entrusted to him.

The delay of a week in Puteoli gives the believers in that city time to send word to Rome, whence others then set out in order to meet Paul and his companions. Some of these Christians from Rome, perhaps the stronger and younger ones, or perhaps those who were traveling on horseback, meet Paul and his companions at the Forum of Appius, some sixty-five kilometers from Rome. The rest, perhaps a day later, meet him at Three Taverns, sixteen kilometers closer to Rome. Luke tells us that upon seeing them "Paul thanked God and took courage."

2. Paul in Rome (28:16–31)

Finally we reach Rome. Some other translations include in verse 16 a phrase taken from the Western text (and also from an Antiochene tradition): "The centurion delivered the prisoners to the military prefect." This was the normal procedure, and that is probably why the Western text adds it; but the Alexandrian text does not, and therefore the NRSV and other recent translations do not include it. At any rate, Paul "was allowed to live by himself, with the soldier who was guarding him." This is the *custodia militaris,* discussed previously. In 28:30 Luke lets us know that Paul rented a place in which to live—or at least that is one of the possible readings of that verse.

Three days after his arrival (possibly the time it would take to determine the status of his imprisonment, to find a dwelling, and to make other arrangements), Paul gathers the local leaders of the Jews in Rome. This is done on his own initiative in order to explain to them why he is imprisoned, and to summarize the events that have led to the present situation. They respond that although they have heard about Christianity, and what they have heard is not good, they have received no communications from Judea about him, nor has anyone come accusing him. This is surprising, for in earlier chapters we have

---

59. The Western text, apparently in order to avoid the impression that Paul could make such a decision on his own and at the invitation of the Christians in Puteoli, simply says that he remained there for seven days, without mentioning the invitation.

encountered Jews who followed Paul in order to impede his mission, and the leaders of Judea had also taken an unusual interest in him. On this score, it is important to remember that a few years before, as a result of the disorders that took place in Rome surrounding the preaching of a certain "Chrestus"— probably Christ—Emperor Claudius had expelled the Jews from the city, or at least their leaders. Therefore, quite likely Jews in Rome were eager to avoid similar incidents, and those in Jerusalem, knowing the situation in Rome, may have decided to forego further accusations against Paul.[60] At any rate, the leaders in Rome decide to allow him to explain the matter in further detail.

On the appointed day, "great numbers" came to Paul's dwelling, and he spent the entire day trying to persuade them, "both from the law of Moses and from the prophets." As he did at the beginning of the book, Luke again summarizes the Christian message as "testifying to the kingdom of God" (28:23 and 31). And, as has happened before, some believe and some do not. In response, Paul quotes Isaiah 6:9–10, which speaks of the hardened heart of the people of God, and concludes saying that "this salvation of God has been sent to the Gentiles, they will listen." On hearing this, according to some manuscripts that the NRSV does not follow, the Jews departed divided among themselves.

In a way, this episode summarizes what has been shown repeatedly in the book: the message is first of all for Jews, but when they reject it, it is offered to the Gentiles. What has taken place throughout the history that Luke is concluding is precisely that, as has been illustrated in numerous incidents.

Finally, Luke ends his book with a summary that includes two years during which Paul preaches about the reign of God and teaches about Jesus Christ "with all boldness and without hindrance."

That is the end of the book. Not one word is said about what eventually became of Paul. Perhaps the two years mentioned are a reference to the maximum time that a person could remain in prison without being taken to trial (see commentary on 24:27). On the basis of other writings and traditions there are a number of conjectures about the rest of Paul's life. But Luke remains silent.

EPILOGUE: THE ACTS OF THE SPIRIT

In a way the end of the book gives unity to Luke's double work. His Gospel begins by placing the advent of the Lord in its political context: "in the days of King Herod of Judea" (Luke 1:5); "a decree went out from Emperor Augustus" (Luke 2:1); "this was the first registration and was taken while Quirinius was governor of Syria" (Luke 2:2). The Book of Acts ends on a similar note, with Paul left a prisoner in Rome as a consequence of the actions of certain Jewish leaders. The first book begins among Jews, and refers to Rome; the second ends at Rome, with reference to Jews.

---

60. On the decree of Claudius, see the commentary on 18:2.

But in fact the book does not end; it simply quits. On reading its last words, we wish to turn the page to see what happens next. But there is no next page. What became of Paul? What happened next? What about the other apostles? Perhaps, instead of a final period, the book should end with ellipsis points. . . .

Why does the book not end? The matter has been endlessly discussed, leading to various theories. But perhaps the explanation is quite simple: the book does not end because the acts of the Spirit do not end. If his book were indeed about the "acts of the apostles," Luke would have told us what each of the apostles did after the ascension of the Lord. But that is not Luke's purpose. The real protagonist of this second book is the Spirit. As long as we await the final coming of God's reign, the acts of the Spirit continue.

This is the main reason the book is so relevant for us today. If it were only a matter of stories and anecdotes about the apostles or about the early Church, it would probably be very inspiring, but it would still be an old book of mostly antiquarian interest. But that is not the case. The same Spirit whose action we see in Acts continues acting among us; we are still living in the times of the acts of the Spirit; we live, so to speak, in chapter 29 of Acts; and for as long we live in such times, this book will be a Word of God for our benefit and direction.

Index

Made in the USA
Las Vegas, NV
25 August 2023

76562816R10171